THE LAW RELATING TO
COHABITATION

AUSTRALIA
The Law Book Company
Brisbane . Sydney . Melbourne . Perth

CANADA
Ottawa . Toronto . Calgary . Montreal . Vancouver

Agents
Steimatzky's Agency Ltd., Tel Aviv;
N.M. Tripathi (Private) Ltd., Bombay;
Eastern Law House (Private) Ltd., Calcutta;
M.P.P. House, Bangalore;
Universal Book Traders, Delhi;
Aditya Books, Delhi;
MacMillan Shuppan KK, Tokyo;
Pakistan Law House, Karachi, Lahore.

THE LAW RELATING TO COHABITATION

by

MARTIN L. PARRY, LL.B.

Solicitor, Senior Lecturer in Law
The University of Hull

Third edition

London
Sweet & Maxwell
1993

First Edition 1981
Second Edition 1988

Published in 1993 by
Sweet and Maxwell Limited of
South Quay Plaza, 183 Marsh Wall,
London E14 9FT
Computerset by York House Typographic Ltd., London W13
Printed and bound in Great Britain by
Butler & Tanner Ltd, Frome and London

No natural forests were destroyed to
make this product: only farmed
timber was used and re-planted.

ISBN 0-421-46390-2

**A catalogue record for this book
is available from the British Library**

Index prepared by Patricia Baker

PREFACE

The model adopted in the second edition, of providing an analysis for the lawyer of the substantive law relating to unmarried couples and their children, was well received and has been maintained in this third edition. The most significant changes in the intervening period have been in the context of the law relating to parent and child. The rationalisation of child law by the Children Act 1989 is reflected in the rewriting of Chapter 5, a task made more complex and less rational as a result of the Child Support Act 1991, so that the revised Chapter is somewhat longer than its predecessor. Other significant legislative developments which are incorporated include taxation changes and changes in the assessment of unmarried couples for legal aid purposes. Of the numerous case law developments, the most significant has been the reformulation of the constructive trust by the House of Lords in *Lloyds Bank plc* v. *Rosset*, which is fully considered in Chapter 2. In the context of the wider policy issues, which are drawn together in the Conclusion, particular attention is given to the Scottish Law Commission Discussion Paper No. 86, *The Effects of Cohabitation in Private Law* and its subsequent *Report on Family Law*.

I am again indebted to a number of current or former colleagues in the University of Hull Law School for their guidance. In particular Paul Fairest and Nicholas Parry for their help on a number of Chapters, and Hugh Bevan, Valerie Cromack, Ada Kewley, and Christopher Riley for their help on individual Chapters. A very special debt is owed to my wife Deborah for reading the entire manuscript and her patient tolerance of my word processing skills! Finally, thanks to our young son Adam for so willingly accepting the delayed start to our football matches whilst the book was completed.

The manuscript was finished on May Day 1993 and seeks to state the law at that date. I have squeezed into the footnotes at proof stage a few subsequent cases which illustrate, rather than alter, the principles applicable to the law relating to cohabitation.

Martin Parry
July 1993

TABLE OF CONTENTS

TABLE OF CASES

TABLE OF STATUTES

TABLE OF STATUTORY INSTRUMENTS

Chapter 1

INTRODUCTION

1. Terminology

It is necessary at the outset to define cohabitation. "To cohabit" generally means to live together as husband and wife, and is usually used of a man and a woman who are not married to each other. "Cohabitation" similarly describes the relationship of a heterosexual couple who cohabit, and the parties are frequently referred to as "cohabitees". The term "cohabitee" is, however, grammatically incorrect and purism offers "cohabitant" or "cohabiter", neither of which has popular appeal. Official preference is for "cohabitant" which will no doubt receive legislative authority.[1] "Concubine", in respect of a woman, is correct but rather technical; in popular use are "common law wife" and "mistress", both of which are expressive but inaccurate. Reported American alternatives include "meaningful associate", "special friend", "current companion", "live-in-lover", "significant other", and "domestic associate", none of which, it is suggested, is helpful or meaningful. Various judicial alternatives[2] may be appropriate for the law reports but not for everyday use; for example, "illegitimate wife and illegitimate husband", "family partner", "de facto spouse", "unmarried housewife". It is proposed to follow the popular rather than the official line and use the term "cohabitee" when referring to a man and a woman who are living together as husband and wife.

The terms "common law husband" and "common law wife" are misleading and their use is not to be encouraged, for they suggest a particular kind of legal relationship which in fact does not exist. The terms arose when the law of marriage was part of ecclesiastical law and there were strict penalties for sexual relationships outside marriage. At common law, however, no religious ceremony was necessary; parties could marry by merely declaring that they took each other as husband and wife (*per verba de praesenti*) or by declaring an intention to do so (*per verba de futuro*), in which case the marriage was binding when the parties had sexual intercourse, *i.e.* consummated the marriage. The rule was later modified so that a marriage was valid only if conducted in the

---

1 See in particular the Draft Family Homes and Domestic Violence Bill, cl. 1(*a*), below, p. 184.
2 See further Sparkes, "The Language of Cohabitation" [1989] Fam. Law 328.

presence of a priest (*in facie ecclesiae*) but the law was in a state of uncertainty until the Marriage Act 1753.[3] That Act, which is the basis of the modern law of formation of marriage, removed the common law marriage[4] and required a church ceremony after the calling of banns, the consent of a minor's parents or guardians and the entry of the ceremony in an official register. Marriage by civil ceremony was not permitted until the Marriage Act 1836.

Common law marriages can still be contracted in other countries, for example, in certain parts of the United States of America. In Scotland such marriages were effective until the Marriage (Scotland) Act 1939.[5] Certain customs, similar to the common law marriage, were followed by wandering groups, particularly in the north of England, to gain social acceptability for relationships outside marriage. One such custom was the marriage over the broom (or living over the brush) where the group provided its own ceremony in which the couple joined hands and jumped over a broom which was swung in circles near the ground.

The term "mistress" is often used synonymously with cohabitee but the two are not the same, nor are the legal rights respectively attaching to them. Mistress suggests a woman who has been provided with a home by a man so that he may visit her and enjoy a sexual relationship[6] and it will be used in that context hereafter. The relationship of mistress and lover is not that of husband and wife, nor can it be described as one of cohabitation. The legal recognition of relationships outside marriage has concentrated on couples who have lived as married couples and the preparedness to extend to cohabitees certain legal protection enjoyed by spouses has not been accorded to mistresses.[7] For example, matrimonial injunctions under the Domestic Violence and Matrimonial Proceedings Act 1976,[8] apply to " . . . a man and a woman who are living with each other in the same household as husband and wife . . . " and not to mistresses. In the words of one Law Lord they apply to the "unmarried housewife".[9] A cohabitee may be described as an unmarried housewife but the description does not include a mistress. Moreover, the term cohabitee describes both partners of the relationship; mistress clearly

---

3 For an analysis of modern cohabitation and the legal responses to it as part of an historical process, see Parker, *Informal Marriage, Cohabitation and the Law, 1750-1989* (Macmillan, 1990).

4 On the current possibility of a common law marriage, see Hall, "Common Law Marriage" (1987) C.L.J. 106 and, for an historical perspective, see Lucas, (1990) C.L.J. 117.

5 It is still possible in Scotland to have a marriage "by cohabitation with habit and repute" where a couple have set up home together and live together as husband and wife. The Marriage (Scotland) Act 1977, s.21, provides for the registration of such "irregular marriages". See also *R(S) 4/85*. The Scottish Law Commission has recommended the abolition of such marriages, but without prejudice to the validity of any such marriage already contracted: see Scot. Law Com. No. 135, Pt. VII.

6 See, *e.g. Horrocks* v. *Forray* [1976] 1 W.L.R. 230, below, p. 53.

7 See Welstead, "Mistresses in Law Deserving of Protection" [1990] Fam. Law 72.

8 See below, p. 160.

9 *Per* Lord Kilbrandon in *Davis* v. *Johnson* [1979] A.C. 264 at 339 and see below, p. 161.

does not. Yet, if recognition is to be given to a relationship, is it realistic to talk just in terms of one partner?

It may be difficult, of course, in a particular case to determine whether a woman is a cohabitee or a mistress, for example, the woman with whom a man lives from Monday to Friday to be near his job, the man leaving to live with his wife at weekends. One definition of cohabitation used in the United States and in some European countries is two persons of opposite sex sharing a bedroom during at least four nights per week for at least three consecutive months.[10]

It is important, however, to distinguish between a mistress and a cohabitee since it is relationships which can be equated with marriage which tend to receive legal recognition.[11] So, for example, in the Consumer Credit Act 1974,[12] references to a husband and wife include, in certain contexts, a reputed husband or wife and the Pneumoconiosis etc. (Workers' Compensation) Act 1979 refers to a "reputed spouse".[13]

The tendency to define cohabitees in terms of spouses is consistent with the tendency to presume that a couple living together are married. Thus in *Re Taplin*[14] a couple lived together for 10 years and held themselves out as husband and wife. They and their children were received into local society. The children's birth certificates recorded the marriage of their parents but there was no record in the appropriate register of marriages and there was a reference in a deed of covenant by the children's paternal grandfather to his son's "reputed children". The court held that the absence of any entry in the register of marriages, and the words in the deed of covenant, were insufficient to rebut the presumption of marriage.

The legal response to cohabitation depends upon the qualitative and quantitative nature of the cohabitation and the purpose for which it is being claimed, or denied, that a couple are cohabiting. A distinction is drawn, for example, between short-term and long-term cohabitation, between the casual affair and the stable relationship, between relationships which have resulted in the birth of children and those which have not, and between couples who live together and couples who do not. It is not perhaps surprising, therefore, that the legal response to relationships outside marriage has been as variable as the relationships themselves. So, for example, in certain contexts the legal test is one of financial dependency rather than cohabitation.[15] A mistress might well be dependent upon her lover notwithstanding the lack of cohabitation.[16] When considering the legal position outside marriage it will be essential,

---

10 See Macklin (1972), referred to in Eekelaar and Katz (eds.), *Marriage and Cohabitation in Contemporary Societies* (1980), p. 21.
11 See, *e.g. Bernard* v. *Josephs* [1982] Ch. 391 at 402, *per* Griffiths L.J.
12 s.184.
13 See below, p. 231.
14 [1937] 3 All E.R. 105.
15 See, for example, the Inheritance (Provision for Family and Dependants) Act 1975, below, p. 211.
16 See, *e.g. Malone* v. *Harrison* [1979] 1 W.L.R. 1353.

therefore, to consider not only the nature of the relationship, but also the particular legal issues arising from that relationship.

Where the relationship is no more than a casual encounter there is unlikely to be either cohabitation or dependency and the relationship is unlikely to warrant special recognition.[17] To give it that would defeat one of the objects of such a relationship, namely the lack of commitment. The difficulty remains, however, of where to draw the line between the stable union and the casual encounter.

This book is chiefly concerned with cohabitation between a man and a woman living together as husband and wife. It is only where the test is one other than cohabitation, for example, ownership of property,[18] that parties to a homosexual or lesbian relationship may currently be included. There are also many instances of members of a family living together in a relationship of companionship. Such domestic relationships do not amount to cohabitation in the sense of a couple living together as husband and wife and will be described hereafter, in so far as they are discussed, as family cohabitations. Where the law has recognised cohabitation it has done so largely on the basis of relationships which essentially run parallel with marriage.

2. COMPARISON WITH MARRIAGE

English family law is based on the legal rights and duties arising from marriage. The law regards cohabitation and the sharing of lives and a home as the essence of marriage and recognises rights and duties arising from cohabitation within marriage. Parties who cohabit outside marriage do not have the legal responsibilities of a married couple; nor do the benefits and burdens of matrimonial law extend to them. This is so because our social structure is based on marriage, a formal contract giving rise to a particular status. As Lord Denning put it[19]: "The only basis for a sound family life is a Christian marriage — the personal union of one man with one woman, to the exclusion of all others . . . " The acceptance of marriage as the basis of our social structure inevitably means that the law will differentiate between marriage and cohabitation. Yet increased recognition is being given to cohabitation,[20] so that cohabitation, like marriage, is giving rise to a particular status.

Marriage does, of course, impose duties as well as confer rights; there is a tendency to talk solely in terms of rights, but to do so is inaccurate. One of the attractions of cohabitation is that it does not impose upon the parties the duties imposed by marriage. The more the law recognises

---

17 See below, p. 243.
18 For a British Columbia decision where the Court invoked the doctrine of the constructive trust to award a lesbian woman a share in property acquired by her partner in a 10-year relationship, see *Anderson* v. *Luoma* (1986) 50 R.F.L. (2d) 127.
19 Denning, *The Due Process of Law* (1980), p. 201 adapting the definition of Lord Penzance in *Hyde* v. *Hyde* (1866) L.R. 1 P. & D. 130.
20 As, for example, in the cohabitation rule for welfare benefit purposes.

cohabitation and confers rights on cohabitees, the more it will be inclined to impose obligations upon them and the more their freedom of choice is infringed. It is not readily apparent how many couples cohabit through choice and how many are not free to marry.[21] The reform of the divorce law has made remarriage easier and would suggest that the need to cohabit because of an existing marriage of one of the parties is not as great as previously. In some cases it may be that the parties are free to marry but only one of them wishes to do so. If a couple live together because they have chosen not to marry, is it right that the law should treat them as if they were married? To treat them differently does not preclude some other form of recognition within the framework of the family, for both marriage and cohabitation can be seen as constituting changing patterns of family formation.[22]

Cohabitation can be seen as an informal contract, just as marriage is a formal one, and each can be seen as giving rise to its own status. The terms of a marriage contract are, however, legally prescribed; it is not possible to enter into a contract of marriage except in accordance with the formalities of the Marriage Acts and any private agreement to live together[23] will not constitute a marriage. The law has as yet shown little inclination to recognise private agreements to live together outside marriage[24] but there is here scope for the development of the legal response to cohabitation.[25]

The legal consequences of marriage are identifiable within a general framework of matrimonial law which gives rise to a status which does not extend to those who cohabit. The legal consequences of cohabitation have developed in other areas of the law on an ad hoc basis depending upon both the context in which the relationship falls to be considered and the nature of the cohabitation. This development has taken place under the general umbrella of family law, rather than matrimonial law, thereby reflecting an acceptance that those who cohabit as husband and wife can properly be described as members of a family, provided that the relationship is of sufficient permanence and stability.[26] There remains the problem of defining the appropriate degree of permanence and stability. The judicial and legislative approaches have been tentative and piecemeal, the matter being considered very much in individual legal contexts, for example, property and contract. It is suggested that there is a need for a reappraisal of the role of family law in the light of the current assessment of family ties,[27] so that those who live together outside

---

21 See further Scottish Law Commission, Discussion Paper No. 86, *The Effects of Cohabitation in Private Law* (1990), para. 1.4.
22 See The Study Commission on the Family, *Values and the Changing Family* (1982); Blake, "Family Law or the Law of Relationships?" (1982) 12 Fam. Law 95.
23 See, *e.g.* the American case of *Peck* v. *Peck* 30 N.E. 74 (1892).
24 See below, p. 235.
25 See below, p. 246.
26 See, *e.g. Dyson Holdings Ltd.* v. *Fox* [1976] Q.B. 503.
27 See also Ghandi and Macnamee, "The Family in U.K. Law and The International Covenant On Civil and Political Rights 1966" (1991) 5 I.J.L.F. 104.

marriage can be advised with some degree of certainty whether legally they cohabit as a family or, as is currently so often the case, as strangers.

3. OCCURRENCE

Marriage is self-proving, cohabitation is not. There is a register of marriages but not of cohabitations; the latter by their uncertain nature preclude precise statistics. One of the objects of the divorce law reforms in 1971[28] was to enable those who were unable to marry to regularise by marriage their "stable illicit unions".[29] The object was realised in the short term rather than the long term in so far as the subsequent increase in the divorce rate has not been matched by a decrease either in cohabitation, or in the number of births outside marriage.

The increasing interest in and incidence of cohabitation has been reflected in a number of studies.[30] There is evidence that increasing numbers of couples cohabit before marriage in what have come to be called trial marriages. The General Household Survey 1988 showed that the number of couples who lived together before marriage had risen from 4 per cent. in the late 1960s to 37 per cent. in 1988.[31] Some indication of the frequency of cohabitation resulting in the birth of children may be gained from the registration of births of children whose parents have never been married to each other. In 1966, 38 per cent. of such births were registered on the joint application of both parents. Ten years later, this figure had risen to 51 per cent. and by 1990 it was up to 73 per cent. It can be argued from these figures that as the fathers were prepared to acknowledge paternity there is a strong likelihood that in many cases the mother and father were living together, particularly in view of the fact that in three-quarters of the 1990 joint applications the parties gave the same address.[32] These figures give no indication, of course, of the incidence of cohabitation without the birth of children, on which any speculation is even more tentative, but one statistical analysis on cohabitation in Great Britain in 1986/87 estimated there to be approximately 900,000 cohabiting couples and 444,000 dependent children living in such families. About 4 per cent. of all dependent children were estimated to be living in cohabiting-couple families.[33]

---

28 With the implementation of the Divorce Reform Act 1969 and the Matrimonial Proceedings and Property Act 1970: see now the Matrimonial Causes Act 1973.
29 See Law Commission, *Reform of the Grounds of Divorce. The Field of Choice*, Cmnd. 3123 (1966), paras. 33-37.
30 For a useful consideration, see Barton, *Cohabitation Contracts* (1985), pp. 6-10; Freeman and Lyon, *Cohabitation Without Marriage* (1983), pp. 56-60; Hoggett and Pearl, *The Family Law and Society* (3rd ed., 1991), pp. 320-331.
31 Office of Population Censuses and Surveys (H.M.S.O., 1990). For the findings of a survey on post-divorce cohabitation, see Maclean and Eekelaar, "Cohabitation after Divorce" [1985] Fam. Law 180.
32 See *Population Trends 65* (1991).
33 Haskey and Kiernan, "Cohabitation Some Demographic Statistics" [1990] Fam. Law 442.

4. CONSEQUENCES

Detailed analysis of the differing legal consequences of marriage and cohabitation must be left until the following Chapters when specific issues are discussed and marriage and cohabitation are contrasted. Some general observations will, however, provide a useful introduction to that analysis.

While the common law doctrine of unity, whereby spouses were treated as one person with that one being the husband, is that of a bygone age, its ghost still haunts certain areas of the law relating to husband and wife.[34] It is visible in the practice of a woman taking the surname of her husband on marriage. There is, however, no legal requirement that she should do so. People are free to be known by whatever surname they choose, provided that they do not choose one for a fraudulent purpose. A married woman can retain her maiden name if she so wishes and a cohabitee can use his or her own surname or that of the partner or indeed any surname. No legal formalities are necessary, but are available should it be felt necessary ever to prove the change of name, for example, to obtain a passport or in dealings with official bodies such as the Inland Revenue or the Departments of Health and Social Security. The simplest formal method of providing evidence of a change of name is by statutory declaration,[35] which is likely to suffice for most purposes. Occasionally evidence is required in the form of a deed poll which must be duly stamped and may then be enrolled in the Central Office of the Supreme Court and formally advertised.[36] Such steps are not, however, necessary in order to effect a change, but only if required to evidence one. Cohabitees may, like spouses, prefer to retain separate names and identities and the woman avoid the title "Mrs." in preference to "Miss" or the equivocal "Ms", for all are courtesy titles without legal significance. The fact that the parties use different surnames does not reflect legally upon the nature of their relationship if they are married, but may do so if they are not, for example, when determining whether or not they are living together as husband and wife for the purposes of social security law.[37]

The legal recognition of marriage means that certain relatives are prohibited by law from marrying. The prohibited degrees of affinity which arise from marriage do not attach to cohabitation. Whereas a man may not marry his wife's mother or wife's daughter except as provided for by the Marriage (Prohibited Degrees of Relationship) Act 1986 he is quite free to marry his cohabitee's mother or cohabitee's daughter.[38] Cohabitation, therefore, may arise as a result of the prohibited degrees of relationship, for example, between a man and his step-daughter where

---

34 See below, p. 187.
35 See below, p. 254.
36 See the Enrolment of Deeds (Change of Name) Regulations 1983 (S.I. 1983 No. 680).
37 See below, p. 85.
38 See, *e.g. Wing* v. *Taylor* (1861) 2 Sw. & Tr. 278.

their marriage is not permitted by the Marriage (Prohibited Degrees of Relationship) Act 1986 because the younger party has, at some time before attaining the age of 18, been a child of the family in relation to the other party.[39]

Certain people cannot marry because of a blood relationship. They may cohabit, but in the case of these prohibited degrees of consanguinity, some relatives are prohibited also from having a sexual relationship, for example, father and daughter, mother and son, brother and sister. A man or woman[40] who knowingly has such a relationship commits the criminal offence of incest.[41] Not all those within the prohibited degrees commit incest by having intercourse, for example, uncle and niece, even though they cannot marry.[42]

In addition to complying with the prohibited degrees of relationship two people have capacity to marry each other in England and Wales only if both are over the age of 16, both are unmarried and one male and the other female.[43] Any marriage between two people not so qualified is void. Whilst, of course, they are free to cohabit the fact that they have been through a ceremony of marriage does, in some respects, legally distinguish their relationship from that of two people who cohabit without having purported to contract a marriage. In particular, on granting a decree of nullity of marriage, or at any time thereafter, the court has power to make financial provision and property adjustment orders in the same way as on granting a decree of divorce.[44] No such power exists in relation to those who cohabit without celebrating a marriage, whether valid or void. The court in nullity proceedings has jurisdiction also in respect of the children of the family.[45] Moreover, any child of a void marriage may benefit from the doctrine of the putative marriage so as to be treated as the legitimate child of his parents.[46]

Two people of the same sex cannot marry but can cohabit.[47] Any purported marriage between two people manifestly of the same sex cannot, it is suggested, even be termed a void marriage. If it were, the court would have power to grant a decree of nullity and exercise its power to make ancillary orders. A cohabitation between two people of the same sex may be one of companionship. If, however, there is a sexual

---

39 s.1(1). See, *e.g. Smith* v. *Clerical Medical and General Life Assurance Society* [1993] 1 F.L.R. 47.
40 Provided, in the case of a woman, she is aged 16 or over.
41 Sexual Offences Act 1956, ss.10 and 11.
42 See Barton, "Incest and the Prohibited Degrees" (1987) 137 N.L.J. 502.
43 Matrimonial Causes Act 1973, s.11.
44 *Ibid.* ss.23-24A.
45 *Ibid.* s.52 and see below, p. 189.
46 Legitimacy Act 1976, s.1 (as amended): see below, p. 107.
47 For the recognition of such marriages in Denmark, see below, p. 244. For marriage law purposes in English law, a person's sex is fixed at birth and is a biological question. Hence, a sex change operation undergone by a transsexual does not change that person's sex for the purpose of capacity to marry: see *Corbett* v. *Corbett* [1971] P. 83.

relationship between two men sexual acts are only legal if both men are over 21, both consent and the act takes place in private.[48]

Sixteen is the minimum age for both parties to a marriage.[49] If, however, either party is under the age of 18, the parents of the party under age must consent to the marriage (unless the person under age is a widow or widower).[50] If the parents refuse to consent the parties wishing to marry may apply to the court for permission. A marriage without such consent, however, is legally valid. A couple, in such circumstances, may choose instead to live together and are free to do so subject only to such powers of restraint as may be available to the parents. Although theoretically parents have parental responsibility until the child attains majority[51] the exercise and enforcement of these rights diminishes as the child grows older.[52] It is open to the parents to apply to the court to have the child made a ward of court[53] and ask the court to direct that the couple shall not live together. It is likely, however, that the court in wardship would see its role as one of advice, for the jurisdiction is currently used far less frequently to restrain children who are considered to have reached the age of discretion.

If either of the cohabiting parties is under the age of 16, then the need for intervention may be greater. Parental authority is not, however, absolute. In *Gillick* v. *West Norfolk and Wisbech Area Health Authority*,[54] which was concerned with the prescription of contraceptive advice and treatment to a girl under the age of 16, it was recognised that if the girl had sufficient understanding and intelligence to enable her to understand what is involved, the doctor has a discretion to give such advice and treatment without parental knowledge or consent provided he is satisfied on five caveats identified by Lord Fraser.[55] Lord Scarman, agreeing with the opinion of Lord Fraser, said that the underlying principle of the law " . . . is that parental right yields to the child's right to make his own decisions when he reaches a sufficient understanding and intelligence to be capable of making up his own mind on the matter requiring decision".[56] Taken at its widest this could be seen as establishing that children of sufficient age and understanding can assert their own rights including where and with whom they should live.[57] This self-assertive view of the

---

48 Sexual Offences Act 1967, s.1.
49 Marriage Act 1949, s.2.
50 *Ibid*. s.3.
51 See below, p. 116.
52 See, *e.g.* Children Act 1989, s. 9(6), (7).
53 See below, p. 129.
54 [1986] A.C. 112.
55 [1986] A.C. 112 at 174, namely (1) that the girl (although under 16 years of age) will understand his advice; (2) that he cannot persuade her to inform her parents or to allow him to inform the parents that she is seeking contraceptive advice; (3) that she is very likely to begin or to continue having sexual intercourse with or without contraceptive treatment; (4) that unless she receives contraceptive advice or treatment her physical or mental health or both are likely to suffer; (5) that her best interests require him to give her contraceptive advice, treatment or both without the parental consent.
56 [1986] A.C. 112 at 186.
57 See, *e.g.* Eekelaar, "The Emergence of Children's Rights" (1986) 6 O.J.L.S 161.

child's rights is, it is submitted, going further than the combined opinions warrant in the light of Lord Fraser's five caveats which stress the protective nature of the parental/child's rights dichotomy.[58] Nevertheless, a parental right to challenge his child's decision to cohabit must be open to doubt if the child can be regarded as of sufficient understanding and intelligence to make his own decision. One way of seeking a judicial assessment of the issue would be by making the child a ward of court so as either to invoke the court's custodial jurisdiction on the argument that the child's upbringing is directly in issue and, hence, section 1 of the Children Act 1989 applies[59] or to invoke the protective jurisdiction which would "enable the court to protect a ward who is sufficiently mature to be entitled to make a decision himself even though . . . the custodial jurisdiction may cease to apply".[60]

This need for protection is enhanced if either party to a cohabitation is under the age of 16 because it is a criminal offence for a boy over 14 or a man to have sexual intercourse with a girl under 16.[61] There is no corresponding offence where a girl or woman has sexual intercourse with a boy under 16, although she may be guilty of an indecent assault.[62] In addition, it is a criminal offence to take a girl under 16 away from her parent or guardian against his will, even if there is no sexual motive.[63]

The following Chapters examine the legal recognition and consequences of cohabitation. They are concerned both with the mutual responsibilities of cohabitees and with those owed to and by third parties. It is necessary to consider not only the nature of the relationship, but also the purpose for which it is being claimed that a relationship exists. In view of the recognition that the law is giving to cohabitation, the concluding Chapter contains some thoughts on the future development of the law relating to cohabitation.

---

58 See also *Re W. (A Minor)(Medical Treatment)* [1992] 4 All E.R. 627.
59 See below, p. 125.
60 See further Lowe and White, *Wards of Court* (2nd ed., 1986), p. 158.
61 Sexual Offences Act 1956, s.6. See also Sexual Offences (Amendment) Bill 1993.
62 See *Faulkener* v. *Talbot* [1981] 1 W.L.R. 1528.
63 Sexual Offences Act 1956, s.20. Alternatively circumstances may justify a person under the age of 17 who is at risk of significant harm being made subject to care proceedings under the Children Act 1989, particularly if either cohabiting party is under the age of 16.

CHAPTER 2

HOME OWNERSHIP

The courts have been prepared to apply the principles applicable
between husband and wife during marriage to questions of home ownership between the unmarried.[1] This is perhaps not surprising in so far as it
has been said of husband and wife that:

> " . . . the rights of the parties must be judged on the general
> principles applicable in any court of law when considering ques-
> tions of title to property, and though the parties are husband and
> wife these questions of title must be decided by the principles of law
> applicable to the settlement of claims between those not so related,
> while making full allowances in view of that relationship."[2]

Yet the courts have made very full allowances for that relationship and
this has been so also where there is a relationship outside marriage,
depending upon the particular circumstances. The fundamental difference is that ownership of property between unmarried partners is
determined in accordance with the principles of property law, not
matrimonial law. The issue is who owns it, not who ought to own it. The
adjustive jurisdiction available to the divorce court[3] which has largely
removed the need to decide spouses' property rights according to property law, unless the issue arises either in relation to a third party's claim
or during the subsistence rather than on breakdown of marriage, does
not apply to the unmarried. Thus in *Hammond* v. *Mitchell*[4] it was said of
an unmarried couple:

> "Had they been married, the issue of ownership would scarcely
> have been relevant, because the law these days when dealing with
> the financial consequences of divorce adopts a forward looking
> perspective in which questions of ownership yield to the higher

---

1 See, *e.g. Cooke* v. *Head* [1972] 1 W.L.R. 518, below, p. 26; *Bernard* v. *Josephs* [1982]
 Ch. 391, below, p. 12; *Gordon* v. *Douce* [1983] 1 W.L.R. 563. Contrast *Diwell* v.
 Farnes [1959] 1 W.L.R. 624.
2 *Per* Lord Upjohn in *Pettit* v. *Pettit* [1970] A.C. 777 at 813. For a special statutory rule
 regarding improvements to the home see Matrimonial Proceedings and Property Act
 1970, s.37, below, p. 28.
3 See Matrimonial Causes Act 1973, ss.24 and 24A, below, p. 194.
4 [1991] 1 W.L.R. 1127 at 1129.

11

demands of relating the means of both parties to the needs of each, the first consideration given to the welfare of the children. Since this couple did not marry, none of that flexibility is available to them, except a limited power to direct capital provision for their children. In general, their financial rights have to be worked out according to their strict entitlements in equity, a process which is anything but forward looking and involves, on the contrary, a painfully detailed retrospect."

The development of the equity principles relating to home ownership have thus been of particular significance to the unmarried,[5] notwith-standing that the leading cases[6] on that development of principle have concerned married partners. One difference, of course, is that marriage is self-proving whereas cohabitation is not. Where a party to a cohabi-tation wishes to rely on the cohabitation as a basis for asserting a property right, it will be necessary to go into the detailed facts of the cohabitation. In so doing, it is only in those cases where the parties intend the relationship to involve the same degree of commitment as marriage that the courts are likely to consider it appropriate to regard them as no different from a married couple.[7]

One influential factor is, for example, the parties' future intention to marry. In particular, recognition is given, for certain purposes, to an engagement, *i.e.* an agreement to marry. When the Law Reform (Miscel-laneous Provisions) Act 1970[8] abolished actions for breach of promise to marry, consequential provision was made with regard to property of engaged couples. On termination of the engagement, any rule of law relating to the rights of spouses in relation to property in which either or both of the parties had a beneficial interest[9] applies also to any property in which either of the engaged couple had an interest while the engage-ment was in force.[10] Whilst this provision makes a summary procedure available and applies the proprietary principles in cases of married couples to determining the beneficial interests in property acquired during an engagement, it was made clear by the Court of Appeal in *Mossop* v. *Mossop*[11] that it confers no power upon the court to make a property adjustment order under the Matrimonial Causes Act 1973, s.24. The legislation is clear that power is available only on granting a decree of divorce, nullity or judicial separation. The procedural advantages of

---

5 See Griffiths L.J. in *Bernard* v. *Josephs* [1982] Ch. 391 at 401.
6 From *Pettit* v. *Pettit* [1970] A.C. 777 and *Gissing* v. *Gissing* [1971] A.C. 886 to *Lloyds Bank plc.* v. *Rosset* [1991] 1 A.C. 107.
7 See *Bernard* v. *Josephs* [1982] Ch. 391 at 402, *per* Griffiths L.J.
8 s.1.
9 Including the provisions relating to improvements to the home.
10 Law Reform (Miscellaneous Provisions) Act 1970, s.2(1), and see Matrimonial Proceedings and Property Act 1970, s.37, below, p. 28.
11 [1989] Fam. 77.

section 17 of the Married Women's Property Act 1882[12] also apply where an agreement to marry is terminated whereas cohabitees cannot avail themselves of this summary procedure.

The legislation does not make clear what constitutes an "agreement to marry". It is certainly open to a cohabitee who has been living with another as husband and wife to argue that there was such an agreement, but there may be difficulties of proof, particularly if it was an unannounced engagement. Provided that it can be shown that there was an agreement, however, the court has jurisdiction notwithstanding, it has been held, that the agreement would have been unenforceable at common law, for example, if as in *Shaw* v. *Fitzgerald*[13] one party was already married to someone else.

It can be argued that the principles applicable between cohabitees should be the same whether or not there was an agreement to marry. A long-term cohabitee's case may be just as deserving, if not more so, than that of the short-term fiancé(e):

> "As it happened Parliament had in 1970 passed an Act which put engaged couples on the same footing as husband and wife . . . Our decision in *Cooke* v. *Head*[14] does the same for couples living together as if they were husband and wife, even though they have not made any agreement to marry. This is very desirable. There is no good reason for making any difference between the two kinds of case. Especially when their relationship of 'engaged' or 'not engaged' to be married is so often undetermined and indeterminable."[15]

As home ownership between unmarried partners is determined in accordance with general principles of property law, the starting point is the legal title.

1. JOINT NAMES

Where both cohabitees are, if the title to the land is registered,[16] the registered proprietors or, in the case of unregistered title,[17] the land is conveyed into both their names, they are joint legal owners and both have a right to live in the home by virtue of that ownership.[18] Joint legal

---

12 As extended by Matrimonial Causes (Property and Maintenance) Act 1958, s.7. Application must be made within three years of the termination of the agreement: see Law Reform (Miscellaneous Provisions) Act 1970, s.2(2). See also *Marsh* v. *Von Sternberg* [1986] 1 F.L.R. 526.
13 [1992] 1 F.L.R. 357.
14 [1972] 1 W.L.R. 518.
15 *Bernard* v. *Josephs* [1982] Ch. 391 at 399, *per* Lord Denning M.R.
16 Hereafter "registered land".
17 Hereafter "unregistered land".
18 See further pp. 45 *et. seq.*

ownership does not tell the full story because joint legal owners prima facie hold the property on trust for themselves as beneficiaries (jointly or in common) under a trust for sale.[19] Ownership of the proceeds of sale depends upon the division of the beneficial ownership, which should be clearly spelt out in the conveyance or legal transfer or in a separate trust deed. The latter is particularly appropriate if the division of the beneficial ownership is subsequent to the acquisition of the property or if the parties agree to vary the beneficial ownership.

Where the parties hold the property jointly upon trust for themselves as "joint tenants beneficially"[20] they are both equally entitled to the whole of the beneficial interest. Should either of them die, the whole interest passes automatically to the survivor, subject to the power of the court to order that the deceased's share be treated as part of his or her estate so as to meet claims under the Inheritance (Provision for Family and Dependants) Act 1975.[21]

If it is intended that the parties should own distinct shares (not necessarily equal) then the property should be conveyed to them jointly upon trust for themselves as "beneficial tenants in common" and their respective shares identified. If the property is conveyed to the parties "in equal shares" this will be construed as a beneficial tenancy in common with each party owning a half share. A declaration that the parties hold the property as tenants in common in specified shares will likewise be conclusive, in the absense of fraud or mistake. On death of a tenant in common, his or her equitable share does not pass to the survivor, but passes in accordance with the deceased's will or the law of intestacy.[22]

If it is intended that the parties should jointly own the whole beneficial interest in the property, the conveyance or legal transfer should state that they hold the property upon trust for themselves as joint tenants beneficially which presupposes equality. If joint beneficial interests are spelt out in this way such a declaration will be conclusive in the absence of fraud or mistake.[23]

Thus in *Goodman* v. *Gallant*[24] a house was purchased in the name of the plaintiff's husband. Some years later he left and the plaintiff cohabited with the defendant in the property which in due course they purchased. The conveyance to the plaintiff and defendant declared that "the purchasers shall hold the property upon trust to sell the same with power to postpone the sale thereof and shall hold the net proceeds of sale . . . upon trust for themselves as joint tenants". The plaintiff later severed the equitable joint tenancy. The Court of Appeal rejected her

---

19 See Law of Property Act 1925, ss.34-36. For proposals for reform see Law Commission Report No. 181, *Trusts of Land* (1989).
20 Hereafter "joint tenants".
21 See below, p. 219.
22 See below, p. 223.
23 See *Leake* v. *Bruzzi* [1974] 1 W.L.R. 1528; *Godwin* v. *Bedwell, The Times*, March 10, 1982.
24 [1986] Fam. 106. See Juss, [1986] C.L.J. 205; J.E.M., [1986] Conv. 355. Applied in *Turton* v. *Turton* [1987] 3 W.L.R. 622: see below, p. 31.

contention that when her husband originally purchased the property she had a half beneficial interest in it from the outset and the effect of the purchase from him was to leave her owning three-quarters. The Court held that if the conveyance contains an express declaration of trust which comprehensively declares the beneficial interests, there is no room for the application of the doctrine of resulting, implied or constructive trusts[25] unless and until the conveyance is set aside or rectified; until that event the declaration in the document speaks for itself.[26] The defendant was therefore entitled to a half share of the beneficial interest in the property.

Problems have arisen where the title documents have not clearly stated that the parties are to hold the property as joint tenants beneficially. In *Huntingford* v. *Hobbs*[27] the parties who were not married were registered as joint proprietors and the transfer contained a standard declaration by the parties that "the survivor of them can give a valid receipt for capital money arising on the disposition of the land". The Court of Appeal, by a majority, rejected the argument that this constituted a declaration of trust by the parties declaring themselves as holding the legal title upon trust for themselves as joint tenants beneficially. The Court distinguished *Re Gorman*[28] where the declaration included the statement that the parties were entitled for their own benefit, which thus negated any third party involvement. The Court followed *Harwood* v. *Harwood*[29] and held that the declaration, although entirely consistent with the existence of a beneficial joint tenancy, was no less consistent with the parties holding the property as trustees for a third party and so the words could not be read as constituting a declaration of the beneficial interests. Moreover the meaning of the words alone was the material factor and so extrinsic evidence was neither relevant nor admissible. In the absence of any declaration of trust, the parties' beneficial interests fell to be determined by reference to the principles governing the creation of resulting, implied or constructive trusts. Hence, if the parties intend to hold as joint tenants beneficially, their intentions should be given explicit effect in the title documents and failure by their legal advisers to do so may result in the advisers being liable in negligence.[30]

If the title only states joint legal ownership and is silent as to beneficial ownership, the extent of the parties' interests will be determined in accordance with the law of trusts[31] paying regard to their common intention inferred from the contributions which they have made to the acquisition of the property. There is a presumption that the property is held on resulting trust for the parties in the proportions in which they have contributed to its acquisition unless there is sufficient specific

---

25 See below, p. 19.
26 See also *Wilson* v. *Wilson* [1963] 1 W.L.R. 601.
27 [1993] 1 F.L.R. 736.
28 [1990] 1 W.L.R. 616, where the parties had not even signed the declaration.
29 [1991] 2 F.L.R. 274.
30 See below, p. 17.
31 See *Walker* v. *Hall* [1984] F.L.R. 126; *Huntingford* v. *Hobbs* and below, p. 19.

evidence of their common intention that they should be entitled in other proportions.[32] The parties' shares in equity are thus ascertained according to their respective contributions to the acquisition cost,[33] which may not be too difficult to determine where the house is bought for cash but is more difficult in the usual case of purchase funded by a mortgage. Thus in *Huntingford* v. *Hobbs*[34] a majority of the Court of Appeal thought the man's initial assumption of liability to pay the mortgage, rather than his making actual payment towards the purchase, entitled him to a share of the balance of the net proceeds of sale (assessed at 39 per cent.) based on that contribution.[35]

The time at which the parties' common intention regarding the size of their respective shares is to be ascertained is the date of acquisition,[36] subject to evidence of subsequent events from which it can be inferred that the parties agreed to alter their shares in the beneficial interest. In order to take into account contributions up to the time of separation,[37] and perhaps thereafter, the conduct subsequent to the time of acquisition is relevant only in so far as it is evidence of what the parties originally agreed. It cannot affect the original agreement.[38] In *Springette* v. *Defoe*[39] the Court of Appeal held that if it is sought to rebut the presumption of resulting trust by specific evidence of a common intention that the parties should be entitled in other proportions, that intention must have been a shared one communicated between the parties. It is not sufficient for there to be a common but uncommunicated intention. In the words of Steyn L.J.: "Our trust law does not allow property rights to be affected by telepathy."[40]

The significance attached to the parties' respective contributions and their common intention is comparable with the approach where the property is purchased in the name of one party and the other seeks to assert a beneficial interest.[41] This raises the question in this context, however, of whether or not sufficient regard is being paid to the fact of purchase in joint names. So, for example, in *Young* v. *Young*[42] the plaintiff and defendant lived together as husband and wife and bought a house in joint names with the woman plaintiff providing £4,150 of the £15,900 purchase price and the remainder being raised on mortgage.

---

32 See *Springette* v. *Defoe* [1992] 2 F.L.R. 388.
33 See, *e.g. Crisp* v. *Mullings* (1976) 239 E.G. 119; *Lawrence* v. *McFarlane*, *The Times*, May 19, 1976.
34 See above, and below, p. 17.
35 See also *Bernard* v. *Josephs* [1982] Ch. 391.
36 See Griffiths L.J. in *Bernard* v. *Josephs* [1982] Ch. 391 at 404.
37 See Lord Denning M.R. and Kerr L.J. in *Bernard* v. *Josephs* [1982] Ch. 391.
38 Moreover: "The practitioner must be on guard not to confuse the proportion of the contributions (which is assessed at the date of the agreement and which does not change unless there is an express or implied variation of the agreement) and the assessment of the value, which occurs on the dissolution of the trust." *Per* Bush J. in *Marsh* v. *Von Sternberg* [1986] 1 F.L.R. 526 at 533 and see below, p. 29.
39 See above, n. 32.
40 [1992] 2 F.L.R. 388 at 394.
41 See below, p. 18.
42 [1984] F.L.R. 375.

They pooled their earnings in a joint account from which the mortgage instalments were paid during the 16 months before they separated. The Court of Appeal held that as only about £200 had been paid off the mortgage capital it would be unrealistic to decide that even a small proportion of the equity was held in trust for the defendant, accordingly, the plaintiff was entitled to the whole beneficial interest. The decision is open to criticism that insufficient regard was paid to the joint repayment of the interest and the joint liability under the mortgage and is hard to reconcile with *Huntingford* v. *Hobbs*.[43] It seems preferable to credit the parties with their joint liability[44] rather than their actual payments. Indeed where the property is conveyed into joint names it ought to be relatively easy to infer that the parties were each to have a beneficial interest.[45]

The uncertainty associated with a claim based upon the law of trusts can be avoided by careful drafting at the time of purchase. Beneficial ownership as joint tenants is the more usual arrangement, certainly amongst married couples, but may not suit the needs of all couples, as in the case of cohabitees who wish to own separate shares. The practitioner should take steps to ascertain from his client at the time of purchase what the parties' common intention is as to the beneficial interests and to declare it in the documents.[46] Failure to do so may result in the solicitor being liable in negligence.[47] If a solicitor is acting for both parties and a conflict, or potential conflict, arises he should not continue to act for both.

A beneficial joint tenancy[48] may be severed by either of the joint tenants, thereby converting it into a beneficial tenancy in common. Such action should always be considered if the parties' relationship breaks down, and a solicitor who is consulted in such circumstances and who fails to address the issue may be sued for professional negligence.[49] If the joint tenancy is severed the right of survivorship no longer applies and the parties will need to address the succession implications and if necessary alter or make a will.

Severance can be achieved in any of the following ways[50]: by giving written notice to the other joint tenant[51]; by agreement[52]; by one joint tenant dealing with his own beneficial share, for example, by way of sale

---

43 See above, p. 16 and *Savill* v. *Goodall* [1993] 1 F.L.R. 755.
44 As in *Marsh* v. *Von Sternberg* [1986] 1 F.L.R. 526.
45 See *Walker* v. *Hall* [1984] F.L.R. 126.
46 See Bagnall J. in *Cowcher* v. *Cowcher* [1972] 1 W.L.R. 425 at 442.
47 *Per* Dillon L.J. in *Walker* v. *Hall* [1984] F.L.R. 126 at 128. See also *Bernard* v. *Josephs* [1982] Ch. 391; *Springette* v. *Defoe* [1992] 2 F.L.R. 388.
48 But not a legal joint tenancy: see Law of Property Act 1925, s.36(2).
49 See, *e.g. McDowell* v. *Hirschfield Lipson & Rumney and Smith* [1992] Fam. Law 430.
50 But not by will.
51 Law of Property Act 1925, s.36(2). See, *e.g. Turton* v. *Turton* [1987] 3 W.L.R. 622. A memorandum should be endorsed on the conveyance if title is unregistered and a restriction entered if title is registered.
52 *Burgess* v. *Rawnsley* [1975] Ch. 429, but subject now to the Law of Property (Miscellaneous Provisions) Act 1989.

or mortgage; or by a course of dealing between the joint tenants showing an intention that the property should be held in common and not jointly. The latter was considered in *Barton* v. *Morris*[53] in relation to property in which the joint owners, Miss Barton and Mr. Morris, had lived for seven years, prior to Miss Barton's death in an accident. The conveyance included an express declaration that they held the property for themselves as beneficial joint tenants. Mr. Morris provided £900 of the purchase price of £40,000, the balance being provided by Miss Barton either at the time of purchase or by her subsequently paying off the mortgage. The parties carried on their business as a partnership and the property was shown as a partnership asset in the business accounts. That was held insufficient to show an intention that the property was to be held as tenants in common for that would have represented a fundamental change in the parties' intention from what was expressed at the time of purchase and there was no evidence of such change. Accordingly the property passed to Mr. Morris by right of survivorship.

It was held by the Court of Appeal in *Goodman* v. *Gallant*[54] that, on severance of a beneficial joint tenancy, a tenancy in common in equal shares is created and not, as was suggested in *Barton* v. *Morris*, a tenancy in common in shares proportionate to the parties' contributions. Credit may be given, however, for financial outlay, for example, in the form of mortgage repayments or improvements to the property since separation.

2. SOLE NAME

Where the property is in the name of one party to a relationship outside marriage only (usually the man), then that person is the sole legal owner and prima facie the legal estate carries with it the whole beneficial interest so that the other party has no share in the property.[55]

In the case of married partners the court can reallocate matrimonial resources on divorce, notwithstanding property rights.[56] A spouse has been given increased protection in recent years so that the contributions made by each of the parties to the welfare of the family, including any contribution made by looking after the home or caring for the family, are taken into account on divorce, when the court decides how to exercise its powers in relation to property adjustment orders.[57] By contrast, the rights of unmarried partners are determined according to strict property

---

53 [1985] 1 W.L.R. 1257.
54 [1986] Fam. 106: see above, p. 14.
55 See *Burns* v. *Burns* [1984] Ch. 317, below, p. 27.
56 Matrimonial Causes Act 1973, s.24: see below, p. 194. Before so doing, the court has jurisdiction to determine not only the rights and interests of the spouses in the property but also the rights of third parties who claim an interest in the property: see *Tebbutt* v. *Haynes* [1981] 2 All E.R. 238.
57 Matrimonial Causes Act 1973, s.25(2)(*f*).

principles; there is no power to order a property transfer on breakdown of the relationship. As Millet J. made clear in *Windeler* v. *Whitehall*[58]:

> "English courts exercise a statutory jurisdiction to adjust the property rights of married persons on the dissolution of their marriage, but there must be a marriage to dissolve. The courts possess neither a statutory nor an inherent jurisdiction to disturb existing rights of property on the termination of an extra-marital relationship, however long established the relationship and however deserving the claimant."[59]

It may be possible for a cohabitee (usually the woman) who is not the legal owner to establish that she has a beneficial interest in the home by showing that the other cohabitee, as legal owner, holds the property on trust for them both. This is because:

> "When a man (it usually is a man) purchases property and his companion (married or unmarried, female or male) contributes to the purchase price, or contributes to the payment of a mortgage, equity treats the legal owner as trustee of the property for himself and his companion in the proportions in which they contribute to the purchase price because it would be unconscionable for the legal owner to continue to assert absolute ownership unless there is some express agreement between the parties, or unless the circumstances in which the contributions were made established a gift or loan or some relationship incompatible with the creation of a trust."[60]

Establishing a trust

A deed is required to convey or create any legal estate in land.[61] The legal owner can declare a trust stating that the property is to be held on trust for himself and another, for example, a cohabitee, and setting out their respective shares. The declaration can be quite simple in form, but must be evidenced in writing and signed by the creator of the trust; and no interest in land can be created or disposed of except by writing signed by the creator. These formalities prescribed by section 53(1)(*b*) of the Law of Property Act 1925 do " . . . not affect the creation or operation of resulting, implied or constructive trusts".[62]

---

58 [1990] 2 F.L.R. 505 at 506.
59 See also, *e.g. Re Evers' Trust* [1980] 1 W.L.R. 1327, below, p. 24; *Burns* v. *Burns* [1984] Ch. 317, below, p. 27; *Cousins* v. *Dzosens* (1984) 81 L.S.Gaz. 2855; *Hammond* v. *Mitchell* [1991] 1 W.L.R. 1127, below, p. 25. By contrast there is power to make a property adjustment order in favour of a child of the relationship: see below, p. 153.
60 *Per* Lord Templeman in *Winkworth* v. *Edward Baron Development Co. Ltd.* [1987] 1 All E.R. 114 at 118.
61 Law of Property Act 1925, s.52.
62 Law of Property Act 1925, s.53(2). See also *Midland Bank PLC* v. *Dobson and Dobson* [1986] 1 F.L.R. 171.

Usually there is no express declaration of trust and reliance is placed on the doctrine of resulting, implied or constructive trusts. These trusts are not easy to distinguish; indeed the courts frequently do not distinguish between them.[63] In so far as a distinction is still made, it seems to be between, on the one hand, a resulting or implied trust and, on the other hand, a constructive trust. The concept of the resulting trust is narrower in scope as it is based on the parties' intention where there has been a financial contribution by the claimant to the acquisition of the property, and the claimant's beneficial interest is in proportion to his or her contribution. Whilst such cases can be argued as giving rise to a beneficial interest under a constructive trust, such a trust is wider, and more uncertain, in not necessarily depending upon any financial contribution, but extending to the claimant having acted to her detriment in reliance on the parties' intention that they should both have a beneficial interest in the property.

In the absence of a common intention[64] there is no trust, leaving the claimant to seek a remedy, if any, in proprietary estoppel which may now provide the safety net previously provided by a broad interpretation of the constructive trust as a means of providing justice in terms of result, rather than proprietary principle.[65] An agreement or common intention is not sufficient in itself, however, to give rise to a trust, because a voluntary declaration of trust of land is unenforceable, in the absence of writing. There must be some action or conduct by the claimant in reliance on that intention to her detriment, so that it would be inequitable to deny her a beneficial interest in the property. Otherwise equity will not assist a volunteer.

The proliferation of case law in this area has obscured rather than clarified the legal principles regarding both the classification and creation of these trusts. The time has not " . . . yet arrived when it is possible to state the law in a way which will deal with all the practical problems which may arise in this difficult field, consistently with everything said in the cases".[66] That caveat applies to the following analysis as it does to any analysis of this continually developing area of law. The development of the constructive trust, in particular by Lord Denning during the 1970s,[67] in order to achieve the just and equitable result was countered during the 1980s by a return to more settled principles of property law[68] derived from the decisions of the House of Lords in *Pettit* v. *Pettit*[69] and

---

63 See, *e.g.* Lord Diplock in *Gissing* v. *Gissing* [1971] A.C. 886 at 905; Lord Denning in *Hussey* v. *Palmer* [1972] 1 W.L.R. 1286 at 1289-1291; Fox L.J. in *Burns* v. *Burns* [1984] Ch. 317 at 326.
64 See Clarke, "The Family Home: Intention and Agreement" [1992] Fam. Law 72.
65 See below, p. 37.
66 *Per* Mustill L.J. in *Grant* v. *Edwards* [1986] Ch. 638 at 651.
67 See in particular *Cooke* v. *Head* [1972] 1 W.L.R. 518, below, p. 26; *Hussey* v. *Palmer* [1972] 1 W.L.R. 1286, discussed in the second edition of this book, para. 2-17; *Eves* v. *Eves* [1975] 1 W.L.R. 1338.
68 See, *e.g. Burns* v. *Burns* [1984] Ch. 317, below, p. 27.
69 [1970] A.C. 777.

Gissing v. *Gissing*.[70] Their Lordship's decision in *Lloyds Bank plc* v. *Rosset*[71] confirmed that return to orthodoxy.

Resulting or implied trust

Where the legal title to the property is in the name of a party other than the one who provided some or all of the purchase money, the law infers (or implies) that the parties had a common intention that the non-owner should have a beneficial interest in the property and a presumption of resulting trust arises.[72] If, for example, one cohabitee provides all (or part) of the purchase money and the home is conveyed into the name of the other cohabitee, the latter holds the property on trust for the former (and himself) in the proportions in which the purchase money was provided.[73] Similarly, in the case of a wife providing all or part of the purchase money where the house is conveyed to the husband, he owns the legal estate subject to a resulting trust for the wife. Where the home is purchased by a husband and conveyed to his wife this may be presumed to be a gift to her and the presumption of advancement applies. The presumption of advancement does not apply between the unmarried,[74] save where a man transfers property to his fiancée.[75]

The presumption of resulting trust is rebuttable by evidence that to apply it would be inconsistent with the parties' intention,[76] for example, evidence that the contribution was a loan or a gift. There has been occasional reluctance in the case of an unmarried couple for the court to imply a common intention to share the beneficial interest in such circumstances. Thus in *Richards* v. *Dove*,[77] an unmarried couple bought a house which was conveyed into the man's name. The house cost £3,500, of which Mr. Dove provided £350 and Miss Richards provided £150, the balance being obtained by mortgage granted to Mr. Dove. He paid the household bills and she paid for food and gas. The relationship broke up and Miss Richards claimed that Mr. Dove held the property on trust for them both. Her claim failed. The judge held that although the trust concept applies to cohabitees as well as spouses, there is a difference in the application of the concept, because a husband is under a legal duty to maintain his wife, whereas no such obligation arises as a result of cohabitation. A cohabitee must, therefore, show that the home has been acquired by their joint efforts and that her contribution was made with

---

70 [1971] A.C. 886.

71 [1991] 1 A.C. 107: see below, p. 23.

72 See, *e.g.* Crane v. Davis, *The Times*, May 13, 1981.

73 *Re Roger's Question* [1948] 1 All E.R. 328; *Sekhon* v. *Alissa* [1989] 2 F.L.R. 94.

74 *Soar* v. *Foster* (1858) 4 K. & J. 152, and must be applied with caution as between spouses: see *Harwood* v. *Harwood* [1991] 2 F.L.R. 274 at 294, *per* Slade L.J.

75 *Moate* v. *Moate* [1948] 2 All E.R. 486.

76 Where there is an illegal transaction, a party can recover if he can establish his title without relying on his own illegality even if it emerges that the title was acquired in the course of carrying through an illegal transaction: see *Tinsley* v. *Milligan* [1993] 3 All E.R. 65.

77 [1974] 1 All E.R. 888. Compare *Sekhon* v. *Alissa* [1989] 2 F.L.R. 94 where the court was not satisfied that a mother's contribution to purchase of property in her daughter's sole name was a gift or loan and so the presumption of resulting trust was not rebutted.

the intention of helping with the purchase of the home, and thus with the aim of acquiring some interest in the property. The judge held that Miss Richards had lent the money and could not have intended to acquire an interest in the home, and her contributions to the household expenses could not be regarded as giving her any interest in the home. His finding was at a time when cohabitation was less accepted than it has become and the case does not seem to reflect current attitudes to cohabitation.

So as a general principle, a cohabitee who is claiming a beneficial interest under a resulting trust must show a common intention that she should have a beneficial interest in the home and that she has financially contributed towards its acquisition. If the parties have made an agreement that the claimant is to have an interest, this will go some way to showing their intention,[78] unless the agreement is regarded as a "cohabitation contract", in which case it may be void as contrary to public policy, or unenforceable as not intended to give rise to a legal relationship.[79] The decided cases on trusts between cohabitees have not been argued on such grounds and it seems that such agreements will be given effect. In the absence of any express agreement, the courts resort to the inferred common intention and seek to determine the parties' original intention, on the basis that the claimant can only acquire an interest on the strength of the parties' common intention at the time of acquisition of the property,[80] not at any subsequent time. This may give rise to a fiction. When a couple buy a home, its ultimate division is unlikely to be contemplated.[81] In determining the parties' intention, there is an element of artificiality; the court will seek to draw such inferences as are reasonable from the parties' words or conduct, for example, regular mortgage repayments may be relevant in so far as it helps to imply the parties' intention at the time of acquisition. Once the relationship has broken down, events thereafter will rarely be of assistance in the search for the original intention.

The repayment of an outstanding mortgage debt may count as a contribution towards the purchase price, as may mortgage repayments, provided the repayments are regular and substantial. So in *Diwell* v. *Farnes*,[82] a woman who lived with a man as his wife but who was not married to him was held entitled to a share, by way of resulting trust, in the proceeds of sale of the property owned by him, since her payments towards the repayment of the mortgage were contributions towards the purchase price of the property. Her share was in proportion to her contributions. In such a case, the amount of the share will be more difficult to calculate than a cash contribution to the purchase price. There must, however, be a financial contribution, as the basis of a resulting trust, the limitations of which have reduced its significance as an effective remedy.

---

78 See also *Grant* v. *Edwards* [1986] Ch. 638, below, p. 25.
79 See below, p. 235.
80 See *Burns* v. *Burns* [1984] Ch. 317.
81 See *Midland Bank PLC* v. *Dobson and Dobson* [1986] 1 F.L.R. 171.
82 [1959] 1 W.L.R. 624.

Constructive trusts

An alternative course of action is to seek to establish the existence of a constructive trust. It is still necessary to show that the parties had a common intention that the claimant should have a beneficial interest in the property.[83] Such intention can arise either by express but informal agreement, arrangement or understanding between the parties[84] or, in the absence of such evidence, where the parties' conduct is such as to provide a basis from which a common intention to share the property can be inferred. In the words of Lord Bridge in the single opinion in *Lloyds Bank plc* v. *Rosset*[85]:

"The first and fundamental question which must always be resolved is whether, independently of any inference to be drawn from the conduct of the parties in the course of sharing the house as their home and managing their joint affairs, there has at any time prior to acquisition, or exceptionally at some later date, been any agreement, arrangement or understanding reached between them that the property is to be shared beneficially. The finding of an agreement or arrangement to share in this sense can only, I think, be based on evidence of express discussions between the partners, however imperfectly remembered and however imprecise their terms may have been. Once a finding to this effect is made it will only be necessary for the partner asserting a claim to a beneficial interest against the partner entitled to the legal estate to show that he or she has acted to his or her detriment or significantly altered his or her position in reliance on the agreement to give rise to a constructive trust or proprietary estoppel.

In sharp contrast with this situation is the very different one where there is no evidence to support a finding of an agreement or arrangement to share, however reasonable it might have been for the parties to reach such an arrangement if they had applied their minds to the question, and where the court must rely entirely on the conduct of the parties both as the basis from which to infer a common intention to share the property beneficially and as the conduct relied on to give rise to a constructive trust. In this situation direct contributions to the purchase price by the partner who is not the legal owner, whether initially or by payment of mortgage instalments, will readily justify the inference necessary to the

---

83 For cases of an unmarried couple where there was no evidence of a common intention, see *Howard* v. *Jones* [1989] Fam. Law 231; *Windeler* v. *Whitehall* [1990] 2 F.L.R. 505, below, p. 40.

84 For examples of express agreement between cohabitees, see *Risch* v. *McFee* [1991] 1 F.L.R. 105 (claimant assured that her name was as good as being on the title deeds); *Stokes* v. *Anderson* [1991] 1 F.L.R. 391, below, p. 25; *Hammond* v. *Mitchell* [1991] 1 W.L.R. 1127, below, p. 25.

85 [1991] 1 A.C. 107 at 132: see Thompson, [1990] Conv. 314; Davies, (1990) 106 L.Q.R. 539; Gardner, "A Woman's Work" (1991) 54 M.L.R. 126.

creation of a constructive trust. But, as I read the authorities, it is at least extremely doubtful whether anything less will do."

Lord Bridge, who declined to undertake "an elaborate and exhaustive analysis of the relevant law", did not distinguish between either resulting, implied, and constructive trusts or between constructive trusts and proprietary estoppel. With regard to the issue of common intention he distinguished between, first, evidence capable of establishing an *express* agreement or representation that the partner who is not the legal owner is to have a beneficial interest and, secondly, evidence of conduct alone as a basis for an *inferred* common intention. Only in the case of an express common intention is it sufficient merely for the claimant to show an acting to his or her detriment in reliance on the intention. His Lordship considered that on the facts there was no evidence of an express common intention between Mr. and Mrs. Rosset[86] and so her supervising building work and redecorating the house were not sufficient conduct from which to infer a common intention *and* acts of reliance thereon to qualify her for a beneficial interest in the property, which was in her husband's name as required by the trustees of his family trust which provided the purchase money. Indeed it was doubted that her contribution would have been sufficient even if her husband had clearly represented that he intended that they should share the property.

Lord Bridge gave as an example of an express agreement the case of *Eves* v. *Eves*.[87] Mr. and Mrs. Eves were cohabitees and she was the mother of his children. They bought a house in a dilapidated condition and it was conveyed into Mr. Eves' sole name, after he had told Mrs. Eves that as she was under 21 the house could not be in joint names. He provided the purchase price, partly by cash and the balance on mortgage and she did a great deal of work to the house and garden. On breakdown of the relationship she claimed that Mr. Eves held the house on trust for them both. Lord Denning held that, in view of Mr. Eves' behaviour in telling her that the property was to be their joint home and that it would have been conveyed into their joint names but for her age, it would be "inequitable" to deny her a share. Browne L.J. and Brightman J. found in her favour, on the basis that there was an agreement between the parties that she should contribute her labour towards the property in return for a share in the beneficial interest. The judges were therefore saying different things. Lord Denning's finding was irrespective of the parties' intention. He said that the trust arose not because that was the

---

86 The case concerned a claim by a spouse against a third party creditor rather than one between spouses or between cohabitees, but is to be regarded as the leading authority in that regard: see, *e.g. Hammond* v. *Mitchell* [1991] 1 W.L.R. 1127; *Stokes* v. *Anderson* [1991] 1 F.L.R. 391; *Savill* v. *Goodall* [1993] 1 F.L.R. 755.
87 [1975] 1 W.L.R. 1338.

parties' intention, but because that was the equitable result.[88] The other members of the Court said that a trust arose because that is what the parties had intended. That intention was interpreted in *Rosset* as being an express agreement and not one inferred from conduct.

A second case referred to and approved in the opinion in *Rosset* as being an outstanding example of express intention was *Grant* v. *Edwards*,[89] where a female cohabitee was told by her male partner that her name would have been on the title deeds but for her divorce proceedings with her husband and that if the property was acquired jointly, that might operate to her prejudice in those proceedings. There was evidence that she had made substantial indirect contributions to the mortgage instalments and that was conduct on which she could not reasonably have been expected to embark unless she was to have an interest in the house.

The dicta in *Rosset* have subsequently been applied in a number of cases concerning former cohabiting couples. In *Stokes* v. *Anderson*[90] Mr Stokes' saying he would put Miss Anderson's name on the deeds when he had got it all sorted out was evidence of a common intention and that payments of £5000 and £7000 by her were not loans but conduct amounting to an acting on the common intention so as to give her a beneficial interest. In *Hammond* v. *Mitchell*[91] there were express discussions which, although not directed with any precision to proprietary interests, were sufficient to give rise to an understanding that the property was to be shared beneficially. Miss Mitchell's participation in commercial activities based on the property was conduct consistent with that intention and was also to her detriment because their speculative nature might have led to the sale of the property.

In *Rosset* the subsequent conduct of the women in *Eves* and *Grant* v. *Edwards* was not considered as having been sufficient conduct by itself to have supported the claim of a constructive trust in the absence of the express representation. So, where the claimant is relying on the parties' conduct as the basis for both an *inferred* common intention and as giving rise to a trust, the courts have become far more restrictive regarding the conduct which will suffice. The suggestion in *Rosset* is that such conduct is limited to direct contributions to the purchase price either initially or

---

88 For examples of similar reliance on the constructive trust doctrine in the Commonwealth, see *Dwyer* v. *Love* (1976) 58 D.L.R. (3d) 735; *Pettkus* v. *Becker* (1981) 117 D.L.R. (3d) 257; *Baumgartner* v. *Baumgartner* (1987) 164 C.L.R. 137; Bryan, "Constructive Trusts in the Beehive" (1982) 12 Fam. Law 21; Bates, "More Trusts and Antipodean Concubinage" [1982] Conv. 424; Hodkinson, "Constructive Trusts: Palm Trees in the Commonwealth" [1983] Conv. 420; Hayton, "Remedial Constructive Trusts of Homes; An Overseas View" [1988] Conv. 259; Bryan, "Constructive Trusts: A New Zealand Development" (1990) 106 L.Q.R. 213; Gardner, "Rethinking Family Property" (1993) 109 L.Q.R. 263.
89 [1986] Ch. 638.
90 [1991] 1 F.L.R. 391.
91 [1991] 1 W.L.R. 1127; Lawson, [1992] Conv. 218; Clarke and Edmunds, "*H* v. *M*: Equity and the Essex Cohabitant" [1992] Fam. Law 523. See also *Savill* v. *Goodall* [1993] 1 F.L.R. 755.

by payment of mortgage instalments. In view of this narrow interpretation of the circumstances in which the court can find an inferred common
intention, there may be a greater preparedness to find an express
intention, as occurred in *Grant* v. *Edwards*, in the woman's favour than
where the claimant cohabitee is the male partner as in *Thomas* v. *Fuller-
Brown*.[92] Mrs. Thomas paid the purchase price of the property and they
both applied for an improvement grant. They agreed that he should carry
out the work in return for her keeping him. He built a two-storey
extension, created a through lounge, carried out minor electrical and
plumbing works, replastered and redecorated the property throughout,
landscaped the garden, laid a driveway, repaired the roof, built an entry
hall, rebuilt the kitchen and installed a new stairway. The Court of
Appeal held that there was no express agreement and, furthermore, Mr.
Fuller-Brown had not established that a common intention should be
inferred from their conduct and his claim for a beneficial interest failed.

In *Grant* v. *Edwards* it was suggested[93] that:

> " . . . where, although there has been no writing, the parties have
> orally declared themselves in such a way as to make their common
> intention plain . . . the court does not have to look for conduct
> from which the intention can be inferred, but only for conduct
> which amounts to an acting upon it by the claimant."

The case did not make clear what connection there must be between the
conduct and the original intention. It seems, however, after *Rosset*, that
if an express intention is established, then the claimant must go on to
show that she has acted to her detriment in reliance on the intention and
the acts in reliance are referable to the intention.[94] It is in this context
that the detriment to the claimant may be, but need not be, of a financial
nature. A direct contribution by labour towards the acquisition of the
home may also suffice as, for example, in *Eves*. It is also possible to
justify the decision in the earlier case of *Cooke* v. *Head*[95] on that basis.
Miss Cooke and Mr. Head, a married man, decided to acquire land and
build a bungalow on it. He paid a deposit of £390 and raised £3,000 on
mortgage. The conveyance was taken in his name. Miss Cooke contributed nothing in cash, but helped by doing a lot of heavy work. She used
a sledgehammer to demolish old buildings, worked a cement mixer, filled
a wheelbarrow with rubble and helped with the painting. When the
bungalow was nearly completed, they separated and Miss Cooke brought
an action claiming a beneficial interest. The Court of Appeal held that
Mr. Head held the property on trust for himself and Miss Cooke. The
different treatment of Miss Cooke's claim from that of Mr. Fuller-

---

92 [1988] 1 F.L.R. 237.
93 [1986] Ch. 638 at 647, *per* Nourse L.J. See also Browne-Wilkinson V.-C. at 657;
    Warburton, [1986] Conv. 291; Hayton, [1986] C.L.J. 394; Sufrin, (1987) 50 M.L.R. 94.
94 See also *Midland Bank PLC* v. *Dobson and Dobson* [1986] 1 F.L.R. 171.
95 [1972] 1 W.L.R. 518.

Brown[96] can be explained, in the light of recent case law, on the basis that there was an express agreement in the former's case which there was not in the latter's.

Where there is no express common intention then, after *Rosset*, it seems that the courts will infer an intention to share the beneficial ownership only if there is evidence of a financial contribution to the acquisition of the property which manifests an intention that beneficial ownership is to be shared. On one analysis such cases can be classified as giving rise to a presumed resulting trust,[97] although that classification was not considered in *Rosset*. The contribution will be evidence from which a common intention can be inferred and from which it can be shown that the claimant has acted to her detriment in reliance on that intention. Such a contribution may include a financial contribution to the purchase or the payment of mortgage instalments[98] as both can be seen as being a direct contribution to the acquisition of the property.

What remains uncertain is the extent, if any, to which account will be taken of indirect contributions, *i.e.* contributions such as to relieve the other party from paying sums which he would otherwise have had to pay. In so far as such contributions have been recognised as giving rise to a beneficial interest, they must, it seems, be substantial and in money or money's worth, and be referable to the acquisition of the property.[99] There must also be evidence that the contributions show an intention that the beneficial ownership is to be shared.

Although there have been suggestions that the court can take into account looking after the other cohabitee and caring for the children,[1] such conduct is not enough. Indirect contributions, in so far as they are relevant after the extreme doubts expressed in *Rosset*, must be made with the intention of helping towards the purchase of the property and, arguably, be essential to the purchase, for example, by releasing the other partner's income to pay the mortgage. So a better classification, it has been suggested, is to require "referable" financial contributions, be they direct or indirect.[2] On this basis it is not enough to contribute towards household expenses or to do the housekeeping.[3] So in *Burns* v.

---

96 See above, p. 26.
97 See above, p. 21.
98 *Bernard* v. *Josephs* [1982] Ch. 391; *Marsh* v. *Von Sternberg* [1986] 1 F.L.R. 526.
99 *Winkworth* v. *Edward Baron Development Co. Ltd.* [1987] 1 W.L.R. 1512, H.L.; Warburton, [1987] Conv. 217.
1 See *Eves* v. *Eves* [1975] 1 W.L.R. 1338; Lord Denning in *Hall* v. *Hall* (1982) 3 F.L.R. 379 at 381. In that case counsel conceded that there was a resulting trust in favour of the applicant, a concession described in *Burns* v. *Burns* as wrongly made ([1984] Ch. 317 at 341, *per* May L.J.).
2 See Dixon, "Acquiring An Interest In Another's Property" [1991] C.L.J. 38.
3 Thus, *e.g.* a contribution towards rent has been held not to create a beneficial interest in favour of the contributor: *Diwell* v. *Farnes* [1959] 1 W.L.R. 624; *Savage* v. *Dunningham* [1974] Ch. 181. See also *Spence* v. *Brown* [1988] Fam. Law 291 (money advanced by mother to daughter and son-in-law for improvement to their house in return for being allowed to live there held not to give rise to a beneficial interest); compare *Hussey* v. *Palmer* [1972] 1 W.L.R. 1286.

Burns[4] the parties, although not married, had lived together for 19 years as husband and wife and the woman brought up their two children. Only towards the end of the relationship was Mrs. Burns in a position to work, her earnings then going into the housekeeping. She bought certain fixtures, fittings and household items as well as doing some decorating. She claimed a share in the house bought by Mr. Burns in his sole name and for which he provided the purchase price and mortgage instalments. None of her expenditure was seen by the Court of Appeal as indicating a common intention that she was to have a beneficial interest in the property, for that requires a substantial contribution in money or money's worth towards the expenses of the household which can be related to the acquisition of the property. One can question whether Mrs. Burns' contribution over the years was any less than the muscle power of Miss Cooke, Mrs. Grant and Mrs. Eves. Their more favourable treatment can be explained on the basis that they had an express agreement with their partners that the beneficial ownership was to be shared, whereas Mrs. Burns was seeking to establish an inferred intention. As Fox L.J. acknowledged[5]: " . . . she lived with him for 18 years as man and wife, and, at the end of it, has no right against him. But the unfairness of that is not a matter which the courts can control. It is a matter for Parliament." The emphasis that the courts have placed upon financial contributions puts a cohabitee whose contribution has been to the relationship and the family alone at a considerable disadvantage.[6]

Also disadvantaged is the claimant whose relationship with the legal owner arose after he acquired the property, following the suggestion in *Rosset* that only exceptionally will there be an agreement at some later date than acquisition of the property. It may be that there is no express agreement, or the evidence is so conflicting that one cannot be shown, in which event it will be difficult for the claimant to establish conduct both as the basis to infer a common intention to share the property and such as was sufficiently relied upon to give rise to a constructive trust and she may well have to fall back on arguing proprietary estoppel.[7]

Special mention must be made of contributions by way of improvements to the home. Where a husband or wife makes such a contribution he, or she, subject to any agreement between them to the contrary, is treated as having acquired a beneficial interest in the home, provided that the contribution is of a substantial nature and is in money or money's worth.[8] This provision does not apply to cohabitees who must rely on the trust concept and, as has been seen, the law is uncertain. The uncertainty has been dispelled in relation to improvements made by spouses and engaged couples whose engagement is terminated but not in relation to

---

4 [1984] Ch. 317. See Ingleby, [1984] C.L.J. 227.
5 [1984] Ch. 317 at 332.
6 See Eekelaar, "A Woman's Place - A Conflict Between Law And Social Values" [1987] Conv. 93.
7 See below, p. 37.
8 Matrimonial Proceedings and Property Act 1970, s.37.

improvements made by cohabitees who have not been engaged.[9] One thing is clear:

> " . . . under English law the mere fact that A expends money or labour on B's property does not by itself entitle A to an interest in the property. In the absence of express agreement or a common intention to be inferred from all the circumstances or any question of estoppel, A will normally have no claim whatever on the property in such circumstances."[10]

A cohabitee who claims a beneficial interest arising from improvements to the home must satisfy the general constructive trust principles and establish that the improvements were made with the common intention that the claimant should have a beneficial interest in the property. The parties' intention at the time of purchase is normally the determining factor. If there was an express agreement or understanding at that time both to share the beneficial interest and that the claimant would contribute by way of improvements, then the performance of those improvements, provided they are substantial and extend beyond routine maintenance and minor improvements, will give rise to a beneficial interest. If the parties did not so agree, the question is whether the common intention to confer a beneficial interest on the claimant may be inferred from their conduct and that the improvements are such that the claimant could only be expected to perform them if he or she were to acquire a beneficial interest.

3. QUANTIFYING THE BENEFICIAL INTEREST

Whether the legal ownership is in joint names[11] or sole name, if the claimant cohabitee is successful in establishing entitlement to a beneficial interest, it is then necessary to quantify the parties' shares, first, as to the proportions and, secondly, as to the date at which those proportions are valued.[12]

As to the parties' shares, in the less usual case of an initial direct contribution to the purchase price giving rise to a resulting trust, the parties' shares are in the proportions in which the purchase money was provided,[13] in the absence of an intention to share equally.[13a] If the

---

9 See above, p. 12.
10 *Thomas* v. *Fuller-Brown* [1988] 1 F.L.R. 237 at 240, *per* Slade L.J. and see above, p. 26. See also *Pettit* v. *Pettit* [1970] A.C. 777 and *per* Griffiths L.J. in *Bernard* v. *Josephs* [1982] Ch. 391 at 404. Compare *Hussey* v. *Palmer* [1972] 1 W.L.R. 1286.
11 On which, in this context, see also above, n. 38.
12 Either party can apply for an order for sale under s.30 of the Law of Property Act 1925: see below, p. 45.
13 *Re Roger's Question* [1948] 1 All E.R. 328.
13a *Savill* v. *Goodall* [1993] 1 F.L.R. 755; but in that particular case the plaintiff's agreement to discharge the mortgage meant that his share had to be debited with the principal outstanding and costs of redemption.

parties have expressed a common intention as to their shares under a constructive trust, that will presumably also be conclusive. More usually there is no such evidence and although the amount of any financial contribution will be important, particularly where the claimant has contributed towards the mortgage repayments,[14] each party's share of the beneficial interest does not depend solely on the monetary contribution each has made towards the acquisition of the home. The cases are looked at broadly in the light of *all* the particular circumstances[15] for as Nourse L.J. put it in *Stokes* v. *Anderson*[16]:

> "..the starting point must be Lord Diplock's speech in *Gissing* v. *Gissing*, from which it is clear that this question, like the anterior one, depends on the common intention of the parties, either expressed or, more usually, to be inferred from all the circumstances. That does not mean that in the latter case you have to infer a common intention that the extent of the claimant's beneficial interest is to be ascertained once and for all at the date of its acquisition . . . all payments made and acts done by the claimant are to be treated as illuminating the common intention as to the extent of the beneficial interest. Once you get to that stage, as Lord Diplock recognised, there is no practicable alternative to the determination of a fair share. The court must supply the common intention by reference to that which all the material circumstances have shown to be fair."

In this context rarely is the maxim "equality is equity" considered appropriate.[17] In *Stokes* v. *Anderson* the Court of Appeal's "fair view" of all the circumstances was that Miss Anderson was entitled to one-quarter, rather than one-half of the beneficial interest. On occasions the court has adopted an approach similar to that applied as a starting point in awarding financial provison on divorce and the claimant has received a one-third share,[18] others have received a quarter[19] others one-fifth[20] or two-fifths[21] and a few have received a half share.[22] Hence the uncertainty

---

14 See above, p. 17, and Sparkes, "The Quantification of Beneficial Interests: Problems Arising From Contributions to Deposits, Mortgage Advances and Mortgage Instalments" (1991) 11 O.J.L.S. 39. See also *Passee* v. *Passee* [1988] 1 F.L.R. 263; *Huntingford* v. *Hobbs* [1993] 1 F.L.R. 736, above, p. 16, where the majority of the Court of Appeal treated a commitment to discharge the mortgage as equivalent to payment of cash: see Wylie, "Mortgages and Ownership of the Family Home" [1993] Fam. Law 176.
15 See *Passee* v. *Passee* [1988] 1 F.L.R. 263; Warburton, [1988] Conv. 361.
16 [1991] 1 F.L.R. 391 at 399.
17 See *Hammond* v. *Mitchell* [1991] 1 W.L.R. 1127 at 1137.
18 *Cooke* v. *Head* [1972] 1 W.L.R. 518; *Cousins* v. *Dzosens* (1984) 81 L.S.Gaz. 2855.
19 *Eves* v. *Eves* [1975] 1 W.L.R. 1338; *Gordon* v. *Douce* [1983] 1 W.L.R. 563; *Walker* v. *Hall* [1984] F.L.R. 126 (property in joint names).
20 *Hall* v. *Hall* (1982) 3 F.L.R. 379.
21 *Risch* v. *McFee* [1991] 1 F.L.R. 105.
22 *Bernard* v. *Josephs* [1982] Ch. 391 (property in joint names): *Grant* v. *Edwards* [1986] Ch. 638; *Hammond* v. *Mitchell* [1991] 1 W.L.R. 1127.

surrounding the determination of a beneficial interest extends also to its quantification. This uncertainty complicates the job of the practitioner and is a further illustration of the advantage of clearly identifying the legal and beneficial ownership so as to obviate the need for negotiation, and in many cases litigation, to clarify ownership.

So far as the date at which the value of each party's share is determined, it was held by the Court of Appeal in *Turton* v. *Turton*[23] that the beneficial interests are to be regarded as held under a trust for sale with the result that they endure until the property is sold and then attach to the proceeds of sale.[24] Although the time of the parties' separation may indicate that the purpose of the trust, *i.e.* the provision of a home for the parties, has ceased, there is no discretion, as had been earlier suggested,[25] to determine the valuation of the beneficial interests at that time. Thus in *Walker* v. *Hall*[26] the property was in the joint names of Mrs. Walker and Mr. Hall but with no statement of their respective beneficial interests. On termination of the cohabitation the Court of Appeal held that the purpose of the trust had come to an end as the property was no longer used as a family home. Nevertheless the trust for sale continued until either the property was sold in execution of the trust or one party, by buying the other out, became solely and absolutely entitled. The parties' beneficial interests neither ceased nor were to be quantified as fixed on the cessation of cohabitation.

If one of the parties has spent money on the property after they have separated, it may be necessary for that expenditure to be taken into consideration by way of equitable accounting if it has preserved or enhanced the value of the property.[27] The party remaining in occupation may also be required to pay an occupation rent to the other party depending upon the circumstances.[28]

4. Protecting Rights Arising from a Beneficial Interest

If legal ownership is in joint names then the parties' beneficial interests are protected because any sale or mortgage requires the consent of both parties. Where legal ownership is in the name of one party (usually the man), then if the other party has a beneficial interest she is at risk of the legal owner dealing with the legal title without her knowledge. Such a dealing could prejudice the benefical owner's rights in the proceeds of

---

23 [1987] 3 W.L.R. 622: see Warburton, [1987] Conv. 378; Montgomery, "Back to the Future - Quantifying the Cohabitee's Share" [1988] Fam. Law 72; see also *Passee* v. *Passee* [1988] 1 F.L.R. 263.
24 Presumably the parties could agree some other date.
25 *Hall* v. *Hall* (1982) 3 F.L.R. 379.
26 [1984] F.L.R. 126. See also *Cousins* v. *Dzosens* (1984) 81 L.S.Gaz. 2855; *Gordon* v. *Douce* [1983] 1 W.L.R. 563.
27 See, *e.g. Bernard* v. *Josephs* [1982] Ch. 391.
28 See below, p. 47, and on the issue of credit for payment of mortgage instalments, see p. 50 and *Savill* v. *Goodall* [1993] 1 F.L.R. 755.

sale and rights of occupation.[29] In cases of co-ownership the legislation[30] imposes a trust for sale. Where there is a sole legal owner, the beneficiary may protect her rights arising from her beneficial interest in the proceeds of sale, *inter alia*,[31] by seeking the appointment of a second trustee[32] (*e.g.* herself, if adult). It was confirmed by the House of Lords in *City of London Building Society* v. *Flegg*[33] that dispositions of the property by two trustees, by way of sale or mortgage, will overreach the beneficial interests[34] which are transferred to the proceeds of sale. If the legal owner will not consent to the appointment of a second trustee, application should be made to the court.[35] In the absence of a second trustee, the circumstances in which a beneficial interest of a non-owner will bind a puchaser depend upon whether the title of the property is registered or unregistered.

Where the title is registered, the beneficial interest may be protected by the entry on the register of a restriction,[36] notice or caution[37] and this step should be taken if the beneficial owner is not in occupation. The interest then becomes a protected minor interest which is binding on any purchaser or mortgagee. The entry of a notice or caution will mean that the beneficiary will also have notice of any disposal and can then, if necessary, seek an injunction to prevent the transaction.[38]

The problem, of course, is that a cohabitee with a beneficial interest is unlikely to appreciate the subtleties of conveyancing law, in which case, if the interest is not protected as a minor interest by registration, it may nevertheless be an overriding interest if the beneficiary is in actual occupation of the home. The list of overriding interests is contained in section 70 of the Land Registration Act 1925, and the relevant paragraph is section 70(1)(g): "The rights of every person in actual occupation of the land or in receipt of the rents and profits thereof, save where enquiry is made of such person and the rights are not disclosed."It is not the occupation which is binding, but the rights arising under the beneficial

---

29 *Bull* v. *Bull* [1955] 1 Q.B. 234 and see p. 46.
30 Law of Property Act 1925, ss.34 and 36.
31 Also by injunction or by application under s. 30 of the Law of Property Act 1925: see below, p. 45.
32 Under Trustee Act 1925, s.41.
33 [1988] A.C. 54. See Smith, (1987) 103 L.Q.R. 520; Harpum, [1987] C.L.J. 392; Swadling, [1987] Conv. 457; Gardner, (1988) 51 M.L.R. 365; Sparkes, [1988] Conv. 141.
34 Law of Property Act 1925, ss.2 and 27. See also Harpum, "Overreaching Trustees' Powers and the Reform of the 1925 Legislation" [1990] C.L.J. 277.
35 Notice of which should be registered as a caution if title is registered and a *lis pendens* if it is unregistered. In the case of unregistered title, notice of appointment should be endorsed on the title deeds.
36 Which requires production of the land certificate (see Land Registration Act 1925, s.64(1)(c)), and hence the co-operation of the registered proprietor. If there is a restriction, there cannot be a sale unless its terms are complied with.
37 A notice, but not a caution, also requires production of the land certificate: see Land Registration Act 1925, ss.54, 101(3). See also *Elias* v. *Mitchell* [1972] Ch. 652; *Belcourt* v. *Belcourt* [1989] 1 W.L.R. 195.
38 *Waller* v. *Waller* [1967] 1 W.L.R. 451.

interest because of the occupation. The interest is overriding because any purchaser or mortgagee takes the property subject to that interest even though it is not registered, for an interest can only be an overriding interest if it is not protected as a minor interest by registration.[39]

In *Williams and Glyn's Bank Ltd. v. Boland*,[40] a husband bought the home with a substantial contribution from his wife, but he was registered as sole owner. The wife had a beneficial interest by virtue of her contribution. In order to raise money for his business, the husband later mortgaged the property to the bank without his wife's knowledge. His business failed and the bank sought possession. The question was whether or not the wife's beneficial interest took priority over the bank's mortgage. The House of Lords held that it did. A spouse who buys the home with the help of a contribution from the other spouse holds the home, and not merely the proceeds of sale, on trust for them both. The trust confers a right which is binding as an overriding interest because the contributor is in actual occupation. The overriding interest entitles the contributor to remain in possession.[41]

The result is that any purchaser or lender ought to make inquiries of every person in actual occupation. If an occupier discloses any interest the purchaser or lender takes subject to the interest, unless he obtains a release from the occupier, for example, by getting the occupier to join in the conveyance or mortgage,[42] otherwise it is only where inquiry is made of such person and the rights are not disclosed that the purchaser or lender takes free from any interest.

Whether a person is in actual occupation or not is a question of fact and as Lord Oliver said in *Abbey National Building Society v. Cann*[43]:

> "It is, perhaps, dangerous to suggest any test for what is essentially a question of fact, for 'occupation' is a concept which may have different connotations according to the nature and purpose of the property which is claimed to be occupied. It does not necessarily, I think, involve the personal presence of the person claiming to occupy . . . On the other hand, it does in my judgment involve some degree of permanence and continuity which would rule out mere fleeting presence."

Certainly a wife who is physically present and living in the home is in actual occupation, and the same, it seems, applies between cohabitees. In *Hodgson v. Marks*[44] the Court of Appeal decided that a purchaser must pay heed to anyone occupying the home. In *Boland* the case of

---

39 Land Registration Act 1925, s.3(xvi).
40 [1981] A.C. 487.
41 Subject to the rights of the trustee in bankruptcy if the owner is insolvent.
42 See, *e.g.* *Hammond* v. *Mitchell* [1991] 1 W.L.R. 1127 at 1132. Such a release may be questionable for undue influence: see *Barclays Bank* v. *O'Brien* [1992] 3 W.L.R. 593.
43 [1991] 1 A.C. 56 at 93. For an *obiter* discussion of the term in a case where title was unregistered, see *Kingsnorth Trust Ltd.* v. *Tizard* [1986] 1 W.L.R. 783.
44 [1971] Ch. 892.

cohabitees was considered and the suggested solution[45] was to read section 70(1)(g) for what it said, so that anyone in occupation who had proprietary rights in the home was entitled to have those rights protected, so long as they were in actual occupation. Personal rights, for example, those of a lodger, are not protected, but rights arising from a beneficial interest are protected, whether the beneficiary is a wife, a cohabitee, a mistress or whatever. Parties to a family cohabitation or homosexual cohabitation, with a beneficial interest, will thus qualify. The need to make inquiries of occupiers as to their rights could, of course, be embarrassing for potential purchasers and mortgagees. Whilst it is standard practice for them to inquire of the legal owner, section 70 envisages inquiries of any person in actual occupation. To rely on an inquiry of the legal owner may neither elicit the true picture nor afford protection.

In *Boland* the beneficial interest was not overreached because the mortgage money was not paid to two trustees and the case is thus distinguishable from *City of London Building Society* v. *Flegg*. In both cases there was an interest capable of being overriding but only in *Flegg*, where there were two trustees, was it overreached.[46]

The decision in *Boland* is subject to a number of significant qualifications, which have had the effect of confining its effect to second, or subsequent, rather than first mortgages.

It was held by the House of Lords in *Abbey National Building Society* v. *Cann*[47] that the relevant date for determining whether an interest in registered land is protected by actual occupation is the date of completion of the relevant transaction and not when it is registered. So in the usual case of a purchase and contemporaneous first mortgage, the mortgagee is likely to take priority either because the party with the beneficial interest will not have been in occupation at the time the mortgage was completed, or because even if she is in occupation there is no point in time at which the legal owner takes the title unencumbered by the mortgage; "the acquisition of the legal estate and the charge are not only precisely but indissolubly bound together".[48] So there is no unencumbered legal estate to which the beneficial interest can attach.

Moreover, in *Boland*, the wife was ignorant of the mortgage to the bank. Where, however, the beneficiary knows of the disposition to the third party, the decision in *Cann* confirms in *Bristol and West Building Society* v. *Henning*[49] that an intention can be inferred that her beneficial interest is to be subject to the third party's charge. Mr. and Mrs.

---

45 [1981] A.C. 487 at 506, *per* Lord Wilberforce.
46 The Law Commission has proposed that a beneficiary who is living in the property would have to consent to a sale: see Law Com. No. 181, *Trusts of Land: Overreaching* (1989). This proposal would in effect reverse the decision in *Flegg* as the beneficial interest would be overreached without that consent.
47 [1991] 1 A.C. 56: see Oakley, [1990] C.L.J. 397; Baughen, "Some Lessons of Cann" [1991] Conv. 116; Evans, [1991] Conv. 155; Smith, [1990] L.Q.R. 545.
48 *Per* Lord Oliver at 92.
49 [1985] 1 W.L.R. 778; Welstead, [1985] C.L.J. 354; Thompson, (1986) 49 M.L.R. 245.

Henning, although not married, lived together as husband and wife and they bought a house, title to which was unregistered, and it was conveyed in Mr. Henning's sole name. The property was mortgaged to the plaintiff building society with Mrs. Henning's full knowledge and approval. It was held that there was a common intention that Mr. Henning, as trustee, should have power to mortgage the property and that the mortgage should have priority over any beneficial interests in the property. The decision in *Henning* was applied to registered land in *Paddington Building Society* v. *Mendelsohn*,[50] a case involving a mother and son who agreed that the son should take the transfer and mortgage of a leasehold flat in his name. An intention was imputed to the mother that the building society should take priority. The case also involved a mortgage granted at the time of acquisition when it is more likely that the beneficiary will be aware of it, as opposed to the situation when a mortgage is used subsequently, as in *Boland*, to fund one party's financial dealings. In both *Henning* and *Mendelsohn* the beneficiary benefited from the mortgage, without which the purchase could not have proceeded. In the *Boland* situation the purchase had already occurred. If the beneficiary knows of the subsequent mortgage, it has been argued[51] that this may not be decisive unless the beneficiary also benefits from the mortgage, in which case there is then the uncertainty as to what constitutes such benefit.

The decision in *Henning* was extended by the Court of Appeal in *Equity and Law Home Loans Ltd.* v. *Prestidge*[52] to the case where the beneficial owner agreed to the mortgage but was unaware of its later redemption and the property's remortgage. The defendants, Mr. Prestidge and Mrs. Brown, cohabited in a house, the legal title to which was in his name. It was conceded that he held the entire beneficial interest upon trust for Mrs. Brown who financed £10,000 of the purchase price with the balance of approximately £30,000 being raised on mortgage, between Mr. Prestidge and the Britannia Building Society, to which Mrs. Brown consented. Later, unbeknown to Mrs. Brown, the plaintiffs advanced approximately £43,000 secured by a mortgage on the property. Mr. Prestidge used some of the moneys to pay off the first mortgage and kept the balance. The defendants' cohabitation broke down and Mr. Prestidge made no repayments to the plaintiffs who claimed possession. It was accepted that if the mortgage had remained where it was, Mrs. Brown would have had no answer to a claim for possession. The new mortgage was held to have been made against the background of consent to the creation of an encumbrance entered into in order to enable the purchase to proceed. That imputed consent applied to the creation of a replacement mortgage, provided it did not change the beneficial owner's

---

50 [1987] Fam. Law 121. See Thompson, [1986] Conv. 57.
51 See Martin, "Co-ownership and the Mortgagee: A Tangled Web" [1986] Fam. Law 315.
52 [1992] 1 W.L.R. 137: see Dixon, [1992] C.L.J. 223; Greed, "Mortgagees and contributors" (1992) 142 N.L.J. 539; Thompson, [1992] Conv. 206; Smith, (1992) 108 L.Q.R. 371.

position for the worse, so Mrs. Brown was bound only up to the extent of the first mortgage.[53] This was so whether or not she was aware of the remortgage and irrespective of whether the mortgagees should have been put on notice of her interest.

Where title to the property is unregistered and there is a disposition by a sole trustee, protection of the beneficial interest as an interest in the property depends upon any purchaser or mortgagee having prior notice of the interest, for which purpose details of the beneficial interest should be endorsed on the title deeds. Notice may be either actual where the person has knowledge of it or constructive where the person ought to have knowledge of it, for example, if he had made such inquiries and inspections as he ought reasonably to have made.[54] The authorities do not support the registration of the interest as a land charge.[55] There is nothing to be lost, other than the risk of the costs involved, in registering the interest as a Class C(iii) land charge, for even if it is later ordered to be cleared from the register, it will have given any purchaser or mortgagee notice of the beneficial interest and any purchaser should then pay the purchase money to two trustees. If necessary, the beneficiary can seek an injunction to restrain any dealing with the home. If proceedings have begun, it is possible to register a pending land action.[56]

Even if the beneficial interest is neither endorsed on the deeds nor registered, it may nevertheless be protected. The decision in *Boland*, although a case on registered land, suggests that a purchaser or mortgagee of unregistered land will be regarded as having notice of the beneficial interest of anyone in occupation of the property. There have been earlier statements to the contrary, as in *Caunce* v. *Caunce*,[57] where it was held that a bank to whom the property was mortgaged was not to be regarded as having constructive notice of the wife's beneficial interest merely because she was living in the property, together with the husband. Such statements, however, are out of line with subsequent decisions, and it is doubted that they have survived *Boland*.[58] It is necessary, however, not only for the beneficiary to be in occupation but also that the occupation is discoverable "if such inquiries and inspection had been made as ought reasonably to have been made".[59]

Thus in *Kingsnorth Trust Ltd.* v. *Tizard*,[60] Mr. Tizard was the sole legal owner of the matrimonial home, title to which was unregistered, and in which his wife had a half share of the beneficial interest. The marriage broke down and Mrs. Tizard went to live nearby returning to

---

53 *Quaere* whether the terms of the remortgage were no less favourable to her: see Lunney, "Never Trust a Man" (1993) 56 M.L.R. 87.
54 Law of Property Act 1925, s.199(1).
55 *Re Rayleigh Weir Stadium* [1954] 1 W.L.R. 786; Land Charges Act 1972, s.2(4)(iii)(*b*): *Kingsnorth Trust Ltd.* v. *Tizard* [1986] 1 W.L.R. 783.
56 Land Charges Act 1972, s.17(1), and see further Murphy and Clark, *The Family Home* (1983), p. 164.
57 [1969] 1 W.L.R. 286.
58 [1981] A.C. 487 at 506, *per* Lord Wilberforce.
59 Law of Property Act 1925, s.199(1).
60 [1986] 1 W.L.R. 783.

sleep in the home only during the husband's frequent absences. She also came to the house during the daytime to help look after the children. The husband applied to Kingsnorth for a mortgage stating that he was single. A surveyor acting for Kingsnorth inspected the property by arrangement on a Sunday afternoon when Mr. Tizard made sure his wife was away. After receiving the mortgage moneys the husband emigrated. In an action by Kingsnorth to enforce the mortgage the issues were whether the wife was in occupation and if so whether the mortgagee had notice of the occupation. On the facts, the wife was held to have been in occupation of the property. Mr. Tizard having informed the surveyor he was married but separated, but having described himself as single on the mortgage application form, meant that there was a duty to look for signs of occupation by a third party. The pre-arranged inspection was not sufficient to be such inspection as ought reasonably to have been made and the mortgagee had constructive notice of the interests of the wife who was in occupation. The decision places a considerable burden upon mortgagees and purchasers as to the extent of the inspection which they are required to carry out[61] but without identifying what constitutes reasonable inspection.

What would the position have been if Mr. and Mrs. Tizard had not been married? Presumably an unmarried Mrs. Tizard would still have been in occupation, for Mrs. Tizard's marital status did not seem to be relevant in determining that issue. It was relevant, however, in relation to the subsequent issue of the inquiries and inspection that ought reasonably to have been made. If there is no evidence of a cohabitee's occupation from an inspection and the mortgagor or vendor in reply to a question as to his marital status indicates that he is single, must the mortgagee or purchaser inquire further as to relationships outside marriage? To be guaranteed priority he would be best advised to take that precaution. If there is evidence of occupation by a possible cohabitee, it seems the third party will have notice of such person's rights if he does not make reasonable inquiry and inspection.

It must be remembered that the beneficial interest will not be protected if the beneficial owner knows of the disposition, as, for example, in the case of an acquisition mortgage, and an intention can be inferred that the third party's interest is to take priority.[62]

5. Estoppel

As an alternative to a claim based on a trust, it may be possible to argue that the legal owner is estopped from denying the claimant's belief that

---

61 See Luxton, "Clandestine Co-owners An Occupational Hazard for Mortgagees?" (1986) 136 N.L.J. 771; Thompson, "The Purchaser As Private Detective" [1986] Conv. 283; McHugh, "Overreaching The Undiscoverable" [1987] C.L.J. 28.
62 See *Bristol and West Building Society* v. *Henning* [1985] 1 W.L.R. 778, above, p. 34.

she has or would be given a proprietary interest in the property. For the claim to succeed five elements must be established[63]:

(1) the plaintiff must have made a mistake as to her legal rights;
(2) the plaintiff must have expended money or done some act on the faith of the mistaken belief;
(3) the defendant must know of the existence of his own right which is inconsistent with that claimed by the plaintiff;
(4) the defendant must know of the plaintiff's mistaken belief; and
(5) the defendant must have encouraged the plaintiff in the expenditure of money, or in the acts performed, either directly or by abstaining from asserting his legal right.

Once established, an equitable proprietary right arises in favour of the claimant which will be satisfied by the defendant giving effect to the expectations which he has encouraged, provided that any order is workable in the light of relations between the parties.[64] Such an order can relate just to occupation[65] or can extend to ownership, in which case the consequences can be very rewarding to the claimant. Thus in *Pascoe* v. *Turner*[66] Mrs. Turner moved into Mr. Pascoe's house as his housekeeper. They subsequently cohabited as man and wife. Some years later Mr. Pascoe left to live with another woman, but told Mrs. Turner "the house is yours and everything in it". The property was never conveyed to her. Mrs. Turner, with Mr. Pascoe's knowledge and encouragement, spent £230, about a quarter of her capital, on repairs and improvements. After a quarrel, Mr. Pascoe claimed possession. Mrs. Turner argued that the property was held on trust for her or, in the alternative, she had a licence to occupy for her lifetime.

The Court of Appeal decided that there was nothing on the facts from which an inference of a constructive trust could be drawn, but invoked the doctrine of estoppel, having regard to the way in which she had changed her position for the worse by spending money on the property, with the acquiescence and encouragement of Mr. Pascoe. He was required by the court to give effect to his promise and perfect the imperfect gift by transferring the property outright to Mrs. Turner. The case is significant for the generosity with which Mrs. Turner's claim was treated. Her contribution to the acquisition of the property was insufficient to establish a trust, yet her reward was greater than if she had. Indeed, she could not have hoped for more had she been married to Mr. Pascoe. The case is the closest yet to the court's wide powers to make property transfer orders on divorce. It has not opened the floodgates,

63 *Per* Fry J. in *Willmott* v. *Barber* (1880) 15 Ch.D. 96 at 105-106, approved by Scarman L.J. in *Crabb* v. *Arun District Council* [1976] Ch. 179 at 194-195. See also *Coombes* v. *Smith* [1986] 1 W.L.R. 808, below, p. 39.
64 See *Burrows and Burrows* v. *Sharpe* [1991] Fam. Law 67 and Jones, "Proprietary estoppel - satisfying the equity" (1992) 142 N.L.J. 320.
65 See below, p. 56 and *Baker* v. *Baker* (1993) 90/14 L.S. Gaz. 43.
66 [1979] 1 W.L.R. 431.

however, and the generosity extended to Mrs. Turner cannot be accepted as the norm.[67] More usually the court will make a lesser order, for example, a right to occupy the property for life, or monetary compensation if such satisfies the equity.

In *Greasley* v. *Cooke*[68] the equity was satisfied by granting the defendant a declaration that she be entitled to occupy the property rent-free for the rest of her life. The case is interesting because unlike Mrs. Turner the defendant had not incurred any expenditure on the property,[69] and the acts relied upon as giving rise to the estoppel (namely looking after her deceased cohabitee partner and his mentally ill sister as unpaid housekeeper, in the belief, induced by assurances from her cohabitee and his co-owner brother, that she could remain in the house rent-free for the rest of her life) were not referable to the property.[70] Moreover, these assurances were seen as giving rise to a presumption that she had acted to her detriment and raised an equity in her favour. The burden of proof was seen as lying not on her but on the plaintiffs to show that she had not acted to her detriment by remaining in the house. This they had not established, so the equity was not defeated. The decision has been described as appearing to stretch the doctrine of proprietary estoppel to its utmost limits[71] and should not be interpreted as saying that there is no need for detriment to be proved in order to establish estoppel.[72]

The finding in *Greasley* v. *Cooke* regarding the burden of proof was taken in *Coombes* v. *Smith*[73] to mean that where, following assurances by the defendant, the claimant had adopted a course of conduct which is detrimental to her in reliance upon the alleged assurances, the burden of proof does not shift to the defendant to prove the absence of detriment, but there is a rebuttable presumption that she had adopted a course of conduct in reliance upon those assurances. In that case, the plaintiff's becoming pregnant by the defendant, leaving her husband and moving into a house bought but not occupied by the defendant, doing the housekeeping and gardening, looking after their child and redecorating the house were held insufficient to establish that she acted to her detriment. In any event, the defendant's assurance that he would always look after her was held not to establish a mistaken belief on the part of the plaintiff that she had a legal right to remain in occupation against his wishes so as to give rise to an equity.

The uncertain scope of the doctrine of estoppel[74] applies also to the specificity of the property. A claim against the deceased's estate in *Layton* v. *Martin*[75] based on proprietary estoppel failed because the

---

67 See, *e.g. Thomas* v. *Fuller-Brown* [1988] 1 F.L.R. 237, above, p. 26.
68 [1980] 1 W.L.R. 1306.
69 See also *Re Basham, dec'd* [1986] 1 W.L.R. 1498, below, p. 40.
70 Hence the case has been classified as one of a licence by estoppel rather than proprietary estoppel: see below, p. 56.
71 See Annand, [1981] Conv. 154.
72 *Watts & Ready* v. *Storey* [1983] C.A.T. 319.
73 [1986] 1 W.L.R. 808.
74 See also *Maharaj* v. *Chand* [1986] A.C. 898.
75 [1986] 2 F.L.R. 227.

representations did not relate to a specific asset whereas in *Re Basham, decd* [76] proprietary estoppel was seen as being in the nature of a constructive trust which was described as follows[77]:

> "where one person, A, has acted to his detriment on the faith of a belief, which was known to and encouraged by another person, B, that he either has or is going to be given a right in or over B's property, B cannot insist on his strict legal rights if to do so would be inconsistent with A's belief. The principle is commonly known as proprietary estoppel, and since the effect of it is that B is prevented from asserting his strict legal rights it has something in common with estoppel. But in my judgment, at all events where the belief is that A is going to be given a right in the future, it is properly to be regarded as giving rise to a species of constructive trust. . ."

The belief on which A relies does not have to relate to an existing right nor to a particular property. In that case the plaintiff was the deceased's step-daughter who was encouraged by the deceased to come and look after him for many years without payment on the understanding that she would inherit all of the deceased's estate, including a cottage in which she had never lived. Since that understanding had been encouraged by the deceased and she had acted to her detriment in subordinating her own interests to the deceased's wishes, she had established a proprietary estoppel and was entitled to his estate. Whereas, in the later case of *Windeler* v. *Whitehall*,[78] where a couple cohabited as man and wife and the woman looked after the man's house and he made a will leaving her his residuary estate, there was held, on breakdown of the relationship, to be no proprietary estoppel in her favour for at least four reasons. First, it was not pleaded; secondly, there was no evidence that the defendant ever promised to leave his property to her; thirdly, there was no evidence that she believed that whatever happened she would inherit and that the defendant had encouraged her in that belief; and finally, even if she had been encouraged to believe she would inherit if she continued to live with him until he died, she herself had destroyed the contingency on which her claim depended.

The correlation between proprietary estoppel and a constructive trust has been commented upon in a number of cases[79] and resulted in the suggested assimilation of the principles of the two concepts.[80] One difference is that an interest arising under a constructive trust exists from its creation, whereas proprietary estoppel is rather in the nature of a remedy than a right and exists only from when it is declared by the court. A further difference is that a constructive trust requires, *inter alia*,

---

76 [1986] 1 W.L.R. 1498. See Hayton, [1987] C.L.J. 215; Martin, [1987] Conv. 211.
77 *Per* Edward Nugee Q.C. sitting as a Deputy High Court judge at 1503.
78 [1990] 2 F.L.R. 505.
79 *Grant* v. *Edwards* [1986] Ch. 638 at 656 and 675; *Austin* v. *Keele* [1987] A.L.J.R. 605 at 609; *Lloyds Bank plc.* v. *Rossett* [1989] Ch. 350 at 387.
80 *Per* Nourse L.J. in *Stokes* v. *Anderson* [1991] 1 F.L.R. 391 at 399.

evidence of a common intention[81] whereas proprietary estoppel requires evidence that the claimant acted to her detriment in consequence of a mistaken belief encouraged by the defendant. Some of the leading constructive trust cases, in particular *Grant* v. *Edwards*, might well have been so argued. The point has been argued in a scholarly way that[82]: "[i]t is time that the English courts accepted that the apparent distinction between common intention constructive trusts and equitable estoppel claims is illusory".

6. PROCEDURE

In *Hammond* v. *Mitchell*[83] certain procedural guidance was given so as to minimise the length of proceedings, which in that case had extended to 19 days in the High Court and cost the parties £125,000 in legal fees. It is desirable that all possible issues in dispute, including maintenance and property orders for children,[84] are raised as early as possible so that the appropriate forum and procedure can be identified and so as to obviate the need to consolidate proceedings commenced either in different courts or different Divisions of the same court. In the High Court the appropriate forum for these "family" cases, it has been suggested,[85] is the Family Division. There is no procedure for automatic discovery in the Family Division where reliance on questionnaires, as in cases of marital breakdown, is inappropriate to proprietary claims between cohabitees based upon evidence. Hence discovery orders should be made early in the proceedings and enforced strictly.

As to formulation of the claim, the emphasis placed upon express discussions between the parties "means that the tenderest exchanges of a common law courtship may assume an unforeseen significance many years later when they are brought under equity's microscope".[86] Hence such discussions should be pleaded in the greatest detail, both as to language and as to circumstance. This may prevent the claimant's case foundering for vagueness and it should ensure that the respondent knows exactly what case he has to meet. It may also provide a basis for reasonable compromise which

> "will be an especially desirable objective in the case of separating unmarried couples, whose distress or bitterness is often found, paradoxically, to have been increased rather than diminished by

---

81 See above, p. 23.
82 Hayton, "Equitable Rights of Cohabitees" [1990] Conv. 370 at 387. For a contrary argument, see Ferguson, "Constructive Trusts - A Note of Caution" (1993) 109 L.Q.R. 114 and reply by Hayton at (1993) 109 L.Q.R. 485.
83 [1991] 1 W.L.R. 1127 at 1138-1139
84 See below, p. 153. In *Hammond* v. *Mitchell* the judge considered that it would be inappropriate to make a capital order for the parties' child.
85 *Per* Lord Denning in *Bernard* v. *Josephs* [1982] Ch. 391 at 407.
86 *Hammond* v. *Mitchell* [1991] 1 W.L.R. 1127 at 1139.

their decision not to undertake a commitment to each other in marriage".[87]

7. CONTENTS OF THE HOME

In determining ownership of the contents of the home, rarely will there be title documents as a starting point. In any event, where it is established that one of the co-habiting partners is the legal owner, it is open to the other to establish that the property is held upon resulting, implied or constructive trust for them both.[88] It has been said in relation to disputes over chattels that[89]:

> "While no one suggests that English law recognises or should develop a doctrine of community of property regarding the household goods of those who settle for an unmarried union, the parties must expect the court in ordinary cases to adopt a robust allegiance to the maxim 'equality is equity' if only in the interests of fulfilling the equally salutary maxim *'sit finis litis'*."

Property belonging to each at the start of the cohabitation, and personal items acquired during cohabitation, will remain the property of each, as will personal gifts between the parties.

If there has been an engagement which has been terminated, ownership of gifts given by the parties to one another depends upon whether or not they were given conditionally upon the wedding taking place. If they were, they must be returned to the donor, but not otherwise, regardless of which party broke off the engagement.[90] An engagement ring does not normally have to be returned, even if the woman changes her mind. It is presumed to be an absolute gift, unless the man can prove that the ring was given on condition that is should be returned if the marriage did not take place.[91] As with other gifts, proving that it was conditional will not be easy. If the man makes it expressly conditional when slipping the ring on her finger, he is likely to get it back more quickly than he expected. The condition can be implied as, for example, where the ring is a family heirloom.

Engagement presents from other people, like wedding presents, are presumed to be given conditionally on the wedding taking place. If the wedding is called off, for whatever reason, the gifts should be returned to the donors.

---

87 *Ibid.* at 1139.
88 See above, p. 20. Reference is made elsewhere to the special rules applicable to ownership of money (for example, savings and joint bank accounts) and property bought with money withdrawn from a joint account: see below, p. 77.
89 *Per* Waite J. in *Hammond* v. *Mitchell* [1991] 1 W.L.R. 1127 at 1138.
90 Law Reform (Miscellaneous Provisions) Act 1970, s.3(1).
91 *Ibid.* s.3(2).

As with all disputes between a couple on breakdown of their relationship, the matter should be resolved, if at all possible, between those involved, if necessary with legal advice, but without recourse to litigation.[92] This is particularly so with regard to the contents of the home, for their value will soon disappear in costs.

If recourse has to be had to the courts, then the correct procedure is a claim for a declaration or inquiry as to the beneficial interest, supported by affidavit evidence, on similar lines to disputes under section 17 of the Married Women's Property Act 1882, rather than by actions in conversion or detinue.[93]

---

92 *Per* Millett J. in *Windeler* v. *Whitehall* [1990] 2 F.L.R. 505 at 516; *per* Waite J. in *Hammond* v. *Mitchell* [1991] 1 W.L.R. 1127 at 1138.
93 *Per* Waite J. in *Hammond* v. *Mitchell* [1991] 1 W.L.R. 1127 at 1138-1139.

CHAPTER 3

HOME OCCUPATION

Cohabitation, unlike marriage, confers no right to live in the family home.[1] Occupation rights are linked with ownership rights and depend upon principles of property law. Hence entitlement to live in the home depends in part upon whether or not the parties are owner-occupiers.

1. OWNER-OCCUPIERS

Where legal and beneficial ownership of the home are in both parties, they both have a right to live in the home by virtue of that co-ownership. Neither party can exclude the other unless an exclusion injunction is obtained from the court.[2] Of particular importance is the need for both parties to join in any sale of the house. Both their names are on the title documents, or they are both registered proprietors, therefore both signatures are needed for any transfer.[3] If they cannot agree on a sale then as the property is co-owned it is held on trust for sale[4] and there is a duty to sell subject to a power to postpone sale.[5] Either of the parties can apply to the court under section 30 of the Law of Property Act 1925 for an order that the property be sold[6] and the proceeds of sale be divided in accordance with the parties' respective beneficial interests.[7] The order for sale may be postponed, at the discretion of the court, if one party agrees to let the other remain in the home and the remaining party purchases the other's share.[8] The party wishing to remain in occupation will argue for the sale to be postponed notwithstanding that the primary purpose of the trust for sale may be the sale of the property. Section 30 is of particular relevance to unmarried co-owners as a means of resolving

---

1 See below, p. 52.
2 See below, p. 164.
3 Law of Property Act 1925, ss.2(2) and 27(2).
4 *Ibid.* ss.34-36.
5 Unless excluded: see *ibid.* s.25(1).
6 See Thompson, "Cohabitation, Co-ownership and Section 30" [1984] Conv. 103; Schuz, "Section 30 Law of Property Act 1925 and Unmarried Cohabitees" (1982) 12 Fam. Law 108.
7 See p. 19.
8 See, *e.g. Bernard* v. *Josephs* [1982] Ch. 391. For postponement until the occupier finds alternative accommodation, see below, p. 48.

disputes regarding their rights of occupation, because the Matrimonial Homes Act 1983 rights of occupation apply only to spouses.[9]

Where the legal estate is vested in one cohabitee alone (usually the man) he prima facie has the sole right to live in the home. If the other party can establish that she has a beneficial interest in the property,[10] that interest prima facie gives her a right to live there[11] and is not limited to a beneficial interest in the proceeds of sale. She is at a disadvantage, however, compared with a cohabitee whose name appears on the title documents or who in the case of registered land is a registered proprietor, for her interest will not be there for all the world to see. According to the title documents there is nothing to prevent the legal owner disposing of the home, either by way of sale or mortgage, for the purchaser or mortgagee will not know of the beneficial interest. He may, however, take subject to it, if he knows, or ought to know, of it, and the beneficiary will need to consider protecting her rights arising from the beneficial interest.[12] If a cohabitee has a beneficial interest in her partner's home, the property is also held on trust for sale subject to a power to postpone sale. She could seek the appointment of herself as second trustee[13] and refuse to join in any sale of property, leaving it to the legal owner to apply under section 30 of the Law of Property Act 1925. Where she has not been appointed as second trustee, an application by her under section 30 is only appropriate if her partner refuses to sell. If he intends to sell or in some other way deal with the property contrary to her wishes she may seek an injunction to restrain him.[14]

Under section 30 the matter of whether the property should be sold is at the court's discretion, save that it has no power to adjust property rights as it has under section 24 of the Matrimonial Causes Act.[15] In exercising its discretion the court will normally order a sale if the underlying purpose for which the property was bought, for example, cohabitation, has come to an end,[16] whether the parties are married or unmarried.[17] An important consideration will be the needs of any children. If the property is still needed to provide them with a home, the court might postpone sale until a later date or dismiss the application for sale leaving it to the applicant to apply again later if circumstances change. So in *Re Evers' Trust*,[18] where the parties were not married to

---

9 See below, p. 52.
10 See above, p. 19.
11 *Bull* v. *Bull* [1955] 1 Q.B. 234; *per* Lord Wilberforce in *Williams and Glyn's Bank Ltd.* v. *Boland* [1981] A.C. 487 at 507. See also *Barclay* v. *Barclay* [1970] 2 Q.B. 677.
12 See above, p. 31.
13 See above, p. 32.
14 See Cretney, *Principles of Family Law* (5th ed., 1990), p. 259 and *Waller* v. *Waller* [1967] 1 W.L.R. 451. The Law Commission has made a number of proposals for reform: see Law Com. No. 181, *Trusts of Land* (1989).
15 See *Re Evers' Trust* [1980] 1 W.L.R. 1327; *Cousins* v. *Dzosens* (1984) 81 L.S. Gaz. 2855.
16 *Jones* v. *Challenger* [1961] 1 Q.B. 176.
17 *Per* Nourse L.J. in *Re Citro (A Bankrupt)* [1991] Ch. 142 at 147.
18 [1980] 1 W.L.R. 1327.

each other, it was held that the approach to be adopted in "family" cases is to see whether the primary purpose of the trust, *i.e.* for sale, has been affected by the underlying purpose of providing a home not only for the parents but also for the children.[19] As the underlying purpose of the particular trust was to provide a home for the parties and their children for the indefinite future, the application for sale was dismissed. The approach in such cases is the same as that where the parties are married and application is made under section 30.[20] This approach favours the party with care of the children, who will usually be the children's mother. Where there are no children, however, and the parties' relationship has broken down, the court is likely to give effect to the trust for sale unless in the circumstances the underlying purpose is continuing.[21] The court may postpone sale for a specified period, usually in terms of a few months, but not an indefinite period, for some particular purpose, for example, to allow the other co-owner to find suitable alternative accommodation.[22]

Where an order for sale is not made, consideration should be given to compensating the outgoing party in such a way as is reasonable in the circumstances, for example, by requiring the remaining party to undertake to pay the whole of the mortgage repayments, or other outgoings. In *Dennis* v. *McDonald*[23] the applicant had left her cohabitee partner some years previously because of his violence and was afraid to return. In the circumstances the court did not make an order for sale but the man was ordered to pay a so-called "occupation rent"[24] to the applicant. So where one party has been ousted by the other, this may justify a departure from the general rule that if one co-owner enjoys property to the exclusion of the other that enjoyment does not give rise to any right of compensation. Section 30 confers no powers on the court unless an order for sale is in fact made,[25] but the same result may be possible, in practice, by the court threatening to make an order for sale unless, for example, the party in occupation undertakes to pay rent[26] or on condition that he pays the mortgage. In *Cousins* v. *Dzosens*[27] the purposes of the particular trust were not regarded as having been fully discharged until the plaintiff was

---

19 The children's needs will not necessarily be conclusive: see *Burke* v. *Burke* [1974] 1 W.L.R. 1063.

20 On which see *Williams (J.W.)* v. *Williams (M.A.)* [1976] Ch. 278; *Chhokar* v. *Chhokar* [1984] F.L.R. 313 and Lord Denning M.R. in *Bernard* v. *Josephs* [1982] Ch. 391 at 400. In view of the court's powers under the Matrimonial Causes Act 1973, s.24, s.30 of the Law of Property Act 1925 is of less significance as between spouses. Although as between cohabitees the court does not possess the adjustive powers available under the Matrimonial Causes Act 1973, s.24, the exercise of the discretion under s.30 has been analogous with the exercise of the discretion under s.24.

21 See, *e.g. Bedson* v. *Bedson* [1965] 2 Q.B. 666.

22 See *Cousins* v. *Dzosens* (1984) 81 L.S.Gaz. 2855.

23 [1982] Fam. 63: see Annand, "The Tenant in Common as a Tenant" (1982) 132 N.L.J. 526.

24 It is strictly a form of compensation paid by a trustee for exclusive enjoyment of the property: see Sir John Arnold, [1982] Fam. 63 at 81.

25 *Per* Kerr L.J. in *Bernard* v. *Josephs* [1982] Ch. 391 at 410.

26 See also *per* Purchas J. in *Dennis* v. *McDonald* [1982] Fam. 63 at 74.

27 (1984) 81 L.S.Gaz. 2855.

able to move to alternative accommodation.[28] On that basis the judge ordered the sale of the house and until the sale the plaintiff was required to pay an occupation rent to the defendant. Unlike *Dennis* v. *McDonald*, the occupier in *Cousins* had not ousted the other party and the case is a departure from the principle that one co-owner is not liable to another unless he has excluded the other.[29] It suggests that whenever there is a breakdown of a relationship, an occupation rent may be payable where the home remains unsold with one party in occupation.[30]

The preceding analysis relates to an application under section 30 between cohabitees, rather than with a third party. Where, as in *Stott* v. *Ratcliffe*,[31] one cohabitee has died, the purpose of the trust, *i.e.* the provision of a home, may be seen as continuing until the death of the surviving trustee, in which case it will be inappropriate to require an occupation rent to be paid to the person who has become entitled to the deceased's beneficial interest.

Where the issue of occupation arises on a cohabitee's bankruptcy[32] the bankrupt's interest in the home forms part of his estate and the trustee in bankruptcy is under a duty to realise the bankrupt's assets for the benefit of the creditors. A cohabitee with no beneficial interest in the property cannot resist the vesting of the home in the trustee in bankruptcy. The provision in the Insolvency Act 1986 conferring a limited right of occupation upon a spouse or former spouse[33] (with or without a beneficial interest) does not avail a cohabitee.

Where a bankrupt's cohabitee has a beneficial interest in the property, however, this beneficial interest will not vest in the trustee in bankruptcy who holds the legal estate on trust. If the home is in joint names, the trustee in bankruptcy steps into the shoes of the bankrupt. In either case, if the bankrupt's cohabitee objects to a sale of the property by the trustee in bankruptcy, she will have to apply as "any person interested"[34] for an order for sale of the property under section 30 of the Law of Property Act 1925. In such a case, considerations different from those discussed above apply. The court must consider which of the competing claims, *i.e.* that of the trustee seeking to realise the bankrupt's share in the home for the benefit of the creditors and that of the other party to the relationship seeking to preserve a home for herself (and any children), ought to prevail in equity. So in *Re Holliday*[35] it was held that the need to preserve

---

28 See also *Walker* v. *Hall* [1984] F.L.R. 126.
29 *M'Mahon* v. *Burchell* (1846) 2 Ph. 127; *Jones (A.E.)* v. *Jones (F.W.)* [1977] 1 W.L.R. 438. See Martin, "A Co-owner's Liability to Pay Rent" [1982] Conv. 305; Webb, "Co-habitational Homes" (1982) 98 L.Q.R. 519.
30 See also Lord Denning M.R. in *Bernard* v. *Josephs* [1982] Ch. 391 at 400-401.
31 (1982) 126 S.J. 310; (1983) 133 N.L.J. 303.
32 See Murphy and Clark, *The Family Home* (1983), Chap. 8; Insolvency Act 1986; Furey, "Bankruptcy and the Family - The Effect of the Insolvency Act 1986" [1987] Fam. Law 316.
33 s.336.
34 *Re Solomon* [1967] Ch. 573. The trustee in bankruptcy is also a person interested.
35 [1981] Ch. 405. See Hand, (1981) 97 L.Q.R. 200. See also *Burke* v. *Burke* [1974] 1 W.L.R. 1063.

the house as a home for the children, where they are not beneficiaries under the trust for sale, was not a secondary or collateral object of the trust. The existence of children is, however, an incidental factor to be taken into account. Only exceptionally, however, as in *Re Holliday*, where the creditors were likely to receive full payment in any event, have the circumstances resulted in a deferment of the order for sale.[36] Hence a narrower property-based approach regarding the trust for sale has been taken in bankruptcy cases than in "family" cases[37] for in the latter greater emphasis has been placed on the underlying purpose of the trust to provide a home for the parties and the children. The majority decision of the Court of Appeal in *Re Citro (A Bankrupt)*[38] marked a further retreat from its more enlightened approach in *Re Holliday* and confirmed that the voice of the creditors will usually prevail and a sale of the property ordered within a short time save in exceptional circumstances. Such circumstances do not include eviction of a wife, or it is submitted a cohabitee, with young children notwithstanding that there may be schooling and other problems.

Although the Insolvency Act 1986 confers limited rights of occupation upon a bankrupt's spouse or former spouse but not a cohabitee[39] there is a limited right of occupation in favour of the bankrupt for a 12-month period.[40] It applies where the bankrupt is entitled to occupy the property by virtue of a beneficial estate or interest and includes any person under the age of 18, with whom the bankrupt had at some time occupied the property, who had their home with the bankrupt at the time when the bankruptcy petition was presented and at the commencement of the bankruptcy. Although the provision is probably intended for children of the bankrupt it could include, for example, a minor cohabitee. In such circumstances the bankrupt has a right not to be evicted or excluded except with the leave of the court and, if not in occupation, a right with the court's leave to enter and occupy the property. If the trustee applies for leave to evict or exclude the bankrupt, the court must make such order as it thinks just and reasonable having regard to the creditors' interests, to the bankrupt's financial resources, to the needs of the children and to all the circumstances of the case other than the bankrupt's needs. All the circumstances might therefore include a cohabitee's

---

36 For an example of a deferred sale, see *Re Gorman* [1990] 1 W.L.R. 616. For examples of immediate sale, see *Re Turner* [1974] 1 W.L.R. 1556; *Re Bailey* [1977] 1 W.L.R. 278; *Re Lowrie* [1981] 3 All E.R. 353.

37 The bankruptcy cases have involved claims between a trustee in bankruptcy and a spouse or former spouse but it is submitted that the principles are the same where the parties are not married. The same principles also apply where the person interested is a chargee and not a trustee in bankruptcy: see *Lloyds Bank PLC* v. *Byrne and Byrne* [1993] 1 F.L.R. 369.

38 [1991] Ch. 142: see Hall, [1991] C.L.J. 45; Cretney, (1991) 107 L.Q.R. 177; Lawson, [1991] Conv. 302; Clarke, [1991] J.C.L. 116; Brown, (1982) 55 M.L.R. 284.

39 The Cork Committee was of the view that the terms "husband" and "wife" should include persons of the opposite sex living as husband and wife. See Report of the Review Committee on Insolvency Law and Practice, Cmnd. 8558 (1982), para. 1125.

40 Insolvency Act 1986, s.337.

needs. If, however, the application is made more than a year after the vesting of the bankrupt's estate in the trustee in bankruptcy, the court must assume, unless the circumstances are exceptional, that the interests of the bankrupt's creditors outweigh all other considerations.[41]

The appropriate venue for section 30 proceedings is either the High Court or the County Court and the latter's jurisdiction is no longer subject to a financial limit.[42] High Court proceedings have usually been commenced in the Chancery Division, although it has been suggested that cases concerning the homes of couples living together are so similar to those of husband and wife that they should be started in the Family Division or transferred to it.[43] In the County Court application is by originating application setting out the terms of the order sought and the grounds relied upon in support. The application is filed in the court for the district in which the respondent lives or where the property is situated.[44]

Section 30 proceedings should not be undertaken lightly in view of the costs of litigation. This is particularly important in this context where the claimant is legally aided, because of the statutory charge in favour of the Legal Aid Board in respect of property recovered or preserved as a result of the proceedings. The Board's discretion to postpone the statutory charge on dwelling houses does not apply to section 30 proceedings and the exemption from the charge of the first £2,500 does not apply to such proceedings whereas they do, for example, to proceedings under section 17 of the Married Women's Property Act 1882 and under section 24 of the Matrimonial Causes Act 1973.[45]

Mortgage obligations

Associated with rights of occupation will be the liability for mortgage repayments, particularly in the event of separation. If cohabitees are joint mortgagors they are jointly and severally liable for the repayments. If they separate, the party remaining in occupation may be under an obligation to pay the other an occupation rent for the use of the property.[46] The interest element of the mortgage repayment may be regarded as equivalent to such a rent to be borne by the occupying party[46a] on principles of equitable accounting. The capital element of such repayments, however, remains the obligation of both parties and if the occupier meets the full amount the non-occupier must give credit for

---

41 See also *Re Citro (A Bankrupt)* [1991] Ch. 142.
42 High Court and County Court Jurisdiction Order 1991 (S.I. 1991 No. 724), art. 2. Application for leave under the Insolvency Act 1986, s.337, must be made to the court having jurisdiction relating to the bankruptcy: see s.337(4).
43 *Per* Lord Denning M.R. in *Bernard* v. *Josephs* [1982] Ch. 391 at 401. Application is by originating summons supported by affidavit.
44 C.C.R., Ord. 4, r. 8, and see below, p. 255.
45 See The Civil Legal Aid (General) Regulations 1989, regs. 94-97.
46 See above, p. 47.
46a See *Savill* v. *Goodall* [1993] 1 F.L.R. 755.

one-half.[47] If an occupation rent is not considered to be justified, the occupier must additionally be credited with one-half of the interest element,[48] although the precise inter-relationship of payment of mortgage instalments and occupation rent is one of complexity and uncertainty.

If the mortgage is in the name of only one cohabitee, the other is under no obligation to the mortgagee although he or she may wish to assume responsibility if the mortgagor defaults. Where a cohabitee has no legal or beneficial interest in the property owned by her partner and the partner defaults on his mortgage payments, the non-owner has no right to make the payments so as to prevent the mortgagee taking proceedings for possession, and no right to be given notice of such proceedings. By contrast a spouse with rights of occupation has the right to pay mortgage arrears,[49] thereby preventing the mortgagee from gaining possession of the home. Moreover, a spouse's statutory right of occupation under the Matrimonial Homes Act 1983 is a charge which if registered either before or after the completion of the mortgage, but by the time of the proceedings, entitles the spouse concerned to be served with notice of any action for the enforcement of the mortgage.[50] It is advisable for a non-owning cohabitee to see if the mortgagee will accept payment, but there is no obligation on the mortgagee to do so and he may well refuse to accept payment, because to accept might estop him from taking later possession proceedings. In such proceedings, the non-owner should make it clear to the court that payment has been offered and ask the court to adjourn the proceedings or postpone the possession order. The non-owner could not claim the benefit of the Administration of Justice Act 1970, s.36,[51] which gives the court power in possession proceedings to adjourn the proceedings, stay or suspend execution of the possession order, or postpone the date for possession, because this power applies only where the mortgagor (and not his cohabitee) is likely to be able to pay all sums due within a reasonable time.

The issue could also arise in proceedings brought by a cohabitee under the Domestic Violence and Matrimonial Proceedings Act 1976.[52] Suppose a man is ordered out of the home owned by him and he defaults on his mortgage payments. In any possession proceedings by the mortgagee, it is suggested that the woman's right of occupation arising from the injunction ought to be good reason, during the continuance of the injunction, for postponement of the possession order, otherwise the injunction would be worthless. Notwithstanding that the Administration

---

47 *Leake* v. *Bruzzi* [1974] 1 W.L.R. 1528; *Suttill* v. *Graham* [1977] 1 W.L.R. 819 and see above, p. 47.

48 In *Re Gorman* [1990] 1 W.L.R. 616 the court did not distinguish between capital and interest repayments and the trustee in bankruptcy was required to give credit for half the mortgage instalments paid by the wife.

49 Matrimonial Homes Act 1983, s.1(5).

50 Matrimonial Homes Act 1983, s.8(3).

51 As amended. A wife may claim such benefit if the Matrimonial Homes Act 1983, s.8, applies.

52 See below, p. 159.

of Justice Act 1970, s.36, is of no help because it only protects a mortgagor, the court should at least adjourn proceedings to enable the woman to find alternative accommodation.

Licences

Where a cohabitee enjoys neither a legal nor beneficial interest in the property, she cannot seek to rely on the cohabitation to give her a right of occupation. Marriage confers on the parties a duty to cohabit and a duty to support. A wife has a right, arising from the marriage, to be provided with a home. A spouse with no legal title to the home (whether or not he or she has a beneficial interest) has a statutory right of occupation.[53] This right is a charge on the interest of the owning spouse and can be protected either by registering a Class F land charge if the home is unregistered land, or by registering a notice[54] if the home is registered land (the right cannot be an overriding interest).[55] Once the right of occupation is registered, it is binding on third parties except the trustee in bankruptcy,[56] so, for example, anyone who buys a house which has such a charge registered against it will buy it subject to the spouse's right to remain there.

A cohabitee has no right of occupation under the Matrimonial Homes Act 1983 and, in the absence of any beneficial interest or other equity or right to live in the home,[57] will only be able to establish a right to live in the home if he or she has a licence to do so or can establish a right of occupation in equity or under the Settled Land Act 1925.[58]

Establishing a licence

Cohabitation itself is insufficient to confer rights of occupation. A cohabitee with no legal or beneficial rights in her partner's property will have a licence to occupy but in order that the licence cannot be revoked at the wish of the owner on giving reasonable notice[59] (a bare licence), the claimant must show either that the parties have entered into a contract by which one party has agreed, for consideration, that the other shall have a right to occupy the home (a contractual licence), that the legal owner has induced the claimant to believe that she has a right to occupy the home and that she has acted in reliance of that assurance so that equity will impose a licence (an equitable licence) or that the legal

---

53 Matrimonial Homes Act 1983, s.1.
54 Not by a caution: see Matrimonial Homes Act 1983, s.2(8) and (9).
55 Matrimonial Homes Act 1983, s.2(8).
56 See above, p. 48.
57 See above, p. 19. In Scotland a "non-entitled partner" of "a cohabiting couple" has a limited right of occupancy but only on application to the court: see further Matrimonial Homes (Family Protection) (Scotland) Act 1981, s.18.
58 For limited rights of occupation under the domestic violence legislation, see below, p. 164.
59 *I.e.* sufficient to find alternative accommodation which will usually be about 28 days.

owner is estopped from denying her right of occupation (a licence by estoppel).

Contractual licence For an agreement to constitute a contractual licence it may be express or implied. In either case there must be clear terms of agreement, an intention to create a legal relationship[60] and consideration. Finally, the agreement must not be illegal or contrary to public policy.[61]

The leading case is *Tanner* v. *Tanner*,[62] which was part of the Denning era of the emergence of unmarried women's rights. Mrs. Tanner was neither a wife nor a cohabitee, but rather a mistress[63] who was the mother of twins fathered by Mr. Tanner, a married man. He provided a house for her and the children and she gave up the tenancy of a rent-controlled flat. He made it clear to her, however, that he did not intend to marry her. The house was in his name and he provided the purchase price by way of mortgage. Mr. Tanner later divorced his wife and married another woman. He wanted to evict Mrs. Tanner and the twins so that he could occupy the house with his new wife. The Court of Appeal decided that Mrs. Tanner had made no contribution from which it could be inferred that she was to have any beneficial interest, but there was an agreement between the parties under which she had a contractual licence to live in the house with the children so long as they were of school age and required the accommodation. She had provided consideration for the licence by giving up her rent-controlled flat and looking after the children.[64] As she and the children had been rehoused by the local authority, she was not seeking to reoccupy the house and it was thus no longer practicable to enforce the licence. Had it been so, the court could have issued an injunction restraining Mr. Tanner from revoking the licence. Instead, Mrs. Tanner was awarded compensation of £2,000 for loss of the licence.

Since *Tanner* the courts have displayed a more restrictive interpretation of the contractual licence. In *Horrocks* v. *Forray*,[65] a married man, who lived with his wife, kept a mistress (Mrs. Forray) for 17 years before his death. They had a daughter and he bought a house for mother and daughter. The house was in his name, although he had contemplated transferring it to her or creating a trust for his daughter, but for tax reasons did neither. Only on his death did his wife discover the existence of the house and the mistress. His executors gave the mistress notice to quit so that the house could be sold with vacant possession, otherwise it was probable that the deceased's estate would be insolvent. In reply the mistress claimed a contractual licence. The case differed from that of

---

60 See *Layton* v. *Martin* [1986] 2 F.L.R. 227, below, p. 233.
61 See below, p. 233.
62 [1975] 1 W.L.R. 1346.
63 See above, p. 2.
64 It is questionable whether or not the mother's looking after the children was consideration in itself, because she was under an existing duty to do so: see below, p. 150 and *Ward* v. *Byham* [1956] 1 W.L.R. 496.
65 [1976] 1 W.L.R. 230.

Mrs. Tanner, for there "consideration was perfectly clear"[66] whereas that was not so in Mrs. Forray's case. In all the circumstances, there was no contractual licence and the widow's claim for possession was granted.

The law is again unclear as to precisely what must be established. There is the impression that the courts are trying to achieve the equitable result in the particular case, thus in *Horrocks* v. *Forray* the court's sympathy was with the widow rather than the mistress, yet such reasoning leads to uncertainty. There is a suggestion that arrangements made between two people living happily together are not intended to affect their legal relationships. In *Horrocks* v. *Forray* the fact that the man had provided well for his mistress and child was taken as not indicating a contract. This suggests, therefore, that a contract is less likely in a happy relationship (as in *Horrocks*) than one that is breaking down (as in *Tanner*) — but is this realistic?

The need to provide children of the union with a home is an influencing factor, but Lord Denning in *Tanner* suggested that the duty extends beyond the children: "This man had a moral duty to provide for the babies of whom he was the father. I would go further. I think he had a legal duty towards them. Not only towards the babies. But also towards their mother."[67] The duty to the mother must, presumably, be as a mother and not as a cohabitee, for there is no duty to support a cohabitee. For such a duty to arise there has to be a contract under which the claimant has given consideration, for example, has suffered a detriment by moving into the home. The claimant must, however, establish some detriment. Moving into the home of itself will not by itself suffice; thus in *Coombes* v. *Smith*[68] Mrs. Coombes's leaving her husband and moving into the home provided by the defendant was held not to provide consideration. *Tanner* was distinguished because Mrs. Tanner had given up a rent-controlled flat. The distinction appears to be a fine one.

One of the factors influencing the courts in finding a beneficial interest arising under a trust rather than a licence to occupy is the parties' intention to marry. This influenced the courts in favour of a trust for Miss Cooke and Mrs. Eves, whereas it was clear that Mr. Tanner never intended marriage with Mrs. Tanner. This seems a somewhat artificial limitation. Surely what is important is their intention with regard to the home, not their future marital status? There is the impression that some judges regard an intention to marry as giving the relationship an air of respectability, justifying the award of a beneficial interest, which is not justified in cases of cohabitation with no plans of marriage. So, for

---

66 *Per* Megaw L.J. at 239.
67 [1975] 1 W.L.R. 1346 at 1350.
68 [1986] 1 W.L.R. 808. The plaintiff's claim was dismissed on the defendant's undertaking to provide accommodation for her in the property as long as their child was under 17 and to pay the mortgage instalments during that time. So the result was similar to that which might have been expected from a divorce court exercising its adjustive jurisdiction. The case also raised the issue of proprietary estoppel: see above, p. 39.

example, the relationship in *Richards* v. *Dove*[69] was seen as one of convenience, with no thought of marriage on the part of either party.

Also significant is the presence or absence of cohabitation. The status of Mrs. Tanner, Mrs. Forray and Mrs. Coombes was that of a mistress, not cohabitee.[70] The relationship was not equivalent to that of husband and wife and the preparedness to extend to cohabitees the legal protection enjoyed by spouses has not been accorded so readily to mistresses.

Equitable licence Consistent with the impression that the courts are seeking to achieve the equitable result, there is some support for the view that the courts may not insist upon the need to prove an express or implied contract and may instead impose the equivalent of a contract. This form of licence has been referred to as an "equitable licence"[71] and is one the terms of which the court has to spell out. In *Re Sharpe*,[72] an aunt's loan to her nephew, on the common assumption that she was to have a right to occupy the home, meant that she had acted to her detriment and the court implied an irrevocable licence to occupy the house until the loan was repaid. Furthermore, the aunt's irrevocable licence was held to be not merely a contractual licence, but one which arose under a constructive trust.[73]

One case in which the court held that rights of occupation existed under a constructive trust *rather* than under a licence was *Ungurian* v. *Lesnoff*[74] where the defendant gave up a promising academic career in Poland to live with the plaintiff in England. She entered into a marriage of convenience with a third party in order to be able to live in England and gave up her flat in Poland. The plaintiff bought a house of which he was sole registered proprietor for himself and the defendant to live in as man and wife with her two sons and his son. The defendant carried out considerable improvements over the next four years until the relationship came to an end, whereupon the plaintiff claimed possession. The judge held that the intention to be attributed to the parties was not that he bought the house for her but that she was to have the right to live in the property during her lifetime. Full effect would not be given to that intention by inferring an irrevocable licence but by the plaintiff holding the house on trust for the defendant to reside in during her life unless and until the plaintiff, with the defendant's consent, sold the property and bought another for her in substitution. The house became settled land and the defendant was a tenant for life with all the statutory powers of a tenant for life. One surprising result was that she could decide when and if the house was to be sold, which was hardly within their common

69 [1974] 1 All E.R. 888: see above, p. 21.
70 See above, p. 2.
71 *Per* Lord Denning M.R. in *Hardwick* v. *Johnson* [1978] 1 W.L.R. 683 at 688.
72 [1980] 1 W.L.R. 219.
73 See below, p. 57.
74 [1990] Ch. 206; Oldham, [1990] C.L.J. 25; Sparkes, [1990] Conv. 223; Hill, "The Settled Land Act 1925: Unresolved Problems" (1991) 107 L.Q.R. 596.

intention. That intention could have been accommodated more happily, it is submitted, by either a contractual licence or a licence by estoppel.

Licence by estoppel   An alternative remedy to those discussed so far is that of a right of occupation arising under a licence by estoppel, where the legal owner has led the other cohabitee to believe, or acquiesced in her belief, that she has a long-term right to live in the property and she has acted to her detriment in reliance on that belief. It is very similar to proprietary estoppel, save that the belief is as to occupation rather than ownership and hence the acts in reliance may not be referable to the acquisition of the property. It is on the basis of that distinction that the case of *Greasley* v. *Cooke*[75] can be characterised as one of licence by estoppel rather than proprietary estoppel.

Duration of a licence

If a licence can be established, there will be the further question of its duration. Mrs. Tanner's licence was said to be one to occupy the home so long as the children were of school age. Such an order will not be appropriate in all cases, however, and, in the absence of express agreement, the licence may be terminated on giving reasonable notice. In *Chandler* v. *Kerley*,[76] Mr. Chandler bought the house of his mistress, Mrs. Kerley, and her husband who were living apart. He paid substantially less than the asking price, on the understanding that Mrs. Kerley would continue to live in the house until she obtained a divorce and he joined her there. Six weeks after the purchase, the relationship between Mr. Chandler and Mrs. Kerley ended and he ordered her out of the house. On the strength of his assurance at the time of purchase that he would not put her out if they parted, Mrs. Kerley claimed a licence to occupy for the rest of her life. The Court of Appeal decided that, although Mr. Chandler knew that Mrs. Kerley wanted the house as a home for her children as well as herself, it would be wrong to infer that he had assumed the burden of another man's wife and children indefinitely. Mrs. Kerley's contractual licence was terminable on reasonable notice and 12 months' notice was reasonable. What constitutes reasonable notice must depend upon the circumstances of the case and in particular whether or not there are children in need of a home. Thus one week's notice is unlikely to be sufficient and, as a very minimum, a month seems more likely. Once the licence has been terminated, a licensee who remains in occupation becomes a trespasser and the owner may seek a possession order. Alternatively an injunction can be sought to prevent re-entry by the licensee and, if necessary, to restrain violence.[77]

---

75 [1980] 1 W.L.R. 1306: see above, p. 39 and see also *Maharaj* v. *Chand* [1986] A.C. 898.
76 [1978] 1 W.L.R. 693.
77 *Egan* v. *Egan* [1975] Ch. 218.

Effect on third parties

A contractual licence gives rise to a personal right in favour of the licensee. Rights arising under a contract cannot generally bind a person who is not a party to that contract. If the owner sells the home, the purchaser will not be bound by a contractual licence even if he has notice of it, because the licence does not create a property right.[78]

The position may be different if the contractual licence can be said to give rise to an interest under a constructive trust, in which case the interest will be enforceable against a purchaser of the home, provided that the purchaser bought the home with notice of the licence if the title is unregistered, or if it constituted an overriding interest, if title is registered. However, in *Ashburn Anstalt v. Arnold*, it was not felt desirable that "constructive trusts of land should be imposed in reliance on inferences from slender materials".[79] It is a question of what is the reasonable inference to be drawn from the facts. The court will only impose a constructive trust if the conscience of the estate owner is affected. Whilst circumstances may justify such a finding,[80] earlier cases based upon the notion that a contractual licence gives rise to a constructive trust must be treated with extreme caution.[81]

If the licence arises by estoppel the position of third parties is uncertain and views differ.[82] Whilst there is authority that estoppels bind both the parties and their successors in title[83] it is submitted that in view of the similarity between the two types of licence[84] it would be anomalous if a claimant relying on estoppel were in a stonger position than one relying on agreement.[85]

2. TENANCIES

As a general principle, cohabitation gives rise to no special rights in relation to rented property and the law treats cohabitees in the same way as those who live in tenanted property without cohabiting. The parties' rights of occupation depend upon the nature and terms of the tenancy.

---

78 *Ashburn Anstalt* v. *Arnold* [1989] Ch. 1 disapproving dictum to the contrary of Lord Denning in *Errington* v. *Errington* [1952] 1 K.B. 290; see Sparkes, (1988) 104 L.Q.R. 175; Hill, (1988) 51 M.L.R. 226; Thompson, [1988] Conv. 201; Oakley, [1988] C.L.J. 353. Contrast *Midland Bank Ltd.* v. *Farmpride Hatcheries Ltd.* (1981) 260 E.G. 493; Annand, [1982] Conv. 67; Dewar, "Licences and Land Law: An Alternative View" (1986) 49 M.L.R. 741.

79 *Per* Fox L.J. at 26. The issue of whether or not a contractual licence can bind third parties was *obiter*, because the Court had found there to be a tenancy.

80 See, *e.g. Binions* v. *Evans* [1972] Ch. 359.

81 *e.g. D.H.N. Food Distributors* v. *London Borough of Tower Hamlets* [1976] 1 W.L.R. 852; *Re Sharpe* [1980] 1 W.L.R. 219, discussed in the second edition of this book, para 3-14 and above, p. 55.

82 See, *e.g.* Hill, (1988) 51 M.L.R. 226 at 233.

83 *Ives Investments Ltd.* v. *High* [1967] 2 Q.B. 379.

84 See, *e.g. Hardwick* v. *Johnson* [1978] 1 W.L.R. 683.

85 See further Battersby, "Contractual and Estoppel Licences as Proprietary Interests in Land" [1991] Conv. 36.

There is not the scope here to do more than identify the general principles applicable in the context of cohabitation.

Private sector tenancies

The Housing Act 1988 fundamentally reformed the law relating to landlord and tenant with effect to tenancies granted on or after January 15, 1989. Tenancies in existence before that date which were governed by the Rent Act 1977 continue to be so and will be considered first.

Rent Act 1977 tenancies

If the tenancy is taken in joint names both parties have the right to live in the property; one cannot exclude the other without a court order and both will be liable for all the obligations, for example, to pay the rent, whether or not in occupation. On the death of one joint tenant the other becomes sole tenant by survivorship. Problems may arise on breakdown of the relationship if the tenants split up. If they agree on who should continue to occupy the property then the assignment of the tenancy to the occupying tenant is dependent upon the terms of the tenancy relating to assignment. If there is no covenant against assignment, or where there is but the landlord consents, the tenancy can be assigned to the occupying tenant as sole tenant.

In the absence of an assignment, protected[86] and statutory tenants have security of tenure under the Rent Act. A tenant in occupation under a contractual tenancy is protected from eviction by the terms of his contract. On the determination of the contractual (*i.e.* protected) tenancy, for example, when a fixed-term tenancy expires or notice to quit has been given in accordance with the periodic tenancy and section 5 of the Protection from Eviction Act 1977, a statutory tenancy arises if and so long as the tenant occupies the dwelling-house as his residence. The landlord can terminate a protected or statutory tenancy only on proof of one of the statutory grounds.[87]

If the tenancy in joint names is a protected tenancy and one of the cohabitees leaves the home during the tenancy, the other will be regarded as the protected tenant so as to become the statutory tenant under the Rent Act at the end of the protected tenancy.[88] So in contrast to the position under the Housing Act 1988 and in the public sector,[89] where one joint tenant under a joint periodic tenancy gives notice to quit, the notice terminates the protected tenancy but a statutory tenancy then arises in favour of the tenant remaining in occupation. A joint tenant in

---

86 A tenancy to which Pt. I of the Rent Act applies is a protected tenancy where a dwelling-house is let as a separate dwelling.
87 s.98 and Sched. 15.
88 *Lloyd* v. *Sadler* [1978] Q.B. 774.
89 See below, p. 61.

occupation may serve notice to quit to the landlord to bring the contractual tenancy to an end[90] with a view to obtaining a new sole statutory tenancy and to deny the non-occupying tenant security of tenure, but the occupying tenant thereby gives the landlord a statutory ground for possession.[91]

Where the tenancy is in the name of only one cohabitee, it will be very difficult to prove other than that he or she is the sole tenant. The other cohabitee is likely to be merely a licensee. In the absence of any evidence sufficient to give rise to a contractual licence, equitable licence or licence by estoppel[92] he or she will be a bare licensee who can be required to leave the property on being given reasonable notice by the tenant.[93]

Under the Rent Act a statutory tenant has security of tenure if and so long as he occupies the dwelling-house as his residence, subject to the landlord establishing any ground for possession.[94] If the statutory tenant leaves the home intending to return at some future time and leaves some indication in the home of that intention, his tenancy will continue. Leaving a cohabitee in occupation with an intention by the tenant to return will be sufficient to continue the tenancy.[95] If the statutory tenant leaves the home with no intention of returning, the tenancy will not continue. A non-tenant cohabitee who is left in the home is not entitled to remain in possession, whereas the Matrimonial Homes Act 1983[96] provides that a spouse's occupation under section 1 of that Act shall, for the purposes of the Rent Act 1977, be treated as possession by the tenant spouse. In *Colin Smith Music Ltd.* v. *Ridge*,[97] an unmarried couple lived together as man and wife in premises of which the man was statutory tenant. They had two children. The man later left and surrendered his tenancy and the landlords claimed possession. The Court of Appeal held that a cohabitee's position was not analogous to that of a wife and it could not be said that a woman who had borne the tenant's children occupied the home on his behalf. She was therefore a mere licensee and the landlords were entitled to possession. It is interesting to compare this situation with that on the death of a statutory tenant, in which event a surviving cohabitee may qualify as a statutory successor and thus be entitled to remain in possession.[98]

---

90 In accordance with *Hammersmith and Fulham London Borough Council* v. *Monk* [1992] 1 A.C. 478.
91 Under Rent Act 1977, Case 5, Pt. 1. Sched. 15. The ground is discretionary as the court must consider it reasonable to make an order: see s.98.
92 See above, p. 52. For the position where there is an injunction under the domestic violence legislation, see below, p. 64.
93 As the essence of cohabitation is the sharing of a common life within a relationship akin to that of husband and wife, it is not proposed here to discuss arrangements between parties such as to give rise to a restricted contract (Rent Act 1977, s.19) or a sub-tenancy (Rent Act 1977, s.137).
94 Rent Act 1977, s.98.
95 *Brown* v. *Brash* [1948] 2 K.B. 247; see also *Thompson* v. *Ward* [1953] 2 Q.B. 153; Brierley, "The Rent Act 1977 and the Absent Tenant" [1991] Conv. 345 and 432.
96 s. 1(6), and see *Griffiths* v. *Renfree* [1989] 2 F.L.R. 167.
97 [1975] 1 W.L.R. 463.
98 See below, p. 224.

A cohabitee has no right to pay the rent if her tenant partner defaults on his payments. In addition the court's power on or after breakdown of marriage to order the transfer of a tenancy does not apply on breakdown of cohabitation.[99]

Housing Act 1988 tenancies

The Housing Act 1988 introduced assured tenancies[1] for tenancies created on or after January 15, 1989 and, save in limited circumstances, no protected tenancy can be created after that date.[2] The assured tenancy is modelled on the public sector secure tenancy under the Housing Act 1985 [3] rather than the contractual and statutory tenancy under the Rent Act 1977. An assured tenancy is one under which a dwelling-house is let as a separate dwelling; the tenant, or each of the joint tenants, is an individual and the tenant or at least one of the joint tenants occupies the dwelling-house as his or her only or principal home.[4]

Where the tenancy is a joint tenancy, each tenant has the right to live in the property and each is jointly and severally liable for all the obligations such as the rent. On the death of one tenant the other becomes sole tenant by survivorship. On breakdown of the relationship, a fixed-term tenancy can be assigned[5] unless prohibited by the agreement. A periodic tenancy can be assigned with the landlord's consent[6] and the parties should seek to have the tenancy transferred into the sole name of the proposed occupier so that that party alone is responsible for all the obligations.

Security of tenure is conferred by section 5 on the basis that an assured tenancy cannot be brought to an end by the landlord except by court order in accordance with the Act or, in the case of a fixed-term tenancy which contains power for the landlord to determine the tenancy, by his exercising that power. On the termination of a fixed-term tenancy, either by effluxion of time or because the landlord exercised a right to terminate, then, provided the tenant is occupying the property as his only or principal home, the tenancy will be replaced by a statutory periodic tenancy on the same terms.[7] The tenant can terminate a periodic tenancy by notice to quit or surrender, and a fixed-term tenancy by surrender.

In contrast to a joint periodic tenancy under the Rent Act and in line with a secure periodic tenancy under the Housing Act 1985, a notice to quit given by one of two joint tenants terminates a periodic tenancy.[8] So,

---

99 See below, p. 61.
 1 There is not the scope within this book to consider assured shorthold tenancies which the Act also created.
 2 See Housing Act 1988, s.34.
 3 See below, p. 62, except that the grounds for possession are much less fair to the tenant.
 4 s.1, subject to the exceptions in Sched. 1, Pt. 1.
 5 By deed of assignment.
 6 s.15.
 7 s.5(2).
 8 See *Hammersmith and Fulham London Borough Council* v. *Monk* [1992] 1 A.C. 478, below, p. 62.

where one tenant remains in occupation after breakdown of cohabitation, the absent tenant may determine the tenancy by giving notice to quit and the occupying tenant is at risk of the landlord thereafter seeking an order for possession. Alternatively the landlord may be willing to grant the occupying tenant a new sole tenancy. Notice to quit by one joint tenant of a fixed-term tenancy does not determine the tenancy,[9] which requires all joint tenants to determine it.[10]

Where the assured tenancy is a sole tenancy, the other cohabitee is likely to be a bare licensee who can be required to leave on being given reasonable notice.[11] Any assignment of the tenancy would require the landlord's consent. A notice to quit served by the tenant will operate to surrender the tenancy. If the tenant leaves the property with no intention of returning, that will bring the tenancy to an end as residence by a cohabitee is not sufficient.[12]

A cohabitee has no right to pay the rent if her partner defaults on his payments. A spouse with statutory rights of occupation under the Matrimonal Homes Act 1983 has this right[13] and can thus prevent the landlord from gaining possession. Moreover, on granting a decree of divorce, nullity or judicial separation or at any time thereafter, the court may transfer a protected, statutory or assured tenancy from one spouse to the other.[14] The courts have no such power on breakdown of cohabitation. It is advisable for a non-tenant cohabitee to inquire of the landlord whether he is prepared to accept rent from her. He is under no obligation to do so, however, and may be reluctant, for fear of granting a new tenancy, particularly if the tenant has left for good.

Public sector tenancies

The granting of a tenancy in respect of local authority property depends upon the particular authority's practice, for authorities have a wide discretion which is generally exercised in favour of families with children. In the case of spouses, there has been a move away from granting tenancies to husbands alone in favour of granting a joint tenancy to husband and wife and this practice is slowly being extended to cohabitees.

Prior to the Housing Act 1980 local authorities had a wide discretion to terminate or transfer tenancies so, for example, on breakdown of cohabitation a parent (usually the mother) with care of the children had a strong claim to remain in the property. Since the 1980 Act the issues are essentially the same as those applicable to private sector tenancies and rights of occupation on breakdown of cohabitation depend primarily

---

9 ss.5(2)(b) and 45(2).
10 See *Leek & Moorlands Building Society* v. *Clark* [1952] Q.B. 788.
11 See above, p. 52.
12 See *Colin Smith Music Ltd.* v. *Ridge* [1975] 1 W.L.R. 463, above, p. 59.
13 Matrimonial Homes Act 1983, s.1(5).
14 Matrimonial Homes Act 1983, s.7 and Sched. 1; Matrimonial Causes Act 1973, s.24.

upon in whose name the tenancy is. The law is now in the Housing Act 1985.[15]

If the parties are joint tenants, both have the right to occupy the home and both are liable for the rent. On the death of one joint tenant, the other becomes sole tenant by survivorship. On breakdown of the relationship, then, provided that the tenancy is a secure tenancy,[16] the tenancy can be assigned, *inter alia*, to a person who could have been a qualified successor had the tenant died immediately before the assignment,[17] which includes a joint tenant, so that that party alone is responsible for all the obligations. In the event of a disagreement as to occupation of a secure tenancy, the landlord cannot terminate it without a court order,[18] and the tenancy remains secure subject to the property being occupied as the only or principal home by at least one of the tenants.[19] The security of tenure provisions, however, only prevent termination by the landlord. The tenant may terminate his tenancy in the usual way by notice to quit or surrender. In the case of a joint periodic tenancy it was held by the House of Lords in *Hammersmith and Fulham London Borough Council* v. *Monk*[20] that notice to quit given by one joint tenant without the concurrence of the other is effective at common law to determine a periodic joint tenancy subject, however, to both the terms of the tenancy[21] and the Protection from Eviction Act 1977.[22] So where one periodic joint tenant gives notice to quit to the local authority landlord, this will bring the tenancy to an end and does not give security to the remaining tenant. When the notice to quit expires, the local authority is entitled to possession. It is open to the authority to grant a new sole tenancy and it could be agreed between one joint tenant and the local authority that, on that joint tenant giving notice to quit, the authority will grant him or her a sole tenancy. This could be appropriate, for example, where there has been domestic violence.[23] It has been argued that the giving of notice to quit without consent constitutes a breach of trust and if there is a regrant of a tenancy to an occupying tenant she is a trustee attempting to benefit from a breach of trust and will hold the equitable estate on constructive trust for herself and the other tenant.[24] However, in *Hammersmith* Lord Bridge said that the existence of a trust for sale can make no difference to the principles applicable to the determination of a

---

15 As amended.
16 Housing Act 1985, s.79.
17 ss. 91-92.
18 *Ibid*. s.82.
19 *Ibid*. s.81.
20 [1992] A.C. 478, applying *Greenwich London Borough Council* v. *McGrady* (1983) 81 L.G.R. 288; (1983) 267 E.G. 515. See Dewar, (1992) 108 L.Q.R. 375; Goulding, [1992] Conv. 279.
21 See *Hounslow L.B.C.* v. *Pilling* [1993] 2 F.L.R. 49. One joint tenant cannot unilaterally serve a notice operating a break clause in the tenancy agreement.
22 s.5 requires a notice to quit to be given by a landlord or tenant not less than four weeks before the date on which it is to take effect.
23 See below, p. 64.
24 Williams, "Ouster Orders, Property Adjustment and Council Housing" [1988] Fam. Law 438 at 443.

tenancy and Lord Browne Wilkinson considered a breach of trust to be "very dubious".

It was accepted in *Hammersmith* that if the joint tenancy is for a fixed term, notice to quit by one joint tenant does not determine the tenancy which requires the joint tenants to act together.[25]

If the tenancy is taken in the name of only one cohabitee, the other is likely to be a bare licensee[26] lacking any right of occupation should he or she be required to leave by the tenant giving reasonable notice. The tenant alone will be liable for the rent and the non-tenant cohabitee has no right to pay the rent if the tenant defaults. If the tenant leaves the home with no intention of returning, the tenant condition[27] is no longer satisfied so the secure tenancy will cease and the local authority will be entitled to possession.[28] It is open to the non-tenant cohabitee to request the grant of a new tenancy, but the matter is entirely within the authority's discretion in the light of all the circumstances. The need to provide any children with a home ought to be a major factor and the local authority will need to be mindful of its obligations should the family become homeless.[29] The authority is not entitled to require payment of rent arrears in respect of the original tenancy from the non-tenant and ought not to make the payment of such arrears a condition of the grant of a new tenancy.

It is generally not possible for a secure tenant to assign his tenancy but one of the exceptions is an assignment to a person who would be qualified to succeed the tenant, if the tenant died immediately before the assignment.[30] A surviving cohabitee may qualify for that purpose.[31] If a tenancy is assigned in this way, the new tenant is regarded as a successor so as to deny subsequent succession on the death of the new tenant.[32]

A secure tenant has the right to buy subject to certain conditions and exceptions.[33] A secure tenant is entitled to require that not more than three members of his family who are not joint tenants but occupy the house as their only or principal home should share the right with him.[34]

---

25 See *Leek & Moorlands Building Society* v. *Clark* [1952] Q.B. 788.
26 See above, p. 52. Again it is not proposed here to discuss the possibility of a sub-tenancy.
27 s. 81. See also *Crawley Borough Council* v. *Sawyer* (1988) 20 H.L.R. 98.
28 Whereas occupation by a non-tenant spouse is to be treated as occupation by an absent tenant spouse for the purpose of the security of tenure provisions of the Housing Act 1988.
29 See below, p. 65.
30 Housing Act 1985, s.91(3)(*c*), and notwithstanding an absolute prohibition on assignment: see *Peabody Donation Fund Governors* v. *Higgins* [1983] 1 W.L.R. 1091. Any such assignment ought to be by deed (Law of Property Act 1925, ss.52-53 and *Crago* v. *Julian* [1992] 1 W.L.R. 372).
31 See below, p. 227.
32 Housing Act 1985, ss.87 and 88(1)(*d*).
33 See Housing Act 1985, Pt. V (as amended). There is also a right to a mortgage: see s.132.
34 Housing Act 1985, s.123: see, *e.g. Savill* v. *Goodall* [1993] 1 F.L.R. 755. An established claim by a secure tenant is enforceable by a member of his family after his death: see *Harrow London Borough* v. *Tonge* (1993) 25 H.L.R. 99.

Thus a secure tenant cohabitee could seek to join the non-tenant who is a member of his family[35] as a purchaser, provided the non-tenant has been residing with him for the 12 months prior to the notice claiming to exercise the right to buy or the landlord consents.

The power of the court to order the transfer of a secure tenancy on or after breakdown of marriage[36] is not of course available on breakdown of cohabitation.

3. INJUNCTION

Where a cohabitee is in need of protection for herself or her children from her partner, she may be entitled to an injunction under the Domestic Violence and Matrimonial Proceedings Act 1976, excluding him from the home.[37] The court's powers under the Act are irrespective of property rights,[38] so a "battered" cohabitee with or without property rights in the home can apply for an injunction to exclude his or her partner, even if the party against whom the order is sought is the sole owner or sole tenant of the home. An injunction gives a right of occupation, usually for a temporary period, so as to enable the applicant to find other accommodation. In the words of Lord Scarman[39]:

> "I find nothing illogical or surprising in Parliament legislating to over-ride a property right, if it be thought to be socially necessary. If in the result a partner with no property rights who obtains an injunction . . . thereby obtains for the period of the injunction a right of occupation, so be it. It is no more than the continuance by court order of a right which previously she had by consent: and it will endure only for so long as the County Court thinks necessary."

If the injunction is granted against a sole owner or sole tenant and the applicant has no proprietary interest in the home, her position will be very precarious if the respondent decides to dispose of his interest in the home.[40] The applicant's right of occupation is not a proprietary right. If the respondent is sole tenant and he leaves the home with no intention of returning the applicant will have no right to remain in possession[41] other than by arguing that the injunction confers a limited right of occupancy pending the applicant finding alternative accommodation.[42] In the case

---

35 A cohabitee will be a member of the tenant's family if they live together as husband and wife, which is the same definition as applies to succession on death: see Housing Act 1985, s.186, and below, p. 227: see also *Savill* v. *Goodall* [1993] 1 F.L.R. 755.
36 Matrimonial Homes Act 1983, s.7, and Sched. 1; Matrimonial Causes Act 1973, s.24.
37 See below, p. 164.
38 *Davis* v. *Johnson* [1979] A.C. 264. See below, p. 164.
39 [1979] A.C. 264 at 348.
40 See below, p. 165.
41 See above, p. 59.
42 See below, p. 165.

of a local authority tenancy, the power available to the authority prior to the Housing Act 1980 to transfer the tenancy is no longer available. If the respondent has no intention of surrendering the tenancy his security of tenure will prevail notwithstanding the injunction, unless either the authority has grounds for taking possession proceedings or the injunction is, unusually, of unlimited duration.[43] In the latter case it can be argued that the security of tenure is lost because the tenant condition has lapsed.[44] In either case it would be open to the authority to grant a sole tenancy to the cohabitee remaining in occupation.

Where the tenancy is in joint names there is the possibility of the victim of domestic violence, who remains in possession after the other tenant has left, giving notice to quit so as to leave the landlord free to grant her a new tenancy.[45]

4. HOMELESSNESS

Either or both of the parties to a relationship outside marriage who becomes homeless may look to the local authority for accommodation under Part III of the Housing Act 1985[46] which places a duty upon local authorities to house the homeless and those threatened with homelessness. The duty[47] is on the housing authority[48] and it varies depending upon whether or not the applicant:

(a) is homeless or threatened with homelessness;
(b) has a priority need;
(c) is intentionally homeless or threatened with homelessness;
(d) has a local connection.

A *Code of Guidance*[49] has been issued to local housing authorities and social services authorities which explains how the Act is to be applied. Authorities are under a duty to have regard to the Code,[50] but having done so they are not bound to follow it.[51] Hence practice varies depending upon the extent to which authorities, having had regard to the Code,

---

43 See below, p. 168.
44 Housing Act 1985, s.81. See also *Warwick* v. *Warwick* (1982) 12 Fam. Law 60; (1982) 1 H.L.R. 139.
45 *Hammersmith and Fulham London Borough Council* v. *Monk* [1992] 1 A.C. 478, above, p. 62.
46 Consolidating and amending the Housing (Homeless Persons) Act 1977.
47 See below, p. 71 and generally *Garlick*. v. *Oldham Metropolitan Borough Council* [1993] 2 All E.R. 65.
48 Application is to the housing unit of the Housing Department.
49 3rd ed., 1991.
50 Housing Act 1985, s.71.
51 See, *e.g. De Falco* v. *Crawley Borough Council* [1980] Q.B. 460.

then adhere to it. The greater the adherence the more sympathetic the treatment that the applicant is likely to receive.[52]

Homelessness and threatened homelessness

The first inquiry is whether or not the applicant is homeless or threatened with homelessness. A person is homeless,[53] if there is no accommodation in England, Wales or Scotland, which he, together with any other person who normally resides with him as a member of his family or in circumstances in which it is reasonable[54] for that person to reside with him, is entitled to occupy, *inter alia*, by virtue of an interest, court order or licence.[55] So a cohabitee who has a beneficial interest in the home is prima facie not homeless and even a bare licence may prevent her from being so.[56] If, however, the licence has been terminated, she is homeless.[57]

As to the meaning of "member of the family" the *Code of Guidance* indicates that "any other person . . . in circumstances in which it is reasonable for that person to reside with him" includes "any cohabiting couples".[58] Hence a cohabitee ought to be taken into account as a member of the applicant's family if normally residing with the applicant without the need to consider whether or not "it is reasonable for that person to reside with him". In line with the policy of the legislation to keep families together, whether married or unmarried, the Code also indicates that:

> "Persons who normally live with the applicant but are unable to do so for no other reason than that there is no accommodation in which they can live together should be included in the assessment . . . When dealing with a family which has split up, authorities need to take a decision on a matter of fact - does the other person normally live with the applicant?"[59]

A period of cohabitation may be so transient an arrangement, however, as not of itself to constitute a period of accommodation from which

---

52 Research has shown a wide variation of policies: see Thornton, "Homelessness Through Relationship Breakdown: The Local Authorities' Response" [1989] J.S.W.L. 67. For a report on how local authorities in Wales respond to the housing needs of women leaving violent homes, see *The Answer is Maybe . . . And That's Final!* published by Welsh Women's Aid.
53 Housing Act 1985, s.58(1).
54 Not whether the housing authority considers it reasonable as in the Housing (Homeless Persons) Act 1977, s.1.
55 Housing Act 1985, s.58(2). A person shall not be treated as having accommodation unless it is accommodation which it would be reasonable for him to continue to occupy: see s.58(2A) (as inserted).
56 See Thornton, [1989] J.S.W.L. 67 at 73.
57 See further *Code of Guidance*, para 5.5.
58 Para. 5.3.
59 *Ibid*. paras 5.3 and 5.4.

the applicant can become homeless. So in *R. v. Purbeck District Council, ex p. Cadney*[60] the applicant left the matrimonial home of which she was joint tenant and for three months lived with another man until he required her to leave. In considering whether this accommodation was a settled home which she left intentionally the local authority was held to be entitled to take the view that it was a transient arrangement for which she was leaving a secure home. Any homelessness could arise only by her departure from the matrimonial home which in the circumstances was intentional.[61]

If a cohabitee has suffered violence or there is a likelihood of violence[62] if he or, more likely, she continues to occupy the home she will be homeless, for a person is homeless if she has accommodation but cannot secure entry to it, or it is probable that occupation of it will lead to violence from someone else living in it, or to threats of violence from someone else living in it which are likely to be carried out.[63] The accommodation must be such that it is reasonable for her to continue to occupy it,[64] which requires the local authority to take into consideration the physical and mental needs of the applicant as well as the quality of the accommodation. In *R. v. Broxbourne Borough Council, ex p. Willmoth*[65] the Court of Appeal held that the authority should take into account the fact that the man whom the applicant had been living with violently assaulted her and seized their child in the street. Violence is not to be disregarded because it took place outside the home.[66]

Not all authorities require proof of violence, but in practice the applicant may be required to establish that violence has occurred by using the domestic violence legislation in order to obtain evidence and as part of a long-term solution.[67] The existence of a domestic violence injunction[68] should be sufficient evidence but the applicant ought not to be required to obtain an injunction,[69] nor should the fact that she has obtained an exclusion injunction preclude the applicant from being homeless in view of the temporary nature of such injunctions.[70] The *Code of Guidance* says authorities:

---

60 [1986] 2 F.L.R. 158.
61 See further below, p. 69.
62 See Bryan, "Domestic Violence: A Question of Housing?" [1984] J.S.W.L. 195.
63 Housing Act 1985, s.58(3). See *R. v. Purbeck District Council, ex p. Cadney* [1986] 2 F.L.R. 158, where on the facts it was held that there was nothing to show that the wife had made any attempt to secure entry to the matrimonial home and only the most indirect evidence that if she did enter it violence from the husband would result.
64 s. 58(2A) (as inserted), reversing *R. v. Hillingdon London Borough Council, ex p. Puhlhofer* [1986] A.C. 484.
65 (1989) 22 H.L.R. 118.
66 See *R. v. Kensington and Chelsea Royal London Borough Council, ex p. Hammell* [1989] 1 All E.R. 1202; *Code of Guidance*, para. 5.8(*d*).
67 See Thornton, [1989] J.S.W.L. 67 at 71; *The Answer is Maybe . . . And That's Final!*, p. 30.
68 See below, p. 160.
69 See *Warwick v. Warwick* (1982) 12 Fam. Law 60; (1982) 1 H.L.R. 139.
70 See below, p. 168.

" . . . should respond sympathetically to applications from men and women who are in fear of violence. The fact that violence has not yet occurred does not, on its own, suggest that it is not likely to occur. Injunctions ordering persons not to molest, or enter the home of, the applicant will not necessarily deter people and the applicant should not necessarily be asked to return to their home in this instance. Authorities may inform applicants of the option to take out an injunction, but should make clear that there is no obligation to do so if s/he feels it would be ineffective."[71]

The fact that an applicant has been driven out of her home and sought refuge in a Women's Aid Centre does not relieve the authority of its duty under Part III of the Housing Act 1985.[72]

If a person is not homeless, he will be threatened with homelessness if it is likely that he will become homeless within 28 days.[73]

Priority need

Homelessness is not in itself sufficient to give rise to a duty to house, for in the absence of a priority need there is merely a duty to give advice and assistance.[74] Once an authority is satisfied that the applicant is homeless or threatened with homelessness, it must make further inquiries to decide whether or not the applicant falls within a priority need category. There is a priority need for accommodation,[75] *inter alia*, if the applicant:

(a) is a pregnant woman, or a person with whom a pregnant woman lives or might reasonably be expected to live, such as, for example, a cohabitee;

(b) is a person with whom dependent children live or might reasonably be expected to live. A dependent child need not necessarily be a child of the applicant and need not be wholly and exclusively dependent on the applicant or live only with him.[76] The *Code of Guidance* currently states that court orders are an obvious starting point, but authorities should take care that each case is fully assessed on its individual circumstances[77] whereas previous guidance indicated court orders should not be required.[78] It is to be

---

71 Para. 5.9.
72 *R.* v. *Ealing London Borough Council, ex p. Sidhu* (1983) H.L.R. 45.
73 Housing Act 1985, s.58(4).
74 See below, p. 71.
75 See Housing Act 1985, s.59.
76 *R.* v. *London Borough of Lambeth, ex p. Vagliviello* (1990) 22 H.L.R. 392 (child lived with each parent for three and a half days a week, applicant could have a priority need.)
77 Para. 6.3.
78 See the second edition of the *Code of Guidance*, para. 2.12a. See also *R.* v. *Ealing London Borough Council, ex p. Sidhu* (1983) H.L.R. 45.

hoped, however, that authorities are aware of the presumption of no order in the Children Act 1989[79];

(c) or any person with whom he or she lives or might reasonably be expected to live is vulnerable as a result of old age, mental illness or handicap or physical disability or other special reason. The latter may include men and women without children who have suffered violence at home or are at risk of further violence if they return home[80];

(d) is homeless or threatened with homelessness as a result of an emergency such as flood, fire or other disaster.

Intentionally homeless or threatened with homelessness

Before the full duty to secure permanent accommodation arises under the Act the authority must be satisfied that the applicant has not become homeless intentionally.[81] A person becomes homeless intentionally if he deliberately does or fails to do anything in consequence of which he has ceased to occupy accommodation which is available for his occupation and which it would have been reasonable for him to continue to occupy.[82] Any act or omission in good faith by a person who is unaware of any relevant fact is not to be treated as deliberate.[83]

Where one member of a family unit, such as a cohabitation, becomes homeless intentionally, the other member remains entitled to apply for accommodation notwithstanding that the intentionally homeless party might benefit from the application.[84] The housing authority is entitled, however, to look at the conduct of the family as a whole and assume, in the absence of evidence to the contrary, that conduct of one party, which was such that he should be regarded as having become homeless intentionally, was conduct to which the other member of the family was a party. So in *R.* v. *North Devon District Council, ex p. Lewis*,[85] as there was evidence on which the local authority could come to the conclusion that the applicant had acquiesced in the decision by her cohabitee to become homeless intentionally by giving up his job, knowing that they would have to leave their tied cottage, it was entitled to take the view that she had herself become homeless intentionally. If, however, an applicant acts in good faith in ignorance of a relevant fact, she will not be regarded as having acquiesced. [86]

---

79 s. 1(5): see below, p. 125.
80 *Code of Guidance*, para. 6.17.
81 Provided also there is a local connection: see below, p. 72. The burden of proving intentional homelessness is on the authority: see *Code of Guidance*, para. 7.1.
82 Housing Act 1985, s.60(1). A similar test applies in the context of threatened homelessness: see s.60(2).
83 *Ibid.* s.60(3).
84 See *R.* v. *Mole Valley District Council, ex p. Burton* (1988) 20 H.L.R. 479.
85 [1981] 1 W.L.R. 328. See also *R.* v. *Swansea City Council, ex p. Thomas* (1983) 9 H.L.R. 64.
86 See *R.* v. *Mole Valley District Council, ex p. Burton* (1988) 20 H.L.R. 479.

A wilful and persistent refusal to pay rent or mortgage repayments leading to repossession is likely to be regarded as rendering the person homeless intentionally but a cohabitee, like a spouse, ought not automatically to be held jointly responsible for the arrears incurred by the other partner. As well as considering legal responsibility for payment, the authority should seek to establish whether responsibility for the arrears was shared in practice, before treating the applicant as intentionally homeless. If the default is against the wishes or without the knowledge of the applicant, or if the applicant was aware of the default and did all that could reasonably be expected to prevent it, she should not be regarded as intentionally homeless.[87]

The authority has to establish that it would have been reasonable for the applicant to continue in occupation.[88] If the applicant is homeless in consequence of breakdown of cohabitation then it will depend upon the circumstances as to whether or not it is reasonable for the applicant to remain in occupation. If the couple drift apart the authority may well take the view that the homelessness is intentional. Where the breakdown occurs because of a dispute the housing authority will need to satisfy itself about its severity. If there has been domestic violence the applicant will have a good case for saying that she cannot reasonably be expected to continue to live in the property. The *Code of Guidance* says that it:

> "would not normally be reasonable for someone to continue to occupy accommodation if s/he . . . was a victim of domestic violence, or threats of violence from inside or outside the home. (Authorities should not normally treat an applicant as intentionally homeless because s/he has failed to use legal remedies.)"[89]

In line with the policy of the legislation to keep families together, accommodation is only available for a person's occupation if it is available for occupation both by him and by any other person who might reasonably be expected to reside with him.[90] In *R. v. Wimborne District Council, ex p. Curtis*[91] the applicant lived with her cohabitee in property provided for her sole occupation under a separation agreement entered into on the breakdown of her marriage. The agreement provided for the sale of the property if she cohabited or remarried. Her husband obtained an order for sale and the applicant applied for accommodation as a homeless person. The local authority decided that she was homeless and had a priority need but had become homeless intentionally. It was held on appeal that the local authority had not directed its mind to the question of whether the property was accommodation for occupation by the applicant and any person who might reasonably be expected to reside with her (*i.e.* her cohabitee). If it was not, the question of intentionality

---

87 *Code of Guidance*, para. 7.6.
88 Housing Act 1985, s.60(1).
89 Para. 7.11.
90 Housing Act 1985, s.75. See *Code of Guidance*, para. 4.2.
91 [1986] 1 F.L.R. 486.

did not arise. Similarly in *R*. v. *Peterborough City Council, ex p. Carr*[92] the court held that section 60 must be read incorporating section 75 and the local authority had failed to address its mind to whether the applicant's fiancé, who was the father of her child, was a person who might reasonably be expected to live with her.

The duty

If a person applies for accommodation the authority must make inquiries[93] and satisfy itself as to whether it is under a duty to assist. If the authority has reason to believe that the applicant may be homeless and have a priority need it must secure that temporary accommodation is made available for the applicant's occupation and for any person who might reasonably be expected to reside with him,[94] for example, a cohabitee, pending any decision it may make as a result of its inquiries.[95]

If the authority is satisfied that the applicant is homeless, has a priority need and is not satisfied that he became homeless intentionally, it is under a duty to secure that accommodation becomes available for his occupation[96] and that of any person who might reasonably be expected to reside with him.[97] If he is threatened with homelessness, has a priority need and did not become threatened with homelessness intentionally the duty is to take reasonable steps to secure that accommodation does not cease to be available for his occupation.[98] Where it is satisfied that the applicant is homeless and has a priority need but is satisfied that he became homeless intentionally, there is a temporary housing duty owed to secure that accommodation is made available for his occupation for such period as it considers will give him a reasonable opportunity of securing accommodation for his occupation and a duty to give advice and such assistance as it considers appropriate.[99] Where the applicant is threatened with homelessness and has a priority need but became threatened with homelessness intentionally, the duty is only to give advice and assistance.[1] Similarly, where there is homelessness or threatened homelessness but the authority is not satisfied that the applicant has a priority need, there is merely a duty to give advice and assistance in finding accommodation.[2]

---

92 (1990) 22 H.L.R. 206.
93 See further Housing Act 1985, s.62, and the *Code of Guidance*, para. 3.2.
94 *Ibid.* s.75.
95 *Ibid.* s.63.
96 *Ibid.* s.65(1) and (2). Unless there is no local connection with their area: see below, p. 72.
97 *Ibid.* s.75.
98 *Ibid.* s.66(1) and (2): see also s.66(4) (and that of any person who might reasonably be expected to reside with him).
99 *Ibid.* s.65(1) and (3).
1 *Ibid.* s.66(1) and (3)(*b*).
2 *Ibid.* s.65(1) and (4), 66(1) and (3)(*a*). See *Code of Guidance*, paras. 6.1-6.5.

Local connection

Even where it has been accepted that there is a duty to secure permanent accommodation[3] the housing authority may be of the opinion that there is no local connection with their area and that the conditions are satisfied for referral of the application to another local housing authority.[4] These conditions are that neither the applicant nor any person who might reasonably be expected to reside with him has a local connection[5] with the authority's area, that one of them has a local connection with another housing authority's area and neither of them will run the risk of domestic violence in that other authority's area. A person runs the risk of domestic violence for this purpose if he runs the risk of (a) violence from any person with whom, but for that risk, he might reasonably be expected to reside or from a person with whom he formerly resided, or (b) threats of violence from such a person which are likely to be carried out.

If the notified authority agrees that the conditions for referral are satisfied it is then under a duty to secure accommodation. In the absence of agreement, the notifying authority remains responsible to provide temporary accommodation until the dispute is settled.[6] If the notifying authority does not establish a local connection with another authority's area they are under a duty to secure accommodation even if there is no local connection with the area of any housing authority.[7]

Performance of the duty

If a housing authority is required to secure that accommodation becomes available, it may perform that duty by providing suitable local authority accommodation, by securing that the applicant obtains suitable accommodation from some other person or by giving such advice and assistance as will secure that suitable accommodation is obtained from some other person.[8] In so advising, the housing authority is not confined to ensuring that the accommodation is obtained from someone else within the housing authority's area.[9] An applicant should be cautious about rejecting an offer of permanent accommodation, for if the housing authority can show that it has discharged its duties by making a single reasonable offer of suitable accommodation, no further offer will be made.[10]

---

3 *I.e.* under ss.65(1) and (2).
4 *Ibid.* s.67, in which case they must notify that other authority.
5 For meaning, see *ibid.* s.61, and *Code of Guidance*, para. 8.3.
6 *Ibid.* s.68.
7 *R.* v. *Hillingdon London Borough Council, ex p. Streeting* [1980] 1 W.L.R. 1425.
8 Housing Act 1985, s.69 (as amended).
9 *R.* v. *Bristol City Council, ex p. Browne* [1979] 1 W.L.R. 1437.
10 *R.* v. *Westminster City Council, ex p. Chambers* (1983) 81 L.G.R. 401.

CHAPTER 4

MONEY

At some stage in every relationship, matters of money are important. The relationship between cohabitees has been described as that of "stranger in law",[1] a statement which is certainly true in relation to direct support obligations during the parties' lifetime.[2] A contrast can be drawn between this lack of financial obligation *inter vivos* and the right to seek financial provision on death,[3] thereby highlighting the different legal approaches to cohabitation, depending upon the context in which the relationship is under consideration. The distinction has been justified by the Law Commission[4] on the basis that the deceased may have been providing for the applicant and may have wished to continue doing so, but his will or the law of intestacy does not give effect to those wishes. The distinction arises because any claim during a couple's lifetime has to be made under matrimonial law, which by its nature excludes the unmarried, whereas on death a claim may be based upon dependency, which can occur outside marriage.[5] This Chapter is concerned with financial obligations between cohabitees during their lifetime; their financial obligations upon death and to their children are considered later.[6]

I. MAINTENANCE

Whereas spouses are under a reciprocal statutory duty to maintain each other,[7] cohabitees are not.[8] English law recognises the duty to maintain and the right to be maintained as arising out of the marriage relationship; without such a relationship such rights and obligations do not arise.

---

1 *Per* Hodson L.J. in *Diwell* v. *Farnes* [1959] 1 W.L.R. 624 at 629.
2 See below.
3 See below, p. 210.
4 See Law Commission, Second Report on Family Property, *Family Provision on Death* (Law Com. No. 61) (1974), para. 90.
5 For further consideration of this apparent lack of consistency in the legal response to cohabitation, see below, Chap. 10.
6 See below, pp. 210 and 142. Funeral payments and inheritance tax are, however, considered in this Chapter: see below, pp. 92 and 95.
7 See, *e.g.* Matrimonial Causes Act 1973, s.23; Domestic Proceedings and Magistrates' Courts Act 1978, s.1; Social Security Administration Act 1992, ss.78(6) and 105(3).
8 See *Windeler* v. *Whitehall* [1990] 2 F.L.R. 505.

If cohabiting parties subsequently marry, can account be taken of the cohabitation when assessing marital obligations?[9] In *Campbell* v. *Campbell*,[10] a couple lived together for three and a half years before marrying. The marriage lasted just two years. In divorce proceedings brought by Mrs. Campbell, she argued that the pre-marital cohabitation should be taken into account in determining the length of the marriage,[11] when assessing maintenance. Sir George Baker P. rejected the argument on the basis that[12]:

> "It is the ceremony of marriage and the sanctity of marriage which count; rights, duties and obligations begin on the marriage and not before. It is a complete cheapening of the marriage relationship, which I believe, and I am sure many share this belief, is essential to the well-being of our society as we understand it, to suggest that pre-marital periods, particularly in the circumstances of this case, should, as it were, by a doctrine of relation back of matrimony, be taken as part of marriage to count in favour of the wife performing, as it is put, 'wifely duties before marriage'."

The courts, however, have been prepared to take into account cohabitation after divorce[13] and the trend is for pre-marital cohabitation to have some relevance, particularly if it has resulted in the creation of family assets.[14] In *Kokosinski* v. *Kokosinski*[15] the parties lived together for only four months after their marriage, having cohabited for 25 years before marrying. Wood J. stressed that the court should not construe the legislation too narrowly. He held that the Matrimonial Causes Act 1973 requires the court to have regard to the conduct of the parties[16] and also to all the circumstances of the case,[17] under both of which behaviour which occurs outside marriage can be taken into account, at least in a

---

9 See Deetch, "The Relevance of Cohabitation" (1982) 98 L.Q.R. 630.

10 [1976] Fam. 347.

11 See Matrimonial Causes Act 1973, s.25(2)(*d*) (as substituted). See also Domestic Proceedings and Magistrates' Courts Act 1978, s.3(2)(*d*) (as substituted).

12 [1976] Fam. 347 at 352.

13 *Chaterjee* v. *Chaterjee* [1976] Fam. 199.

14 See *Gojkovic* v. *Gojkovic* [1992] Fam. 40 where the whole of the spouses' relationship, including nine years' pre-marital cohabitation, was considered when the court had regard to all the circumstances of the case in assessing the wife's exceptional contribution to the creation of the family assets.

15 [1980] Fam. 72. See also *Day* v. *Day* [1988] 1 F.L.R. 278, where the court looked at the whole of the relationship, consisting of a four-year association (not amounting to continuous cohabitation) followed by marital cohabitation for six weeks and held that the husband had taken on a financial commitment in marrying and accepting his wife's children as children of the family.

16 s.25(2)(*g*), as since substituted by the Matrimonial and Family Proceedings Act 1984, s.3. For a consideration of the effect of the substituted wording, see below, p. 192. See also Domestic Proceedings and Magistrates' Courts Act 1978, s.3(2)(*g*).

17 *Ibid.* s.25(1) and see *Gojkovic* v. *Gojkovic* [1992] Fam. 40, above, n. 14. See also Domestic Proceedings and Magistrates' Courts Act 1978, s.3(1), and *Day* v. *Day* [1988] 1 F.L.R. 278, above, n. 15.

case where the conduct affected the finances of the other spouse. The court, it was said, could not do justice between the parties unless it took into account the wife's conduct during the 25 years that she and the husband had been cohabiting. She had been faithful, loving and hard-working and had helped to build up the family business, manage the home and bring up their son. The judge considered that a lump sum payment to her of £8,000 was appropriate. In so deciding, he expressed the perhaps too sanguine view that[18]:

> " . . . it will be said by some that to recognise the relationship which existed before marriage as relevant to financial redistribution, is to encourage relationships outside marriage. To them I would answer that the occasions on which a court is likely to feel that justice requires such recognition are likely to be few, possibly very few. It would, however, not be helpful to speculate on situations which may never arise. In my judgment, upon the particular facts of the present case my decision will do nothing to undermine the institution of marriage."

It is ironic that, had the parties not been married for the four months, the wife could have claimed nothing.

The decisions turned very much on their individual facts. The relationship in *Campbell* drew judicial disapproval whilst that in *Kokosinski* drew judicial sympathy. The courts exercise a wide discretion. In *Foley* v. *Foley*[19] the parties cohabited for seven years and had three children before marrying. They separated after five years of marriage and were divorced three years later. The Court of Appeal accepted the judge's view that the duration of the marriage begins with the date of the ceremony but that cohabitation may be a relevant factor when the court is considering all the circumstances of the case:

> " . . . the two periods, namely cohabitation and marriage, are not the same. What weight will be given to matters that occurred during those periods will be for the judge to decide in the exercise of his discretion, but one cannot say that those two periods are the same. Ten years of cohabitation will not necessarily have the same effect as ten years of marriage. During the period of cohabitation the parties were free to come and go as they pleased. This is not so where there is a marriage. In the great majority of cases public opinion would readily recognise a stronger claim founded upon years of marriage than upon years of cohabitation. On the other hand, in deciding these difficult financial problems there may be cases where the inability of the parties to sanctify and legitimise their relationship calls for a measure of sympathy which will enable

---

18 [1980] Fam. 72 at 88.
19 [1981] Fam. 160.

the court to take what has happened during the period of cohabitation into account as a very weighty factor. *Kokosinski* v. *Kokosinski* [. . .] is one such case. *Campbell* v. *Campbell* [. . .] is certainly not."[20]

The wife received a lump sum payment of £10,000.

At the same time as the Court of Appeal was deciding *Foley*, Balcombe J., who had been the first instance judge in that case, was deciding *H.* v. *H. (Financial Provision: Short Marriage).*[21] The parties cohabited sporadically for nearly six years before contracting a marriage which lasted only seven weeks. The judge adopted the approach in *Campbell* which he had applied in *Foley*, accepting also that a period of pre-marital cohabitation may be relevant as one of the circumstances of the case particularly where, as in *Kokosinski*, there are children.[22] As, however, the parties' relationship lacked any semblance of permanence, there were no children and the wife had not suffered financially as a result of the on and off period of cohabitation it would have been "cynical in the extreme"[23] to have considered it as equivalent to a true period of marriage. The pre-marital cohabitation was held to be of no relevance. The courts have thus embarked upon a difficult value-laden exercise, the outcome of which will depend upon the judicial attitudes to cohabitation as well as the facts of the case.

Maintenance agreement

In the absence of a duty to maintain, can cohabitees impose such a duty by agreement? Maintenance agreements between spouses are common and enforceable[24] giving effect as they do to the matrimonial responsibility to maintain, but agreements between cohabitees are another matter.[25] They have in the past been viewed as contrary to public policy.[26] Society's changed attitude to cohabitation no longer warrants the law's refusal to recognise such agreements, particularly if the agreement is one of maintenance within a stable relationship, rather than payment for a sexual relationship.[27] In *Horrocks* v. *Forray*[28] Scarman L.J., referring to the child of unmarried parents, said: "there is certainly nothing contrary to public policy in the parents coming to an agreement, which they intend to be binding in law, for the maintenance of the child and the mother." The law now recognises agreements relating to the

---

20 [1981] Fam. 160 at 167, *per* Eveleigh L.J.
21 (1981) 2 F.L.R. 392.
22 Which may include children accepted as children of the family: see *Day* v. *Day* [1988] 1 F.L.R. 278, above, n. 15.
23 (1981) 2 F.L.R. 399.
24 See, *e.g.* Matrimonial Causes Act 1973, s.34.
25 See below, p. 233.
26 See, *e.g. per* Lord Wright in *Fender* v. *St. John Mildmay* [1938] A.C. 1 at 38.
27 See below, p. 236.
28 [1976] 1 W.L.R. 230 at 239.

home by virtue of the concepts of the trust and the licence[29] and a duty to support is recognised indirectly by granting a share in the home to a cohabitee who has contributed to its acquisition.[30] Similar recognition ought not to be denied to an agreement between cohabitees to provide financial support for each other, provided that the agreement satisfies the ordinary principles applicable to the formation of contracts.[31] In view of the personal nature of the subject-matter of such an agreement, it is particularly important that the parties have shown an intention to create a legal relationship and that the agreement is more than a gratuitous promise. Hence it is advisable that it be made by deed so as to avoid problems of inadequacy of consideration, whilst simultaneously evidencing the intention that the agreement should be legally binding.

2. SAVINGS

Entitlement to savings is based upon the general principles applicable to other items of personal property,[32] although there are certain presumptions relating to joint accounts. Where cohabitees have separate incomes and maintain separate accounts, then generally each will be entitled to his or her income and savings. The position is more complicated if they operate a joint savings fund. To what share is each entitled should the cohabitation cease, either by break-up or on death? Most of the reported cases have concerned savings belonging to spouses, but it can be argued that savings belonging to cohabitees should be treated in the same way.

Many couples have joint bank accounts or joint building society accounts. If the account is in joint names and is one into which both parties pay their incomes and from which both take out money, the fund belongs to them jointly as joint tenants beneficially.[33] On breakdown of cohabitation, the fund (or debt if there is an overdraft) belongs to the parties equally and not in the proportions in which they contributed. On death of either of the parties, the right of survivorship[34] operates. By regarding such accounts as belonging to the parties jointly, the law is purporting to give effect to the parties' intentions. It will do so, only in so far as their intentions do not indicate something other than joint ownership. It is advisable, therefore, for the parties to spell out their intentions when the account is opened. This can be done quite simply by a short written statement, of which both parties keep a signed and dated copy, that the account is intended for their joint use and is to be regarded as

---

29 See above, pp. 19 and 52.
30 See above, p. 20.
31 See below, p. 233.
32 See above, p. 42.
33 Such accounts are sometimes referred to as a "common purse": see *Jones* v. *Maynard* [1951] Ch. 572.
34 See above, p. 14.

owned by them jointly. Alternatively, such ownership could be dealt with as part of a cohabitation contract.[35]

Property bought with money withdrawn from a joint account will generally belong not to the parties jointly, but to the person who bought it, unless the property was intended for their joint use.[36] So personal items purchased by either party will be the property of the purchaser, whereas an investment which is intended to represent the original fund will be joint property. Similarly, where the parties have demonstrated a joint intention that the survivor is to receive the benefit of a life insurance endowment policy and have acted upon that intention, the survivor is beneficially entitled to the proceeds of the policy in pursuance of the parties' joint intention, notwithstanding the personal representatives' contractual rights under the policy.[37]

If the parties wish to be regarded as owning separate shares (not necessarily a half each), they should make this clear, in which case they will jointly own the fund as beneficial tenants in common and not as beneficial joint tenants. On death of either party the right of survivorship does not operate and the deceased's share passes in accordance with his will or the law of intestacy. If the fund is owned jointly as joint tenants beneficially, the joint tenancy can be severed by notice or by agreement,[38] whereupon a tenacy in common in equal shares is created. In the absence of such severance, however, either party can draw upon the entire fund. Such is particularly likely either upon, or in anticipation of, breakdown of the relationship, in which event it is advisable to notify the bank or building society that the single signature withdrawal mandate is cancelled.

Where only one party contributes to an account in joint names, this may be evidence that the parties did not intend a joint interest and that the fund belongs to the person who paid the money in on a presumption of resulting trust.[39] Where only one party so contributes, this presumption will operate unless there is evidence to the contrary, so if the parties intend that they should have a joint interest they should make this clear. Thus, if only one of the parties has an income and the income is paid into a joint account so that the other can draw on the account as a matter of convenience, the money in the account belongs to the contributor. An account which was originally opened in joint names for convenience may become a common purse, if the contributor changes his intention so as to benefit the other party.[40]

The fact that a savings account is in the name of one cohabitee alone does not necessarily mean that the other has no claim to a share. The fund will belong to the party in whose name the account is held, unless

---

35 See below, p. 235.
36 *Re Bishop* [1965] Ch. 450.
37 *Smith* v. *Clerical Medical and General Life Assurance Society* [1993] 1 F.L.R. 47, applying constructive trust principles: see above, p. 23.
38 See above, p. 17.
39 See above, p. 21.
40 *Re Figgis* [1969] 1 Ch. 123.

there is evidence that it was intended to belong to both jointly. In *Paul* v. *Constance*,[41] a cohabitee successfully claimed half the money in a deposit account opened in the sole name of her partner who had since died. On many occasions he had said that the money was as much hers as his. The court decided that his words showed that he had declared an express trust in which both of them had an interest. In effect he had declared himself as trustee of the money in the account for them both in equal shares so as to create a tenancy in common in equal shares.

Ownership of savings from a housekeeping fund would prima facie result to the party providing the fund. Cohabitees are not included within special rules which apply to such funds made by a husband,[42] for the expenses of the matrimonial home, or for similar purposes, in which case the money is regarded as belonging to the husband and wife equally, unless they have made alternative arrangements.[43] If, however, there is evidence that in providing the fund one cohabiting partner intended the other to retain or to share any such savings or property bought therefrom, this ought to be sufficient to rebut the presumption of resulting trust.

3. INSURANCE

The Life Assurance Act 1774[44] requires the person for whose benefit a life assurance policy is made to have an insurable interest in the life of the assured; any policy made contrary to this requirement is void and illegal. The interest must be of a financial nature. The purpose of the Act was to prevent people gambling upon the death of another where there was no other interest. Marriage, but not cohabitation, is seen as giving the parties an insurable interest in the life of each other without the need to prove financial loss.[45] The Insurance Ombudsman has decided that parties who are engaged to be married also have an insurable interest in each other's life, so that if the engagement is broken off the premiums are not repayable.[46] Other relationships have not been held to constitute an insurable interest unless there is a financial interest,[47] capable of valuation in money and founded on a legally recognised obligation. The amount of the insurable interest will be the loss which the person for

---

41 [1977] 1 W.L.R. 527.
42 Where a wife provides such a fund the general rule applies.
43 Married Women's Property Act 1964, s.1. Little use is made of the legislation which is under review. The proposed reforms do not relate to cohabitees: see Law Commission Working Paper No. 90, *Transfer of Money between Spouses—the Married Women's Property Act 1964* (1985); de Cruz, "Transfer of Money between Spouses: New Law Commission Proposals" (1985) 135 N.L.J. 797.
44 s.1.
45 *Griffiths* v. *Fleming* [1909] 1 K.B. 805; Married Women's Property Act 1882, s.11.
46 See the Insurance Ombudsman, *Annual Report 1989*, paras. 2.31-2.35. He did not believe that, had the policy been illegal, the policy-holder would not have been entitled to recover the premiums: see para. 2.33.
47 *Halford* v. *Kymer* (1830) 10 B. & C. 724.

whose benefit the assurance is taken will sustain by reason of the assured's death.

It is open to argument that a cohabitee, who is supported financially by his or her partner, has an insurable interest in the other's life, up to the amount of financial support which will be lost by the assured's death. In so far as the law indirectly recognises a support obligation between cohabitees,[48] there will be the loss of a benefit which the law recognises as one of financial value. There will be the difficulty, of course, of establishing the support obligation and the resulting financial loss. Such an obligation is recognised, for example, for purposes of claims under the Inheritance (Provision for Family and Dependants) Act 1975[49] on the basis of dependence. It is submitted that a life assurance policy would be providing for the same dependence. Moreover, such a policy is not within the gambling mischief of the legislation and could be argued as valid for that reason.[50]

4. SOCIAL SECURITY

The law treats cohabitees as independent persons for maintenance law purposes, but it does not follow, therefore, that they are to be treated independently for purposes of social security law. There is a tendency for them to be treated independently if to do so is to their disadvantage, but not if it is to their advantage. In particular, the treatment of married and unmarried couples is based upon the principle that the latter should not, by virtue of being unmarried, receive preferential treatment compared with the former. There is not the scope within this book to undertake a general consideration of social security law, so the following is an examination of the special rules which apply in cases of cohabitation.

Income-related benefits

There are five income-related benefits, namely income support, family credit, disability working allowance, housing benefit and council tax benefit.[51] In relation to each of these means tested benefits the unit of claim is the "family" which, put simply[52] means a married or unmarried couple; a married or unmarried couple with a child; and single-parent families. If one member of a family is entitled to an income-related

---

48 See above, p. 77.
49 See below, p. 210.
50 See the Insurance Ombudsman, *Annual Report 1989*, para. 2.34.
51 Social Security Contributions and Benefits Act 1992, s.123 (as amended). For a brief outline of each, directed to cohabitation, see below, p. 86, and for a detailed consideration see Mesher, *CPAG's Income Related Benefits: The Legislation* (1993).
52 For the precise meaning, see Social Security Contributions and Benefits Act 1992, s.137(1), and Income Support (General Regulations) 1987 (S.I. 1987 No. 1967), reg. 2(3) and Pt. III; Family Credit (General) Regulations 1987 (S.I. 1987 No. 1973), Pt. III; Housing Benefit (General) Regulations 1987 (S.I. 1987 No. 1971), Pt. IV.

benefit, then any other member is excluded from entitlement to that benefit during the same period.[53] As a general rule when applying the means test the income and capital of the family members are aggregated and the legislation provides[54] that:

> "Where a person claiming an income-related benefit is a member of a family, the income and capital of any member of that family shall, except in prescribed circumstances,[55] be treated as the income and capital of that person."

The policy behind this so-called "cohabitation rule"[56] is that an unmarried couple should not be more favourably treated than a married couple, which they would be if they were able to claim as single persons.[57] The rule assumes, however, a support obligation between cohabiting parties which the law does not recognise. It assumes also that any benefit received will be used for the support of the family including any children living with the cohabiting parties, whether or not they are children to whom a maintenance obligation is owed.[58] If one spouse fails to support the other, that other can enforce the right to maintenance,[59] whereas a cohabitee cannot and a spouse has the possibility of such action as a bargaining chip, whereas a cohabitee does not. If a couple are cohabiting as man and wife and one of them is engaged in remunerative work but does not support the other, that other is entitled neither to maintenance nor to income support. Even where neither party is engaged in remunerative work, the resources and requirements of one will be treated as the resources and requirements of the other. In view of the lack of any obligation to maintain, or for the recipient of income support to use it for the benefit of his cohabiting partner, the important issue ought to be each party's own resources and requirements, not his or her living arrangements. It nevertheless remains crucial for a cohabiting couple to know whether or not they come within the concept of an "unmarried couple" for income-related benefit purposes.

Unmarried couple

The Social Security Contributions and Benefits Act 1992[60] preserved the earlier definition[61] of an unmarried couple as meaning "a man and a

---

53 Social Security Contributions and Benefits Act 1992, s.134(2), except in prescribed circumstances.
54 Social Security Contributions and Benefits Act 1992, s.136(1).
55 See S.I. 1987 No. 1967, Pt. V.
56 Which has its origins in the national insurance widow's schemes introduced by the Widows' and Orphans' and Old Age Contributory Pensions Act 1925, s.21.
57 For an official justification of the rule, see Supplementary Benefits Administration Papers 5, *Living Together as Husband and Wife* (1976). For an interesting insight to the background of the report, see Donnison, *The Politics of Poverty* (1982), pp. 108-116.
58 See below, p. 142.
59 See above, p. 73.
60 s.137.
61 Supplementary Benefits Act 1976, s. 34; Social Security Act 1986, s. 20(11).

woman who are not married to each other but are living together as husband and wife otherwise than in prescribed circumstances".[62] The requirement that the relationship must be between a man and a woman limits the cohabitation rule to heterosexual cohabitations. Parties to a homosexual cohabitation are assessed individually. A "married couple" continues to mean "a man and a woman who are married to each other and are members of the same household".[63] A "couple" means a married or unmarried couple.[64] The retention of these concepts meant that their interpretation remained unchanged.

The phrase "living together as husband and wife" has been taken to be synonymous with the earlier phrase "cohabiting as man and wife". The change was proposed because:

> " . . . the term 'cohabitation' has come to acquire a pejorative meaning in the public mind, and its use tends to perpetuate the mistaken assumption that the benefit rule is somehow intended to be a punishment for misconduct."[65]

If a couple admit that there is cohabitation, there is no difficulty. Where it is denied then, in deciding what constitutes living together as husband and wife for the purposes of the rule, certain criteria have been laid down. They are to be found both in decided cases[66] and in official policy, formerly in the *Supplementary Benefits Handbook*, the latter being judicially described as " . . . admirable signposts to help a tribunal . . . to come to a decision whether in fact the parties should be regarded as . . . 'living together as husband and wife'".[67] The criteria are currently to be found in the *Adjudication Officers' Guide*.[68] The value judgment involved in borderline cases makes the issue one of considerable complexity.[69]

(i) Members of the same household For the rule to operate, it is essential that the couple live together in the same household.[70] This does not mean, however, that all couples living in the same household will be

---

62 The Regulations prescribe the circumstances in which a person is to be treated as being or not being a member of the household: see the Income Support (General) Regulations 1987 (S.I. 1987 No. 1967), reg. 16.

63 See S.I. 1987 No. 1967, reg. 16.

64 See S.I. 1987 No. 1967, reg. 2. See also the definition in that regulation of "close relative", "partner" and "lone parent".

65 See *Living Together as Husband and Wife*, para. 52.

66 Of the courts and the Social Security Commissioners. The same principles should apply to both income-related benefits and widow's benefit (see *R(SB) 17/81*; *R(G) 3/81*, p. 229) and between the income-related benefits (see *R* v. *Penwith District Council, ex p. Menear, The Times*, October 21, 1991).

67 *Per* Woolf J. in *Crake* v. *Supplementary Benefits Commission* [1982] 1 All E.R. 498 at 505, referring to an earlier version of the Handbook.

68 See Pt. 15, available at DSS offices, and see the *Income Support Manual*, paras. 5.901-5.955.

69 See Donnison, *op. cit.*, Chap. 5.

70 See, *e.g. R(G) 11/55*.

cohabiting,[71] for one could be a lodger, or a housekeeper. The couple must regularly live in the same house or flat, apart from absences in connection with work[72] or visits to relatives, etc., and neither party must usually have another home.

Some help in determining whether the parties are members of the same household may be found in the "two households test" adopted for the purposes of determining in matrimonial law whether or not a couple are living apart,[73] subject, however, to the important qualification that such cases are not dealing with the inception of living together as man and wife but with the termination of such a relationship. Once it is established that such a relationship exists, its continuance is easier to show.[74]

In *Crake* v. *Supplementary Benefits Commission; Butterworth* v. *Supplementary Benefits Commission*[75] Woolf J. held that if it is established that a couple are living together in the same household, it is necessary then to consider whether they are doing so as husband and wife by ascertaining, in so far as is possible, the manner in which they are living in the same household[76] and their intention in so doing. If as in *Butterworth* the reason for one party living in the same household as another is to look after that person because of illness or incapacity, the parties are not living together as husband and wife. There has not, however, been judicial consistency in the application of this subjective approach. Thus in *Campbell* v. *Secretary of State for Social Services*,[77] notwithstanding the appellant's contention that the relationship was one of housekeeper and employer and the tribunal's having made no reference to the question whether sexual relations had taken place, Woolf J. found that the tribunal was not unreasonable in coming to the decision that the parties were living together as husband and wife, in particular because Mrs. Campbell had sold the majority of her furniture before taking up residence and because the parties intended to apply for a joint local authority tenancy.

The objective approach places emphasis upon the parties' conduct towards one another on the basis that intention cannot be ascertained otherwise than by what the parties do and say at the relevant time.[78] In *Robson* v. *Secretary of State for Social Services*[79] the determination of whether or not cohabitation constitutes living as husband and wife was

71 *Robson* v. *Secretary of State for Social Services* (1982) 3 F.L.R. 232.
72 Which could include absences for higher education: see *R(SB) 30/83*.
73 See *Hopes* v. *Hopes* [1949] P. 227; *Mouncer* v. *Mouncer* [1972] 1 W.L.R. 321; *Fuller* v. *Fuller* [1973] 1 W.L.R. 730 and see below, p. 162.
74 *Per* Woolf J. in *Crake* v. *Supplementary Benefits Commission* [1982] 1 All E.R. 498 at 502, commenting on the wording of the Domestic Violence and Matrimonial Proceedings Act 1976, s.1(2), and *Adeoso* v. *Adeoso* [1980] 1 W.L.R. 1535: see below, p. 162.
75 [1982] 1 All E.R. 498.
76 See also *R(SB) 35/85*.
77 (1983) 4 F.L.R. 138. See also *Kaur* v. *Secretary of State for Social Services* (1982) 3 F.L.R. 237.
78 *R(G) 3/81*.
79 (1982) 3 F.L.R. 232.

regarded as frequently depending upon the objective facts, because usually the intention of the parties is either unascertainable or, if ascertainable, is not to be regarded as reliable. If it is established, however, that the parties concerned did not intend to live together as husband and wife then "it would be a very strong case indeed sufficient to justify a decision that they are, or ought to be treated as if they are, husband and wife".[80]

Where the parties have given detailed evidence of the relationship and have said in unequivocal terms that they are not living together as husband and wife and have sought to show that they are not, then they are entitled to know how any contrary conclusion is reached.[81] Proper reasons go beyond a mere statement of the conclusion.

If either party has another home it is unlikely that they will be regarded as being members of the same household, as a person cannot simultaneously be a member of more than one household. Moreover, where one member of an unmarried couple is also a member of a married couple and there is no evidence to suggest that the marriage has broken down, there is a presumption that that member is part of a married couple and not, simultaneously, a member of an unmarried couple.[82] What is required is evidence of a stable cohabitation, which may exist, however, notwithstanding temporary absences.[83]

(ii) Stability   If the relationship is of a temporary nature, the couple are unlikely to be living together as husband and wife, for that implies more than an occasional or brief relationship. No time limits are laid down and each case depends upon its own facts. In some cases it may be apparent from the outset that the relationship is that of husband and wife. A couple's continued living together is strong evidence that the relationship has become that of husband and wife, provided that there are other indicators of such a relationship, for many landlady and lodger relationships are of long duration. Indications of a stable relationship may include the birth of a child of the parties,[84] the parties using the same surname[85] or their following a joint social life by, for example, going on holiday together.

(iii) Financial support   If either one of the parties is financially dependent upon the other, or there is some mutual financial support, for example, by a joint bank account, this will go some way to establishing that the parties are living together as husband and wife, although such evidence is not conclusive. Likewise, the fact that the parties retain financial independence is not conclusive evidence that they are not so living, for in some marriages the parties retain financial independence.

80 *Per* Webster J., *ibid.* at 236. Contrast *R(SB) 17/81*.
81 *Kingsley* v. *Secretary of State for Social Services* (1983) 4 F.L.R. 143.
82 *R(SB) 8/85*.
83 *R(SB) 30/83*, but see also *R(SB) 19/35*.
84 See below, p. 85.
85 See below, p. 85.

So, if the other indications of a stable marital-like relationship are present, the lack of evidence of financial support may not be sufficient to rebut the presumption of cohabitation. Payment for board and lodging will normally be evidence that the parties are not living as husband and wife.

(iv) Sexual relationship Sexual intercourse is a normal part of marriage and so the fact that a couple have a sexual relationship is, in practice, of great importance in showing that they are living as husband and wife, even though officers are instructed not to initiate questions about sexual relationships but to note statements and evidence presented by the claimant. The relationship as a whole must be considered, so the fact of a sexual relationship does not automatically mean that the couple must be regarded as so living. Failure to establish a sexual relationship will not necessarily rule out such a finding,[86] but if there is no evidence of a sexual relationship ever having existed it may be wrong to regard a couple as living together as husband and wife, unless an analogy can be drawn with a companionship marriage of an elderly couple. Actual proof of a sexual relationship is unnecessary if it can be inferred from the circumstances in which the couple are living together.

(v) Children The birth of a child of the relationship will go a long way towards establishing that the parents are living together as husband and wife, particularly if they jointly care for the child; likewise if they jointly care for the child or children of one of them.[87]

(vi) Public acknowledgment The fact that a couple are known publicly as husband and wife and the woman uses the man's surname will indicate that they are living as husband and wife.[88] It does not follow, however, that the fact that a couple do not represent themselves as married means that they cannot be so regarded.[89] The couple's dealings with third parties are also relevant; thus in *Campbell* v. *Secretary of State for Social Services*[90] the parties' intention to apply for a joint tenancy of the home was regarded as not the kind of step a lodger or housekeeper could be expected to take with a person with whom she is lodging or for whom she is housekeeping.

It may be that in the light of these factors a decision can be reached as to the nature of the relationship, but inevitably there will be doubtful

---

86 See, *e.g. Campbell* v. *Secretary of State for Social Services* (1983) 4 F.L.R. 138, above, p. 83; *Kaur* v. *Secretary of State for Social Services* (1982) 3 F.L.R. 237.
87 But see *Kingsley* v. *Secretary of State for Social Services* (1983) 4 F.L.R. 143 where the claimant, who returned to her former husband's house to look after the child of his second marriage, successfully challenged a finding of living together as husband and wife.
88 See, *e.g. R(G) 5/68.*
89 See, *e.g. CP 97/49.*
90 (1983) 4 F.L.R. 138.

cases in view of the fact that the criteria are not in any way conclusive. In cases of doubt the claim is supposed to be dealt with by an adjudication officer who has received special training.

If a couple deny that they are living together as husband and wife, it is in practice up to them to prove that they are not, for once it has been decided that they are cohabiting, there can be only one claimant in respect of the family and any further benefit will be withdrawn, leaving the couple to appeal. Likewise, once cohabitation has been established, if it later ends, it is up to the claimant to prove that it has ended, which is very difficult if the couple still live in the same premises.[91] In such a case, they will need to establish that they are living as two separate households and the issue is then the discontinuance rather than the inception of living together as husband and wife.[92]

Brief consideration will now be given to each of the income-related benefits.

Income support

Income support is the successor to supplementary benefit and is a means-tested benefit designed to take the resources of those who satisfy the relevant criteria with respect to availability for employment, up to subsistence level.[93] The legislation lays down the general framework of the benefit leaving it to regulations to prescribe the detailed operation of the system.[94] Everyone who is of, or over, the age of 16[95] is entitled to income support if[96]:

(1) he has no income or his income does not exceed the applicable amount[97];

(2) he is not engaged in remunerative work[98] and, if he is a member of a married or unmarried couple, the other member is not so engaged; and

---

91 See, *e.g. R(P) 6/52.*

92 See above, p. 83.

93 Income support was introduced by the Social Security Act 1986 following from a review of the social security scheme, the result of which was published in a Green Paper, Cmnd. 9517 (1985) followed by a White Paper, "Reform of Social Security", Cmnd. 9691 (1985).

94 See in particular the Income Support (General) Regulations 1987 (S.I. 1987 No. 1967) (as amended).

95 The Social Security Act 1988 amended the basic conditions of entitlement to income support so that persons under 18 cannot receive benefit except in certain narrowly prescribed circumstances: see now Social Security Contributions and Benefits Act 1992, s.125.

96 See Social Security Contributions and Benefits Act 1992, s.124.

97 See *ibid.* s.135 and S.I. 1987 No. 1967, Pt. IV.

98 See S.I. 1987 No. 1967, regs. 5-6.

(3) except in prescribed circumstances he is available for, and actively seeking, employment[99] and is not receiving relevant education.[1]

The income and capital resources of family members are aggregated[2] and a married couple and an unmarried couple are treated alike. There can be only one claimant in respect of the family, the claimant being whichever partner the parties agree should claim. In default of agreement the Secretary of State shall determine.[3]

Where mortgage interest is payable by a borrower who is entitled, or whose "partner, former partner or qualifying associate" is entitled, to income support and assistance has been provided by way of a housing addition to income support, then provision has been made by the Social Security (Mortgage Interest Payments) Act 1992[4] for that part of the benefit to be paid directly to the lender. A "partner" includes "any person to whom the borrower is not married but who lives together with the borrower as husband and wife, otherwise than in prescribed circumstances" and "former partner" means "a person who has at some time been, but no longer is, the borrower's partner". The definition differs from that of unmarried couple used for income support purposes[5] in referring to any person rather than to a man and a woman. It is arguable that a homosexual cohabiting couple are living together as husband and wife. Such a person may also come within the definition of "qualifying associate" which means:

"a person who, for the purposes of income support, falls to be treated . . . as responsible for so much of the expenditure which relates to housing costs . . . as consists of any of the mortgage interest payable by the borrower, and who falls to be so treated because—
    (a)   the borrower is not meeting those costs, so that the person has to meet them if he is to continue to live in the dwelling occupied as his home; and
    (b)   the person is one whom it is reasonable, in the circumstances, to treat as liable to meet those costs."

---

99 *Ibid.* regs. 7-11. The claimant is exempted from this requirement, *inter alia*, where he is a member of a married or unmarried couple one of whom is pregnant, or where either or both of them are responsible for a child or young person; and the adjudication officer is satisfied that unless income support is paid hardship will be suffered: see reg. 10A(2) (as amended).
1 *Ibid.* regs. 12-13.
2 Social Security Contributions and Benefits Act 1992, s.136: see above, p. 81.
3 Social Security (Claims and Payments) Regulations 1987 (S.I. 1987 No. 1968), reg. 4(3). See also regs. 2, 4(4) and 7(2).
4 See now Social Security Administration Act 1992, s.15A.
5 See above, p. 81.

Family credit

Family credit, which replaced family income supplement, is paid where a man or woman[6] is normally engaged in remunerative work, their "family"[7] includes at least one child or young person of a prescribed description for whom either party is responsible and all live in the same household. The family's income must not exceed the applicable amount, or exceed it but only by a certain percentage.[8] It is intended for families with at least one dependent child who are not entitled to income support or disability working allowance and have a low income.[9]

An unmarried couple has the same meaning as in the context of income support[10] and is once again equated with a married couple, so that, for example, the parties' income and capital are aggregated,[11] and only one of the parties can claim. One difference from income support is that the claim must be made by the woman unless the Secretary of State is satisfied that it would be reasonable to accept a claim by the man.[12] Either or both of the parties can be engaged in remunerative work and either party can be responsible for the child or young person. Family credit is normally payable for 26-week periods regardless of any change in the family's circumstances, which will be reviewed upon renewal of the claim. Provision is made, however, for regulations to provide for family credit to terminate if a person who was a member of the family at the date of the claim becomes a member of another family and some member of that other family is entitled to family credit or if income support or a disability working allowance becomes payable in respect of a person who was a member of the family at the date of the claim for family credit.[13]

Disability working allowance

A person who has attained the age of 16 and who has a physical or mental disability which puts him at a disadvantage in getting a job is entitled to disability working allowance if he is normally engaged in remunerative work, his income does not exceed the applicable amount or exceeds it only by a certain percentage and, except in prescribed circumstances, neither he, nor any member of his "family", is entitled to family credit.[14] "Family" has the same meaning as for other income-related

---

6 Or both.
7 See Social Security Contributions and Benefits Act 1992, s.137(1), above, p. 80.
8 *Ibid.* s.128.
9 Entitlement is again prescribed chiefly in regulations: see the Family Credit (General) Regulations 1987 (S.I. 1987 No. 1973), especially the definition in reg. 2 of "close relative" and "partner", and regs. 3, 43 and 49.
10 See p. 81.
11 Social Security Contributions and Benefits Act 1992, s.136, above, p. 81.
12 Social Security (Claims and Payments) Regulations 1987 (S.I. 1987 No. 1968), reg. 4(2). See also regs. 2 and 36.
13 Social Security Contributions and Benefits Act 1992, s.128(4): no regulations have as yet been made.
14 Social Security Contributions and Benefits Act 1992, s.129, and see Disability Working Allowance (General) Regulations 1991 (S.I. 1991 No. 2887).

benefits[15] and so includes an unmarried couple. Their resources are aggregated in calculating the allowance.[16] If both parties satisfy the conditions for the allowance, a claim can only be made by whichever one of them they agree should claim or, in default of agreement, by whichever one the Secretary of State decides.[17] Like family credit it is normally payable for 26-week periods regardless of any change in the family circumstances. Provision is also made for the allowance to terminate if a disability working allowance becomes payable in respect of someone else who was a member of his family at the date of his claim or income support or family credit becomes payable in respect of someone who was a member of the family at that date.[18]

Housing benefit

Housing benefit is designed to help with the payment of rent[19] and is administered by local authorities and not the Department of Social Security. Entitlement[20] arises where the claimant is liable for payment in respect of residential accommodation[21] which he occupies as his home,[22] there is an appropriate maximum housing benefit in his case and, *inter alia*, he has no income or his income does not exceed the applicable amount.[23] As with other income-related benefits, the unit of claim is the family and the income and capital of one of an unmarried couple is treated as that of the other[24] and married and unmarried couples are generally treated alike[25] so that entitlement of one party excludes the other. A claim may be made by whichever one of them they agree should claim or, in default of agreement, by such one as the appropriate authority shall determine.[26]

The administering local authority will decide whether or not a couple are cohabiting and also the procedures to be followed by its officers in

---

15 Social Security Contributions and Benefits Act 1992, s.137, above, p. 80.
16 *Ibid*. s.136.
17 Social Security (Claims and Payments) Regulations 1987 (S.I. 1987 No. 1968), reg. 4(3A).
18 Social Security Contributions and Benefits Act 1992, s.129(7).
19 Not mortgage repayments, assistance with which is only available from income support.
20 For full details, see Social Security Contributions and Benefits Act 1992, s.130, and the Housing Benefit (General) Regulations 1987 (S.I. 1987 No. 1971) and in particular reg. 2 definitions of "close relative", "family", "partner" and "unmarried couple".
21 See Social Security Contribution Act 1992, s.137(1), definition of "dwelling".
22 See S.I. 1987 No. 1971, reg. 5.
23 Social Security Contributions and Benefits Act 1992, s.135, and S.I. 1987 No. 1971, Pt. V.
24 See Social Security Contributions and Benefits Act 1992, s.136, and above, p. 81, and S.I. 1987 No. 1971, Pt. VI.
25 See, *e.g.* Social Security Contributions and Benefits Act 1992, s.134(2); S.I. 1987 No. 1971, Pt. V, reg. 52, Pt. VIII. For differential treatment, see reg. 96, dealing with payment on death of a person entitled which refers to next of kin.
26 See S.I. 1987 No. 1971, reg. 71, and, generally on claims, Pt. X.

obtaining the evidence upon which to base that decision.[27] The administering officer's decision may be challenged before a housing benefit review board but the onus is then in practice on the claimant. Moreover if the Department of Social Security has decided that a couple are not cohabiting for income-related benefit purposes, that decison binds the local authority for housing benefit purposes.[28]

Council tax benefit

Council tax benefit was introduced by the Local Government Finance Act 1992 as the successor to community charge benefit.[29] It is available to those on low incomes to assist with their liability to pay the council tax.[30] Like housing benefit it is administered by local authorities and entitlement to the council tax benefit is aligned to entitlement to housing benefit. "Couples", married or unmarried,[31] are generally treated alike.[32] An unmarried couple's income and capital are aggregated and only one of them can claim.

Miscellaneous provisions

Being a member of an unmarried couple is relevant also in the following contexts:

(1) for the purpose of calculating income support where a person is engaged in a trade dispute[33];
(2) where any amount paid in respect of an unmarried couple is recoverable,[34] it may be recovered, without prejudice to any other method, by deduction from prescribed benefits payable to either of them[35];
(3) in calculating entitlement to pensioners' Christmas bonus.[36]

The Social Fund

The Social Fund[37] replaced the previous regulation-based system of single payments with payments by way of loan or grant,[38] entitlement to

---

27 For an analysis of the diverse practices of three local authorities to the issue of the cohabitation rule in the housing benefit scheme, see Loveland, "The Micro-Politics of Welfare Rights: The Interpretation and Application of the Cohabitation Rule in the Housing Benefit Scheme" [1989] J.S.W.L. 23.
28 *R.* v. *Penwith District Council, ex p. Menear,The Times*, October 21, 1991.
29 Social Security Contributions and Benefits Act 1992, s.131 (as substituted).
30 On liability to council tax, see below, p. 102.
31 For meaning, see above, p. 81.
32 Social Security Contributions and Benefits Act 1992, s.132 (as amended) and Council Tax Benefit (General) Regulations 1992 (S.I. 1992 No. 1814), reg. 2.
33 Social Security Contributions and Benefits Act 1992, s.126.
34 See Social Security Administration Act 1992, s.71(8).
35 See *ibid.* s.71(9).
36 Social Security Contributions and Benefits Act 1992, ss.148 and 150(3).
37 Introduced by the Social Security Act 1986 in April 1988.
38 See now Social Security Contributions and Benefits Act 1992, s.138.

which is largely dependent upon discretionary powers conferred by the legislation and by regulations.[39] The questions whether such a payment, other than maternity, funeral and cold weather payments, is to be awarded and how much it is to be are determined by a Social Fund officer,[40] who may determine also that an award is to be repayable. Such an award may be recovered:

(a) from the person to or for the benefit of whom it was made;
(b) where that person is a member of a married or unmarried couple, from the other member of the couple;
(c) from a person who is liable to maintain the claimant.[41]

The concepts of married and unmarried couple are to be construed in the same way as in relation to income-related benefits.[42] Additionally where the concept of "partner" is used it means "one of a married or unmarried couple or a member of a polygamous relationship".[43]

The amount payable from the Social Fund is subject to the amount allowed to each local office in any given year. There is no right of appeal from the determination of a Social Fund officer to an independent tribunal but merely a limited right of review[44] by a Social Fund officer with the right to a further review by a Social Fund inspector.

The following payments have particular relevance for cohabiting partners.

Maternity payment

Maternity payment is a non-discretionary payment[45] to meet maternity expenses[46] referred to as a maternity payment. A single payment in respect of each child is made[47] where:

(a) the claimant or the claimant's partner[48] has in respect of the date of the claim for a maternity payment been awarded either income support, family credit or disability working allowance;

---

39 Thereby reverting to the practice prior to the Social Security Act 1980.
40 Social Security Contributions and Benefits Act 1992, s.139. Directions and guidance on how Social Fund officers should exercise their powers are contained in the *Social Fund Manual*. Maternity, funeral and cold weather payments are governed by regulations (see below) and the Social Fund Cold Weather Payments (General) Regulations 1988 (S.I. 1988 No. 1724). Decisions are made made by adjudication officers and there is the usual right of appeal.
41 Social Security Administration Act 1992, s.78(3). For the benefits from which an award may be recovered, see the Social Fund (Recovery by Deductions from Benefits) Regulations 1988 (S.I. 1988 No. 35).
42 *Ibid.* s.33(12): see above, p. 81.
43 See, *e.g.* Social Fund Maternity and Funeral Expenses Regulations 1987 (S.I. 1987 No. 481), reg. 3.
44 Social Security Administration Act 1992, s.66. See further Social Fund (Application for Review Regulations) 1988 (S.I. 1988 No. 34).
45 Which replaced the former maternity grant and single payments for maternity items from April 1987.
46 Social Security Contributions and Benefits Act 1992, s.138(1).
47 See S.I. 1987 No. 481, reg. 5 (as amended).
48 See above, p. 82.

(b) either: (1) the claimant or, if the claimant is a member of a family, one of the family is pregnant, or has given birth to a child, or still-born child; or (2) either or both of them have adopted a child not more than 12 months old at the date of the claim;

(c) the claim is made within the specified period.[49]

"Family" is defined[50] in this context as meaning:

"(a) a married or unmarried couple and any children who are members of the same household and for whom one of the couple is or both are responsible;

(b) a person who is not a member of a married or unmarried couple and any children who are members of the same household and for whom that person is responsible;

(c) persons who are members of the same household and between whom there is a polygamous relationship and any children who are also members of the same household and for whom a member of the polygamous relationship is responsible."

Any capital of the claimant or the claimant's partner in excess of £500, or £1000 if either of them is aged over 60, is deducted from the payment.[51]

Funeral payment

For the purposes of this non-discretionary payment, married and unmarried couples are also treated alike. A single payment is made where[52]:

(1) the claimant or the claimant's partner[53] has, in respect of the date of the claim for a funeral payment, been awarded an income-related benefit[54]; and

(2) the claimant or, if he is a member of a family,[55] one of his family takes responsibility for the costs of a funeral (the responsible member) which takes place in the United Kingdom; and

(3) the claim is made within the specified period.

Payment is subject to certain deductions in respect of moneys available to the responsible member or any other member of his family.[56]

---

49 Where the claimant or the claimant's partner is affected by a trade dispute, there is an additional time limit: see reg. 6 (as amended).
50 See S.I. 1987 No. 481, reg. 3 (as amended).
51 *Ibid.* reg. 9 (as amended).
52 See S.I. 1987 No. 481, reg. 7 (as amended).
53 See above, p. 82.
54 See above, p. 86.
55 Which has the same meaning as in the context of maternity payment: see above.
56 S.I. 1987 No. 481, reg. 8. See also reg. 9, above, n.51, for the effect of any capital.

The remaining payments are from the discretionary part of the Social Fund.

Budgeting loans

These interest-free loans are to help with important intermittent expenses that may be difficult to budget for. Eligibility depends upon the applicant satisfying the following conditions at the date of the application[57]:

(1) he or his partner has been in receipt of income-support for a continuous period of 26 weeks;
(2) neither of them is disqualified under the trades disputes disqualification or would be so disqualified if they were otherwise entitled to claim unemployment benefit.

Where the capital of the applicant and his partner exceeds £500, a budgeting loan shall be awarded only to the extent that the loan exceeds the amount by which their capital exceeds £500.

Crisis loans

These interest-free loans are payable[58] in an emergency or as a consequence of a disaster provided, *inter alia*, that the provision of such assistance is the only means by which serious damage or serious risk to health or safety of the applicant or a member of his family may be prevented. They are not limited to applicants in receipt of income support or any other benefit.

Community care grants

These are grants and not loans which may be payable[59] to help an eligible person or a member of his family to stay in the community rather than enter institutional or residential care, or to move out of such care into the community, or to ease exceptional pressures on the claimant and his family, or in certain circumstances to assist him, or a member of his family, with travel expenses. Capital resources of the applicant and his partner are again taken into account if they exceed £500, as they are with a budgeting loan.

Contributory benefits

In the context of contributory (or non-means tested) benefits, cohabitees are treated as single persons and entitlement is based on the claimant's own national insurance contributions and not those of a partner. A more detailed consideration may be found in Bonner, Hooker and White, *Non-Means Tested Benefits: The Legislation* (1993).

---

57 Social Fund Directions 8-92.
58 See *ibid*. Directions 14-23.
59 See *ibid*. Directions 25-29.

Widow's benefits

Marriage is a prerequisite for widow's benefits[60]; moreover, a widow who was cohabiting with another man at the time of her husband's death is not entitled to the widow's payment,[61] and any entitlement to widowed mother's allowance or a widow's pension is suspended during cohabitation.[62] So cohabitation is not taken into account when assessing entitlement to this benefit, yet may be taken into account to deprive a cohabiting widow of benefit to which she would otherwise have been entitled. The test of cohabitation is the same as that applicable to income-related benefits.[63]

Retirement pension

Entitlement to a retirement pension depends upon the type of pension, but in any event is based on either the claimant's contributions or those of a spouse or former spouse.[64] No such pension is available by virtue of a cohabitee's contributions. The use of a former spouse's contributions ceases on remarriage[65] but not on cohabitation.

Other benefits

Provision is made for a claimant for unemployment benefit, sickness benefit or maternity allowance to receive an increase for a spouse where certain conditions are satisfied.[66] The increase in favour of a spouse does not extend to a cohabitee.[67] If, however, a cohabitee qualifies as an adult dependant of the claimant and the cohabitee has the care of a child or children in respect of whom the claimant is entitled to child benefit, then an increase will be payable provided the claimant is not entitled to an increase in respect of some other person, for example a spouse. The test is one of dependency, however, and not cohabitation.

5. LEGAL AID AND ADVICE

The Legal Aid and Advice scheme[68] follows social security law in requiring that a man and a woman who are living together with each other in the same household as husband and wife are to be treated in the same way as spouses for the purpose of assessment of resources and so their income and capital are aggregated, unless one has a contrary

---

60 See below, p. 229.
61 Social Security Contributions and Benefits Act 1992, s.36(2).
62 *Ibid*. ss.37(4)(*b*) and 38(3)(*c*).
63 See *R(G) 3/81* and above, p. 81.
64 Social Security Contributions and Benefits Act 1992, ss.43-55.
65 Social Security Contributions and Benefits Act 1992, s.48.
66 See Social Security Contributions and Benefits Act 1992, s.82.
67 See *R(S) 6/89*.
68 The Civil Legal Aid (Assessment of Resources) Regulations 1989 (S.I. 1989 No.338), reg. 7; Legal Advice and Assistance Regulations 1989 (S.I. 1989 No.340), Sched. 2 paras. 2 and 7; Legal Aid in Criminal and Care Proceedings (General) Regulations 1989 (S.I. 1989 No. 344).

interest to the other in the matter.[69] The policy of the law is once again to equate heterosexual, but not homosexual, cohabitation and marriage so that a financial penalty arising from marriage is extended to the unmarried.

6. TAX

Cohabitees are treated like any other individual taxpayer[70] and hence are denied the tax planning opportunities available to married couples. The tax system's[71] differential treatment of married and unmarried couples was substantially altered[72] by the Finance Act 1988 in consequence of the changes to the taxation of married couples where the spouses are living together, with the aim of removing those tax rules which either favoured cohabitation or penalised marriage. Since that Act, spouses, like cohabitees, are taxed separately on all income, earned and unearned, and are entitled to separate personal allowances. Spouses, however, are entitled to an extra personal allowance, namely the "married couple's allowance", which is equivalent to the difference between the single person's allowance and the married man's allowance under the former system. The differential treatment was also reduced by changes which affected the taxation of cohabitees, for example, in relation to mortgage interest relief, covenanted payments and by limiting single parent relief to one child per cohabiting couple. For tax purposes it remains the case that it is generally more advantageous to be married than to cohabit, particularly if there are no children. Indeed the current trend is to remove the disincentives to marriage and the incentives to cohabitation, as a response to the difficult policy issues associated with the taxation of the family unit.

Income tax

It is worth emphasising, should such emphasis be necessary, that for the purposes of income tax legislation, and it is submitted for tax purposes generally:

> "the term 'wife' is used only to denote a woman who has entered into a marriage with a particular man, and that this term is not apt to cover a woman who has not entered into such a marriage but who

---

69 The Regulations provide other discretionary exceptions.
70 Except in relation to council tax: see below, p. 102.
71 There is not the scope in this book for a detailed analysis of revenue law and the following is a guide to the general principles of tax law by way of comparison between cohabitation and marriage.
72 From April 6, 1990.

is merely cohabiting with a man, however permanent or close the relationship may be".[73]

The same principle of interpretation must apply to terms such as husband and spouse. Similarly the concept of marriage does not include cohabitation or the so-called common law marriage.

Hence each cohabitee is treated as a single person for income tax purposes and the income of each, after deducting his or her personal allowance, is taxed at the applicable rate. Married couples are, since implementation of the relevant parts of the Finance Act 1988,[74] taxed likewise, save that the married couple's allowance is awarded to a man if he establishes that for the whole or part of the year of assessment he is a married man whose wife is living with him.[75] This allowance is not dependent upon the married couple having children and so the childless married couple receives preferential treatment to a childless unmarried couple, each member of which receives a single person's allowance. This tax concession to married couples ensured that they continued to receive the benefits which were available prior to the introduction of separate taxation but having made the concession the policy seems to be to allow it to diminish in real terms by not increasing the allowance. In effect it was a form of transitional relief designed to protect married couples from any loss of allowances under the reformed tax system.

This disadvantageous aspect of an unmarried couple's tax position is removed, however, if they have a qualifying child[76] who is living with the claimant for the whole or part of the year of assessment so that the claimant is eligible for the additional personal allowance.[77] This allowance, which is currently equal to the married couple's allowance, is available to a woman who is not throughout the year of assessment married to and living with her husband. A married woman who is permanently separated from her husband can claim the allowance if, during the part of the year in which she was separated from her husband, a qualifying child is resident with her.[78]

The allowance is available to a man, in the case of cohabitees, provided that either he is neither married to and living with his wife for the whole or part of the year of assessment nor entitled to claim married couple's allowance[79] because his wife is wholly maintained by voluntary maintenance payments.

Under the pre-Finance Act 1988 law this additional allowance could be particularly beneficial to cohabitees with more than one qualifying child

---

73 *Per* Ferris J. in *Rignell* v. *Andrews* [1991] 1 F.L.R. 332 at 335, decided in the context of the Income and Corporation Taxes Act 1970.
74 On April 6, 1990.
75 Income and Corporation Taxes Act 1988, s.257A (as substituted). From 1993/94 a married couple can elect to allocate the allowance to the wife, or the wife can claim half the allowance: see *ibid.* s.257BA(1),(2) (as substituted).
76 See below.
77 *Ibid.* s.259(1), (2).
78 *Ibid.* s.259(4).
79 *Ibid.* s.257 F.

where each cohabitee wholly or partly maintained at least one of the children, for each could claim an additional personal allowance in respect of one child and thus obtain greater relief than was available to a married couple.[80] This adverse taxation on marriage no longer[81] applies because section 259(4A) of the Income and Corporation Taxes Act 1988 provides that:

> "Where–
> (a) a man and a woman who are not married to each other live together as husband and wife for the whole or any part of the year of assessment, and
> (b) apart from this subsection each of them would on making a claim be entitled to a deduction under subsection (2) above,
> neither of them shall be entitled to such a deduction except in respect of the youngest of the children concerned (that is to say, the children in respect of whom either would otherwise be entitled to a deduction)."

So, an allowance can only be made for the youngest child in respect of whom either of them may claim.

The Inland Revenue practice[82] in such cases is that if both parties can claim for the youngest child, one of them can give up his or her claim or the allowance may be split between them.[83] If only one party can so claim, the other party receives no allowance, even if there are other qualifying children in respect of whom he could otherwise claim, and this is so throughout the cohabitation, including the year in which it commences and the year in which it ceases.

Section 259(4A), it should be noted, applies to "a man and a woman", so parties to a homosexual cohabitation do not fall within its terms and each party can claim the allowance if there is more than one qualifying child and each party wholly or partly maintains at least one of the children.

A qualifying child must have been born in, or be under the age of 16 at the start of, the year of assessment, or be over the age of 16 and receiving full-time education (or training for not less than two years)[84] and be either a child of the claimant or be under the age of 18 at the start of the year of assessment and maintained by the claimant for all or part of the year.

The reference to a child of the claimant includes a step-child, an adopted child and an illegitimate child, provided in the latter case that the claimant has married the other parent after the child's birth.[85] Hence,

---

80 See the second edition of this book, para. 4-34.
81 Since 1989-90.
82 See I.R. 92, *A guide for one parent families*.
83 See the Income and Corporation Taxes Act 1988, s.260, the basis of the split being a consideration in tax planning.
84 See *ibid*. s.259(5), (6).
85 See *ibid*. s.259(8).

notwithstanding the reforms in the Family Law Reform Act 1987,[86] an unmarried parent cannot claim on the basis of parenthood and can only claim on the basis that the child is being maintained by the claimant, in which case the child must be under the age of 18. A claim is thus not possible in such cases in respect of child over that age who is in full-time education or training.[87]

The Finance Act 1988 also substantially affected the tax advantages of covenanted payments by one cohabitee to another as a means of "income splitting" where one partner's income is below and the other's is above his personal allowance so as to transfer tax liability.[88] For tax purposes, such payments made on or after March 15, 1988 remain the income of the payer and do not form part of the income of the person to whom it is made or any other person.[89]

Payments by a cohabitee direct to his or her child made under a court order were, prior to the Finance Act 1988, regarded as the income of the child, who was not liable for tax thereon provided the child's income, including the payments, did not exceed his personal allowance.[90] The Finance Act 1988,[91] in line with its other reforms, provided that such payments do not form part of the recipient's income and must be paid from the payer's taxed income.

Some other personal reliefs are available only to married persons, for example, certain age reliefs,[92] the widower's or widow's housekeeper relief,[93] the widow's bereavement allowance, the dependent relative relief in respect of a relative of the claimant's spouse and blind person's relief claimed by the blind person's spouse.[94] Reference has already been made to the possibility that a cohabitee who is financially dependent upon his or her partner has an insurable interest in the other's life.[95] In so far as tax relief is available on life assurance premiums, however, it is available only in respect of premiums on the life of the policy-holder or policy-holder's spouse.[96]

---

86 See below, p. 105. The reforms are disapplied in this context: see Income and Corporation Taxes Act 1988, s.831(4).
87 It may be that the Inland Revenue will not insist on drawing this distinction: see *Butterworths Family Law Service*, para. D[1029] and Schuz, "Discrimination and anomalies in personal tax reliefs" [1990] 140 N.L.J. 766.
88 See the second edition of this book, paras. 4-34–4-35, including payments to a child who is not the child of the payer.
89 See Income and Corporation Taxes Act 1988, s.347A(1) (as inserted). Covenants, particulars of which were received by the Inland Revenue before June 30, 1988, remain subject to the old Rules.
90 See the second edition of this book, para. 4-35.
91 s.36, inserting Income and Corporation Taxes Act 1988, ss.51A and 51B with effect from March 15, 1988. For transitional provisions, see s.36(3)-(5).
92 See Income and Corporation Taxes Act 1988, s.257(2).
93 *Ibid.* s.258, except in so far as a widower's or widow's cohabitee qualifies as a housekeeper within the terms of the section.
94 *Ibid.* ss.262, 263 and 265 respectively.
95 See above, p. 79.
96 See further Income and Corporation Taxes Act 1988, s.266(2)(b).

Mortgage interest relief

The income tax advantage in being unmarried and cohabiting (that each partner could claim mortgage interest relief on interest payments on loans not exceeding £30,000 for the purchase of one's main residence) was limited by the Finance Act 1988[97] with regard to loans taken out on or after August 1, 1988. Such relief now applies up to a maximum of £30,000 per residence and not per individual. Each partner paying interest on a loan used to purchase the residence qualifies only for interest relief in respect of so much of the interest as arises from that partner's share of the loan. It is important that each cohabitee pays the interest due on his or her part of the loan. Where there is a joint mortgage then, for purposes of mortgage interest relief, the total amount borrowed is allocated equally between the borrowers.[98] If, for example, cohabitees have a joint mortgage but only one of them pays the interest, he or she would only get tax relief on half the loan and would not get relief on their partner's half, nor would the partner. In contrast, spouses living together may, by an allocation of interest election, allocate interest payments to either of them for income tax purposes irrespective of who pays the interest[99] and may vary the position from tax year to tax year to achieve the best financial planning. Cohabitees cannot so elect and from a planning point of view should arrange to finance the repayment of interest in such a way as to maximise the overall tax relief in relation to their respective incomes. For example, if A and B have a joint mortgage, but only A has sufficient income to fund his or her part of the loan, then if they wish to receive maximum tax relief A would need to provide B with the resources to fund B's part so that each pays his or her part of the loan. It seems that the Inland Revenue is more concerned with the form of the payment rather than in the substance of who is paying.[1]

If the loan was taken out by cohabitees before August 1, 1988, then each borrower remains entitled to mortgage interest relief on a loan up to £30,000, if on that date at least two sharers were entitled to claim mortgage interest relief on money borrowed, by either separate or joint loans, to purchase the same residence.[2] Each party continues to be entitled to relief up to £30,000 whilst he or she continues to pay interest on that loan and at least one other person continues to be entitled to mortgage interest relief on the same residence. A joint loan is apportioned according to the amount of interest being paid by each borrower at July 31, 1988. So, if there is a loan of £60,000 on which the interest is paid one-quarter by A and three-quarters by B, then A receives interest relief on £15,000 of the loan and B is limited to relief on a loan of £30,000. If at any time only one person entitled to relief occupies the house, for example, on breakdown of cohabitation, then the "per residence" relief

---

97 s.42, inserting Income and Corporation Taxes Act 1988, s.356A.
98 See *ibid.* s.356D(8).
99 See *ibid.* s.356B. This advantage is of less significance now that interest can only be set off against basic tax rate.
1 See *Butterworths Family Law Service* , para. D[1034].
2 See Income and Corporation Taxes Act 1988, s.356C(2).

applies. If cohabiting borrowers marry they will only be entitled to mortgage interest relief up to £30,000. They are required to inform the lender who has the reponsibility for administering the MIRAS[3] scheme that interest which had qualified for MIRAS relief has ceased to do so,[4] and the borrowers are liable to make good any excess relief.[5]

Another limited context in which cohabitees still have an advantage compared with spouses is where each pays interest on a loan for a separate residence used or to be used as his or her main residence. Each can claim separate mortgage interest relief on a loan up to £30,000, whereas in the case of spouses the residence first bought is treated as the only or main residence of both of them.[6]

Capital gains tax

Capital gains tax is levied on chargeable gains on the disposal of chargeable assets after deducting allowable losses and the annual exemption.[7] Cohabitees are treated as separate individuals; hence each can claim the annual exemption, and their chargeable gains and allowable losses are assessed separately so that losses of one cannot be deducted from gains of the other. As part of the tax reforms in the Finance Act 1988,[8] independent taxation of married couples applies also in the context of capital gains. Spouses, too, are entitled to their own annual exemption, each is assessable and chargeable on his or her own gains and the allowable losses of one spouse are not deductable from gains made by the other. Any excess of allowable losses over chargeable gains may only be carried forward and deducted from future gains of that spouse. However, some differences in taxation of capital gains remain.

Special rules apply to disposals between a married couple who are living together which may, depending upon the circumstances, confer an advantage on a married couple compared with an unmarried couple. The effect put simply is that such a disposal is deemed to be for a consideration such that neither a gain nor a loss accrues to the transferring spouse on the disposal.[9] The receiving spouse who transfers the asset to a third party might bear less capital gains tax than the transferring spouse because each spouse has an annual exemption and each spouse pays the tax at their marginal rate. So, for example, if the asset-owning spouse A has already used up his annual exemption whereas the other spouse B has not, then if A disposes of it directly to a third party, he will be taxed on the full disposal, whereas if A disposes of it to B, A makes no gain and no loss. If B then disposes of the asset to the third party, B can use his annual

3 Mortgage Interest Relief At Source.
4 See Income and Corporation Taxes Act 1988, s.375(1).
5 See *ibid*. s.375(3).
6 See *ibid*. s.356B(5), if the conditions of s.365B(5)(*a*)-(*c*) apply, otherwise it is a question of fact which is the main residence.
7 Taxation of Chargeable Gains Act 1992, ss.1-3.
8 Now consolidated in the Taxation of Chargeable Gains Act 1992.
9 *Ibid*. s.58.

exemption. Even if both have used their annual exemption, if A pays tax at a higher rate than B, then it still makes sound tax planning for A to dispose of it to B and for B to realise the gain on the subsequent disposal. There is also a link with income tax[10] if spouse A pays income tax at a higher rate than spouse B: A can transfer income-producing assets to B without incurring a capital gains tax liability on the transfer. Capital gains tax is, however, chargeable in the usual way on disposals between cohabitees.

There is generally no chargeable gain on the disposal of a dwelling-house or part thereof which is or has been that person's only or main residence.[11] In the case of a man living with his wife there can be only one principal private residence.[12] There is no such limitation in the case of cohabitees, who will thus be at an advantage if they each own a residence and come within the terms of the principal private residence exemption as each will receive relief on disposal. The difficulty facing parties who are cohabiting in one residence is in satisfying the exemption provisions in respect of any other residence. Where a person has two or more residences he or she may elect which shall be his main residence.[13]

Inheritance tax

Inheritance tax[14] is payable on transfers of value made *inter vivos* and on death. Most gifts during lifetime are exempt, however, provided that the donor survives for seven years.[15] A transfer of value is a disposition which reduces the value of the transferor's estate. Tax is levied at progressive rates on the transfer and is chargeable on transfers between cohabitees as if they were strangers. They do not receive the benefit of the exemption from tax in respect of transfers between spouses,[16] who are thus once again treated more favourably for tax planning purposes. The inter-spouse exemption can be particularly beneficial where a spouse's life expectancy is not great and so he cannot rely with confidence upon *inter vivos* transfers.[17]

Inheritance tax is unlikely to be a problem to many cohabiting couples, however, because the nil tax band is £150,000.[18] This figure includes, however, a transfer of a dwelling-house or an interest in a dwelling-house

---

10 It is important that the parties' liability to tax is seen as a whole.
11 See further Taxation of Chargeable Gains Act 1992, ss.222-224.
12 s.222(6).
13 s.222(5).
14 Formerly capital transfer tax. The Capital Transfer Act 1984 was renamed the Inheritance Tax Act 1984 by the Finance Act 1986, s.100.
15 See below, p. 102.
16 Inheritance Tax Act 1984, s.18, which applies whether or not the spouses are living together. The distinction is of less importance than in the case of capital transfer tax because an outright transfer *inter vivos* between individuals is a potentially exempt transfer. Transfers after a decree absolute of divorce or nullity are not exempt transfers.
17 See below.
18 For transfers on or after March 10, 1992.

and hence inheritance tax may well be payable on the death of a cohabitee who lives in an area of high property values. For this reason consideration should be given to taking out life assurance[19] and making maximum use of permissable *inter vivos* transfers.

There is an annual exemption of £3,000 in respect of *inter vivos* gifts and a small gift exemption of £250 per donee.[20] Any unused part of the annual exemption (but not small gifts exemption) can be carried forward for one year. Gifts made more than seven years before the donor's death are in most cases exempt from tax and gifts made within the seven-year period are subject to a tapered rate once the donor has survived three years.[21] Should a cohabiting couple decide to marry it is worth noting that certain gifts in consideration of marriage are exempt from tax.[22]

Although *inter vivos* transfers are advantageous as a means of avoiding inheritance tax, they may not be in terms of capital gains tax and hence the importance of considering the overall tax position and seeking specialist advice in terms of overall tax planning. For example, if a transferor who owns an asset which is showing a large capital gain tansfers it *inter vivos*, he will incur capital gains tax on the capital gain but might thereby avoid inheritance tax on the whole value of the asset. If, however, he retained the asset until his death the gain is wiped out on death and so retention of the asset avoids capital gains tax but preserves the possibility of inheritance tax. It is necessary to balance the two possible charges and decide where the balance of advantage lies after considering all the exemptions in the light of the parties' marital status.

Council tax

Council tax was introduced by the Local Government Act 1992 to replace the community charge.[23] The tax is set locally rather than centrally and is to pay for local services. It is a tax on each "dwelling"[24] whether the property is owned or rented, and is based on the initial assumption that two or more adults occupy the dwelling. The amount payable may be reduced if there is entitlement to a discount, reduction or council tax benefit.[25]

The adult person liable to pay council tax is generally the first of the following categories: a resident freeholder; a resident leaseholder; a resident statutory or secure tenant; a resident contractual licensee; a resident; or the owner if there is no resident. Liability within each category is joint and several.[26] In addition, and of particular relevance to

19 See p. 79.
20 Inheritance Tax Act 1984, ss.19 and 20 respectively.
21 *Ibid*. Sched. 1 (as substituted).
22 See further *ibid*. s.22.
23 With effect from April 1, 1993. The community charge, popularly known as the poll tax, was the short-lived successor to rates.
24 See Local Government Act 1992, s.3.
25 For council tax benefit, see above, p. 90.
26 See further Local Government Act 1992, s.6.

cohabitation, where two persons are married to each other and this includes "a man and a woman — who are not married to each other but are living together as husband and wife",[27] they are jointly and severally liable, where one of them is liable to pay the tax on a dwelling in which he is resident and the other person is also resident there, but would not otherwise be liable to pay.[28] The cohabitation must be between a heterosexual couple and the test of whether a man and a woman are living together as husband and wife is the same, it is submitted, as for income-related benefits including the council tax benefit.[29] On break-down of cohabitation it is important that a party who leaves the family home should notify the local authority.

So, in marked contrast to tax set centrally, cohabitees are not treated like any other individual tax payer for council tax purposes. In equating them with spouses, the law thereby removes the disincentive to marriage and again reflects the policy of equating cohabitation and marriage where to do so ensures that in fiscal matters the disadvantages of marriage, but not the advantages, attach to cohabitation.

---

27 *Ibid*. s.9(3)(*b*).
28 *Ibid*. s.9(1). The rule does not apply for any time when the other person is to be disregarded for the purposes of discount if he is severely mentally impaired: see s.9(2). See also s.18 on death of liable persons.
29 See above, p. 80.

CHAPTER 5

CHILDREN

1. STATUS

The legal relationship between parent and child is not based on parent-hood alone but on whether or not the child's parents are validly married to each other. At common law, a child was legitimate if his natural parents were married to each other at the time of either his conception or his birth. If the parents were not married to each other at either of those times the child was illegitimate. An illegitimate child was *filius nullius* and no-one had rights in respect of him. The law developed by recognis-ing the child's relationship with his mother[1] but not with the father, whereas the legitimate child's father was regarded as the child's natural guardian. The disadvantages attaching to illegitimacy were lessened, however, by piecemeal statutory reform.[2] In particular, the Family Law Reform Act 1987, s. 1 lays down the general principle[3] for that Act and Acts passed and instruments made after the coming into force of section 1,[4] namely that:

> "references (however expressed) to any relationship between two persons shall, unless the contrary intention appears, be construed without regard to whether or not the father and mother of either of them, or the father and mother of any person through whom the relationship is deduced, have or had been married to each other at any time."

The law has generally ceased to use adjectives such as illegitimate to describe a child. In so far as a distinction is drawn it is between parents depending upon their marital status. That distinction, however, affects

---

1 *Barnardo* v. *McHugh* [1891] A.C. 388.
2 See below, p. 107.
3 Following the Law Commission Second Report on Illegitimacy, Law Com. No. 157, Cmnd. 9913 and the Law Reform (Parent and Child) (Scotland) Act 1986 and to that extent departing from the Law Commission Report on Illegitimacy, Law Com. No. 118 (hereafter Law Com. No. 118) which suggested the use of the terms "marital" and "non-marital" child.
4 The Family Law Reform Act 1987, s.30, confers powers on the Lord Chancellor, to be exercised by statutory instrument, to apply the principle in s.1 to past Acts. Such order should so far as practicable ensure they have the same effect.

the legal relationship of parent and child. So as between parents who are not, and have never been, married to each other (for the sake of simplicity but at the cost of some accuracy[5] such parents will be referred to as unmarried parents) only the mother has parental responsibility. References to a "parent", for example, in the Children Act 1989, include the unmarried father as well as the unmarried mother, but the mother alone has parental responsibility for their child,[6] unless the father acquires such responsibility by agreement with the mother, by court order or by being appointed guardian. The Family Law Reform Act 1987 did not go so far as had once been suggested and apply to all children the law applicable to legitimate children.[7] The status of legitimacy has been preserved and in so far as a child does not have that status, the Act preserved the status of illegitimacy. Nevertheless, the principle of referring to a child's relationship with his parents and other relatives regardless of his parents' marital status is to be applauded and is followed throughout this book.

The current legal distinction is between a child whose mother and father were married to each other at the time of his birth[8] and a child whose mother and father were not so married at that date.[9] In the Family Law Reform Act 1987 and subsequent Acts, references to a person whose parents were so married include (and references to a person whose parents were not so married exclude) any person who is treated as legitimate[10]; who is a legitimated person[11]; who is an adopted child[12] or who is otherwise treated in law as legitimate.[13] Section 1(2) and (3) of the Family Law Reform Act 1987 "define references to a person's parents being or not being married at the time of his birth in such a way as to provide what are, in effect, definitions of a legitimate and illegitimate person".[14]

The Children Act 1989, as will be seen, introduced fundamental reforms of the law relating to all children but did not allow parental

---

5 The term unmarried parents would normally exclude a parent married to a third party and include divorced parents and parents whose voidable marriage has been annulled. For the doctrine of putative marriage, where the unmarried parents' marriage is void, see below, p. 107.

6 Children Act 1989, s.2(2): see below, p. 116.

7 See the Law Commission Working Paper No. 74, *Family Law: Illegitimacy*. The Scottish Law Commission so recommended more recently: see below, p. 158. For just such a reform in Jamaica, Barbados and Trinidad, see Poulter, *English Law and Ethnic Minority Customs* (1986), p. 93.

8 For this purpose the time of a person's birth is to be taken to include any time during the period beginning with (a) the insemination resulting in his birth, or (b) where there was no such insemination, his conception, and in either case ending with his birth: see further Family Law Reform Act 1987, s.1(4). The law was so amended because of developments in human assisted reproduction.

9 Family Law Reform Act 1987, s.1(2).

10 By virtue of the Legitimacy Act 1976, s.1: see below, p. 107.

11 Within the meaning of the Legitimacy Act 1976, s.10.

12 Within the meaning of Pt. IV of the Adoption Act 1976.

13 See Family Law Reform Act 1987, s.1(3).

14 Home Office Circular 24/1989, Annex A, para. 3.

responsibility automatically to run with parenthood.[15] The maternal preference in the allocation of parental responsibility may be of little significance during a stable cohabitation, but affects the father's legal position with his child in relation to the State, for example, school authorities, as well as with the mother[16] and may become of particular significance on breakdown of cohabitation or on the mother's death.[17]

The total number of children born of unmarried parents is significant. The birth rate of such children in 1991 was 236,000, being 30 per cent. of births in the United Kingdom.[18] Of this number many later acquire the status of legitimacy on the marriage of the parents.[19]

As the status of legitimacy has been preserved,[20] it is necessary to look at the statutory reform of the common law. Children of a voidable marriage were legitimate at common law unless the marriage was annulled, whereupon the decree of nullity retrospectively rendered them illegitimate. Various statutory reforms[21] modified this rule prior to the reform in 1971 whereby the decree operates prospectively so any child born or conceived during the marriage remains legitimate.[22] The common law rule that children of a void marriage were illegitimate was modified by the doctrine of the putative marriage[23] whereby such children are treated as the legitimate children of their parents, if, at the time of the child's conception,[24] or at the time of marriage if later, at least one of the parents reasonably believed that the marriage was valid.[25] A belief due to a mistake of law that the marriage was valid may nevertheless be a reasonable belief.[26] Moreover, it is to be presumed, unless the contrary is shown, that one of the parties reasonably believed, at the relevant time, that the marriage was valid.[27] Parties to a void marriage, unlike parties to a voidable marriage, never acquire the status of spouse. Hence there is a close similarity between their status and that of cohabiting parties. The doctrine of putative marriage, however, cannot avail cohabitees and

---

15 See below, p. 116. The Act introduced one significant reform in this regard by allowing the private ordering of parental responsibility: see below, p. 117.
16 See Bainham, "When is a Parent not a Parent? Reflections on the Unmarried Father and his child in English Law" (1989) 3 I.J.L.F. 208. For a comparative analysis, see Forder, "Constitutional Principle and the Establishment of the Legal Relationship between the Child and the Non-Marital Father: a Study of Germany, the Netherlands and England" (1993) 7 I.J.L.F. 40.
17 See below, p. 133.
18 (1992; H.C.), Vol. 208, No. 20, col. 465 (June 2, 1992). For an indication of the frequency of cohabitation resulting in the birth of children, see above, p. 6.
19 See below, p. 108.
20 For example, it is possible to seek a declaration of legitimacy: see Family Law Act 1986, s.56 (as substituted).
21 See Bromley and Lowe, *Bromley's Family Law* (8th ed., 1992), p. 282.
22 See now Matrimonial Causes Act 1973, s.16.
23 Introduced by the Legitimacy Act 1959: see now Legitimacy Act 1976, s.1.
24 *I.e.* the insemination resulting in the birth or, where there was no such insemination, the child's conception: see Legitimacy Act 1976, s.1 (as amended).
25 A reasonable belief is judged objectively: see *Hawkins* v. *A.-G.* [1966] 1 W.L.R. 978.
26 Legitimacy Act 1976, s.1(3) (as inserted).
27 Legitimacy Act 1976, s.1(4) (as inserted).

their children are never treated as legitimate. For the most part, however, that distinction is of little significance as the Family Law Reform Act 1987 removed most of the remaining disadvantages attaching to the child of unmarried parents.

The child of unmarried parents is legitimated, however, on his parents' marriage. At common law the decision whether or not to marry in order to confer legitimacy had to be taken before the child's birth. Here too statute has intervened so that a child acquires the status of legitimacy if his natural parents marry after his birth.[28] The child is legitimated from the date of the marriage. Legitimation was introduced by the Legitimacy Act 1926 and at first only applied if the child's parents were free to marry at the time of the child's birth. It was felt that to allow legitimation of a child born of adultery would encourage adulterous relationships. It was not until the Legitimacy Act 1959 that adulterine children could be legitimated by their parents' marriage.

As the legal relationship between parent and legitimated child is virtually identical to that of parent and legitimate child,[29] one of the advantages of cohabitees marrying is to legitimate their children. Where cohabiting parents do marry they should within three months after the marriage re-register the birth and they are under a duty to give the necessary information so that re-registration can take place.[30] Entry of the father's name in the register does not change the child's surname.[31] A child of unmarried parents is also legitimated if he is adopted. He is then treated as the legitimate child of the adopters.[32]

The Family Law Reform Act 1987 marked the high point in a process aimed at removing the legal discrimination against the child of unmarried parents. So, for example, in the context of sucession,[33] the common law rule that a gift in a will to "children" excluded illegitimate children (in the absence of some contrary intention) was reversed by the Family Law Reform Act 1969[34] which also conferred upon the illegitimate child the same succession rights on the intestacy of either parent as the legitimate child.[35] The illegitimate child, however, unlike the legitimate child, had no rights on the intestate death of other relatives, for example, grandparents or brother and sister, however close their links. Likewise such relatives had no inheritance rights on the illegitimate child's death. Other

---

28 See Legitimacy Act 1976, s.2.
29 Legitimacy Act 1976, s.8. See also British Nationality Act 1981, s.47; Legitimacy Act 1976, s.5(3). He is not entitled to succeed, however, to a title of honour: see Legitimacy Act 1976, Sched. 1, para. 4(2).
30 Legitimacy Act 1976, s.9; Births and Deaths Registration Act 1953, ss.14 and 36(d).
31 See below, p. 113.
32 Adoption Act 1976, ss.39 and 41. See also Legitimacy Act 1976, s.4.
33 For the current law see below, p. 156.
34 s.15, in the case of any will made after January 1, 1970.
35 s.14(1), in the case of intestacies after January 1, 1970. For the position before that date, see the second edition of this book, para. 5-06, n. 33.

reforms included the illegitimate child's right to claim against the estate of a deceased parent.[36] An obligation to maintain his illegitimate child could be enforced against the father in affiliation proceedings but their nature and scope, based as they were on the old Poor Law, were such as to operate to the illegitimate child's disadvantage in comparison to proceedings available in respect of the legitimate child under the guardianship of minors legislation.

The legal relationship between a child and his cohabiting but unmarried parents will now be analysed, paying particular regard to the remaining differences between that relationship and the legal relationship of a child and his married parents.

2. PRESUMPTION OF PARENTAGE

A child born to a married woman is presumed to be her husband's child. If the wife is separated from her husband and cohabiting with another man the presumption does not operate if they are separated by court order entitling them to live apart,[37] but continues to apply if they are separated by agreement.[38] At common law the presumption could be rebutted only by evidence beyond reasonable doubt, whereas statute[39] provides for rebuttal on a balance of probabilities. In S. v. S.[40] Lord Reid said "even weak evidence against legitimacy must prevail if there is no other evidence to counterbalance it". The matter has nevertheless been viewed as a grave one and it has been suggested that the standard of proof is more than the ordinary civil standard of balance of probabilities.[41] Such evidence can take the form of proof that the husband was incapable of having intercourse at the time, either because he was impotent or because he did not have access to his wife. It could also be shown by proving that, notwithstanding that the husband could have had intercourse, he is not the father, for example, if the husband was sterile or by evidence from blood tests or DNA profiling.[42] The presumption of legitimacy may also be rebutted by agreement where there is an admission of paternity by a third party.[43]

---

36 Family Law Reform Act 1969, s.18: see now the Inheritance (Provision for Family and Dependants) Act 1975, below, p. 211.
37 *I.e.* now a decree of judicial separation and previously also a Magistrates' Court order incorporating a non-cohabitation clause.
38 *Ettenfield* v. *Ettenfield* [1940] P. 96.
39 Family Law Reform Act 1969, s.26.
40 [1972] A.C. 24 at 41.
41 *Re J.S.* [1981] Fam. 22; *Serio* v. *Serio* (1983) 4 F.L.R. 756; *W.* v.*K.* [1988] 1 F.L.R. 86; *Re G.(No 2)(A Minor)(Child Abuse: Evidence)* [1988] 1 F.L.R. 314.
42 See below, p. 111.
43 See *R.* v *King's Lynn Justices, ex p. M.* [1988] 2 F.L.R. 79.

Whereas the mother's husband is presumed to be a parent there is no such presumption in favour of a cohabiting woman's partner. Cohabitation does not give rise to any presumption of parentage in English law, unlike some Commonwealth countries[44] where cohabitation is regarded as prima facie evidence of paternity. It remains necessary for paternity to be proved, in which context evidence of parental cohabitation will be particularly significant. Whilst a person may seek a declaration as to his own paternity,[45] he may not seek one as to anyone else's for which purpose the issue must be decided in the context of some other issue, for example, upbringing, maintenance or inheritance.[46]

Questions of paternity may arise where a child is born as the result of artificial insemination or as the result of the placement in a woman of an embryo or sperm and eggs. The law again distinguishes between married and unmarried couples. In the case of the former the Human Fertilisation and Embryology Act 1990[47] provides that where a child was born to a married woman as the result of her artificial insemination or the placement in her of an embryo or sperm and eggs, where the embryo was not created by the woman's husband, then, whether or not the treatment was in the course of a licensed treatment service, the presumption of legitimacy, rather than the Act, operates and the child is treated as the child of the husband.[48] If the presumption is rebutted, by showing that the husband is not the father, then the Act applies and the husband is treated as the child's father unless he can show that he did not consent to the treatment.[49]

In the case of an unmarried (heterosexual) couple, special provision[50] is made where the treatment is provided by a licensed provider. If the man is not the donor[51] he will nevertheless be treated as the father if:
(i) the service is provided for the woman and man together; and (ii) the woman is not married to a third party in relation to whom the common law presumption of legitimacy applies. Hence, where an unmarried couple use such a service, the child is regarded as having two parents and two sources of financial support. More generally, the man is treated in law as the child's father for all purposes[52] and no other person, such as the donor, is to be so treated.[53] If the treatment is not provided by a licensed provider, however, the woman's partner will not be treated as the father.

---

44 See Law Com. No. 118, para. 10.53, n. 120.
45 See below, p. 112.
46 See below, pp. 120, 142 and 156.
47 ss.27-29, extending and replacing the Family Law Reform Act 1987, s.27: see s.49(4); on the Family Law Reform Act 1987, s.27, see the second edition of this book, para. 5-04.
48 s.28(5).
49 s.28(2).
50 s.28(3).
51 If he is, he is the father at common law.
52 s.29(1).
53 s.28(4).

3. PROOF OF PARENTAGE

Modern medical techniques, in particular embryo or sperm and egg transfer, increase the possibility of disputes as to maternity, the resolution of which is based upon the principle that the carrying woman is to be treated as the legal mother.[54] Attention is here focused, however, on the situation where a cohabiting woman gives birth to a child and the issue is the child's paternity. In the event of a dispute it is up to the party alleging paternity to prove the allegation. In many cases of cohabitation both parties freely acknowledge the man's paternity and enter his name in the Register of Births[55]; such registration is prima facie evidence of paternity.[56] In the absence of such registration, where the parties have cohabited in a stable relationship, reliance may be placed on the fact of cohabitation and the man's maintenance, if any, of the child. Where a person has been found or adjudged to be the father in any relevant proceedings, that is prima facie evidence of paternity in any subsequent proceedings, so the burden will then lie on the party seeking to disprove paternity.[57] A finding of non-paternity has no formal effect outside the proceedings in which the issue is raised.

Of central importance in proving paternity is blood test evidence and DNA profiling. Although the Family Law Reform Act 1987[58] confers a discretion on the court, either of its own motion or on the application of any party to the proceedings, in any civil proceedings in which the parentage of any person falls to be determined, to give a direction for the use of scientific tests and the taking of bodily samples, the amendment has yet to be implemented. Until such time the courts lack the power to direct DNA profiling of samples other than blood; however, it is open to the parties to agree to such profiling.

A conventional blood test based on blood group investigation cannot directly establish paternity but the current tests are able to provide proof of non-paternity in 97 to 99 per cent. of cases[59] where the man is wrongly alleged to be the father. If the test does not exclude the alleged father, the particular blood group characteristics are determined and the frequency of these occurring is expressed as a percentage of the general population. If such men are not very frequent and the alleged father, not having been excluded, is one of them, the court is likely to decide that, on the balance of probabilities,[60] he is the father.[61] Similarly, if there is evidence that

---

54 Human Fertilisation and Embryology Act 1990, s.27(1).
55 See below, p. 113.
56 See below, p. 115.
57 Civil Evidence Act 1968, s.12 (as amended): see Law Com. No. 118, para. 10.41.
58 s.23, amending Family Law Reform Act 1969, s.20.
59 See Dodd and Lincoln, (1987) 84 L.S. Gaz. 2163. For procedure, see the Blood Tests (Evidence of Paternity) Regulations 1971 (S.I. 1971 No. 1861) (as amended); R.S.C., Ord. 112; C.C.R., Ord. 47, r. 5; Magistrates' Courts (Blood Tests) Rules 1971 (S.I. 1971 No. 1991); Family Law Reform Act 1969, s.20(2) (as substituted).
60 See above, p. 109.
61 See, e.g. T.(H.) v. T.(E.) [1971] 1 W.L.R. 429.

only two men had intercourse with the mother and the blood test evidence excludes one of them, then by elimination the other must be the father. The number of cases in which blood tests neither exclude a man from paternity nor provide evidence in support of paternity are small. The alternative technique of DNA profiling, which examines the deoxyribonucleic acid in chromosomes, allows for positive identification of biological relationships between individuals. This more accurate form of testing is available where it provides further evidence to an earlier finding in affiliation proceedings based upon an inconclusive blood test. The doctine of *res judicata* does not apply in affiliation proceedings and a further application under the replacement legislation to take advantage of DNA testing is not an abuse of the process of the court.[62]

The courts' power is one of discretion and not compulsion so anyone over 16 can refuse to be tested.[63] In the case of a child under 16, the consent of the person with care and control is required.[64] A refusal to be tested entitles the court to draw such inferences as appear proper,[65] for example, that person may not be able to rely on the presumption of parentage.[66] The legislation does not prescribe how the court is to exercise its discretionary power to direct the blood testing of a child. In *S.* v *S.*[67] the House of Lords decided that the issue was to be determined on principles of justice and availability of the best evidence, rather than the principle of the paramountcy of the child's welfare. The court should direct a blood test unless it is satisfied that to do so would be against the child's interests. It is generally best for the child if the truth as to his parentage is ascertained, but there may be circumstances where the court will refuse to order a blood test, for example, where the application is made by a father who has had no relationship with the child and the child has settled into a new family[68] or where the residential parent is unwilling for tests to be carried out.[69] A test should not be directed where paternity is not directly in issue.[70]

4. DECLARATION OF PARENTAGE

Until the Family Law Reform Act 1987 it was not possible for the court to grant a bare declaration of paternity but only to determine paternity if it would have a material bearing on some other issue.[71] The 1987 Act enables a person to apply to the court for a declaration that a person

---

62 See *Hager* v. *Osborne* [1992] 2 All E.R. 494 and below, p. 153.
63 Family Law Reform Act 1969, s.21(1), (2) (as amended).
64 *Ibid*. s.21(3). In the case of a ward of court, the court's consent is required.
65 *Ibid*. s.23 (as amended).
66 See s.23(2) and above, p. 109. See also *B*. v. *B. and E. (B. intervening)* [1969] 1 W.L.R. 1800.
67 See above, p. 109.
68 See *Re F.(A Minor: Paternity Test)* [1993] 1 F.L.R. 598.
69 *Re T.(A Minor: Blood Tests)* [1993] 1 F.L.R. 901.
70 *Hodgkiss* v. *Hodgkiss* [1985] Fam. 87.
71 See *Re J.S.* [1981] Fam. 22.

named in the application is or was his parent.[72] This is in addition to the pre-existing declaration as to legitimacy and legitimation.[73] A person may seek a declaration as to his own parentage but not, however, that of anyone else.[74] So a child[75] can seek a declaration that a man who is not married to his mother is his father, but such a man cannot seek a declaration that a child is his child. It was considered by the Law Commission[76] that a parent who has a valid claim relating to upbringing, financial provision or inheritance can have the question of paternity decided in the context of that issue, it being unnecessary and undesirable to go further and allow applications for a bare declaration in respect of other people's parentage. Any declaration granted is binding *in rem*[77] and achieves finality of litigation regarding the particular status to which it relates. Where a declaration is made, the court must notify the Registrar General[78] who shall, if it appears to him that the birth should be re-registered, authorise the re-registration.[79]

For the purposes of the Child Support Act 1991 special provision is made for the Secretary of State or the person with care of the child to apply to the court for a declaration as to whether or not the alleged parent is one of the child's parents.[80]

5. BIRTH REGISTRATION

The law requires the registration of all births in England and Wales by giving the required particulars to the Registrar of Births within 42 days. In the case of a child whose father and mother were not married to each other at the time of his birth,[81] the father is exempt from the duty to register,[82] which rests with the mother[83] but he may be treated as a qualified informant in certain circumstances.[84]

The choice of the child's forename(s) and surname to be registered for the child of unmarried parents is part of parental responsibility which vests in the mother unless the father has acquired it in accordance with

---

72 s.22, substituting an amended s.56 of the Family Law Act 1986.
73 *I.e.* that he has or has not become a legitimated person. The court has no power to make a declaration that a person is or was illegitimate: s.58(5)(*b*).
74 Thus a man in the position of Mr. J. in *Re J.S.* [1981] Fam. 22 would not be able to seek a declaration as to parentage of the child, for the Act does not provide for a declaration that a person named in the application is or was his child.
75 A child under the age of 18 would have to apply through his next friend.
76 Law Com. No. 118, para. 10.18.
77 s.58(2).
78 s.56(4) (as substituted).
79 See Births and Deaths Registration Act 1953, s.14A (as inserted).
80 Child Support Act 1991, s.27: see below, p. 149.
81 For the meaning of marriage at the time of birth, see above, p. 106.
82 See Births and Deaths Registration Act 1953, s.10(1) (as amended).
83 *Ibid.* ss.2, 10 and 36: registration may also be by a person present at the birth, an occupier of the premises in which the birth took place or a person having charge of the child: *ibid.* s.1.
84 *Ibid.* s.10(2): see below, n.91.

the Children Act 1989.[85] The birth registration regulations[86] prescribe that the surname to be entered shall be that by which at the date of registration it is intended the child shall be known. Where the parents are cohabiting, the mother may prefer to register her partner's surname, rather than her own, particularly if she holds herself out as his wife.

As to the part of the register giving particulars of the father, the birth can be registered or re-registered[87] to show his name in the following circumstances[88]:

(1) at his and the mother's joint request[89];
(2) at the mother's request, on production of a declaration in the prescribed form made by her stating that the man is the father, together with a statutory declaration by him acknowledging paternity;
(3) at the man's request,[90] on production of both a declaration in the prescribed form stating himself to be the child's father and a statutory declaration by the mother acknowledging that he is the father[91];
(4) at the mother's or father's[92] written request on production of:
   (a) a copy of a parental responsibility agreement[93] made between them in relation to the child, together with a declaration (in prescribed form) that the agreement complies with section 4 of the Children Act 1989 and has not been terminated by a court order; or
   (b) a certified copy of any of the following orders (each of which has involved the determination of paternity), together with a declaration (in prescribed form) that the order has not been brought to an end or discharged by a court order
      (i) under section 4 of the Children Act 1989 giving the father parental responsibility for the child[94];

---

85 See below, p. 116.
86 Registration of Births, Deaths and Marriages Regulations 1987 (S.I. 1987 No. 2088), reg. 9(3).
87 See Births and Deaths Registration Act 1953, ss.10 and 10A (as amended). Such registration does not confer parental responsibility: see below, p. 117. If, after registration of the birth, a declaration of parentage is made, the birth may be re-registered by the Registrar-General: see above, p. 113.
88 *Ibid.* ss.10(1) and 10A(1).
89 In the case of registration they both sign the register: see s.10(1)(*a*). Over half the births to unmarried parents are registered on their joint application: see above, p. 6.
90 The Family Law Reform Act 1987 allowed, for the first time, a man alone to request his name be registered.
91 In which case, for the purposes of registration, the man is treated as a qualified informant and by his giving of information concerning the birth and by signing the register any other qualified informant is discharged: see s.10(2). For re-registration there is no requirement that there be a qualified informant.
92 In which case, for the purposes of registration, the man is treated as a qualified informant: see s.10(2), above, n. 91.
93 See below, p. 117.
94 See below, p. 120.

(ii) under Schedule 1 to the Children Act 1989 for the father to make financial provision for the child[95];

(iii) under the pre-Children Act 1989 law[96] which under section 4 of the Family Law Reform Act 1987 gave the father all the parental rights and duties with respect to the child, or which gave him custody or care and control or legal custody under section 9 of the Guardianship of Minors Act 1971, or which required him under section 9 or 11B to make financial provision for the child, or which under section 4 of the Affiliation Proceedings Act 1957 named him as putative father of the child.

If an unmarried couple jointly register the father's name and it is later established that another man is the father (for example, in proceedings by him for parental responsibility) it is possible to use the procedure for correcting errors of fact or substance to alter the record of paternity, where a court order clearly establishes that the man whose name was originally registered is not the father.[97]

Registration of a man as the child's father does not affect the legal relationship between him and the child and does not confer parental responsibility upon the man, but will be prima facie evidence of paternity[98] and can be relied upon, for example, in proceedings for parental responsibility, financial provision or to claim succession rights. The registration shifts the burden of proof on to the party who disputes paternity. Hence birth registration is an important means of proving parentage.[99]

A birth certificate is a certified copy of the entry in the register of births, and is evidence of the birth to which it relates.[1] A "long form" of certificate discloses parentage but a "short form" of certificate makes no reference to the child's parents.[2] The intention of the short form is that it will not reveal that the father's name is not registered, or that the father is not married to the mother. The form merely gives the forename(s), surname, sex, date and place of birth of the child.[3] A short form is issued free on registration of the birth and is usually issued on application for a birth certificate unless the long form is requested.[4]

---

95 See below, p. 152.

96 *I.e.* an order made before October 14, 1991 or made after that date in proceedings pending before that date.

97 Births and Deaths Registration Act 1953, s.29(3) and Registration of Births and Deaths Regulations 1987 (S.I. 1987 No. 2088), reg. 58: see Law Com. No. 118, paras. 10.44 and 10.67.

98 Births and Deaths Registration Act 1953, s.34; *Brierley* v. *Brierley* [1918] P. 257; *Jackson* v. *Jackson* [1964] P. 25.

99 See above, p. 111.

1 Births and Deaths Registration Act 1953, s.34(6).

2 *Ibid.* s.33.

3 Registration of Births and Deaths Regulations 1987 (S.I. 1987 No. 2088), reg. 64 and Forms 21 and 22.

4 For which a fee is payable. The Government has proposed that charges should be made for all certificates issued: see *Registration, a modern service*, Cm. 531, para. 7.10.

6. PARENTAL RESPONSIBILITY

It is not within the scope of this book to undertake an analysis of the nature and extent of parental responsibility.[5] In the words of the Children Act 1989[6] it "means all the rights, duties, powers, responsibilities and authority which by law a parent of a child has in relation to the child and his property". It is sufficient to say that those persons with parental responsibility have considerable power of control over the child. This control diminishes as the child grows older so that parental rights are better seen as parental powers. For, as acknowledged in *Gillick* v. *West Norfolk and Wisbech Area Health Authority*,[7] the parental right to control a child derives from a parental duty and is a dwindling right which exists only in so far as it is required for the child's benefit and protection. This protective nature of the parental right is linked to the self-assertive nature of the child's right to make his own decisions when he reaches a sufficient understanding and intelligence to be capable of making up his own mind.

Notwithstanding the reforms introduced by the Children Act 1989, that Act did not affect the differential exercise of parental responsibility depending upon the parents' marital status. So, as between unmarried parents, the mother alone has parental responsibility and the father does not, unless he acquires it in accordance with the provisions of that Act,[8] whereas married parents each have parental responsibility for their child.[9] The male partner of a stable cohabitation prima facie has no powers over the children of the union, regardless of the length of the relationship. He may, however, have obligations towards the child, for example, he is liable to maintain the child[10] and if, as will be the case in many cohabitations, the child is living with both parents, the father will be under a duty to educate the child and ensure that the child is not neglected or ill-treated, for these responsibilities fall on anyone who has care of a child.[11] Similarly a person who does not have parental responsibility for a child but has care of the child may do what is reasonable in all the circumstances for the purpose of safeguarding or promoting the child's welfare.[12] Such responsibility is, however, of limited nature and subject to the provisions of the Act. What is reasonable "will depend upon the urgency and gravity of what is required and the extent to which it is practicable to consult a person with parental responsibility".[13] So

---

5 See further Cretney and Masson, *Principles of Family Law* (5th ed., 1990), pp. 486-493.
6 s.3(1).
7 [1986] A.C. 112.
8 Children Act 1989, s.2(2).
9 Children Act 1989, s.2(1).
10 See below, p. 142.
11 See Education Act 1944, ss. 36 and 114(1D)-(1F) (as inserted); Children and Young Persons Act 1933, s.1, respectively.
12 Children Act 1989, s.3(5).
13 See *The Children Act 1989 Guidance and Regulations,* Vol. 1, *Court Orders,* para. 2.11.

whilst, for example, the unmarried father would have the necessary authority to arrange medical treatment for an accident to the child, he would not be authorised to consent to major elective surgery.[14]

Consideration needs to be given, therefore, to the manner in which the unmarried cohabiting father can acquire parental responsibility and the consequences of his doing so for him, the mother and the child. He may do so by entering into a parental responsibility agreement with the mother, by obtaining a court order or, on the mother's death, by being appointed guardian. Unmarried parents cannot acquire joint parental responsibility by adoption.[15] If they marry they will of course thereafter have joint parental responsibility.[16]

Parental responsibility agreement

In practice many cohabiting parents agree informally to share parental responsibility. Such an agreement will not be legally effective to transfer parental responsibility,[17] however, unless made in accordance with the Children Act 1989. Notwithstanding the general principle that a person cannot surrender or transfer any part of that responsibility to another[18] there is an exception to this principle relating to an agreement made between a child's mother and father who were not married to each other at the time of the child's birth. Section 4(1)(b) of the Children Act 1989 provides that "the father and mother may by agreement ('a parental responsibility agreement') provide for the father to have parental responsibility for the child". The Children Act 1989 thereby changed the law to allow the private ordering of parental responsibility between unmarried parents by agreement.[19] Previous legislation insisted upon a court order before any unmarried father could acquire that responsibility which was automatically conferred upon all married fathers. A parental responsibility agreement is now available as an alternative to seeking a court order.

This private ordering is purely administrative and requires only that the agreement is in the prescribed form and duly recorded. The father is not required, as he is on application for a court order, to subject his parental suitability to judicial scrutiny to see if it accords with the paramountcy of the child's welfare. There is no check as to whether the

---

14 To use the examples provided by the Law Commission in Law Com. No. 172, para. 2.16.
15 See below, p. 138.
16 See above, p. 108.
17 Save in so far as there is power to delegate: see Children Act 1989, s.2(9)-(11), below, p. 118.
18 Children Act 1989, s.2(9).
19 Previously such agreements were limited to the exercise of parental rights and duties by separated (married or unmarried) parents, which could not be enforced if the court was of the opinion that it would not be for the child's benefit: see Guardianship Act 1973, s.1(2) (as amended), discussed in the second edition of this book, para. 5-19.

117

man is indeed the father.[20] The child too has no say in the creation of the agreement; the only person who does, other than the father, is of course the mother. The prescribed form[21] in which the agreement must be made is endorsed with a warning to both parents that the making of the agreement will seriously affect their legal position and advises them both to seek legal advice before completing the form. It is important that each understands the consequences of the agreement and that the mother is not pressured into making it.[22] In view of the potential conflict of interest it is advisable that each party seeks independent legal advice.

So far as the man is concerned, completion of the form will serve as evidence of paternity. He will by virtue of the agreement share parental responsibility with the mother in the same way as a married father. Each may act alone and without the other in meeting that responsibility, subject to any enactment which requires the consent of more than one person in a matter affecting the child,[23] for example, agreement to adoption,[24] consent to marriage,[25] and removal from the jurisdiction.[26] Any independent action must also be compatible with any order made with respect to the child under the Children Act 1989.[27] So far as the mother is concerned, her parental responsibility continues but is now shared with the father in the way just described and puts her in a similar position to a mother who is married to the father. Thus, for example, she ceases to have the exclusive right to give or withhold agreement to the child's adoption. Moreover, in the event of a dispute with the father, she is not free to revoke the agreement and would have to apply to the court.[28] Neither parent may surrender or transfer any part of his or her parental responsibility but may delegate some or all of it, subject to retaining primary responsibility.[29]

Once the prescribed form has been completed, it is not effective until it has been recorded by filing it, together with two copies, at the Principal Registry of the Family Division.[30] The copies are then sealed and one is

---

20 Whereas a court order may be dependent upon establishing paternity: see below, p. 123.
21 See Parental Responsibility Agreement Regulations 1991 (S.I. 1991 No. 1478), reg. 2 and Sched.
22 For a case where such pressure was alleged, see *Re W. (A Minor)(Residence Order)* [1992] 2 F.L.R. 332.
23 Children Act 1989, s.2(7).
24 See below, p. 139.
25 Marriage Act 1949, s.3(1A) (as inserted).
26 Child Abduction Act 1984, s.1(3) (as amended).
27 Children Act 1989, s.2(8); or any existing order in force at the Act's commencement on October 14, 1991 relating to custody, care and control, access or any matter with respect to a child's education or upbringing: see Sched. 14, paras. 5 and 6.
28 See below, p. 119.
29 s.2(9)-(11).
30 Somerset House, Strand, London WC2R 1LP: see Children Act 1989, s.4(2) and S.I. 1991 No. 1478, reg. 3.

sent to each of the parents. The record of an agreement is open to inspection by any person upon written request and payment of the prescribed fee.[31]

The termination of a parental responsibility agreement, unlike its creation, is not a private matter. It will end automatically when the child reaches the age of 18,[32] if the child is adopted[33] or if the parents marry each other, because the father then has parental responsibility by operation of law.[34] The father is to be relieved of his parental responsibility only by court order made on the application of any person who has parental responsibility for the child, hence including the father, or the child himself provided he has obtained leave of the court, which may only be given if the court is satisfied that the child has sufficient understanding to make the proposed application.[35] In determining the application to end the agreement, the court must apply the principle of the paramountcy of the child's welfare since the matter relates to the child's upbringing,[36] and the court must be satisfied that it is better for the child to end the agreement than not to do so.[37] If the agreement is terminated, then parental responsibility will again vest solely in the mother, which on breakdown of cohabitation may be a powerful reason for her to seek the termination of the agreement, for it is not dependent upon the parents' cohabitation at any time.

Notwithstanding the simplicity of the form and the recording procedures parents who are cohabiting in a stable relationship may not wish to go through the required formalities, although the early signs show a not insignificant number of agreements are being registered.[38] If the relationship breaks down then the mother is unlikely to agree to enter into an agreement and the father will then have to have recourse to the courts if he seeks parental responsibility. That option is available to him during the cohabitation, but the preferred option is likely to be an agreement, unless the mother opposes his wish to share her parental responsibility.

---

31 See S.I. 1991 No. 1478, reg. 3.
32 Children Act 1989, s.91(8).
33 Adoption Act 1976, s.12. This ending of the agreement is not included on the prescibed form.
34 As the child then falls within the definition of a child whose parents were married to each other at the time of his birth: see p. 106. This ending of the agreement is not included on the prescribed form.
35 Children Act 1989, s.4(3), (4).
36 Children Act 1989, s.1(1): see below, p. 125; the checklist in s. 1(3) (see below, p. 125) does not apply but the court ought to consider the child's wishes and feelings if it is to give effect to the paramountcy principle.
37 See Children Act 1989, s.1(5).
38 1510 in the first nine and a half months: see the Children Act Advisory Committee's *Annual Report (1991/92)*, p. 26. The figures do not show the number of agreements in which the parents gave the same address. For the figures to have real significance with regard to cohabitation it would be necessary to ascertain the number of parents cohabiting nationally.

Court order

The unmarried father has a number of options depending upon the family circumstances, only two of which, namely a parental responsibility order and a residence order, confer full parental responsibility. A residence order is the more extensive of the two, in that it determines with whom the child is to live as well as giving the father parental responsibility. In comparison a parental responsibility order does not resolve issues of residence and contact and is more abstract in nature than the practically orientated orders in section 8 of the Children Act 1989.[39] If the father seeks contact with his child but no other parental responsibility, the appropriate order is a contact order. In the highly unlikely event of the statutory jurisdiction failing to provide a suitable option, the father can apply under the inherent wardship jurisdiction.

Parental responsibility order

A parental responsibility order under section 4 of the Children Act 1989 replaced the order under section 4 of the Family Law Reform Act 1987 that gave the unmarried father all the parental rights and duties with respect to the child.[40] If the order is made he will have parental responsibility together with the mother in the same way as under a parental responsibility agreement[41] or, if the mother is dead, together with any guardian appointed under the Children Act 1989, s. 5.[42]

Any such order may be discharged by subsequent court order in the same way as a parental responsibility agreement can only be brought to an end by an order of the court, thereby depriving the father of his parental responsibility, whereas the married father automatically has parental responsibility which cannot be revoked except by adoption. Applications for discharge seem particularly likely on breakdown of cohabitation. The order will end automatically when the child reaches 18,[43] if he is adopted[44] or if the parents marry each other, because the father then has parental responsibility by operation of law.[45]

The Law Commission saw the utility of section 4 orders in three types of case[46]: where the parents are cohabiting and agree to the order being made, where the mother has died without appointing the father to act as guardian and where the parents have separated and the father seeks full parental responsibility. It was envisaged, however, that successful applications by fathers may well be rare.[47] This is more so since the Children

---

39 *I.e.* a residence order, a contact order, a prohibited steps order and a specific issue order: see below, p. 123.
40 Any such order in force on October 14, 1991 is deemed to be a s.4 order under the Children Act 1989: see Sched. 14, para. 4.
41 See above, p. 118.
42 See below, p. 133.
43 Children Act 1989, s.91(7).
44 Adoption Act 1976, s.12.
45 See above, p. 108.
46 Law Com. No. 118, para. 7.29.
47 *Ibid.* para. 7.27.

Act 1989 introduced the alternative of the parental responsibility agreement to meet the first case. There is the alternative of an application to be appointed guardian to meet the second case.[48] So an application seems most likely to meet the third case,[49] in which event the father will need to consider in addition whether to apply for a residence or contact order so that those issues can also be determined. Even if he does not additionally apply for a residence or contact order, the court has the discretion to make such an order in his favour when granting, or indeed refusing to grant, the section 4 application.[50] If he applies for a residence order only and the court grants the application, it must also make a section 4 parental responsibility order.[51] If he applies for a contact order only, however, and the court grants the application the court does not have the power to make a parental responsibility order under section 4. It likewise has no such power on making a prohibited steps order or specific issue order.

It is important to realise that a parental responsibility order does not confer enforceable rights relating to the child's upbringing but "will merely give the father a *locus standi* and place him in the same position as a parent of a legitimate child".[52] Although the extent of enforceability of such an order is a relevant consideration, it is not an overriding consideration:

> "Though existing circumstances may demand that [a natural father's] children see or hear nothing of him, and that he should have no influence upon the course of their lives for the time being, their welfare may require that if circumstances change he should be re-introduced as a presence, or at least as an influence, in their lives. In such a case [an order], notwithstanding that only a few or even none of the rights under it may currently be exercisable, may be of value to him and also of potential value to the children. Although there may be other factors which weigh against the making of [an order] in such circumstances, it could never be right to refuse such an order out of hand, on the automatic ground that it would be vitiated by the inability to enforce it."[53]

Thus in *Re H.(Minors)(Local Authority: Parental Rights)(No. 3)*[54] the Court of Appeal allowed the father's appeal against the judge's refusal to make an order under the Family Law Reform Act 1987, s. 4 and

---

48 See below, p. 135.
49 The reported cases on section 4 of the 1987 Act have come within this category: see below.
50 See Children Act 1989, s.10(1)(*b*).
51 See s.12(1), below, p. 124.
52 *Per* Balcombe L.J. in *Re H.(Minors)(Local Authority: Parental Rights)* [1989] 1 W.L.R. 551.
53 *Per* Mustill L.J. in *Re C.(Minors)(Parental Rights)* [1992] 2 All. E.R. 86 at 89, following *D.* v. *Hereford and Worcester County Council* [1991] Fam. 14; *Re H.(Minors)(Local Authority: Parental Rights)(No. 3)* [1991] Fam. 151.
54 [1991] Fam. 151.

immediately thereafter declared that his consent to an order freeing the child for adoption was unreasonably withheld.[55] In *Re H.(A Minor: Contact and Parental Responsibility)*,[56] decided under the Children Act 1989, the unmarried father who had developed a genuine and loving relationship with his son was denied a contact order because of the attitude taken by the boy's stepfather, but the judge's decision also to refuse him a parental responsibility order was held by the Court of Appeal to be plainly wrong.

Notwithstanding the abstract nature of parental responsibility, the concept relates to the upbringing of the child and as such the court, in determining whether or not to grant an order, must apply the principle of the paramountcy of the child's welfare[57] and it must be satisfied that making an order would be better for the child than making no order at all.[58] The checklist in section 1(3) does not apply[59] but the court and practitioners ought to have regard to the factors therein,[60] so far as they are relevant. In the context of the earlier section 4 orders, where the court applied the same principle of paramountcy of the child's welfare, it became accepted that the court had to ask itself the following question:

> "was the association between the parties sufficiently enduring, and has the father by his conduct during and since the application shown sufficient commitment to the children, to justify giving the father a legal status equivalent to that which he would have enjoyed if the parties had been married, due attention being paid to the fact that a number of his parental rights would, if conferred on him by a P.R.O., be unenforceable under current conditions?"[61]

Thus the court will pay particular regard to the duration and stability of the parents' cohabitation. Even if that relationship was not particularly enduring, it may be that the father's parental commitment to the child has been of sufficient value to the child for it to be in the child's interests that an order should be made. The court will also take into account the degree of attachment between the father and the child and his reasons for applying for the order[62] and, if the child is in care, the reasons for the care

---

55 The father would then be able to take advantage of the provisions in the Adoption Act 1976, ss.19 and 20, relating to progress reports and possible revocation of the freeing order.

56 [1993] 1 F.C.R. 85.

57 Children Act 1989, s.1(1).

58 s.1(5); this presumption of no order did not apply to proceedings under the Family Law Reform Act 1987. If the court decides to make no order, an order should nevertheless be drawn determining the application: see *S. v. R.(Parental Responsibility)* [1993] 1 F.C.R. 331.

59 s.1(4).

60 See below, p. 125.

61 *Per* Mustill L.J. in *Re C.(Minors)(Parental Rights)* [1992] 2 All E.R. 86 at 93.

62 See *Re H.(Minors)(Local Authority: Parental Rights)(No. 3)* [1991] Fam. 151; *S. v. R.(Parental Responsibility)* [1993] 1 F.C.R. 331; *Re C.B.(A Minor)(Parental Responsibility Order)* [1993] 1 F.C.R. 440; *Re T. (A Minor)(Parental Responsibility and Contact)* [1993] 1 F.C.R. 973.

order and the local authority's plans for the child.[63] The mother's attitude will also be a relevant but not a determining factor. Cases where she supports the father's application are likely to be rare in view of the alternative parental responsibility agreement. Where the application is contested, an order may nevertheless be in the child's interests. In *Re C.(Minors)(Parental Rights)*[64] the mother, who was not represented, wrote to the court describing her conviction that the children's interests required them to be cut off from their father altogether; nevertheless, the link which the father had established with the children was considered, by the court, to be worth maintaining. It has been suggested, however, that an application may be rejected where there is such implacable hostility from the mother to the intervention of the father into her life that no benefit would endure to the child.[65]

An order can be made in respect of any child under the age of 18[66] and is not subject to the restrictions in the case of an application for a residence order or any other section 8 order regarding a child who has reached the age of 16 unless the circumstances are exceptional.[67]

Application must be by the father.[68] Where paternity is in issue, it must be determined before the person claiming to be the father can apply.[69] Application can be to the High Court, County Court or the Magistrates' Family Proceedings Court. The father must file the application in respect of each child in Form CHA 1.[70] The procedural rules, which are generally the same for all courts, are governed by the Family Proceedings Rules 1991, Pt. IV, in the higher courts and by the Family Proceedings Courts (Children Act 1989) Rules 1991 in the Magistrates' Family Proceedings Court.

Residence order

If the unmarried father has acquired parental responsibility, then, subject to any court order to the contrary, he and the mother, like married parents, have the power to determine where and with whom the child shall live. If that issue is in dispute, however, it would need to be decided by an application for a residence order under section 8 of the Children Act 1989, *i.e.* "an order settling the arrangements to be made as to the person with whom a child is to live". Similarly an unmarried father without parental responsibility who wishes to have his child living with him, contrary to the mother's wishes, would need to seek a residence order, because the unmarried mother alone has the power to determine

---

63 See *D.* v. *Hereford and Worcester County Council* [1991] Fam. 14.
64 [1992] 2 All E.R. 86.
65 *Per* Ward J. in *D.* v. *Hereford and Worcester County Council* [1991] Fam. 14.
66 Children Act 1989, s.105(1).
67 Children Act 1989, s.9(6), (7): see below, p. 125.
68 Children Act 1989, s.4(1)(*a*).
69 Applying the principle under the Guardianship of Minors Act 1971: see *Re O.* [1985] F.L.R. 716; *Re W.(A Minor)(Interim Custody)* [1990] 2 F.L.R. 86.
70 Family Proceedings Rules 1991, r.4.4(1)(*a*) and Appendix 1; Family Proceedings Courts (Children Act 1989) Rules 1991, r.4(1)(*a*) and Sched. 1.

where the child shall live.[71] In the latter case the court must also make a section 4 parental responsibility order.[72] Any such parental responsibility order must not be terminated while the residence order concerned remains in force.[73] If, however, the residence order is discharged, the father will continue to have parental responsibility until the section 4 order is terminated in response to an application to that end.

The residence order is the successor to, but not the equivalent of, the former order for legal custody under section 9 of the Guardianship of Minors Act 1971. The residence order is practically orientated to the issue of with whom the child is to live. It does not affect other issues of parental responsibility, which continue unaffected. So if the unmarried father is granted a residence order, he will share other aspects of parental responsibility with the mother although each may act alone in meeting that responsibility.[74] He will, by virtue of the residence order, have a greater influence over the child's upbringing, as "parental responsibility largely 'runs with the child'".[75] Whereas under the former law a joint custody, care and control order was stongly discouraged on the ground that it deprived the child of a settled home,[76] the Children Act 1989 allows a residence order to be made in favour of two or more persons who do not themselves all live together. Where such an order is made it may, but need not, specify the periods during which the child is to live in the different households concerned.[77] It is possible for an order to be made in favour of parents who are cohabiting but where as a result of the order the child lives, or is to live, with one of two parents who each have parental responsibility for him, the order ceases to have effect if the parents live together for a continuous period of more than six months.[78]

As the unmarried father is a parent for the purposes of the Children Act 1989, whether or not he has parental responsibility,[79] he is qualified to apply for a residence order.[80] Additionally, the court has the discretion in any family proceedings[81] in which a question arises with respect to the welfare of any child to make a residence order.[82] A court must not

---

71 See, *e.g. F.* v. *S.(Wardship Jurisdiction)* [1991] 2 F.L.R. 349 at 355.
72 Children Act 1989, s.12(1).
73 Children Act 1989, s.12(4).
74 See above, p. 118.
75 Law Com. No. 172, para. 4.8.
76 *Riley* v. *Riley* [1986] 2 F.L.R. 429.
77 Children Act 1989, s.8(4).
78 Children Act 1989, s.11(5).
79 Children Act 1989, s.2(3).
80 Children Act 1989, s.10(4)(*a*) (unless the child has been freed for adoption: see *M.* v. *C. and Calderdale Metropolitan Borough Council* [1993] 1 F.C.R. 431). The application must be in Form CHA 10 for each child. If paternity is in issue, it must be determined before the man claiming to be the father can be said to be a parent: see above, p. 123, n.69. If he is found not to be the father, he is not entitled to apply unless he has lived with the child for at least three years, or has the consent of each of those persons with parental responsibility; if he is not entitled to apply he must obtain leave of the court: see Children Act 1989, s.10(1), (5).
81 As defined in Children Act 1989, s.8(3), (4).
82 Children Act 1989, s.10(1)(*b*).

make a residence order which is to have effect for a period which will end after the child has reached the age of 16 unless it is satisfied that the circumstances of the case are exceptional.[83] Similarly, no order can be made once the child has reached that age unless there are exceptional circumstances.[84]

The question of with whom the child is to live is one clearly relating to the child's upbringing and hence the child's welfare shall be the court's paramount consideration.[85] In making the child's welfare the paramount consideration, the Children Act 1989 made no change in substance from the "first and paramount" principle in the earlier legislation.[86] There is now, however, a presumption against the making of an order and an emphasis upon non-intervention. The Children Act 1989, s.1(5), prohibits a court from making any order under the Act with respect to a child unless it considers that doing so would be better for the child than making no order at all. The onus is upon the applicant for a residence order to satisfy the court that the child's welfare will actually be promoted by the making of an order. In the unusual event of the mother not opposing the father's application, his task is made easier because of the presumption that parents know best. Hence the checklist in the Children Act 1989, s.1(3), applies only where the application for a residence order is opposed.[87] The court must still satisfy itself, however, with regard to the paramountcy principle and the presumption of no order and "have regard to the general principle that any delay in determining the question is likely to prejudice the welfare of the child".[88]

If the making of a residence order is opposed, then the court is required to

"have regard in particular to–
(a) the ascertainable wishes and feelings of the child concerned (considered in the light of his age and understanding);
(b) his physical, emotional and educational needs;
(c) the likely effect on him of any change in his circumstances;
(d) his age, sex, background and any characteristics of his which the court considers relevant;
(e) any harm which he has suffered or is at risk of suffering;
(f) how capable each of his parents, and any other person in relation to whom the court considers the question to be relevant, is of meeting his needs;
(g) the range of powers available to the court under this Act in the proceedings in question".[89]

This so-called checklist is not exhaustive and the court is not thereby

---

83 Children Act 1989, s.9(6).
84 s.9(7).
85 Children Act 1989, s.1(1).
86 *I.e.* Guardianship of Minors Act 1971, s.1.
87 Children Act 1989, s.1(4).
88 Children Act 1989, s.1(2).
89 Children Act 1989, s.1(3).

precluded from considering any other factors which it considers to be relevant to the particular case. The marital status of the child's parents is not listed, nor should it be, for the relevant issue is the quality of the relationship between parent and child, not the parents' marital status. Where the parents have cohabited, the nature of parental cohabitation may provide evidence of how capable each parent is of meeting the child's needs.

Under the former law, if the unmarried father was seeking custody[90] he was at a disadvantage in comparison to the married father in seeking to acquire rather than retain legal responsibility. It is submitted that the change of emphasis in the Children Act 1989 from possessory rights to practical powers is in line with the move away from concern about parental status in favour of concern about parental qualities which the courts had already adopted.[91] The question is thus, in the light of the welfare principles in section 1 of the Children Act 1989, what is in this particular child's best interests? That question is to be resolved in the same way for the child of unmarried parents as for the child of married parents.[92]

If the dispute as to with whom the child shall live is between a parent and a non-parent, then in a series of cases[93] prior to implementation of the Children Act 1989 the blood tie was given particular significance in light of the following dicta from Lord Templeman in *Re K.D.(A Minor) (Ward: Termination of Access)*[94]: "The best person to bring up a child is the natural parent. It matters not whether the parent is wise or foolish, rich or poor, educated or illiterate, provided the child's moral and physical health are not in danger." Thus in *Re O.(A Minor)(Custody: Adoption)*[95] the parents, who were not married to each other but had cohabited briefly, separated on bad terms before the birth of their child. The mother wanted the child to be adopted and the father sought custody. The Court of Appeal held that the father should be preferred over unknown adopters unless he is shown to be unfit to care for his child. That had not been shown and the father was granted custody. Moreover, it was said to matter not whether the father was a putative father who had not applied for parental responsibility, or a father who had parental responsibility, or, indeed, a father who was married to the mother. This latter lack of distinction is in accordance with the welfare principle, but the suggestion that strong evidence against parental care is required before it can be displaced does not sufficiently acknowledge that the issue must be determined by the welfare principle. It is submitted that whilst that principle will usually indicate the need for parental care, the blood

---

90 Or what became legal custody under s. 9 of the Guardianship of Minors Act 1971.
91 See, *e.g. B.* v. *T.(Custody)* [1989] 2 F.L.R. 31.
92 In view of which it is not proposed to analyse the general body of case law which, for the most part, was decided before the Children Act 1989 and was usually only illustrative of criteria now replaced by s.1(3).
93 See, *e.g. Re K.(A Minor)(Custody)* [1990] 2 F.L.R. 64; *Re K.(A Minor)(Wardship: Adoption)* [1991] 1 F.L.R. 57.
94 [1988] A.C. 806 at 812 in a short concurring opinion which should be compared with the main opinion of Lord Oliver.
95 [1992] 1 F.L.R. 77.

tie is relevant only in so far as it relates to the application of that principle.[96]

Contact order

In practice, contact between parent and child is frequently the most contentious aspect of parental responsibility on the breakdown of the parents' relationship, whether or not that relationship is within marriage. If parental contact is in issue, it will need to be resolved by application to the court for a contact order under section 8 of the Children Act 1989, *i.e.* "an order requiring the person with whom a child lives, or is to live, to allow the child to visit or stay with the person named in the order, or for that person and the child otherwise to have contact with each other". Such an order is the successor to the access order and is a more direct equivalent than a residence order is to a custody order. The change of terminology was to avoid doubts which had arisen as to the scope of the meaning of access, so as to put beyond doubt that it extends to contact other than to visit or stay with the person named, for example, it includes letters, telephone calls, cards and presents.

A contact order, unlike a residence order, does not confer parental responsibilty.[97] If an unmarried father seeks parental responsibility in addition to contact then, in the absence of the mother's willingness to enter into a parental responsibility agreement, he would have to seek a parental responsibility order.[98] Such an order does not itself carry enforceable rights such as contact.[99]

The proximity of the concepts of contact and access, and the early case law under the Children Act 1989, indicate that the courts will adopt the same principles in relation to section 8 contact applications as they did in relation to applications for access. The starting point is the child's right to know his birth parents, but there may be cases where there are cogent reasons for denying that right.[99a] In *Re H.(A Minor)(Contact: Parental Responsibility)*[1] the Court of Appeal refused to interfere with the trial judge's finding that the presumption in favour of granting a contact order to an unmarried father who had developed a genuine and loving relationship with his son was displaced because of the hostile attitude taken by the boy's step-father.

Under the law prior to the Children Act 1989, the courts tended to the view that it is in a child's interests to maintain contact with both his

---

96 See *Re H.(A Minor)(Custody: Interim Care and Control)* [1991] 2 F.L.R. 109, approved by the Court of Appeal after the Children Act 1989 in *Re W.(Residence Order)*, *The Times*, April 16, 1993.

97 But a person with care of a child by virtue of a contact order may do what is reasonable in all the circumstances for the purpose of safeguarding or promoting the child's welfare: see Children Act 1989, s.3(5).

98 See above, p. 120.

99 See above, p. 121.

99a *Re D.(A Minor)(Contact)* [1993] 1 F.C.R. 964; *Re T.(A Minor)(Parental Responsibility and Contact)* [1993] 1 F.C.R. 973.

1 [1993] 1 F.C.R. 85.

parents irrespective of their marital status.[2] The longer and more stable the relationship between father and child the greater the father's chances of persuading the court that the maintenance of the link is in the child's best interests. In this context access between parent and child has been regarded as being of particular importance.[3] The maintenance of links through access was seen as desirable not only as a means of encouraging contact between parent and child, but also because a child needs to know his origins. Where a child has a close relationship with, and developed an attachment to, both parents there was a presumption that it will be in the child's interests to continue that contact[4] in the absence of compelling evidence to the contrary. It was held also[5] that the same principles applied in deciding whether existing contact should be terminated or should be reintroduced where it had been broken. The presumption that contact is in a child's best interests will be rebutted if the particular facts suggest otherwise and the courts so found on a number of occasions where the father was not married to the mother,[6] for example, where the mother had found a new partner and contact was seen as likely to destabilise the new family unit.[7]

Refusal of contact was most likely where the father's behaviour or condition was adverse, for example, his cruelty to or abuse of the child,[8] or his strong and dominating attitude towards the mother such as to cause stress and thereby adversely affect the child.[9] Occasionally the hostility on the part of the mother towards the father may be such that to allow contact would have adverse effects on the child.[10] However the fact that the custodial parent's attitude had caused distress to the child did not of itself mean that an access order (which was made in the child's interests) was against those interests.[11] Even committal of the residential parent was exceptionally considered to be in the child's interests.[12]

---

2 See, e.g. Re H. (1965) 109 S.J. 574; Re C. (1981) 2 F.L.R. 163; S. v. O. (1982) 3 F.L.R. 15 and contrast Re G. [1956] 1 W.L.R. 911. This approach was confirmed by the Family Law Reform Act 1987, s.2(1)(c), which put beyond doubt that s.1 of the Guardianship of Minors Act 1971 applied irrespective of the marital status of the child's parents.

3 M. v. M. [1973] 2 All E.R. 81; S. v. O. (1982) 3 F.L.R. 15.

4 M. v. J. (1982) 3 F.L.R. 19.

5 Re H.(Minors)(Access) [1992] 1 F.L.R. 148.

6 See, e.g. Re C.(Minor)(Access) [1991] Fam. Law 417.

7 See, e.g. Re W.(A Minor)(Access) [1989] 1 F.L.R. 163; Re S.M. (A Minor)(Natural Father: Access) [1991] 2 F.L.R. 333, in both of which the parents' relationship ended before the birth of the child and see the post-Children Act 1989 case of Re H.(A Minor)(Contact and Parental Responsibility) [1993] 1 F.C.R. 85, above, p. 127.

8 See, e.g. Re R.(A Minor)(Child Abuse: Access) [1988] 1 F.L.R. 206 where on the facts even limited supervised access was not regarded as beneficial to the child. For cases where supervised access was granted, see C. v. C. (Child Abuse: Access) [1988] 1 F.L.R. 462; H. v. H. [1989] 1 F.L.R. 212.

9 See, e.g. B. v. A. (1982) 3 F.L.R. 27.

10 See, e.g. Re B. [1984] F.L.R. 648; Re B.C. [1985] F.L.R. 639; Re N.(A Minor)(Access: Penal Notice) [1992] 1 F.L.R. 134.

11 Re E. [1987] 1 F.L.R. 368 and see the post-Children Act 1989 case Re D.(A Minor)(Contact) [1993] 1 F.C.R. 964.

12 C. v. C. (Access Order: Enforcement) [1990] 1 F.L.R. 462.

When the court is deciding whether or not to make an order for contact then, as with access, the child's interests are paramount.[13] It is submitted that the House of Lords' decision in *Re K.D.(A Minor)(Ward: Termination of Access)*[14] remains good law and that any "right" which a natural parent has to access and the assumption that a child would benefit from continued contact will always be displaced if the interests of the child dictate otherwise. The paramountcy principle requires that in each case the court must consider what is in the particular child's best interests. The unique nature of those interests means that cases have to be decided on their particular facts. There is now also a presumption against the making of an order[15] so the applicant has the onus of satisfying the court that the child's welfare will be promoted by the making of a contact order.

As the unmarried father is a parent for the purposes of the Children Act 1989 whether or not he has parental responsibility[16] he is qualified to apply for a contact order.[17] Additionally the court has the discretion in any family proceedings[18] in which a question arises with respect to the welfare of any child to make a contact order.[19] A court must not make a contact order which is to have effect for a period which will end after the child has reached the age of 16 unless it is satisfied that the circumstances of the case are exceptional and no order can be made once the child has reached that age unless there are exceptional circumstances.[20] Where the contact order requires one parent to allow the child to have contact with the other parent, the order will cease to have effect if the parents live together for a continuous period of six months.[21]

Wardship
The unmarried father was given the right to apply for custody or access by the Legitimacy Act 1959. His remedy before that date, which remains as an option, was to apply to have the child made a ward of court.[22] In most cases, however, wardship is not to be recommended as its effect is to vest parental responsibility in the court which will decide issues such as with whom the child is to have contact. The ward remains subject to the supervision of the court, although day to day supervision is delegated to the party with care and control. No important step can be taken in the ward's life without the court's consent. Moreover, proceedings have to

---

13 Children Act 1989, s.1(1).
14 [1988] A.C. 806.
15 Children Act 1989, s.1(5): see above, p. 125.
16 s.2(3).
17 s.10(4)(a). The application must be in Form CHA 10 for each child. If paternity is in issue, it must be determined before the man claiming to be the father can be said to be a parent: see p. 123, n.69.
18 As defined in s.8(3), (4).
19 s.10(1)(b).
20 s.9(6), (7).
21 s.11(6).
22 For procedure, see Family Proceedings Rules 1991, Pt. V.

be brought in the High Court[23] which adds to their cost. The proceedings may be of use, however, in cases of emergency. Additionally, as the court's consent is required before any important decision can be taken in the ward's life,[24] the jurisdiction may be of use where there is a dispute over some specific step in the child's life rather than the general exercise of parental responsibility. The need to rely on wardship in this context has been considerably reduced, however, since the introduction of the specific issue order and prohibited steps order which are intended to resolve most of the problems which prior to their enactment gave rise to wardship.[25] Recourse will still have to be had to wardship, however, in those cases where the issue in question is not an aspect of parental responsibility.

Specific issue order and prohibited steps order

A specific issue order "means an order giving directions for the purpose of determining a specific question which has arisen, or which may arise, in connection with any aspect of parental responsibility for a child".[26] Any parent is entitled to apply to the court for such an order[27] which could, for example, relate to the child's schooling or medical treatment. The order is not intended as a substitute for a residence or contact order and hence the court must not exercise its powers to make a specific issue order to achieve a result which could be achieved by making a residence or contact order,[28] but could supplement either such order. As with any question relating to a child's upbringing it will be determined in accordance with the welfare principles in section 1 of the Children Act 1989.

A prohibited steps order "means an order that no step which could be taken by a parent in meeting his responsibility for a child, and which is of a kind specified in the order, shall be taken by any person without the consent of the court".[29] Entitlement to apply extends to the same categories of persons who can apply for a specific issue order and hence includes any parent.[30] Like a specific issue order, it must not be made to achieve a result which could be achieved by making a residence or contact order,[31] but could be made in conjunction with either such order. It is related to imposing a specific restriction, for example, that a parent should not remove the child from the United Kingdom where there is no residence order in force and so the automatic restriction in section 13 of

---

23 But may be transferred to the County Court: see Matrimonial and Family Proceedings Act 1984, ss.32 and 38; *Practice Direction* [1992] 2 F.L.R. 87.
24 *Re S.* [1967] 1 W.L.R. 396.
25 See Law Com. No. 172, paras. 4.18 and 4.20.
26 Children Act 1989, s.8(1), replacing the provision in the Guardianship Act 1973, s.1(3).
27 s.10(1)(*a*), (4). The application must be in Form CHA 10 for each child.
28 s.9(5)(*a*) and see Law Com. No. 172, para. 4.19.
29 Children Act 1989, s.8(1).
30 s.10(1)(*a*), (4).
31 s.9(5)(*a*).

the Children Act 1989 does not apply.[32] Any application will also be determined in accordance with the welfare principles in section 1 of the Children Act 1989.

The prohibition can relate to any person and so is not limited to a person with parental responsibility. An order could therefore be made against an unmarried father who does not have parental responsibility, in relation to any step which he could take if he did have such responsibility.

Choice and change of child's surname

One aspect of parental responsibility which in practice is often of particular significance is the determination of the child's surname. It has already been seen that the initial choice of surname is vested in the unmarried mother unless the father has also acquired parental responsibility in accordance with the Children Act 1989.[33] If both parents have parental responsibility each may act alone and without the other in meeting that responsibility[34] and this would extend to choice of the child's surname. A parent who wishes to prevent such potential independent action would need to apply for a specific issue order and/or a prohibited steps order, depending upon the circumstances. The right of independent action is, of course, subject to any such order which is already in existence on the matter.[35]

As to any subsequent change of the child's surname, this is one part of parental responsibility vested in the mother in the absence of parental responsibility having been acquired by the father. In the latter case the right of independent action applies and either parent may cause the child to be known by a new surname. Where there is a residence order in force, however, no-one may cause the child to be known by a new surname without either the written consent of every person who has parental responsibility for the child or the leave of the court.[36] In the absence of a residence order, if a dispute regarding change of the child's name cannot be resolved by agreement, application would need to be made for a specific issue order and/or a prohibited steps order, depending upon the circumstances. The court will determine any such application in accordance with the welfare principles in section 1 of the Children Act 1989.[37]

---

32 Law Com. No. 172, para. 4.20.
33 See above, p. 116.
34 Children Act 1989, s.2(7).
35 s.2(8).
36 Children Act 1989, s.13(1)(a). Moreover, if it is regarded as being in the child's interests to maintain his links with his natural father in those cases where they have formed a relationship with each other, the marital status of the child's parents should not matter with regard to any change of surname. Hence prior to the Children Act 1989 it was the reported practice of the Central Office of the Supreme Court to require the consent of the unmarried father to any proposed change of name notwithstanding his lack of parental rights: see Law Com. No. 118, para. 9.25. On change of the child's surname after divorce, see below, p. 204.
37 See above, p. 125.

The older the child is, the more relevant will be his wishes and feelings in the light of his age and understanding.[38]

Consent to marriage

Specific provision is made with regard to parental consent to the marriage of a child aged 16 or 17,[39] so that the consent of the following are required:

   (i) each parent who has parental responsibility and each guardian of the child;

  (ii) where a residence order is in force,[40] the person/s with whom the child lives or is to live, as a result of the order, instead of those in (i);

 (iii) where a care order is in force,[41] the local authority in addition to those in (i);

 (iv) where neither (ii) or (iii) applies, but a residence order was in force immediately before the child reached the age of 16, the person/s with whom he lived or was to live, as a result of the order instead of those in (i).

Parental responsibility in favour of a non-parent

If there are children of a cohabitation of whom only one of the partners is the parent, the non-parent will neither have parental responsibility nor be able to enter into a parental responsibility agreement with the mother, as such agreements can only be made between the mother and father.[42] As a non-parent, he or she will not be eligible to apply for a parental responsibility order which can only be sought by the father.[43] It is open to a parent with parental responsibility to delegate some or all of it but he or she retains primary responsibility.[44] A non-parent without parental responsibility but who has care of the child may do what is reasonable in all the circumstances for the purpose of safeguarding or promoting the child's welfare.[45]

---

38 See below, p. 205.
39 Marriage Act 1949, s.3(1A) (as inserted).
40 Such cases will be exceptional: see Children Act 1989, s.9(6), above, p. 125. For the usual case of an order which has been discharged when the child attains the age of 16, see (iv).
41 A residence order and a care order are mutually exclusive: see Children Act 1989, s.91(1), (2).
42 Children Act 1989, s.4(1)(*b*): see above, p. 117.
43 See s.4(1)(*a*).
44 s.2(9): see above, p. 117.
45 s.3(5).

The only option regarding the acquisition of parental responsibility available to a non-parent, save where the parents with parental responsibility are dead,[46] is to seek a residence order, which if granted will confer parental responsibility during the continuance of the order.[47] Parental responsibility will then be shared with those who had it prior to the residence order.[48] If the child has been the subject of a residence order in divorce proceedings, the order could be varied in favour of the parent and his cohabitee. The fact that the parent and cohabitee had obtained a joint residence order would not terminate the parental responsibility of the non-residential parent. A non-parent cohabitee is qualified to apply for a residence order[49] in the following circumstances[50]:

- if the child has lived with him for a period of at least three years;
- if a residence order is in force and the applicant has the consent of each of the persons in whose favour the order was made;
- if the child is in the care of the local authority and the applicant has the authority's consent; or
- in any other case, if he has the consent of each of those who have parental responsibility for the child. So, for example, if an unmarried mother wishes her cohabiting partner of less than three years and who is not the child's father to have a residence order, he is qualified to apply if she consents to his application.

If a non-parent is not entitled to apply, he must seek the leave of the court to make the application.[51] Any application for a residence order will be determined in accordance with the welfare principles in section 1 of the Children Act 1989.[52]

A non-parent can apply for the child to be made a ward of court and seek care and control or contact, but such proceedings are expensive and impractical and do not confer parental responsibility.[53]

Parental responsibility on death

Where unmarried parents are cohabiting, and the child's father has not acquired parental responsibility in accordance with the Children Act 1989, he does not acquire parental responsibility in the event of the mother's death unless she has appointed him to be the child's guardian.[54]

---

46 See below.
47 Children Act 1989, s.12(2), replacing, in this context, the custodianship order.
48 s.2(6); but such an order is not appropriate solely to give a non-parent parental responsibility; see *N. v. B.(Children: Orders as to Residence)* [1993] 1 F.C.R. 231.
49 And also a contact order, but such an order does not confer parental responsibility.
50 Children Act 1989, s.10(5)(*b*), (*c*). A non-parent spouse would additionally qualify under s.10(5)(*a*) if the child is a child of the family.
51 s.10(2)(*b*).
52 See above, p. 125.
53 See above, p. 129.
54 See below, p. 135.

Where, however, the father has acquired parental responsibility during the mother's lifetime, then the surviving parent will continue to exercise that responsibility to the exclusion of any guardian appointed by the deceased parent.[55] The guardian's appointment is postponed while the surviving parent has parental responsibility,[56] unless a residence order in the deceased parent's favour was in force with respect to the child immediately before his or her death[57] and that order was not also in favour of the surviving parent.[58] If such an order was in force in favour of the deceased parent, the appointment of a guardian is effective immediately,[59] and parental responsibility will be shared by the surviving parent and the guardian.[60] If there is disagreement as to the exercise of parental responsibility which cannot be resolved, either the surviving parent or the guardian is entitled to apply for a relevant section 8 order under the Children Act 1989.[61] If the dispute goes to the issue of the appointment of the guardian, then either of them can additionally apply for the guardianship to be terminated.[62] The guardian cannot, however, apply for termination of the parent's parental responsibility save where the parent is the unmarried father, in which case the guardian is qualified to apply for an order that a parental responsibility order or a parental responsibility agreement be brought to an end[63] and for a residence order to be discharged.[64] Any application to the court will be determined in accordance with the welfare principles in section 1 of the Children Act 1989, as the issues relate to the upbringing of the child.

The postponement rule[65] acknowledges that where the first of parents with parental responsibility dies, it will usually be in the child's best interests for the survivor to have sole responsibility, rather than for it to be shared with the guardian who will not normally live with the child.[66] If the prospective guardian is concerned on any matter regarding the child's upbringing by the surviving parent which he cannot resolve with the

---

55 A parent who has parental responsibility for his child may appoint another individual to be the child's guardian in the event of his death: see Children Act 1989, s.5(3). A guardian may also be appointed by a guardian (s.5(4)); or by the court on the application of any individual if the child has no parent with parental responsibility, or a residence order had been made in favour of the deceased parent or guardian: s.5(1). For revocation and disclaimer, see s.6.

56 Children Act 1989, s.5(8). This postponement is a change in the law as a result of the Children Act 1989: for the previous position, see the second edition of this book, para. 5-27.

57 Children Act 1989, s.5(7)(*b*).

58 When the postponement rule continues to apply: see s.5(9).

59 s.5(3), (7).

60 ss.2(6), 5(6).

61 s.10(4)(*a*).

62 s.6(7).

63 s.4(3).

64 ss.8(2), 10(4)(*a*).

65 s.5(8).

66 If the parents are not cohabiting, the residential parent ought to seek a residence order if he or she wishes their appointment of a guardian to have immediate effect in the event of his or her death.

surviving parent, he would need to seek leave of the court to apply for a relevant order under section 8 of the Children Act 1989.[67]

Where the unmarried mother has sole parental responsibility, it is open to her to appoint her partner (whether or not he is the father) to be guardian of her children in the event of her death.[68] The appointment must be in accordance with section 5 of the Children Act 1989[69] and either be by will or made in writing, dated and signed by the appointer or signed at his direction in the presence of two witnesses.[70] No particular form of words need be used[71] but there must be a clear intention to appoint the guardian.

If it is her wish that the father, who has not acquired parental responsibility during her lifetime, should be guardian, she should appoint him as such so as to prevent the need for him to seek a parental responsibility order under section 4, or a residence order under section 8. Alternatively, as there is no parent with parental responsibility the father could apply to the court to be appointed guardian.[72] It has been argued[73] that there are objections in principle and practice to his reliance on the alternative of guardianship; in principle because of the emphasis in the Children Act 1989 upon parenthood rather than guardianship, and in practice because such guardianship may be terminated not only on the application of those persons eligible to apply for termination of a section 4 order, but also by the court of its own motion in any family proceedings.[74]

No matter how close the links between unmarried father and child, the father has no power to appoint a guardian unless he has parental responsibility for his child immediately before his death.[75] This would be the case where he has obtained a parental responsibility order or a residence order[76] which is in force at the time of his death, or if at that date there was a parental responsibility agreement in effect between him and the child's mother,[77] or if he had been appointed guardian.[78] The method of appointment must be in accordance with the Children Act 1989.[79] There is nothing in the Act to exclude the appointment of more than one individual to be guardian. As the appointment takes effect on

---

67 He will not be entitled to apply under the Children Act 1989, s.10(4)(a), as guardian as the appointment as such has been postponed.
68 Children Act 1989, s.5(3).
69 s.5(5), (13).
70 If the appointment is by a will which is not signed by the testator, it must be signed at his direction in accordance with the Wills Act 1837, s.9.
71 For a suggested form, see p. 256.
72 As could anyone else: see Children Act 1989, s.5(1)(a).
73 By Bevan in *Butterworths Family Law Service*, Div. E, para. [222].
74 Children Act 1989, s.6(7).
75 Children Act 1989, s.5(3). Any appointment is subject to the postponement rule: see above, p. 134.
76 Which requires the court also to make a parental responsibility order in his favour: see above, p. 124.
77 See above, p. 117.
78 s.5(4).
79 See s.5(5).

death, it is at that time that the father would have to have parental responsibility, even if he did not have parental responsibility at the time of making the will.

7. CHILD CARE LAW

The Children Act 1989 introduced a number of fundamental reforms in child care law, including the principle that the term "parent" in line with section 1 of the Family Law Reform Act 1987[80] is to be construed without regard to whether or not the child's father and mother were married to each other at any time. Hence, wherever the term parent appears in the Children Act 1989, it includes the unmarried father. The only issue may be as to proof of paternity.[81]

It is only where there is a reference to a parent with parental responsibility or person with parental responsibility that he will be excluded, unless he has acquired it in accordance with the provisions of the Act.[82] For example, where a local authority has provided a child in need with accommodation, any person who has parental responsibility for a child may remove him from such accommodation.[83] The unmarried father may do so only if he has acquired parental responsibility. In contrast, if his child is being looked after by a local authority, whether by being provided with accommodation or because he is in their care,[84] the father is entitled to be consulted by the authority before they make any decision with respect to the child. Similarly where a child is in the care of a local authority, *i.e.* by virtue of a care order,[85] there is a presumption of the child being allowed reasonable contact by the local authority with his unmarried father whether or not he has parental responsibility, as he is a parent.[86] He is not a party to an application for a care or supervision order, however, unless he is believed by the applicant to have parental responsibility for the child[87] but is entitled to written notice of the proceedings[88] and could then seek to be joined as a party. These examples are not exhaustive but rather illustrate the need to look carefully at the wording of the legislation and the rules of court in each context.

---

80 See above, p. 105. For the pre-Act position, see the second edition of this book, paras. 5-45 to 5-47.
81 See above, p. 111.
82 See s.2(2), above, p. 116.
83 s.20(8), subject to the restrictions in s.20(9)-(11).
84 s.22(1).
85 s.105(1).
86 s.34(1)(*a*). If he is dissatisfied with the extent of his contact, he has the right, as a person in whose favour the presumption operates, to apply to the court for contact: see s.34(3).
87 See Family Proceedings Rules 1991, r.4.7 and Appendix 3; Family Proceedings Court (Children Act 1989) Rules 1991, r.7 and Sched. 2.
88 *Ibid.* rr.4.4(3) and 4.3.

The effect of a care order is to place the local authority under a duty to receive the child into their care and to keep him in their care while the the order remains in force and to give the local authority parental responsibility for the child.[89] A care order is the only method by which a local authority can acquire parental responsibility, as parental rights resolutions were abolished by the Children Act 1989 and a local authority may not apply for a residence order.[90]

In line with the principle of concurrent responsibility in the Children Act 1989, any parent with parental responsibility or guardian[91] still retains parental responsibility. In the case of unmarried parents this would be the mother to the exclusion of the father unless he had acquired parental responsibility. The scope of the parent's or parents' continuing responsibility is, however, limited. Although parental responsibility may be exercised independently of the local authority[92] it must not be exercised in a way incompatible with the care order,[93] for example, by removing the child without the authority's permission. As it may not always be apparent whether or not the parental act is incompatible with the care order, the parental exercise of responsibility is further circumscribed by section 33 which gives the local authority power to determine the extent to which a parent may meet his parental responsibility, provided that they are satisfied that it is necessary to do so in order to safeguard or promote the child's welfare.[94]

As a parent with parental responsibility retains that responsibility during a care order, he or she is qualified to apply for the discharge of the care order.[95] Any such application will be determined in accordance with the welfare principles in section 1 of the Children Act 1989, whereas on an application for a care order there are the additional criteria in section 31(2) of the Act. If the father does not have parental responsibility he cannot apply for the discharge of the care order but can apply for a residence order[96] notwithstanding that the child is in care[97] which, if granted, would have the effect of discharging the care order.[98]

The Children Act 1989 reforms of child care law have greatly simplified the position of the unmarried father whilst also stengthening his position so that in relation to many issues he has *locus standi* by virtue of parenthood without having to make out a case to be heard, as was so frequently the case under the former law.

---

89 Children Act 1989, s.33(1), (3).
90 s.9(2).
91 But not any third party who has parental responsibility by virtue of a s.8 order, as such orders are terminated on the making of a care order: see s.91(2).
92 s.2(7).
93 s.2(8).
94 s.33(4).
95 s.39(1)(*a*). For a similar provision in relation to the discharge of a supervision order, see s.39(2).
96 See above, p. 123.
97 s.9(1).
98 s.91(1).

8. ADOPTION

Adoption may concern cohabitees, either as adopters, or as parents whose child is being adopted. A joint adoption application can only be made by a married couple,[99] so cohabitees cannot jointly adopt their own child, the child of one of them, or any other child. In *Re F.*[1] where an adoption order was granted to joint adopters whose marriage was void, the court decided that the adoption was voidable and not void.[2]

An adoption application can be made by one person, provided he is over 21 and not married, or is married but his spouse cannot be found, is incapable of making an adoption application because of ill health, whether physical or mental, or they are living apart and the separation is likely to be permanent.[3] A cohabitee who satisfies these requirements is thus theoretically qualified to apply as a sole adopter, but an adoption agency will need convincing of the benefit to the child of such a placement. In non-agency cases the local authority investigating the proposed adoption will need so convincing. Moreover, a court will be reluctant to make such an order, particularly if the sole applicant is a parent. An adoption order cannot be made in favour of one natural parent unless the other natural parent is dead or cannot be found,[4] or there is some other reason justifying the exclusion of the other natural parent.[5] It is submitted that this restriction applies to the unmarried parent as well as the married parent.[6] It is most likely to affect the former for it is rare for a married parent alone to adopt his or her child. The term "natural parent" suggests a relationship based on parenthood and hence includes the unmarried parent notwithstanding that the unmarried mother is a "parent" for adoption law purposes to the exclusion of the father unless he has parental responsibility.[7] The restriction does not apply if the other parent is dead. The mother is unlikely to apply if the father is dead as she will already have parental responsibility but the provision could help the father without parental responsibility on the mother's death if he wishes to establish a legal relationship with the child, as an alternative to applying either for a parental responsibility order or to be appointed guardian.[8]

---

99 Adoption Act 1976, s.14(1) (as amended).
1 [1977] Fam. 165.
2 Thereby highlighting a further distinction between a cohabiting couple and a couple who are living together after a void marriage: see above, p. 8.
3 Adoption Act 1976, s.15(1) (as amended).
4 Or by virtue of the Human Fertilisation and Embryology Act 1990, s.28, there is no other parent.
5 Adoption Act 1976, s.15(3) (as amended).
6 The Family Law Reform Act 1987 has not put this beyond doubt, as s.1 is prospective and s.2 does not list the Adoption Act 1976.
7 See below, p. 139.
8 See above, pp. 120 and 135.

The adoption of a child of cohabiting parents is most likely to arise either on breakdown of the cohabitation where the mother proposes to marry another man and she and her husband seek to adopt the child or during the cohabitation where the child is placed for adoption. A child cannot be adopted unless the court is satisfied that each parent or guardian of the child agrees to the adoption, or that his agreement can be dispensed with on one of the statutory grounds.[9] The unmarried father is a "parent" for adoption law purposes only if he has parental responsibility,[10] otherwise only the mother's agreement is required. Where the mother is dead and she appointed him guardian or he has been appointed by the court[11] he will be both a parent with parental responsibility[12] and a guardian.

Where the unmarried father does not have parental responsibility he can frustrate an adoption application by applying for a parental responsibility order, a residence order[13] or, less advisably, by applying to make the child a ward of court.[14] If he does so apply his application and the adoption application should be heard together[15] and decided on the basis of the welfare principles in the Children Act 1989, s.1.[16] If the father has sought a residence order and is successful that will resolve both applications. If he has sought instead a parental responsibility order alone, he is then in the position of the married father and it is open to the court to dispense with his agreement.

Where the father has enjoyed a stable relationship with the mother and the child, the ties between him and the child are likely to be as strong as those between married father and child. In past years the courts have not attached much weight to the wishes of the unmarried father on the basis that the advantages of adoption and the removal of the status of illegitimacy outweigh the disadvantages associated with the severance of links with the natural father. More recently the courts have reflected the change in attitude towards children of unmarried parents and given increased recognition to the tie between unmarried father and child as

---

9 Adoption Act 1976, s.16 (as amended).
10 Adoption Act 1976, s.72(1) (as amended). Prior to the Children Act 1989 he could never be a parent for adoption purposes, but was in certain circumstances a guardian: see the second edition of this book, para. 5-38.
11 See above, p. 135.
12 By virtue of the guardianship: see Children Act 1989, s.5(6).
13 Which will also confer parental responsibility: see above, p. 124.
14 If the child is the subject of a care order it cannot be warded: see Children Act 1989, s.100(2)(c); Supreme Court Act 1981, s.41(2A). If the adoption involves a local authority as adoption agency, the court will be reluctant to allow the use of wardship for this purpose: see Re T.D. [1985] F.L.R. 1150.
15 Re Adoption Application 41/61 [1962] 1 W.L.R. 866; G. v. G. [1993] 2 W.L.R. 873.
16 The test applied in proceedings relating to a child's upbringing. In adoption proceedings the child's welfare is the first, but not the paramount, consideration which allows greater weight to be given to the interests of the natural parents including the unmarried father. See Re Adoption Application No. 41/61 [1962] 1 W.L.R. 866; Re C. (M.A.) [1966] 1 All E.R. 838; Re W. [1984] F.L.R. 402; contrast Re E.(P). [1968] 1 W.L.R. 1913.

demonstrated by the decision in *Re O.(A Minor)(Custody: Adoption)*[17] decided shortly before implementation of the Children Act 1989. That Act re-enacts the paramountcy of the child's welfare which will determine such applications.

Where the father's concurrent application is for contact with his child, then in the case of final applications the courts have also followed the principle that both issues must be heard together and resolved in accordance with the paramountcy principle.[18] A court is not, however, bound to apply the same principle to an interim or interlocutory application for contact. Were it to do so, the delay in hearing the contact application is likely to prejudice the child's relationship with his father, should that relationship be in the child's best interests. The court has a complete discretion to make an interim contact order before finally deciding the adoption and contact issues.[19]

Whereas to grant a residence order in the unmarried father's favour would be incompatible with the making of an adoption order, the same is not true of a contact order. Thus in exceptional cases the courts, prior to the Children Act 1989, regarded access by the father as in the child's best interests and made an adoption order conditional[20] upon access by the father,[21] provided all interested parties agree.[22] Alternatively, as adoption proceedings are family proceedings for the purposes of the Children Act 1989[23] the court can make a contact order either of its own motion or on application of a qualified applicant,[24] or a person with leave,[25] provided the contact order is not made before the adoption order.[26] Such orders are, however, open to the objection that they are contrary to the spirit of adoption.[27] If it is felt desirable that the father should not lose all contact with his child, the court can consider making a residence order in favour of the prospective adopters rather than an adoption order,[28] particularly if the proposed adoption is by a relative or step-parent.

---

17 [1992] 1 F.L.R. 77, discussed above, p. 126. Compare *Re M.(A Minor) (Adoption)* [1991] Fam. Law 136, where the child had never lived with his father, who was aged 17 at the time of his birth.

18 *Re G.(A Minor)(Adoption and Access Applications)*[1980] 1 F.L.R. 108; *G. v. G.* [1993] 2 W.L.R. 837.

19 See the pre-Children Act 1989 case of *Re G.(A Minor)(Adoption and Access Applications* [1992] 1 F.L.R. 642, the principle in which would seem equally applicable after the Children Act 1989.

20 See Adoption Act 1976, s.12(6). If the court makes an unconditional adoption order it does not have power to adjourn a parent's application for access: see *Re R.(A Minor)(Adoption: Access)* [1991] 2 F.L.R. 78.

21 See *Re J.* [1973] Fam. 106; *Re S.* [1976] Fam. 1. See also *Re. C. (A Minor) (Adoption: Conditions)* [1988] 1 All E.R. 705.

22 *Re H.* [1985] F.L.R. 519.

23 Children Act 1989, s.8(3), (4)(*d*).

24 Including a parent (see Children Act 1989, s.10(4)(*a*)), unless the child has been freed for adoption, in which case the parents are deprived of their parental responsibility: see *M. v. C. and Calderdale Metropolitan Borough Council* [1993] 1 F.C.R. 431.

25 Children Act 1989, s.10(1).

26 If it is, then it is extinguished by the adoption order: see Adoption Act 1976, s.12(3)(*aa*).

27 *Re C.* [1986] 1 F.L.R. 315.

28 Using its power in the Children Act 1989, s.10(1)(*b*).

Where the court is asked to declare a child free for adoption in respect of a child whose father does not have parental responsibility for him, the court must satisfy itself that anyone claiming to be the father has no intention of applying for either a parental responsibility order[29] or a residence order under section 10 of the Children Act 1989,[30] or if he did apply the application would be likely to be refused.[31] An application for parental responsibility may be granted even though the father cannot immediately exercise all such responsibility. Thus in *Re H.(Minors)(Local Authority: Parental Rights)(No. 3)*[32] the unmarried father was granted an order under section 4 of the Family Law Reform Act 1987[33] even though immediately thereafter his agreement to an adoption order was held to have been unreasonably withheld.

Where the unmarried father without parental responsibility has no intention of seeking parental responsibility, he may still have some *locus standi* in respect of an adoption application. Where his identity is known to an adoption agency there is an obligation upon it, so far as it considers reasonably practicable and in the child's interests, to ascertain certain particulars and whether he intends to apply for parental responsibility or a residence order.[34] Where an application has been made to free the child for adoption, the reporting officer must interview any person claiming to be the father.[35]

Where the father without parental responsibility is liable to maintain a child under any order or agreement, he must be made a respondent to the application,[36] so that his views can be heard. If the father is not so liable, the court is under no duty to seek him out, but if anyone is claiming to be the father and wishes to be heard, the court should be informed.[37] The court has a discretion to add anyone as a respondent.[38] The father's agreement to the adoption is not, however, required. Moreover, if such a father is ignorant of the proposed adoption, the adoption agency has a discretion whether or not to include him in the adoption process,[39] and the court has no power to interfere with the exercise of that discretion, unless it has been improperly exercised.[40]

---

29 Under Children Act 1989, s.4(1) (see above, p. 120); but not it seems whether he has any intention of entering a parental responsibility agreement.
30 See above, p. 123.
31 Adoption Act 1976, s.18(7) (as substituted).
32 [1991] Fam. 151, above, p. 121.
33 The predecessor to s.4 of the Children Act 1989.
34 See Adoption Agencies Regulations 1983 (S.I. 1983 No. 1964), reg. 7(3).
35 See Adoption Rules 1984 (S.I. 1984 No. 265); Magistrates' Courts (Adoption) Rules 1984 (S.I. 1984 No. 611), r.5(4)(e) (as amended).
36 Including a freeing for adoption application, see Adoption Rules 1984 (S.I. 1984 No. 265); Magistrates' Courts (Adoption) Rules 1984 (S.I. 1984 No. 611), rr.4(2)(f), 9, 10 (freeing for adoption); 15 (2)(f), (h), 21 and 23 (adoption).
37 S.I. 1984 No. 265 and S.I. 1984 No. 611, Sched. 2, para. 6.
38 *Ibid.* r.15(3).
39 *Ibid.* Sched. 2, para. 2.
40 *Re L.(A Minor)(Adoption: Procedure)* [1991] 1 F.L.R. 171.

9. FINANCIAL SUPPORT

Financial provision by parent

One of the responsibilities of parenthood[41] is to support one's children financially. Where unmarried parents live together with children, in a stable relationship, the question of enforcing the responsibility is unlikely to arise, but if the parents fail to support their children the responsibility can be enforced in a number of ways.

Liability to maintain under the Child Support Act 1991
The liability of parents to maintain their children was fundamentally restructured by the Child Support Act 1991[42] following on from a government review of the levels of financial support provided by absent parents for their children.[43] That review found the previous court-centred discretionary system to be unnecessarily fragmented, slow and ineffective, such that its effect was uncertain and judicial decisions were inconsistent. The Child Support Act 1991 introduced instead a non-discretionary formula for the calculation of child maintenance payable by all absent parents. The responsibility for tracing absent parents, and the assessment, review, collection and enforcement of maintenance payments, rests not with the courts but with the Child Support Agency accountable to the Department of Social Security. The Agency is headed by a Chief Child Support Officer and staffed by child support officers. It has been estimated that at 1989 figures the new formula will result in an average child maintenance assessment of approximately £40 per week, compared with an average assessment under the court-centred system of £25 per week.[44] The residential parent's freedom of choice is, however, severely curtailed where she is in receipt of income support, family credit or disability working allowance in terms both of being required, subject to certain safeguards, to authorise the Agency to recover child support maintenance and to disclose information to enable the absent parent to be traced and maintenance to be assessed and recovered. So the mother in receipt of benefit who on breakdown of cohabitation with the child's father wishes to have no further involvement with him may find that her wish is not granted.

Where a child support officer is considering the exercise of any discretionary power conferred by the Act "he shall have regard to the

---

41 As opposed to parental responsibility, so an unmarried father is under a duty to support his child.
42 With effect from April 5, 1993, over a phased four-year period: see the Child Support Act 1991 (Commencement No. 3 and Transitional Provisions) Order 1992 (S.I. 1992 No. 2644). Where an absent parent is responsible for maintaining a child living with him, other than the child in respect of whom the application is made, transitional arrangements may mitigate the effects of the increase during the first year: see Sched., para. 7.
43 See White Paper, "Children Come First", Vols. 1 and 2, Cm. 1264 (1990).
44 *Ibid.* para. 3.37.

welfare of any child likely to be affected by his decision".[45] The welfare principle is limited, first, as to its scope and, secondly, as to its nature. As to its scope, it has no application in relation to the assessment of maintenance which is formula based. As to its nature, the child's welfare is neither the paramount consideration, as it is when a court is deciding any question relating to the upbringing of a child,[46] nor the first consideration as it is when a court is deciding how to exercise its powers to make financial provision and property adjustment orders either during or on breakdown of marriage.[47] The officer does, however, have to have regard to the welfare of *any* child likely to be affected by his decision and not just the child in respect of whom his decision is made. The legislation gives the officer no guidance on the exercise of his discretion.

The courts' jurisdiction is a residual one because in any case where a child support officer would have jurisdiction, no court shall exercise any power which it would otherwise have to make, vary or revive any maintenance order in relation to the child and absent parent concerned and this is so even though the circumstances are such that a child support officer would not make an assessment if it were applied for.[48]

The duty to maintain under the Act is imposed upon each parent of a qualifying child.[49] A parent is any person who is in law the mother or father[50] so clearly includes both natural parents irrespective of their marital status, for liability arises from parenthood and not parental responsibility.[51] Hence in this context cohabitation is not relevant and there is no duty to maintain upon a non-parent such as a cohabitee of a parent irrespective of the cohabitee's assumption of responsibility for the child.[52] Cohabitation is relevant, however, in the calculation of parents' resources.[53]

A child is a person who is under the age of 16 or under the age of 19 and receiving full-time non-advanced education, or in prescribed conditions is under the age of 18 and has not been married.[54] A child becomes a "qualifying child" if either or both of his parents are absent parents,[55]

---

45 Child Support Act 1991, s.2.
46 Children Act 1989, s.1: see above, p. 125.
47 See Matrimonial Causes Act 1973, s.25(1); Domestic Proceedings and Magistrates' Courts Act 1978, s.3(1): see below, p. 189.
48 Child Support Act 1991, s.8(1)-(3). The court retains jurisdiction to revoke a maintenance order (s.8(4)); for further exceptions, see below, p. 150.
49 s.1(1).
50 Child Support Act 1991, s.54; where there is a dispute as to parentage, see s.26, below, p. 148.
51 See above, p. 105.
52 Similarly there is no liability on the part of a step-parent under the Act, even though a step-parent, unlike a cohabitee, may be liable to maintain a child of the family in court proceedings: see below, p. 203.
53 See below, p. 147.
54 See Child Support Act 1991, s.55, and the Child Support (Maintenance Assessment Procedure) Regulations 1992 (S.I. 1992 No. 1813), Sched. 1, for the full meaning.
55 s.3(1).

which requires that the parent is not living in the same household with the child and that the child has his home with "a person with care"[56] that is: "a person (a) with whom the child has his home; (b) who usually provides day to day care for the child (whether exclusively or in conjunction with any other person); and (c) who does not fall within a prescribed category of person."[57] In regard to the latter category, parents, guardians and persons in whose favour residence orders are in force must not be prescribed.[58] In short, this means in practice that the child's natural parents are not living together and the child is living with one of them (usually the mother).

There may be more than one person with care in relation to the same qualifying child,[59] for example, the mother and her cohabitee. In such cases no application may be made for a maintenance assessment by such a person who does not have parental responsibility for the child such as a cohabitee unless he has acquired it. If more than one person who is so qualified does apply, only one application may be proceeded with in accordance with the regulations.[60] If the child spends an average of two nights a week (at least 104 nights a year) with the absent parent, that parent will be deemed to have contributed a proportion to the child support maintenance equivalent to the time spent with him[61]; hence the importance in this context of staying contact.

An absent parent is taken as having met his[62] responsibility to maintain a qualifying child under the Act[63] by making such periodical payments of maintenance, referred to as "child support maintenance",[64] as are determined under the Act.[65] Where a maintenance assessment has been made in accordance with the formula, the absent parent is under a duty to comply with it[66]; hence no duty to maintain arises under the Act until the making of such an assessment.

Application to the Child Support Agency for a maintenance assessment may be made by either the person with care of the child or the absent parent.[67] Where the assessment is made, either party may apply to the Agency for it to arrange the collection and enforcement of the child support maintenance.[68] Where the person with care is the child's parent and she, or her partner, is claiming income support, family credit

---

56 s.3(2).
57 s.3(3).
58 s.3(4).
59 s.3(5).
60 See s.5 and S.I. 1992 No. 1813, reg. 4 and Sched. 2.
61 The Child Support (Maintenance Assessments and Special Cases) Regulations 1992 (S.I. 1992 No. 1815), reg. 20.
62 It is assumed that the father is the absent parent notwithstanding that the rules apply whichever parent is absent.
63 But not necessarily other responsibilities to maintain.
64 s.3(6).
65 s.1(2).
66 s.1(3).
67 s.4(1). See also S.I. 1992 No. 1813 (as amended).
68 s.4(2) (for which a charge is made unless the claimant is exempt, for example, if she or her partner is on income support, family credit or disability working allowance).

or disability working allowance, she *must* authorise the Agency,[69] if she is required to do so, to take action to recover child support maintenance from the absent parent,[70] regardless of whether any of the benefits is payable with respect to any qualifying child.[71] She must also, so far as she reasonably can, provide the required information to enable the absent parent, if necessary, to be traced and the amount of child support maintenance payable by the absent parent to be assessed and recovered.[72] Certain specified people are also under a duty to supply information required in connection with the determination of an application.[73] That information may include information and evidence as to "the persons living in the same household as the absent parent or living in the same household as the parent with care, their relationship to the absent parent or the parent with care, as the case may be, and to each other". Such information includes: a cohabitee and the name and address of any current or recent employer of such a person and their earnings; the address from which any such person who is self-employed works together with the business' trading name, gross receipts, expenses and other outgoings; and that person's other income including disability benefits entitlement.[74] State intrusion is not confined to parents' lives but extends to their partners.

On breakdown of the parents' relationship, the residential parent may be concerned for the well-being of herself or the children if she were to comply with any such authorisation, particularly as she may not benefit personally from the maintenance assessment. If the Agency considers that there are reasonable grounds for believing that there would be a risk of the parent with care of the child, or *any* child living with her, suffering harm[75] or undue distress as a result of the parent giving or being required to give the authorisation, then she cannot be required to give it.[76] It is noteworthy, however, that the assessment of whether or not there are reasonable grounds for so believing rests with the Agency[77] and its interpretation will no doubt prove controversial.

The sanction in cases of failure to comply with the obligations in section 6(1) or (9) is also controversial because of the potential penalty to be imposed upon the woman. If a child support officer considers that there are no reasonable grounds for believing that, if she were required

---

69 By completing a maintenance application form: see s.6(6)-(7). For meaning of partner, see below, p. 147.
70 s.6(1). The authorisation extends to all children of the absent parent in relation to whom the other parent is a person with care: see s.6(4).
71 s.6(8), replacing the liable relative procedure in the Social Security Administration Act 1992, ss.78, 105 and 106 in relation to enforcing liability to maintain children.
72 *Ibid.* s.6(9). The obligation does not apply in prescribed circumstances, or where it is waived by the Secretary of State: see further s.6(10).
73 See ss.14-15, Sched. 2, and the Child Support (Information, Evidence and Disclosure) Regulations 1992 (S.I. 1992 No. 1812), reg. 2.
74 S.I. 1992 No. 1812, reg.3(2)(g), (h), (l)-(o).
75 The degree of harm is not specified.
76 s.6(2). The parent can request that s.6(2) be disregarded: see s.6(3).
77 The stated intention is that the residential parent's statement should be believed unless it is implausible.

to comply, there would be a risk of her or of any children living with her suffering harm or undue distress as a result of complying,[78] he has the discretion to give a "reduced benefit direction" with respect to her.[79] In exercising his discretion he must take into account the welfare of any children likely to be affected, but their interests are not paramount.[80] If a direction is given, its effect is that the amount of income support, family credit or other benefit otherwise payable is to be reduced by such amount and for such a period as prescribed, namely 20 per cent. of the benefit[81] of the person with care for 26 weeks and 10 per cent. for the succeeding 52 weeks.[82] Appeal against a decision to give a reduced benefit direction may be made to a child support appeal tribunal.[83]

The highly complex standard formula for the calculation of child support maintenance payable by the absent parent for the qualifying child is based on income support rates[84] and is to be found in Schedule 1 of the Act[85] and regulations made thereunder.[86] It applies irrespective of whether any member of the family is in receipt of welfare benefits. In very brief terms[87] there are four parts to the calculation of child maintenance assessment: (1) the child's maintenance requirement[88]; (2) the parents' assessable income[89]; (3) the maintenance assessment[90]; and (4) protected income.[91]

The child's maintenance requirement (MR) is the minimum amount necessary for the maintenance of a qualifying child. The formula used is $MR = AG - CB$. AG is the aggregate of prescribed sums[92] and CB is child benefit applicable to the child in question. Cohabitation is of particular relevance in the context of AG in that the figures to be taken into account in calculating AG include income support lone parent premium where the parent with care has no "partner". Partner means

---

78 If he considers that there are such reasonable grounds, he must take no further action regarding the failure to comply and give her written notice accordingly: s.46(4).
79 s.46(5). A child support officer may, but is not required, to serve written notice on the parent requiring her, before the end of the specified period, either to comply or to give her reasons for failing to do so: s.46(2).
80 s.2, and see above, p. 143.
81 *I.e.* benefit for herself, not for the child.
82 s.46(11), and see further S.I. 1992 No. 1813, Pt. IX (as amended).
83 s.46(7) (within 28 days of the date on which notification was given, save where the chairman of a tribunal has given leave: see ss.46(8) and 20(2)). For the separate right to apply for a review of the direction, see S.I. 1992 No. 1813, reg. 42.
84 Hence it is regularly updated.
85 s.11(2). Where it appears to a child support officer that he does not have sufficient information, he may make an interim maintenance assessment: see s.12.
86 See further the Child Support (Maintenance Assessment Procedure) Regulations 1992 (S.I. 1992 No. 1813) (as amended) and the Child Support (Maintenance Assessments and Special Cases) Regulations 1992 (S.I. 1992 No. 1815) (as amended).
87 A detailed analysis is outside the scope of this work and reference should be made to the specialist texts on the Act.
88 Sched. 1, para. 1.
89 Para. 5.
90 Paras. 2-4.
91 Para. 6.
92 See S.I. 1992 No. 1815, reg. 3.

"in relation to a member of a married or unmarried couple who are living together, the other member of that couple", and "unmarried couple" means "a man and a woman who are not married to each other but are living together as husband and wife".[93] The definition of unmarried couple is that used in the context of social security law and is to be interpreted, it is submitted, accordingly.[94]

Assessable income is calculated in respect of both the absent parent and the parent with care of the qualifying child, as both are expected to contribute to the child's maintenance requirement if their income is above a certain amount. The formula in respect of the absent parent is $A = N - E$, where A is the assessable income, N is his net income and E is his exempt income. The formula in respect of the parent with care is $C = M - F$, where C is the assessable income, M the net income and F the exempt income of that person. The income of any partner living with a parent is not included in the net income.[95] Cohabitation may be of relevance in the calculation or estimation of exempt income, for example where a parent and a "partner"[96] are the parents of a child living with them there will be an allowance for this child and the partner may be able to contribute to the support of that child.[97] Exempt income does not include an allowance for a partner.

The third part of the calculation is the maintenance assessment based on the formula $(A + C) \times P$ which is the two assessable incomes multiplied by a specified figure which has been set at 0.5, *i.e.* 50 per cent.[98] If this formula gives a result which is equal to, or less than, the child's maintenance requirement, then the absent parent is required to pay half of his assessable income.[99] Where the result is more than the maintenance requirement, the formula provides for an "additional element" so as to provide support above the minimum maintenance requirement.[1]

The final part of the calculation is protected income level, the purpose of which is to prevent payment of child support maintenance leaving the absent parent and any new family, including a cohabitee, with a disposable income below what he would be entitled to if claiming income support. In calculating an absent parent's disposable income, the Act enables regulations to provide that, in prescribed circumstances:

"where the absent parent is living together in the same household with another adult of the opposite sex (regardless of whether or not they are married), income of that other adult is to be treated as the

---

93 See reg. 1.
94 See above, p. 81.
95 See S.I. 1992 No. 1815, regs. 7 and 8, Sched. 1.
96 See above, p. 145.
97 See further regs. 9(2) and 10.
98 Reg. 5(*b*) (the "deduction rate").
99 Child Support Act 1991, Sched. 1, para. 2(2).
 1 See further paras. 2(3), 3 and 4 and S.I. 1992 No. 1815, reg. 6.

absent parent's income for the purposes of calculating his disposable income."[2]

A cohabitation rule thus operates so as to equate heterosexual cohabitation with marriage. The disposable income of the absent parent is the aggregate of his income and that of any member of his "family",[3] which means, *inter alia*, a married or unmarried couple and any child or children living with them for whom at least one member of the couple has day-to-day care.[4]

The regulations list the amounts to be aggregated for the purpose of calculating the protected income, and the first of these amounts differs depending upon whether or not the absent parent has a partner, so that the absent parent's obligations to any current partner may be taken into account. If he does not have a partner the amount is the income support personal allowance for a single claimant aged not less than 25. If he does the amount is the income support personal allowance for a couple where both members are aged not less than 18.[5] The income of any partner of the absent parent is also taken into account in calculating whether the absent parent's income exceeds the total of the various allowances,[6] and in calculating housing costs[7] in which context reference to "close relative" as well as to "partner" and "family" includes the other member of an unmarried couple.[8]

Maintenance is reviewed annually and either parent can seek a review between the annual review if his or her circumstances change significantly,[9] for example, on the birth of a child to a new partner. It is to be noted also that a maintenance assessment ceases to have effect, *inter alia*, if the absent parent and the person with care with respect to whom the assessment was made have been living together for a continuous period of six months.[10]

Of direct relevance also to cohabitation are the provisions in the Act relating to disputes about parentage and applications to the court for a declaration of parentage. These provisions are of central importance in view of the fact that the duty to support is based upon parentage. Where parentage is denied, the child support officer must not make a maintenance assessment on the assumption that the person is one of the child's parents, unless the case falls within one of those set out in section 26(2). They are if he or she:

(i) has adopted the child;

---

2 Sched. 1, para. 6(5)(*b*).
3 S.I. 1992 No. 1815, reg. 12(1).
4 Reg. 1(2).
5 Reg. 11(1)(*a*).
6 Reg. 11(1)(*l*).
7 Regs. 14-18.
8 Sched. 3.
9 Child Support Act 1991, s.17.
10 Sched. 1, para. 16(1)(*d*).

(ii) is a parent by virtue of an order under section 30 of the Human Fertilisation and Embryology Act 1990;
(iii) is declared a parent in a declaration under section 56 of the Family Law Act 1986[11] and the child has not subsequently been adopted;
(iv) is declared as such by a declaration under section 27 of the Child Support Act 1991[12] and the child has not subsequently been adopted;
(v) has been found, or adjudged, to be the father of the child in relevant proceedings in England or Wales or in affiliation proceedings in the United Kingdom, the finding still subsists and the child has not been adopted.

Where a parent (usually the father) denies parentage and the child support officer is not satisfied that the case falls within one of the above, the officer or the person with care may apply to the court[13] for a declaration as to whether or not the alleged parent is one of the child's parents. Such a declaration has effect only for the purposes of the Child Support Act 1991.[14]

The role of the courts is a residual one. If a child assessment officer would have jurisdiction[15] to make a maintenance assessment, "no court shall exercise any power which it would otherwise have to make, vary or revive any maintenance order in relation to the child and absent parent concerned".[16] Reference has already been made to the Act imposing a duty upon absent parents to maintain a qualifying child. Liability of non-parents, so far as it exists,[17] and the limited duty to support children over the age of 18 is not within the scope of the Act and must be enforced by court proceedings. As the duty under the Act falls upon absent parents, the courts retain jurisdiction in respect of maintenance orders against a person with care of the child.[18] Liability under the Act does not affect the courts' powers to make an order for the payment of a lump sum or property adjustment to or for the benefit of the child[19] There is also a power for existing maintenance agreements and certain court orders either to cease to have effect or to have modified effect.[20] The courts also have jurisdiction in the following circumstances:

---

11 See above, p. 112.
12 See below.
13 *I.e.* subject to any provision made under the Children Act 1989, Sched. 11, the High Court, a County Court or a Magistrates' Court: see Child Support Act 1991, s.27(4), and the Family Proceedings Courts (Child Support Act 1991) Rules 1993 (S.I. 1993 No. 627), r.4.
14 See Child Support Act 1991, s.27(3).
15 As a preliminary, an officer has jurisdiction to make an assessment only if the person with care, the absent parent or a qualifying child is habitually resident in the United Kingdom: see s.44.
16 s.8(3).
17 *e.g.* for step-children: see above, p. 143.
18 s.8(10).
19 See below, p. 152.
20 s.10 and regulations thereunder: see in particular the Child Support (Maintenance Arrangements and Jurisdiction) Regulations 1992 (S.I. 1992 No. 2645) (as amended).

(i) to make consent orders in all material respects in the same terms as an existing written agreement which provides for the absent parent to make or secure periodical payments to or for the benefit of the child[21];

(ii) where the amount of child support maintenance was determined by "the alternative formula"[22] and the court is satisfied that it is appropriate to order the absent parent to pay periodical payments in addition to the amount payable under the maintenance assessment,[23] i.e. a topping-up maintenance order;

(iii) where the child is or will be receiving education or undergoing training for a trade, profession or vocation and the court order is solely for the payment of expenses incurred in connection therewith,[24] e.g. school fees;

(iv) where the order is solely for the payment of periodical payments to meet expenses attributable to the child's disability.[25]

The Act does not prevent any person from entering into a maintenance agreement[26] but the existence of such an agreement cannot prevent any party to the agreement, or any other person, from applying for a maintenance assessment under the Act and any clause in the agreement purporting to restrict the right of any person to apply for an assessment is void.[27] Furthermore, where such an agreement has been entered into, it cannot be varied by a court if a child support officer would have jurisdiction.

Maintenance agreement

Subject to the Child Support Act 1991, it is open to the parents to enter into an agreement to maintain their children. It is well established[28] that such an agreement is enforceable[29] except in so far as it attempts to exclude application to the courts for maintenance,[30] in so far as such applications can still be made.[31] If the agreement is by deed there will be no problem regarding insufficiency of consideration. It has been held that, notwithstanding the mother's existing duty to maintain her child, her looking after the child in accordance with an agreement with the father is sufficient consideration for his promise to make the payments under the agreement.[32] This view may be too wide, however, in which case consideration may take the form of the mother's promise not to take

---

21 s. 8(5).
22 In Sched. 1, para. 4(3).
23 s. 8(6).
24 s. 8(7).
25 s.8(8), (9).
26 s.9(2), and see below.
27 s.9(3), (4).
28 See *Jennings* v. *Brown* (1842) 9 M. & W. 496.
29 *Ward* v. *Byham* [1956] 1 W.L.R. 496.
30 *Follit* v. *Koetzow* (1860) 2 E. & E. 730.
31 See above. Such an agreement will be a relevant factor when the court is considering the circumstances of the case: Children Act 1989, Sched. 1, para. 4(1).
32 *Ward* v. *Byham* [1956] 1 W.L.R. 496.

proceedings[33] even though she is not precluded by the agreement from taking such proceedings. Such action would be a breach of the contract and the father would be entitled to consider himself discharged from his promise to pay maintenance and might be able to sue the mother for damages.[34] If the agreement goes further than providing maintenance for the child and provides an allowance for the mother to compensate her for lost earning capacity because of having to look after the child, such an allowance ought to be enforceable as in the case of a court order.[35]

Whilst it had been open to the parties to vary an agreement, until the Family Law Reform Act 1987 there was no power for the court to do so. The Children Act 1989[36] now provides for application to the court[37] for the alteration of a maintenance agreement, being a written agreement which is made between the father and mother of the child and contains financial arrangements for the child's maintenance or education. If the court is satisfied either that (by reason of a change in the circumstances in the light of which any financial arrangements contained in the agreement were made) the agreement should be altered so as to make different financial arrangements, or that the agreement does not contain proper financial arrangements with respect to the child, the court may vary or revoke any financial arrangements as may appear just. Thereafter, the agreement has effect as though the alteration had been made by agreement between the parties for full valuable consideration. Similar provision is made also for the alteration by the County Court or High Court, after the death of one of the parties, of a maintenance agreement which provides for the continuation of payments after the death of one of the parties.[38] An application cannot be made, save with leave of the court, more than six months from the date on which representation in regard to the deceased's estate was first taken out. Any alteration takes effect as if it had been agreed between the parties immediately before the death and for valuable consideration. A maintenance agreement, it has been argued, is terminated by either party giving the other reasonable notice and the father's liability will cease on the mother's death unless agreed otherwise, but may bind his personal representatives after his death.[39]

The law's encouragement of unmarried parents to provide by agreement for the maintenance of their children is to be welcomed. It is noticeable, however, that the law has yet to recognise directly enforceable agreements to maintain made between cohabitees themselves.[40] Support obligations, even to the extent of providing a home, have been enforced indirectly, by the use of the concepts of the trust and the

---

33 *Jennings* v. *Brown* (1842) 9 M. & W. 496.
34 See Bromley and Lowe, *Bromley's Family Law* (8th ed., 1992), p.663.
35 See below, p. 154.
36 Sched. 1, para. 10.
37 *I.e.* the High Court, a County Court or a Magistrates' Court: the latter's powers are more limited.
38 Children Act 1989, Sched. 1, para. 11.
39 See Bromley and Lowe, *op. cit.*, p. 662.
40 See above, p. 76.

licence, particularly where there are children.[41] Once again, however, there is little coherence or consistency in the legal approach and the development of the law has been one of accident rather than design.

Court proceedings
  The liability of both parents to maintain their children is now primarily enforceable through the Child Support Agency and it has been seen that in any case where a child support officer would have jurisdiction the courts are precluded from exercising their powers to make, vary or revive any maintenance order in relation to the child and the absent parent.[42] This is so even where the court is dealing with other aspects of the relationship between the parents and their children. It is only where a child support officer does not have jurisdiction that the parents can have recourse to the courts.[43] In the context of cohabitation this may be where maintenance is sought:

  (i) against the person with care of the child;
  (ii) for the payment of a lump sum or property adjustment;
  (iii) in addition to that payable under the maintenance assessment;
  (iv) to meet expenses incurred in connection with education or training; or
  (v) to meet expenses attributable to the child's disability.

In such cases liability is likely to arise, if at all, under the Children Act 1989.

Children Act 1989
  The amendments to child support maintenance law in the Children Act 1989 were for the most part consequential and the Act's provisions in that regard[44] consist primarily of the re-enactment of provisions of the Guardianship of Minors Acts 1971 and 1973, the Children Act 1975 and the Family Law Reform Act 1987. The last mentioned Act was of particular note because it removed a major form of legal discrimination against the child of unmarried parents, namely affiliation proceedings. Those proceedings, which were based on the old Poor Law and were more akin to criminal proceedings, discouraged applicants. Proceedings under the Guardianship of Minors Act 1971 were previously available only as a means of providing maintenance for the child of married parents. The 1987 Act extended those proceedings so that the financial responsibility of all parents, whether married or unmarried, is enforceable in a like manner. The same is so under its successor the Children Act 1989. Financial responsibility under the Matrimonial Causes Act 1973 and the Domestic Proceedings and Magistrates' Courts Act 1978, however, arises only in the context of matrimonial proceedings; hence the

---

41 See above, p. 52.
42 Child Support Act 1991, s.8(1)-(3), above, p. 149.
43 See above, p. 149.
44 Children Act 1989, s.15, Sched. 1.

importance of Children Act 1989 proceedings in relation to the child of unmarried parents. In the case of unmarried parents, there is also the important difference of needing to prove paternity. Whilst the father's paternity will rarely be in issue if the parents are married, this is less so in the case of unmarried parents. Cohabitation gives rise to no presumption of parentage. If paternity is contested the issue must be resolved.[45] Where there has been an affiliation case involving an inconclusive blood test, the case can be re-opened to take advantage of the more accurate DNA testing and the replacement legislation operates retrospectively to permit applications in respect of children born before it came into force.[46]

Liability under the Children Act 1989 is placed upon parents. It is based primarily, but not exclusively, upon the concept of parenthood because parent has a specially extended meaning so as to include, in addition to both natural parents, "any party to a marriage (whether or not subsisting) in relation to whom the child concerned is a child of the family".[47] So, as with the matrimonial legislation, step-parents as well as natural parents may be liable,[48] but not the cohabitee of a parent. Hence in *J. v. J.(Property Transfer Application)*[49] a mother could not get an order that her cohabitee of 10 years' standing transfer a joint tenancy into her sole name for the benefit of her child who had been a member of their household, because the cohabitee was neither the father of the child nor married to the mother and was not therefore a "parent" for the purpose of that Part of the Act.

An order for financial relief can be made on the application of a parent or a guardian of a child or by any person in whose favour a residence order is in force with respect to the child.[50] An order may be made against either or both parents, to the applicant for the benefit[51] of the child, or to the child. It may be in the form of secured or unsecured periodical payments, a lump sum payment or the transfer or settlement of property, depending upon the court to which application is made. The latter two orders are of particular significance since the Child Support Act 1991. The Magistrates' Court, County Court or High Court may make an order for periodical payments. The County Court and the High Court can also order secured payments and the transfer and settlement of property. All three courts can also order a lump sum payment which in

---

45 See above, p. 123.
46 *Hager* v. *Osborne* [1992] 2 W.L.R. 610, decided under the Guardianship of Minors Act 1971, s.11B, as inserted by the Family Law Reform Act 1987, s.12, now consolidated into the Children Act 1989, Sched. 1, to the same effect.
47 Sched. 1, para. 16(1).
48 See below, p. 203.
49 [1993] F.C.R. 471.
50 For the limited circumstances in which a child who has attained the age of 18 may apply for an order, see Children Act 1989, Sched. 1, para. 2. and below, p. 155.
51 Not necessarily financial: see *K.* v. *K.(Minors: Property Transfer)* [1992] 2 All E.R. 727, below, p. 154.

the County Court and High Court is unlimited and in the Magistrates' Court must not exceed £1000.[52]

Whereas property adjustment orders had been available before the Family Law Reform Act 1987 in respect of the children of married parents, that was so only in proceedings for divorce, nullity or judicial separation, hence no such order was available for the child of unmarried parents. That change represented a major and welcome departure which is of particular use in the case of cohabiting parents on breakdown of their relationship, as a means of securing the position of their children in a similar manner to that of the children of married parents on breakdown of marriage. This form of order is particularly desirable where the father intends to have no further relationship with the child.[53] Moreover, the order is not limited to securing the financial position of the child; thus in *K. v. K.(Minors: Property Transfer)*[54] the Court of Appeal held that there is jurisdiction to order that the father transfer to the mother his interest in the joint tenancy of the family home where the object was to benefit the child by excluding the father. The order thereby has the effect of preserving the family home for the children of unmarried parents, in a similar way to the orders which the divorce court can make to secure the family home for the children of married parents.[55] Such an order also has the indirect effect of benefiting the residential parent, even though there is no power to transfer in favour of an unmarried partner. There is no reason why the unmarried parent, who in practice will usually be the father, should provide less support for his child on breakdown of cohabitation than the married parent should provide for his child on breakdown of marriage. Indeed it had been recognised before the Family Law Reform Act 1987 that, whilst there is no power to order the father to maintain the mother as cohabitee, an order for the benefit of the child may include an allowance for the mother, for example, to compensate her for loss of income if she has had to give up work or is unable to work because she has to look after the child.[56] As an alternative to transferring property to the residential parent for the benefit of the child the court can, for example, order a settlement of property to be made for the benefit of the child.

As proceedings for financial provision of a child under the Children Act 1989 are the same irrespective of the parents' marital status, it is inappropriate here to discuss further the detailed operation of those proceedings save in so far as they relate to parental cohabitation.[57] A periodical payments order made or secured in favour of one parent against another ceases if they live with each other for a period exceeding

---

52 For full details, see the Children Act 1989, Sched 1, paras. 1 and 5(2).
53 See Law Com. No. 118, para. 6.6.
54 [1992] 2 All E.R. 727.
55 See below, p. 194.
56 See *Haroutunian* v. *Jennings* (1980) 1 F.L.R. 62; *Osborn* v. *Sparks* (1982) 3 F.L.R. 90.
57 For the general changes affecting the child of unmarried parents introduced by the Family Law Reform Act 1987, see the second edition of this book, para. 5.31.

six months.[58] A periodical payments order payable to the child is enforceable notwithstanding any such cohabitation. Provision is also made in certain circumstances for a child over 18, whether or not his parents are married, but provided they are not living together, to apply for financial relief[59] from either or both of the parents.[60]

As a result of the Family Law Reform Act 1987, an order for financial relief need not be, although may well be, associated with an application for parental responsibility. It remains the case that a financial provision order imposes upon a parent liability to maintain his child. It does not confer corresponding parental responsibility, which is a separate issue. Subject to the Child Support Act 1991, an application for financial relief may be made independently or in conjunction with other proceedings, for example, for a residence order or contact order and the court can make a financial relief order of its own motion whenever it makes, varies or discharges a residence order.[61] Also, as financial relief proceedings are under Part II of the Children Act 1989, they are "family proceedings" for the purposes of the Act[62] and so the court has the power to make a section 8 order either on application or of its own motion.[63] For example, if the mother sought a financial relief order, the father could apply as part of those proceedings for a contact order.

Other proceedings and other liability to maintain

The financial responsibilities of unmarried parents towards their children have been assimilated with those of married parents in the context of wardship,[64] and liability for contributions from parents towards maintenance of children looked after by local authorities[65] or in residential accommodation.[66] There will of course be the need to prove paternity.

Child benefit

Child benefit is payable to a person who is responsible in any week for one or more children under the age of 16, or under the age of 18 and not receiving full-time education and prescribed conditions are satisfied; or under the age of 19 and receiving full-time non-advanced education at a recognised educational establishment.[67]

---

58 Children Act 1989, Sched. 1, para. 3(4).
59 In the form of periodical payments and lump sum payments but not property adjustment.
60 Children Act 1989, Sched. 1, para. 2.
61 Children Act 1989, Sched. 1, para. 1(6).
62 s.8(3), (4)(a).
63 s.10(1).
64 Children Act 1989, Sched. 1, para. 1(7) (as inserted).
65 Children Act 1989, Sched. 2, Pt. III.
66 National Assistance Act 1948, s.42(1): see Family Law Reform Act 1987, s.2(1)(a), Sched. 2, paras. 5-8.
67 For full details, see Social Security Contributions and Benefits Act 1992, ss.141-142 and Child Benefit (General) Regulations 1976 (S.I. 1976 No. 965) (as amended).

Payment is based on responsibility for a child and not on parenthood. The Social Security Contributions and Benefits Act 1992 provides that a person is "responsible for a child" in any week if he has the child living with him or he is contributing to the cost of providing for the child at a weekly rate which is not less than the weekly rate of child benefit.[68] It may be that both cohabitees are "responsible for a child", in which case only one of them is entitled. The Act provides a scheme of priorities.[69] If benefit has already been paid to a person, he will take priority for a further three weeks after another claim.[70] Otherwise, if one person has the child living with him and another is contributing to the child's maintenance, the former has priority.[71] If the child is living with married parents, the wife is entitled.[72] If the child is living with cohabitees, both of whom are parents, the mother is entitled.[73] If one cohabitee is a parent and the other is not, the parent is entitled.[74] In other cases, if persons are jointly entitled, for example, if neither is a parent, they must decide between themselves who is to receive benefit. If they do not decide, the Secretary of State, through the adjudication officer, will do so.[75]

An extra rate of benefit, known as one-parent benefit, is payable to a person, whether or not a parent, who has the sole responsibility for bringing up a child or children.[76] The claimant must not be residing with a spouse and not living with anyone as his spouse. Where unmarried parents are cohabiting they will be treated as living together during any period of temporary absence on the part of one of them.[77] If the separation is permanent they will be treated as not living together and the separation is not subject to the 91 days time bar applicable to spouses,[78] so in this context cohabitees have an advantage.

10. INHERITANCE

Reference has already been made to the improved succession rights of children of unmarried parents, as a result of the Family Law Reform Act

---

68 s.143.
69 s.144 and Sched. 10. See also Social Security (Claims and Payments) Regulations 1987 (S.I. 1987 No. 1968), regs. 2 and 36, Sched. 8, paras. 2(b), 3, 5, 6(b) and 7.
70 Sched. 10, para. 1.
71 Para. 2, subject to para. 1.
72 Para. 3, subject to paras. 1 and 2.
73 Para. 4(2), subject to paras. 1 to 3.
74 Para. 4(1), subject to paras. 1 to 3.
75 Para. 5.
76 Child Benefit and Social Security (Fixing and Adjustment of Rates) Amendment Regulations 1980 (S.I. 1980 No. 110), reg. 2(1).
77 Child Benefit (General) Regulations 1976 (S.I. 1976 No. 965), reg. 11(3) (as amended).
78 Reg. 11(1) (as amended).

1969.[79] This improvement was continued by the Family Law Reform Act 1987 in the context of both testate and intestate succession.

A child of unmarried parents has always been able to inherit under a will if expressly included. As a result of the 1987 Act[80] the rule in section 15(2) of the 1969 Act that words of relationship are only to be construed presumptively to include an illegitimate person where that person was a potential beneficiary, or where the beneficiary's relationship to the deceased depends on an intermediate illegitimate link,[81] were removed. The use of the term "heir" or any expression used to create an entailed interest is not to be taken as showing an intention to exclude a person whose parents have not been married to each other.[82] Not all discrimination against the child of unmarried parents has been removed, however, for he still cannot succeed to a title of honour or property devolving therewith.[83] Otherwise if a testator wishes to exclude the child of unmarried parents he must do so expressly, for example, by limiting succession to legitimate children only.

Of greater significance was the amendment to the rules of intestate succession. In determining the distribution of the estate of an intestate any relationship between two people is to be construed without regard to whether or not the father and mother of either of them, or the father and mother of any person through whom the relationship is deduced, have or had been married to each other at any time.[84] Thus whereas the Family Law Reform Act 1969 only conferred rights of intestate succession between parents and children, the 1987 Act extended this to all relationships, for example, grandparents and siblings. This is so whether succession is claimed by a person whose parents were not married, or to his estate, or through such a relationship. It remains the case, however, that for the purposes of intestate succession a child is presumed not to have been survived by his unmarried father unless the contrary is shown and this was extended to any person related to him only through his father.[85]

For the purposes of obtaining a grant of probate or administration there is a presumption that the deceased was not survived by any relative whose father and mother were not married to each other at the time of his death, or by any person whose relationship is deduced through such a person.[86]

---

79 See above, p. 108. Independently of the rules of inheritance the child may have a claim under the Inheritance (Provision for Family and Dependants) Act 1975: see below, p. 211.

80 s.19(1), in respect of dispositions, whether *inter vivos*, by will or by codicil, made on or after April 4, 1988, the date on which the Family Law Reform Act 1987, s.19, came into force: see S.I. 1988 No. 425. See also s.19(7).

81 See Law Com. No. 118, para. 8.16.

82 Family Law Reform Act 1987, s.19(2).

83 *Ibid.* s.19(4).

84 *Ibid.* s.18(1): in respect of rights under the intestacy of a person dying after the coming into force of the section, see s.18(4), Sched. 3, para. 8 and S.I. 1988 No. 425.

85 *Ibid.* s.18(2).

86 *Ibid.* s.21, which does not apply in relation to the estate of a person dying before April 4, 1988: see s.21(3) and S.I. 1988 No. 425.

11. CONCLUSION

The removal of legal discrimination against the child of unmarried parents is not yet fully complete. He is still unable to succeed to a title of honour.[87] Of greater significance is that his entitlement to British citizenship is derived solely through his mother.[88] If she is not a British citizen then neither is he even if his father is. This represents an unjustifiable discrimination, for, as the Law Commission acknowledged, there is no reason of principle why children of unmarried parents should be unable to acquire British citizenship from their fathers on the same terms as a child of married parents.[89]

The removal of discrimination against the child of unmarried parents has not extended to the removal of discrimination against the child's father, in whom parental responsibility does not vest legally until he takes steps to acquire it.[90] In that respect a significant distinction remains between those children whose parents are married and those whose parents are not; between those children who are legitimate and those who are not.[91] At least the Children Act 1989, by providing for a parental responsibility agreement, has removed the insistence on a court order before any unmarried father can acquire that which is automatically conferred on all mothers and all married fathers. English law has yet to accept the view of the Scottish Law Commission that in family law "children should just be children, and people should just be people, whether their parents were married to each other or not",[92] and that both parents should automatically have parental responsibility.[93] The Commission rightly questions a law under which a man who abandons his pregnant wife and never sees his child has full parental responsibility, whereas a man who has cohabited with the mother of his child and played a full paternal role has none.

---

87 See above, p. 157.
88 British Nationality Act 1981, s.50(9)(*b*).
89 See Law Com. No. 118, para. 11.9.
90 See above, p. 116.
91 A distinction which has been argued as falling short of what is required under the European Convention on Human Rights: see Bainham, "When is a Parent not a Parent? Reflections on the Unmarried Father and his child in English Law" (1989) 3 I.J.L.F. 208 at 211. Compare the views of Deech, "The unmarried father and human rights" (1992) 4 J.C.L. 3.
92 Scot. Law Com. No. 135, para. 17.4.
93 *Ibid*. paras. 2.36-2.50.

CHAPTER 6

VIOLENCE

It is recognised that domestic violence[1] is not limited to married partners
and that: " . . . a battered wife is a woman who has suffered serious or
repeated physical injury from the man with whom she lives."[2]

The findings of the House of Commons Select Committee on Violence
in Marriage, along with those of the earlier Finer Report on One-Parent
Families,[3] did much to highlight the plight of victims of family violence.
The law cannot prevent people from battering their family partners but it
can help the victim of family violence and legislation has been implemented to this end. Until the Domestic Violence and Matrimonial
Proceedings Act 1976 (the Act) a battered cohabitee was at a particular
disadvantage compared with a battered spouse in being limited to the
spouse's additional remedy of proceedings in tort.[4] Her real need,
however, was for immediate protection, not only for herself but for her
children; hence the need for safe accommodation. Yet the courts had no
power to order a man out of a house of which he was the owner or tenant.
The 1976 Act changed that and is of particular importance to cohabitees
as they cannot avail themselves of the additional protection offered to
spouses by matrimonial legislation.

I. DOMESTIC VIOLENCE AND MATRIMONIAL
PROCEEDINGS ACT 1976

The law

The Act made an injunction a remedy by itself[5] and thus easier to
obtain. It ceased to be necessary for a cohabitee to sue in tort and seek an

---

1 For meaning, see below, p. 162.
2 *Per* Royal College of Psychiatrists: see Report from the Select Committee on Violence
in Marriage (1974-75; H.C. 553), Vols. I and II; Second Report (1976-77; H.C. 431).
3 Report of the Committee on One-Parent Families, Cmnd. 5629 (1974).
4 See below, p. 174.
5 s.1(1).

injunction ancillary to those proceedings.[6] The appropriate court is the County Court.[7] It can make any one or more of the orders in section 1(1).

Orders and applicants

An injunction under the Act can take one of two forms: first, a non-molestation injunction which restrains the other party from molesting the applicant and/or a child living with the applicant; secondly, an exclusion (or ouster) injunction which excludes the other party from the matrimonial home, or a part of it, or from a specified area in which the home is included and/or which requires him to permit the applicant to enter and remain in the matrimonial home or a part of it.[8] The Act applies equally to a man or a woman. The examples given will have the woman as the applicant for in the majority of cases the man is the violent partner, although cases of husband battering are not unknown.[9]

As proceedings under the Act are family proceedings under the Children Act 1989[10] the court may make orders under section 8 of the 1989 Act,[11] for example, relating to residence and/or contact and if it appears to the court that it may be appropriate to make a care or supervision order it may direct the local authority to investigate the child's circumstances.[12]

Section 1(1) applies: "to a man and a woman who are living with each other in the same household as husband and wife as it applies to the parties to a marriage and any reference to the matrimonial home shall be construed accordingly."[13] Although the Act refers to parties who are living with each other the courts have not taken the literal interpretation and have applied the Act provided that the cohabitation existed until the events which led to the application being made.[14] This interpretation seems correct, otherwise much of the good of the Act would have been undone. Except in these circumstances, however, the Act will not apply once there has been a break in the relationship,[15] notwithstanding that the need for protection is often greater in such cases.[16]

---

6 This remedy remains an alternative and, depending upon the nature of the cohabitation, may still have to be relied upon: see below, p. 173.
7 See below, p. 170.
8 See s.1(1). An order under s.1(1)(c) will often be made in conjunction with an order under s.1(1)(d). An injunction should not be granted if the defendant is incapable of understanding the proceedings and the nature and requirements of the order sought: see *Wookey* v. *Wookey* [1991] Fam. 121.
9 See Bates, "A Plea For the Battered Husband" (1981) 11 Fam. Law 90.
10 s.8(3).
11 See s.10, above, p. 24.
12 s.37.
13 s.1(2).
14 See *B.* v. *B.* [1978] Fam. 26; *Davis* v. *Johnson* [1979] A.C. 264; *McLean* v. *Nugent* (1980) 1 F.L.R. 24; *McLean* v. *Burke* (1982) 3 F.L.R. 70; *Rowland* v. *Dyer* (1984) 134 N.L.J. 631; *O'Neill* v. *Williams* [1984] F.L.R. 1.
15 In which event the applicant will have to rely on the pre-Act remedies: see below, p. 173.
16 See *Pidduck* v. *Molloy* [1992] 2 F.L.R. 202 at 206.

Not only must the parties be living with each other but they must also being doing so "in the same household as husband and wife", provided, it seems, that the applicant does not intend to continue to cohabit with the respondent.[17] By using the analogy with the husband and wife relationship, the Act limits its application to those who are cohabiting on a stable basis. The Act has been inaccurately described as protecting battered mistresses. The need for a stable relationship was stressed by Lord Kilbrandon in *Davis* v. *Johnson*[18]:

> "It is unfortunate that [the Act] has been described, in popular language, as an attempt to protect 'battered mistresses'. The English language is poor in this context. 'Mistress', having lost its respectable if not reverential significance, came to mean a woman installed, in a clandestine way, by someone of substance, normally married, for his intermittent sexual enjoyment. This class of woman, if indeed she still exists, is not dealt with by the Act of 1976 at all. The subsection was included for the protection of families — households in which a man and a woman either do or do not bring up children —, the man and the woman being, for whatever reason, unmarried . . . I do not know a single English word which will accurately describe the unmarried housewife, but that is what Parliament is talking about."

It follows that parties to a family cohabitation, for example, brother and sister living together, do not receive the protection of the Act; neither do those who share accommodation for reasons of companionship but not as husband and wife. A former spouse is not protected as a "party to the marriage" but if after a decree absolute former spouses live together in the same household as husband and wife they qualify in the same way as others who cohabit as man and wife.[19] Otherwise they must seek protection by way of ancillary remedy if circumstances so warrant.[20]

The Act does not specify whether a party to a marriage includes a party to a void marriage. It is suggested that in line with the matrimonial legislation[21] and the concept of the putative marriage,[22] parties to a void marriage are protected. If they are not included as parties to a marriage but are living together as husband and wife they will qualify in the same way as parties who cohabit as husband and wife, except perhaps if the marriage is void on the ground that the parties are not respectively male

---

17 See *F.* v. *F. (Protection from Violence: Continuing Cohabitation)* [1989] 2 F.L.R. 451, decided at York County Court, but *quaere* whether it is right to deny protection from molestation where the relationship is to continue, particularly as the denial is not required by the legislation.

18 [1979] A.C. 264 at 338.

19 *White* v. *White* [1983] Ch. 54.

20 See below, p. 173 and *M.* v. *M. (Custody Application)* [1988] 1 F.L.R. 225; *Lucas* v. *Lucas* [1992] 2 F.L.R. 53.

21 Matrimonial Causes Act 1973, s.52(3); Domestic Proceedings and Magistrates' Courts Act 1978, s.88(3).

22 See above, p. 8.

and female,[23] for as such they will not be living as husband and wife. The reference in section 1(2) to a "man and a woman" excludes any application by a party to a homosexual cohabitation.

The fact that the parties are living under the same roof does not necessarily mean that they satisfy the requirement of living "in the same household as husband and wife".[24] The smaller the home, however, the more difficult it is for the parties to live in separate households. In *Adeoso* v. *Adeoso*[25] an unmarried couple lived as man and wife in a flat consisting of one bedroom, a sitting-room, a kitchen and a bathroom. Their relationship broke up. Mr. Adeoso slept in the sitting-room and Mrs. Adeoso slept in the bedroom. They kept their rooms locked. She stopped cooking for him or washing his clothes. They did not speak to one another and communicated by written notes. They continued to share the rent and the cost of electricity. Mrs. Adeoso applied to the court under the Act because of Mr. Adeoso's alleged violence. The Court of Appeal allowed Mrs. Adeoso's appeal against the judge's finding that he could not hear her application because the parties were not living together as husband and wife and hence the Act did not apply. The fact that they lived behind locked doors in separate rooms in a flat with only two rooms did not amount to living separately. Had the home been large enough to be divided into separate parts it would be different. The decision is in line with the spirit of the legislation, if not perhaps the letter. Had Mr. and Mrs. Adeoso been married and Mrs. Adeoso petitioning for divorce on the evidence of living apart the relevant case law[26] suggests that Mr. and Mrs. Adeoso would not have been "living with each other in the same household."[27]

It is only possible to seek an injunction against "the other party". If one partner should bring a new partner into the home, the former partner has no remedy under the Act against the newcomer. Similarly the Act cannot be used against friends or relatives of the other party. If a spouse, therefore, takes a mistress or lover and they cohabit in the matrimonial home, the Act gives no remedy to the other spouse against the mistress or lover. The Act is, however, without prejudice to the jurisdiction of the High Court,[28] to which an aggrieved spouse would have to apply and there are pre-Act examples of a wife being granted an injunction by the High Court ordering her husband's mistress out of the matrimonial home,[29] but such orders are not available under the Act.

Molestation The Act's title refers to "Domestic Violence" but its object is to give protection against molestation, a concept which the Act does

---

23 See Matrimonial Causes Act 1973, s.11(c); *Corbett* v. *Corbett* [1971] P. 83.
24 See *McLean* v. *Burke* (1982) 3 F.L.R. 70.
25 [1980] 1 W.L.R. 1535. See J.M.T., (1981) 97 L.Q.R. 196; Wright, "Living With Each Other In The Same Household As Husband And Wife" (1981) 11 Fam. Law 221.
26 *Fuller* v. *Fuller* [1973] 1 W.L.R. 730; *Mouncer* v. *Mouncer* [1972] 1 W.L.R. 321.
27 Matrimonial Causes Act 1973, s.2(6).
28 s.1(1).
29 *Adams* v. *Adams* (1965) 109 S.J. 899; *Pinckney* v. *Pinckney* [1966] 1 All E.R. 121; *Jones* v. *Jones* [1971] 1 W.L.R. 396.

not define but which "does not imply necessarily either violence or threats of violence. It applies to any conduct which can properly be regarded as such a degree of harrassment as to call for the intervention of the court"[30] provided also that the conduct includes an intent to cause distress or harm.[31] Violence is not therefore necessary, although the applicant's case will be that much stronger if there is evidence of violence and courts have shown a reluctance to grant a non-molestation injunction in the absence of violence.[32] Molestation includes injury to one's mental health and, it is submitted, the courts should be prepared to extend molestation to cases where there is a reasonable apprehension of injury to mental health. As molestation extends beyond violence, the County Court's jurisdiction under the Act is wider than that of the Magistrates' Court under the Domestic Proceedings and Magistrates' Courts Act 1978[33] when a spouse seeks a protection order, for that Act requires evidence of physical violence or a threat of it. The magistrates' jurisdiction is limited, however, to spouses although they are not precluded from relying on the wider powers of the County Court.[34] The 1978 Act did not, therefore, followed the lead of the 1976 Act even though it owed much to that Act. The exclusion of cohabitees from the 1978 Act has been attributed, first, to the problem of Magistrates' Courts having to distinguish between couples living in the same household as husband and wife and couples merely living in the same household and, secondly, to the Magistrates' Court not being the appropriate forum for determining long-term occupation of the home. The limitation is to be regretted as it denies cohabitees the quicker and cheaper magistrates' jurisdiction.

Protection against molestation extends to any child who is living with the applicant. The only restriction is that the child must be living with the applicant. A child living with the other party is unprotected. There is no requirement that the child be a child of the applicant or of the other party, so, for example, a foster child will be protected. The definition is thus wider than that of a "child of the family" in matrimonial legislation.[35] The Act does not define "living with" but it is submitted that it ought not to be restrictively interpreted and so, for example, absence of the child at hospital or boarding school or any other temporary absence should be disregarded. The Act is silent also on the meaning of child; whether, for example, it means offspring so as to include an adult child in need of protection or whether it is limited by age, for example, to a minor child. The former, it is suggested, is the better interpretation as the important issue is the need for protection not the age of the child.

---

30 *Per* Ormrod L.J. in *Horner* v. *Horner* [1982] Fam. 90 at 93.
31 See *Johnson* v. *Walton* [1990] 1 F.L.R. 350 (sending photographs to the press with the intention of causing distress). See also *Vaughan* v. *Vaughan* [1973] 1 W.L.R. 1159 (where a husband pestered his wife).
32 See Edwards and Halpern, "Protection for the victim of domestic violence: Time for radical revision?" [1991] J.S.W.F.L. 94.
33 s.16(2).
34 *Horner* v. *Horner* [1982] Fam. 90.
35 See below, p. 203.

Exclusion The most significant provision is that enabling a court to exclude a cohabitee from the "matrimonial home", a term which includes a house in which a man and a woman are living with each other as husband and wife.[36] The Act applies, therefore, only to a household in which the parties are living (or in certain circumstances have lived)[37] as husband and wife. So if one party to a cohabitation leaves the common home and sets up home elsewhere the new home is not covered. Likewise, if a spouse leaves the matrimonial home and cohabits with someone else in a new home, the other spouse will have no action over the new home as it cannot constitute the matrimonial home. If the leaving spouse wishes to protect the interests of himself and his cohabitee in the new home against the other spouse, he also cannot use the Act and will have to have recourse to the High Court.[38] The absence of a definition of the matrimonial home raises the issue of whether the parties' occupancy is sufficient to constitute a matrimonial home, as, for example, where they are living with relatives. As the Act protects personal rather than proprietary rights, however, it ought to apply in such contexts.

It was settled by the House of Lords in *Davis* v. *Johnson*[39] that the court's powers under the Act to make orders in respect of the home are irrespective of property rights. So, a battered cohabitee with no property rights in the home can apply for an injunction to exclude his or her partner, even if the party against whom the order is sought is the sole owner or sole tenant of the home. A cohabitee now has similar rights to those of a spouse to expel a violent partner, albeit that the former's right solely arises out of the Act, whereas the latter enjoys that right by reason of the marriage, as well as the rights conferred by the Act. This seems correct. The spouse's additional rights arise out of the marriage relationship, a relationship which the cohabitee has not entered into. So a wife has the benefit of the Matrimonial Homes Act 1983 and, if there are matrimonial proceedings, the matrimonial causes legislation. An exclusion injunction granted under the 1976 Act does not affect the legal rights of ownership to the home but only the enjoyment of those rights. It gives a right of occupation. Referring to section 1, Lord Scarman in *Davis* v. *Johnson* said[40]:

> " . . . the purpose of the section is not to create rights but to strengthen remedies. Subsection (2) does, however, confer upon the unmarried woman with no property in the home a new right. Though enjoying no property right to possession of the family home, she can apply to the County Court for an order restricting or

---

36 s.1(2).
37 See above, p. 160.
38 For the situation envisaged, see *Nanda* v. *Nanda* [1968] P. 351.
39 [1979] A.C. 264, overruling the Court of Appeal decisions in *B.* v. *B.* [1978] Fam. 26 and *Cantliff* v. *Jenkins* [1978] Q.B. 47.
40 [1979] A.C. 264 at 349.

suspending for a time her family partner's right to possession of the premises and conferring upon her a limited right of occupancy."

As the applicant acquires no property rights but only a limited personal right, there seems nothing to prevent the respondent, if he is the sole owner or sole tenant, from selling, letting or assigning the property,[41] unless the applicant has any independent property rights,[41] but to do so would take some time and as Lord Salmon said in *Davis* v. *Johnson*[42] it:

> " . . . would accordingly prevent the former mistress [sic] from being thrown out without giving her any breathing space in which to look for suitable accommodation. And this, I believe, is the major object which the Act sought to achieve—first aid but not intensive care for 'battered wives'".

So the right of occupation given to the unmarried woman is not as extensive as that already enjoyed by a wife under the Matrimonial Homes Act 1983. Under that Act a wife can register her right of occupation which is protected even against third parties.[43]

The owner or tenant cohabitee wishing to dispose of the home would be faced with the practical difficulty of being unable to give vacant possession and whilst the injunction is in operation he would be unable to obtain an order for possession of the premises. If the owner or tenant did sell, let or assign to a third party despite the existence of the injunction, the third party could presumably obtain an order for possession, as the injunction does not bind third parties. On the expiration of the injunction, the owner or tenant cohabitee could obtain an order for possession in the absence of the other party's having an independent property right.

If the respondent is a sole tenant it is open to him to surrender the tenancy thereby entitling the landlord to possession. Any attempt to relet to the respondent, however, would be likely to put the respondent in breach of the terms of the injunction. The applicant's position is precarious even if the respondent as sole tenant leaves without surrendering his tenancy. The Act is silent as to the effect of the injunction on the respondent's tenancy.[44] It ought to continue so that the applicant retains the protection of the injunction. If it does there is the issue of liability for outgoings. Arguably the respondent remains liable for his obligations to the landlord although this is by no means certain in view of the lack of any duty between cohabitees to provide a home. If the respondent refuses to pay the rent the landlord is under no duty to accept it from the applicant.[45]

---

41 See above, p. 19.
42 [1979] A.C. 264 at 343.
43 See above, p. 52.
44 See Martin, "Domestic Violence and the Rent Acts" (1978) 128 N.L.J. 154; Sherrin, "Domestic Violence and Property Rights" (1978) 8 Fam. Law 176.
45 See above, p. 61.

In the case of a public sector tenancy, then, prior to the Housing Act 1980, the courts were prepared to take on the role of housing authority.[46] As that Act granted security of tenure to council tenants the courts have lost the power to adjudicate in this way, although they on occasions have shown a preparedness to do so.[47]

There is also the problem of the contents of the home. Orders relate to the home, not its contents. So, for example, when Miss Davis returned to the home which Mr. Johnson had been ordered to vacate, she was greeted by bare floorboards. Whilst it can be argued that the duty on a husband to house his wife extends to the provision of basic household necessities, there is no duty to house a cohabitee.

Principles applicable to the grant of an injunction

The Act's main failing is its silence on the criteria which have to be satisfied before an injunction is granted.

Molestation To obtain a non-molestation injunction there must be evidence of molestation[48] against the applicant or a child living with the applicant and the order must be necessary for the protection of the person on whose behalf it is sought.[49]

Exclusion An exclusion injunction will not be granted as easily as a non-molestation injunction in view of its extreme nature.[50] In considering whether or not to grant an exclusion injunction the Court of Appeal in *Spindlow* v. *Spindlow*[51] held that for the purposes of the Act unmarried couples are to be treated in the same way as married couples. Since the House of Lords' decision in *Richards* v. *Richards*[52] the criteria for the grant of an exclusion injunction in a dispute between spouses are laid down in section 1(3) of the Matrimonial Homes Act 1983, whether the application has been made under that Act or the 1976 Act. Consistent with the earlier decision in *Spindlow* the Court of Appeal in *Lee* v. *Lee*[53] held that on an application for an exclusion order under the 1976 Act the principles in section 1(3) of the 1983 Act apply equally whether the parties are married or unmarried.

Section 1(3) of the 1983 Act provides that:

> "the court may make such order as it thinks just and reasonable having regard to the conduct of the spouses in relation to each other

---

46 See *Spindlow* v. *Spindlow* [1979] Fam. 52. For the position after the Housing Act 1980, see above, p. 61; *Wiseman* v. *Simpson* [1988] 1 All E.R. 245 at 251, *per* Ralph Gibson L.J. and Williams, "Ouster Orders, Property Adjustment and Council Housing" [1988] Fam. Law 438.

47 See *Fairweather* v. *Kolosine* (1986) 11 H.L.R. 61.

48 For meaning, see above, p. 162.

49 *Spindlow* v. *Spindlow* [1979] Fam. 52.

50 See *Tuck* v. *Nicholls* [1989] 1 F.L.R. 283 at 286.

51 [1979] Fam. 52. See also *McLean* v. *Burke* (1982) 3 F.L.R. 70.

52 [1984] A.C. 174.

53 [1984] F.L.R. 243. See also *Thurley* v. *Smith* [1984] F.L.R. 875; *Wiseman* v. *Simpson* [1988] 1 All E.R. 245; *Grant* v. *James* [1993] 1 F.C.R. 850.

and otherwise, to their respective needs and financial resources, to the needs of any children and all the circumstances of the case . . . "

None of these matters is to be treated as prevailing over any other and the weight to be given to any particular matter depends upon the facts of each case.[54] The principle of paramountcy of the child's welfare[55] was held in *Richards* to have no application to exclusion proceedings because the upbringing of a child was not directly in issue. It is still open to the court, however, in deciding the weight to be given to the particular facts in the light of section 1(3), to find, as in *Lee* v. *Lee*, that the needs of the children to be re-established in the family home should carry the greatest weight.

In considering the conduct of the parties it is not essential for the applicant to prove violence on the part of the respondent but the court will look for conduct which goes beyond unpleasantness or inconvenience. Thus in *Wiseman* v. *Simpson*[56] the cohabiting parties quarrelled a great deal but there was no violence and they agreed it was not practical for them to live together under the same roof. The judge ordered the man to leave the council flat of which the parties were joint tenants because the needs of the woman, who was looking after their young son, were greater than the man's, because he was working and had accommodation at his parents' house. The Court of Appeal held that the judge was not entitled to make the order merely because one party's case is stronger than the other. The case must also be such that in all the circumstances and in the light of section 1(3) of the Matrimonial Homes Act 1983 the applicant has proved that it is just and reasonable to make an ouster order, bearing in mind its purpose and drastic nature. The latter is seen by the courts as being of particular importance[57] and hence an exclusion injunction should rarely be granted on affidavit evidence alone.[58] In practice conduct is a major consideration.[59]

When considering the parties' needs one factor is the duty of local authorities to house the homeless. Where a battered cohabitee, particularly if she has a child, will spend an indefinite time in unsatisfactory

---

54 *Gibson* v. *Austin* [1992] 2 F.L.R. 437.
55 Children Act 1989, s.1(1), formerly s. 1 of the Guardianship of Minors Act 1971: see above, p. 125 and *Gibson* v. *Austin* [1992] 2 F.L.R. 437, where the Court of Appeal held that *Richards* had not been overruled by the Children Act 1989.
56 [1988] 1 All E.R. 245, applying *Summers* v. *Summers* [1986] 1 F.L.R. 343. *Spindlow* v. *Spindlow* [1979] Fam. 52 was regarded as no longer good law regarding the matters relevant to the making of an exclusion order, but still relevant in that proof of violence is not necessary. See also *Scott* v. *Scott* [1992] 1 F.L.R. 529; *Grant* v. *James* [1993] 1 F.C.R. 850.
57 See, *e.g. Summers* v. *Summers* [1986] 1 F.L.R. 343; *Grant* v. *James* [1993] 1 F.C.R. 850.
58 See *Shipp* v. *Shipp* [1988] 1 F.L.R. 345; *Whitlock* v. *Whitlock* [1989] 1 F.L.R. 208; *Tuck* v. *Nicholls* [1989] 1 F.L.R. 283.
59 See *Blackstock* v. *Blackstock* [1991] 2 F.L.R. 308.

accommodation it is unlikely to avail the respondent that if an exclusion order is made he will not qualify for rehousing.[60]

Duration of an injunction

The Act makes no provision regarding the duration of an injunction which is at the discretion of the court. A non-molestation injunction is frequently of indefinite duration, leaving the respondent to seek its discharge.

An exclusion injunction, however, is seen as a form of temporary and not permanent relief[61] although there have been cases where the injunction was of a permanent nature.[62] This temporary relief is to enable the applicant cohabitee to find other accommodation and in appropriate cases resolve any dispute regarding her proprietary interest in the home.[63] In view of the temporary nature of an exclusion injunction, it is wrong to delay implementation of an order (other than for a short time for the respondent to find alternative accommodation) pending determination of rights of occupation in the house.[64] A *Practice Direction*[65] states that consideration should be given to imposing a time limit, and that in most cases a period of up to three months will be sufficient, at least to start with.[66] The respondent can, of course, apply within that period for a discharge of the injunction, for example, if the parties are reconciled. Likewise the applicant can apply for an extension. There may be circumstances where it is appropriate for the court to grant the injunction until further order, for example, where the applicant has had to return to the court because of the respondent's continued behaviour.[67] The onus is on the respondent to apply to have the order discharged. The applicant's marital status will be a consideration for, in the case of cohabitees, the court is entitled to take into account the fact that the applicant's only remedy is likely to be under the Act.[68]

Power of arrest

Section 2 of the Act enables a judge to attach a power of arrest to the injunction if:

---

60 See *Thurley* v. *Smith* [1984] F.L.R. 875, applying the principle established in the pre-*Richards* case of *Wooton* v. *Wooton* [1984] F.L.R. 871.
61 *Hopper* v. *Hopper* [1978] 1 W.L.R. 1342; *Freeman* v. *Collins* (1983) 4 F.L.R. 649; *O'Neill* v. *Williams* [1984] F.L.R. 1.
62 Both before the Housing Act 1980 (see, *e.g. Spindlow* v. *Spindlow* [1979] Fam. 52) and since: see, *e.g. Fairweather* v. *Kolosine* (1984) 11 H.L.R. 61, where an exclusion injunction was made against a cohabitee for five years, applying *Spindlow* and stressing the welfare of the children. *Quaere* whether the decision is now consistent with *Richards* v. *Richards* [1984] A.C. 174; see *Wiseman* v. *Simpson* [1988] 1 All E.R. 245. The court may be more prepared to make a permanent order where the excluded party is a joint owner/tenant rather than a sole owner/tenant.
63 *e.g.* under the Law of Property Act 1925, s.30: see above, p. 45.
64 See *Chadda* v. *Chadda* (1981) 11 Fam. Law 142; *Burke* v. *Burke* [1987] 2 F.L.R. 71; *Dunsire* v. *Dunsire* [1991] 2 F.L.R. 314; *Grant* v. *James* [1993] 1 F.C.R. 850.
65 [1978] 1 W.L.R. 1123.
66 See, *e.g. Thurley* v. *Smith* [1984] F.L.R. 875.
67 See *Spencer* v. *Camacho* (1983) 4 F.L.R. 662; *Galan* v. *Galan* [1985] F.L.R. 905.
68 *Spencer* v. *Camacho* (1983) 4 F.L.R. 662.

(1) the injunction contains a provision restraining the other party from using violence against the applicant, or a child living with the applicant or contains an exclusion order; and

(2) the judge is satisfied that the other party has caused actual bodily harm to the applicant or the child concerned; and

(3) the judge considers that he is likely to do so again.

All three conditions must be satisfied[69]; hence a power of arrest cannot be attached to an undertaking. The provisions apply to a man and a woman living together in the same household as husband and wife.[70] If the injunction is a non-molestation injunction, it must restrain the other party from using violence. If it is not so qualified, the judge cannot attach a power of arrest. There is no such qualification if the injunction is an exclusion injunction. A power of arrest is only available against the other party. If the injunction relates to a child, he must be living with the applicant. Actual bodily harm has been widely defined to include "any hurt or injury calculated to interfere with the health and comfort" of another,[71] and includes psychological harm provided that there is a real change in the psychological condition of the person assaulted.[72]

The judge has a discretion whether or not to attach a power of arrest and the Court of Appeal in *Lewis* v. *Lewis*[73] stressed that a power of arrest is not to be regarded as a routine remedy but is designed for exceptional cases where, for example, there are persistent breaches of an injunction. The Court also stressed the need for giving notice to the other party that a power of arrest is being sought. It felt that the respondent might submit to the injunction but would want strenuously to oppose the attachment of a power of arrest. The need for giving notice is in line with the general rule that when the court is granting and enforcing injunctions in matrimonial proceedings, it should only act *ex parte* in an emergency, when the interests of justice or the protection of the applicant or a child clearly demand immediate intervention by the court.[74] Even if the case is an appropriate one for attaching a power of arrest *ex parte*, the power should be limited to the period required to arrange a preliminary hearing *inter partes* which would normally be a matter of days. It is therefore unjustifiable and improper to make an injunction *ex parte* "until further order".[75]

As the power of arrest is regarded as an exceptional remedy, particular regard is paid to the lapse of time since the last act of violence and the likelihood of a repetition.[76] If a power of arrest is attached then, unless the judge is satisfied that a longer period is necessary, it should not

---

69 See, *e.g. McLaren* v. *McLaren* (1980) 1 F.L.R. 85.

70 s.2(2).

71 See *R.* v. *Miller* [1954] 2 Q.B. 282.

72 *Kendrick* v. *Kendrick* [1990] 2 F.L.R. 107.

73 [1978] Fam. 60. See also *Harrison* v. *Lewis*; *R.* v. *S.* [1988] 2 F.L.R. 339, below, p. 171.

74 See *Ansah* v. *Ansah* [1977] Fam. 138.

75 See *Ansah* v. *Ansah* [1977] Fam. 138; *Morgan* v. *Morgan* (1979) 9 Fam. Law 87.

76 *Horner* v. *Horner* [1982] Fam. 90.

normally exceed three months' duration.[77] The applicant may apply for an extension if she reasonably apprehends danger.

The effect of the power of arrest is that a constable may arrest, without a warrant, a person whom he has reasonable cause for suspecting of being in breach of the injunction by reason of the use of violence or entry into the home or area.[78] Anyone so arrested must be brought before a judge within 24 hours from the time of arrest (not counting Christmas Day, Good Friday or any Sunday). During that time, but no longer, the person arrested will be kept in custody, unless a judge has directed that he be released.[79] The police are also under a duty to seek the directions of the court as to the time and place at which that person is to be brought before a judge.[80]

Undertaking

As an alternative to the grant of an injunction, the respondent may be required to give an undertaking, which does not involve any finding of fact and cannot be replaced by an injunction.[81] Enforcement is less strict than in the case of a court order,[82] and no power of arrest may be attached,[83] hence an undertaking is a less effective form of protection in more serious cases where further harm may be anticipated. The relative informality of an undertaking can work to the disadvantage of those it is intended to protect.

Procedure

There is not scope in this book to provide more than a framework of the procedure. Notwithstanding that the Rules[84] provide for applications to the High Court, the appropriate court will usually be the County Court. The procedure is that applicable generally to an application for an injunction,[85] which must be made by originating application to the court for the district in which either the applicant or the respondent lives or where the matrimonial home is situated.[86] It may be necessary also to apply for leave to omit the applicant's address. The application should be supported by an affidavit giving a brief history of the cohabitation

---

77 *Practice Note* [1981] 1 W.L.R. 27.
78 s.2(3). For the procedure following arrest, see *Practice Direction* [1991] 2 All E.R. 9; *Roberts* v. *Roberts* [1991] 1 F.L.R. 294 and below, p. 171.
79 s.2(4) (as amended).
80 s.2(5).
81 *Carpenter* v. *Carpenter* [1988] 1 F.L.R. 121.
82 See below, p. 171.
83 *Carpenter* v. *Carpenter* [1988] 1 F.L.R. 121.
84 Family Proceedings Rules 1991, r. 3.9(2). See also *Crutcher* v. *Crutcher, The Times,* July 18, 1978, where it was held that the Act has not enlarged the High Court's jurisdiction and hence the applicant must seek substantive relief. Application in the High Court is by originating summons and the procedure to be followed is comparable with that applicable in the County Court.
85 C.C.R. 1981, Ord. 13, r. 6.
86 F.P.R. 1991, r. 3.9(2) and see below, p. 171.

together with details of any children and particularising the allegations which form the basis of the application. If the application relates to an exclusion order, the affidavit should give details of ownership and occupation of the home together with the considerations relevant to the operation of the Matrimonial Homes Act 1983, s. 1(3).[87]

The originating application must be filed together with the affidavit, a draft injunction, copy notice of legal aid certificate[88] if appropriate, a notice of acting and the court fee. Duplicate copies of the originating process must be filed for personal service on the respondent by the applicant,[89] giving at least two clear days' notice of the hearing of the application, unless the court orders otherwise.[90] The hearing will be in chambers unless the judge otherwise directs.[91]

An *ex parte* application should only be made in an emergency, when the interests of justice or the protection of the applicant or a child clearly demand immediate intervention by the court.[92] The application is made on affidavit stating the terms of the injunction sought and explaining why the application is being made *ex parte*.[93] An *ex parte* injunction must be limited in time to the shortest period necessary to arrange a preliminary hearing *inter partes* and should specify the date on which it expires. The courts limit *ex parte* injunctions to extreme cases where there is real immediate danger of serious injury or irreparable harm,[94] and rarely grant them if the injunction sought is one to exclude the respondent from the home[95] or where a power of arrest is sought.[96]

Enforcement of an injunction

Enforcement depends upon whether or not a power of arrest is attached to the injunction.

Where a power of arrest is attached, breach of the injunction is itself a ground for arrest and hence protection of the applicant is not dependent upon either commission of a criminal offence or the ordinary committal procedure. A copy of the relevant provisions of the injunction must be delivered to the officer in charge of any police station covering the applicant's address.[97] The burden placed on the police in holding the

---

87 See above, p. 166.
88 The parties' resources will not be aggregated: see above, p. 94.
89 It is advisable to prove service by filing an affidavit of service in case the judge requires proof that the respondent has actual knowledge of the application.
90 F.P.R. 1991, r. 3.9(5).
91 r. 3.9(2).
92 *Practice Direction* [1978] 1 W.L.R. 925; *Ansah* v. *Ansah* [1977] Fam. 138; *Masich* v. *Masich* (1977) 7 Fam. Law 245.
93 C.C.R. 1981, Ord. 13, r. 6(3), (3A).
94 *G.* v. *G.(Ouster: Ex Parte Application)* [1990] 1 F.L.R. 395.
95 *Masich* v. *Masich* (1977) 7 Fam. Law 245. See also *Benesch* v. *Newman* [1987] 1 F.L.R. 262.
96 *Lewis* v. *Lewis* [1978] Fam. 60. See also *Benesch* v. *Newman* [1987] 1 F.L.R. 262; *Harrison* v. *Lewis*; *R* v. *S* [1988] 2 F.L.R. 339.
97 F.P.R. 1991, r. 3.9(6). It is advisable for the police force's criminal records office to be informed in view of the mobility of battered women, a problem which could be alleviated by some form of centralised registry open for use by any police force.

thousands of orders containing a power of arrest is recognised by a *Practice Note*,[98] aimed at enabling the police to concentrate on those cases where action may be required, which indicates that the power of arrest should not normally exceed three months' duration.

Where a power of arrest is not attached to an injunction, the applicant may apply at a later date for this to be done; otherwise enforcement of the injunction will be by committal.

The committal procedure[99] usually requires that the respondent has been served personally with a copy of the injunction endorsed with a penal notice as to the consequences of non-compliance. The injunction may be enforced by committal notwithstanding the absence of personal service if the judge is satisfied that pending such service the respondent has notice by being present when the injunction was made or by being notified of its terms.[1]

The procedural requirements for enforcement are not as strict in the case of an undertaking as in the case of an order because the rules have no direct application to undertakings[2] and failure to comply is a breach of the undertaking and not the order. It has been said, however, that an undertaking has all the force of an injunction.[3]

Contempt proceedings should be dealt with swiftly. The fact that criminal proceedings are pending against the respondent arising out of the same incident need not preclude the hearing of the committal application,[4] and the matter is within the judge's discretion.[5]

If the judge is satisfied he will make an order for committal which must be drawn in clear and unambiguous terms in the prescribed form if the applicant is to receive the protection of the order. Failure to adhere meticulously to the required formalities may invalidate the order[6] but the court has a discretion to remedy an irregularity[7] which is fettered only by the need to do justice.[8] This discretion is to be welcomed, for where a breach sufficient to justify committal has been proved it is unfortunate if the applicant's protection should be defeated by minor procedural irregularities. Even with serious social problems of violence, however, it is apparent that the strict procedural rules should be followed to ensure that a right is not to be without a remedy.[9]

---

98 [1981] 1 W.L.R. 27.
99 See C.C.R. 1981, Ord. 29, r. 1; R.S.C., Ords. 45 and 52.
  1 C.C.R. 1981, Ord. 29, r. 1(6), (7); R.S.C., Ord. 45, r. 7(6), (7). The wider discretion in para. (7) applies at the stage at which the order is being made and the narrower one in para. (6) at the stage at which it is being enforced: see *Hussain* v. *Hussain* [1986] 1 All E.R. 961; *Lewis* v. *Lewis* [1991] 3 All E.R. 251.
  2 *Hussain* v. *Hussain* [1986] 1 All E.R. 961.
  3 *Per* Butler-Sloss L.J. in *Roberts* v. *Roberts* [1990] 2 F.L.R. 111 at 113.
  4 *Szczepanski* v. *Szczepanski* [1985] F.L.R. 468; *Caprice* v. *Boswell* [1986] Fam. Law 52; *R* v. *Green* [1993] Crim.L.R. 46.
  5 *H.* v. *C.* [1993] 1 F.C.R. 1.
  6 See, *e.g. Tabone* v. *Seguna* [1986] 1 F.L.R. 591.
  7 *Nguyen* v. *Phung* [1984] F.L.R. 773; *Burrows* v. *Iqbal* [1984] F.L.R. 844; *Linnett* v. *Coles* [1986] 3 All E.R. 652; *Wright* v. *Jess* [1987] 1 W.L.R. 1076.
  8 *M.* v. *P.(Contempt: Committal); Butler* v. *Butler* [1992] 4 All E.R. 833.
  9 See, *e.g. Clarke* v. *Clarke* [1990] 2 F.L.R. 115.

The courts consider that the real purpose of the committal procedure is to bring the matter back to the court to secure compliance with the order in the future. Whether a committal order is justified or not depends upon the circumstances of the particular case.[10] Where the contempt is sufficiently serious to warrant imprisonment the court has a discretion to imprison for such a fixed period, not exceeding two years,[11] as is necessary for the respondent to purge his contempt. There is a reluctance to commit for more than a short while, and the period is usually about a month. Each case will depend, however, upon its own facts,[12] so, for example, in *Re H.(A Minor) (Injunction Breach)*[13] the defendant's sentence of nine months' imprisonment for a serious breach of an order restraining him from molesting his former cohabitee was reduced by the Court of Appeal to three months in view of his apology to the court and the fact that it was the first time he had breached the order.[14] On release the injunction remains in force.

2. OTHER REMEDIES

In most cases the appropriate course of action for the cohabitee who is the victim of domestic violence will be to seek an injunction under the 1976 Act. That may not always be possible, for example, if the relationship is not of sufficient stability to satisfy the requirement that the couple be living together as husband and wife, or if the couple were living together as husband and wife but are doing so no longer, or if it is a family cohabitation, or a homosexual cohabitation.

Ancillary remedy

The High Court has a general jurisdiction to grant an injunction where it appears just and convenient to do so on such terms and conditions as the court thinks just.[15] In order to minimise costs and delay the appropriate court will usually be the County Court which can grant an injunction in the same way as the High Court.[16] Such an injunction is not a remedy in itself and can only be granted in support of a legal or equitable right,[17]

---

10 *Jones* v. *Jones* [1993] 2 F.C.R. 82. See also *Smith* v. *Smith* [1988] 1 F.L.R. 179.
11 Contempt of Court Act 1981, s.14(1). For the purposes of punishing contempt the County Court is to be treated as a superior court: see County Courts (Penalties for Contempt) Act 1983, reversing *Peart* v. *Stewart* [1983] 2 A.C. 109.
12 For examples of the maximum sentence in a cases concerning cohabitees, see *Wright* v. *Jess* [1987] 1 W.L.R. 1076 and *Mesham* v. *Clarke* [1989] 1 F.L.R. 370. For a lengthy sentence see *Juby* v. *Miller* [1991] 1 F.L.R. 133.
13 [1986] 1 F.L.R. 558.
14 See also *Benesch* v. *Newman* [1987] 1 F.L.R. 262 (12 months' imprisonment for a proven single incident of contempt, namely an assault on a cohabitee respondent, reduced to 28 days on appeal).
15 Supreme Court Act 1981, s.37.
16 County Courts Act 1984, s.38 (as substituted).
17 *Richards* v. *Richards* [1984] A.C. 174.

for example, not to be assaulted.[18] As such it must arise out of a case pending before the court or about to be commenced. A cohabitee cannot use the protectionary powers of the divorce court, there being no marriage which a court can dissolve, so the spouse's remedy of an injunction ancillary to matrimonial causes is not available. Similarly a cohabitee cannot seek an exclusion injunction under the Matrimonial Homes Act 1983. A cohabitee's ancillary remedies are limited, depending upon the circumstances, to an action in tort, in respect of land, or relating to children.

Tort action and injunction

There remains the pre-1976 Act remedy of an action in tort[19] for damages for assault, battery, trespass or nuisance and claiming an injunction as an ancillary remedy,[20] restraining the cohabitee from molesting, assaulting or otherwise interfering with the applicant and the children. It is doubted whether an exclusion injunction can be obtained, save in an action in respect of land or to protect children. The chief object of a tort action is the obtaining of an injunction, for the amount of damages likely to be awarded in most cases will be small. Indeed it has been common practice, once the injunction has been granted, for the applicant to apply for the hearing of the claim for damages to be adjourned indefinitely and the County Court now has jurisdiction to grant an injunction which is not linked to damages.[21]

Although there is no tort of harassment or molestation as such,[22] an injunction can be obtained if the conduct[23] complained amounts to some other tort, in particular nuisance. The Court of Appeal in *Khorasandjian* v. *Bush*[24] reconsidered earlier decisions and widened the scope of the injunction in tort by holding that there is jurisdiction in nuisance to grant an injunction restraining persistent harassment by unwanted telephone calls, nothwithstanding that the parties are not married and have never cohabited, or that the recipient of the calls has no proprietary interest in the premises where the calls have been received. Moreover, the inconvenience and annoyance caused by such calls and the interference with the ordinary and reasonable use of the property are sufficient to constitute

---

18 *Egan* v. *Egan* [1975] Ch. 218.
19 The restriction in the Law Reform (Husband and Wife) Act 1962, s.1(2)(a), whereby inter-spousal tort actions may be stayed where it appears that no substantial benefit will accrue to either party from their continuation is not applicable to tort actions between cohabitees.
20 Such an injunction cannot be a remedy ancillary to a claim under the Inheritance (Provision for Family and Dependants) Act 1975: see *Andrew* v. *Andrew* [1990] 2 F.L.R. 376.
21 County Courts Act 1984, s.3 (as substituted).
22 *Patel* v. *Patel* [1988] 2 F.L.R. 179. See Fricker, "Molestation and Harassment after *Patel* v. *Patel*" [1988] Fam. Law 395: Bainham, (1989) 105 L.Q.R. 9.
23 For meaning of molestation, see above, p. 162 and Fricker, "Personal Molestation or Harassment" [1992] Fam. Law 158; Brazier, "Personal Injury by Molestation - An Emergent or Established Tort" [1992] Fam. Law 346.
24 [1993] 2 F.L.R. 66: see Murphy "The Emergence of Harassment as a Recognised Tort" (1993) 143 N.L.J. 926: Getney, (1993) 109 L.Q.R. 361.

damage which is a necessary element of the tort of nuisance. The Court, by a majority, took a wider view of telephone harassment than taken by the Court of Appeal in *Burnett* v. *George*[25] where it was held that if there is no matrimonial nexus and no children to protect, an injunction to restrain molestation and interference should only be granted if there is evidence that the health of the plaintiff is being impaired. In *Burnett* an order prohibiting the defendant "assaulting, molesting or otherwise interfering with the plaintiff" was qualified by the addition of the words "by doing acts calculated to cause her harm" whereas in *Khorasandjian* interference with the ordinary and reasonable enjoyment of property was seen as a sufficient infringement of a legal right. This division of judicial opinion warrants authoritative and general guidance from either the House of Lords or Parliament.

The procedure to be followed is that applicable generally to an application for an injunction[26] and enforcement is by proceedings for committal.[27] It has been seen that a useful alternative to committal is the power, under section 2 of the 1976 Act, to attach a power of arrest to an injunction. In *Lewis* v. *Lewis*[28] the Court of Appeal decided that section 2 was of general application and applies to any case where a judge, either in the High Court or in the County Court, grants an injunction in one or more of the forms set out in section 2(1). In that particular case the proceedings were divorce proceedings, but the same applies in an action for damages, for there seems no reason to limit the extension to matrimonial proceedings, provided, however, that the parties satisfy the requirement of being parties to a marriage or being a man and a woman living together as husband and wife.[29] In most cases the proviso will not be satisfied, for if it were the applicant would be applying under the 1976 Act.

Action relating to land and injunction

In those cases where the applicant has a property interest in the home and the respondent does not, she may bring an action for an injunction relating to land based on trespass or nuisance, if she can establish entry by the respondent as a trespasser.[30] The widening of the jurisdiction in private nuisance by the Court of Appeal in *Khorasandjian* v. *Bush*[31] irrespective of proprietary rights, has reduced even further the relevance of an action relating to land, save where an exclusion injunction is sought.

---

25 [1992] 1 F.L.R. 525.
26 See C.C.R. 1981, Ord. 13, r. 6 and above, p. 170; R.S.C., Ord. 28, r. 3.
27 See above, p. 172.
28 [1978] Fam. 60.
29 *Harrison* v. *Lewis*; *R* v. *S* [1988] 2 F.L.R. 339.
30 *Lucas* v. *Lucas* [1992] 2 F.L.R. 53.
31 See above, p. 174.

Action relating to children and injunction

It may be possible to obtain an injunction restraining molestation of a child and excluding a violent party from the family home ancillary to an order under the Children Act 1989.[32]

Whilst non-molestation injunctions could be granted under the guardianship legislation to protect a child, case law in relation to the granting of an exclusion injunction under the previous legislation[33] was inconsistent. In accordance with the general principle applicable to ancillary remedies the applicant had to establish a legal right requiring protection by an injunction. Thus in *Re W.*[34] the Court of Appeal upheld the applicant's claim, ancillary to an order for custody, for injunctions restraining the respondent from removing the child from her care and control, restraining the respondent from assaulting, molesting or otherwise interfering with her or the child and an order that the respondent vacate the flat and be restrained from entering or visiting it without leave of the court. The case raised, but did not resolve, a number of important issues,[35] in particular the degree of relationship between the injunctions and the order and the significance of the applicant being the sole tenant of the flat. The latter issue was considered by the Court of Appeal in *Ainsbury* v. *Millington*,[36] which had to consider also the effect of *Richards* v. *Richards*[37] upon such applications. In *Ainsbury* the parties had lived as husband and wife together with their child in a council house of which they were joint tenants. The cohabitation broke down on the respondent's being arrested for burglary. While he was in prison the applicant married another man who moved into the house. On the respondent's release from prison there was a row and the applicant and her husband together with the child went to live in overcrowded conditions. The applicant applied for custody of the child supported by a non-molestation injunction in her favour and an exclusion injunction. The Court of Appeal refused her application for an exclusion order because under the law relating to children the child's welfare is paramount, but following *Richards* the fact that the child's welfare is not paramount on an exclusion application indicates that such an application was inappropriate. The applicant had to show a legal right on which she could rely. As a joint tenant she had an equal right of occupation but not a right to the exclusion of the respondent.

If, as appears to be the case, the Court of Appeal in *Ainsbury* was saying that only if the applicant is the sole owner or sole tenant will she have the legal right on which she can rely to claim ancillary relief by way of an exclusion injunction under the guardianship legislation, then it

---

32 For protection offered directly by that Act see below, p. 177.
33 Guardianship of Minors Act 1971, which in terms of principles applicable to ancillary injunctions arguably remains applicable.
34 [1981] 3 All E.R. 401.
35 See Douglas, "Custody and Injunctions: A New Discovery?" (1982) 45 M.L.R. 468.
36 [1986] 1 All E.R. 73. An appeal to the House of Lords was dismissed without hearing arguments on the merits: see [1987] 1 W.L.R. 379.
37 [1984] A.C. 174: see above, p. 166.

makes an empty shell of the earlier decision in *Re W.* and the scope of such ancillary remedies. No doubt the result of *Ainsbury* was justified in that the application was not a genuine attempt to secure the protection of the child, but rather a device to exclude the former cohabitee. *Re W.*, however, was a genuine application to secure protection for the child. It is submitted that it was that issue alone which justified attaching an exclusion injunction to the custody order. The child's right to be protected ought to be a sufficient legal right, in the context of legislation relating to the upbringing of children, to justify, in appropriate circumstances, the grant to a residential parent of an exclusion injunction whether or not that parent has sole (or indeed joint) occupancy rights.

Ainsbury was followed in *M. v. M. (Custody Application)*[38] where the mother could not make out a proprietary right and the Court of Appeal held it had no jurisdiction to grant an exclusion order to protect the children by preventing their father from returning to the former matrimonial home. Yet in *Wilde* v. *Wilde*,[39] another case arising after dissolution of marriage, the Court of Appeal held that where children are involved the court has an inherent jurisdiction to intervene to protect their interests and has jurisdiction to to exclude one parent no matter what the proceedings, if that is in the children's interests. It is submitted that the *Wilde* interpretation is to be preferred and applies to proceedings under the Children Act 1989.

There is case law under the Children Act 1989 that the County Court does have jurisdiction to grant injunctions ancillary to proceedings under the Act, including an exclusion injunction.[40] There is no jurisdiction to attach a power of arrest to such an injunction save in the event of the applicant satisfying the criteria in section 2 of the Domestic Violence and Matrimonial Proceedings Act 1976.[41]

Proceedings relating to children

Children Act 1989

The new orders available to the courts, including the Magistrates' Courts, under the Children Act 1989 may be sufficiently wide to provide effective protection directly without the need to seek an injunction by way of an ancillary order. Whether or not this is so depends upon the nature and scope of the prohibited steps order. Such an order is one "that no step which could be taken by a parent in meeting his parental responsibility for a child, and which is of a kind specified in the order, shall be taken by any person without the consent of the court".[42] In *W.* v.

---

38 [1988] 1 F.L.R. 225: see also *P.* v. *P.* *(Ouster)* [1993] Fam. Law 283.
39 [1988] 2 F.L.R. 83, following *Quinn* v. *Quinn* (1983) 4 F.L.R. 394. *Re W; Ainsbury* and *M* v. *M* were not cited. See also *Hennie* v. *Hennie* [1993] 1 F.C.R. 886.
40 See *M.* v. *M.(Ouster: Children Act)* [1992] Fam. Law 504; King and Roberts, "Protection from violence: using the Children Act 1989" (January 1992) *Legal Action* 21. See also *S.* v. *C.* (March 1992) *Legal Action* 18.
41 See above, p. 175.
42 Children Act 1989, s.8(1): see above, p. 130.

Hertfordshire County Council,[43] the Magistrates' Family Proceedings Court appears to have given the scope of the order a broad interpretation and made one prohibiting the mother from allowing her cohabitee, or former cohabitee, who she said had caused injury to her child, into her house. The legality of such an order is open to question, however, because the Children Act 1989[44] prohibits the court from making a prohibited steps order, with a view to achieving a result which could be achieved by making a residence or contact order. A contact order includes an order for no contact, thus local authorities cannot circumvent the separate prohibition on their seeking a residence order or contact order[45] by seeking a prohibited steps order requiring that a parent should not live in the same house as his child.[46] On the subject of local authorities they should be mindful also of their power to give assistance, including financial, to the person from whom a child may be at risk of ill-treatment, to enable that person to obtain alternative accommodation,[47] as a means of obviating the need for court proceedings.

It must also be remembered that the County Court and High Court have the power under the 1989 Act to make an order for the transfer or settlement of property for the benefit of a child.[48]

Wardship

In most cases the cost and other disadvantages of wardship proceedings[49] will preclude such an application which should be limited to those cases where there is no alternative. Moreover, the extent of the court's protectionary powers in wardship is unclear. In *Re V.*[50] it was held that there is jurisdiction to grant a non-molestation order in respect of the ward and the custodial party, if it is in the child's interests, but there is no jurisdiction to make an exclusion order. It was suggested in *Spindlow* v. *Spindlow*,[51] however, that the court has power in wardship to make an exclusion order if the child's interests require it. The cases were decided prior to *Richards* v. *Richards*[52] where the House of Lords limited the scope of the principle of paramountcy of the child's welfare in the context of exclusion orders. Where, however, a wardship application and an application under the Matrimonial Homes Act 1983 are heard together, it has been held[53] quite proper for the wardship application to be decided first on the basis of the paramountcy of the child's welfare and for that decision to be taken as one of the considerations relevant to the 1983 Act

---

43 [1993] 1 F.L.R. 118.
44 s.9(5)(*a*).
45 s.9(2).
46 See *Nottinghamshire County Council* v. *P.* [1993] 2 F.L.R. 134.
47 Children Act 1989, Sched. 2, para. 5.
48 See above, p. 152.
49 See above, p. 129.
50 (1979) 123 S.J. 201. See also *Re D. (Minors)* (1983) 13 Fam. Law 111.
51 [1979] Fam. 52 at 58, *per* Ormrod L.J. See also *Rennick* v. *Rennick* [1977] 1 W.L.R. 1455 at 1457.
52 See above, p. 166.
53 *Re T.(A Minor: Wardship)*; *T.* v. *T.(Ouster Order)* [1987] 1 F.L.R. 181.

application. It is submitted that the decision in *Richards* need not be taken as limiting the court's inherent jurisdiction under which the court should have power to make an exclusion order if the ward's welfare so requires and that support for this submission is to be found in *Wilde* v. *Wilde*.[54] There is no power, however, to attach a power of arrest.[55]

The criminal law

An assault by a cohabitee on his[56] partner is, like any other assault, a criminal offence.[57] The victim is therefore entitled to expect the protection of the criminal law either by bringing proceedings herself or, more likely, by seeking the help of the police. Although research indicates that the police may be reluctant to become involved in what may appear to be a purely domestic affair,[58] police attitudes are changing.[59] The Home Office issued a Circular in 1990 to Chief Constables[60] offering guidance to the police on their response to the problem of domestic violence and stressing that they should play an active and positive role in protecting the victim and any children, for example, by establishing dedicated domestic violence units and treating domestic violence as seriously as other forms of violence.

Common assault is now a summary offence[61] for which the the the police may prosecute or leave the victim to pursue her own remedy.[62] Prosecution is more likely if there are more serious acts of violence.[63] Cohabitation, present or past, is no defence to a charge of rape[64] but is a factor to which some weight may be given by the court in sentencing.[65] A cohabitee wishing to prove rape against her current partner is, of course, faced with the considerable burden of proving that the act of intercourse was without her consent.

The complainant, realising that the other party will in many cases be released pending the hearing, may decline, for fear of further violence, from pursuing the complaint and her reluctance to testify may considerably lessen the chance of conviction. A cohabitee of an accused person is

54 [1988] 2 F.L.R. 83, above, p. 177.
55 *Re G.(A Minor)* (1983) 4 F.L.R. 538; *Harrison* v. *Lewis* [1988] 2 F.L.R. 339.
56 In the following discussion it is assumed that the woman is the victim.
57 See Maidment, "The Relevance of the Criminal Law to Domestic Violence" [1980] J.S.W.L. 26; Edwards, "The Real Risks of Violence Behind Closed Doors" (1986) 136 N.L.J. 1191 and the references there cited. The fact that violence occurs in a domestic context is no mitigation: see *R.* v. *Cutts* [1987] Fam. Law 311.
58 See Dewar, *Law and the Family* (2nd. ed., 1992), pp. 226-227 and references there cited. For a comparative view, see Torgbor, [1989] Fam. Law 195.
59 See "Metropolitan Police guidelines for cases of domestic violence" (1987) 84 L.S. Gaz. 1939.
60 Home Office Circular 60/90, *Domestic Violence.*
61 Criminal Justice Act 1988, s.39.
62 *D.P.P.* v. *Taylor; D.P.P. v. Little* [1992] Fam. Law 377.
63 On which see the specialist criminal law texts.
64 See, *e.g. R.* v. *Haywood* (1992) 13 Cr.App.R. (S.) 175.
65 *R.* v. *Berry* (1988) 10 Cr.App.R. (S.) 13; *Attorney General's Reference No. 7 of 1989* [1990] Crim. L.R. 436.

both competent and compellable to give evidence for the prosecution,[66] but the power is used infrequently. As a general rule a spouse too is a competent witness and is compellable where the offence charged involves violence to the potential witness or to a child who was under the age of 16 at the time of the offence or there is a sexual offence against a child under 16.[67]

In cases of less serious violence the court may seek the accused's agreement to being bound over to keep the peace with a financial penalty in case of default. This remedy of taking recognisances, which is available also on the application of the complainant,[68] is rarely used by victims of domestic violence, who are usually in need of a greater degree of protection than this procedure affords.

Compensation for criminal violence

Compensation order

The Powers of Criminal Courts Act 1973[69] provides that a court which convicts a person, in addition to or instead of dealing with him in any other way, may make a compensation order requiring him to pay compensation for any personal injury, loss or damage resulting from the offence or any other offence which is taken into consideration by the court in determining sentence.[70] The significance of these orders must not be over-emphasised, for most compensation orders made by criminal courts are for loss or damage to property and not for personal injury.

Criminal Injuries Compensation Scheme

This Scheme[71] was established in 1964 to make *ex gratia* payments of compensation to, *inter alia*, the victims of violent crime. The Scheme was made statutory by the Criminal Justice Act 1988[72] but the introduction of the provisions has been postponed in favour of a revised non-statutory Scheme.

The original Scheme excluded the payment of compensation where the victim and the offender were living together as members of the same family. The exclusion was because of the difficulty of establishing the facts and of ensuring that compensation did not benefit the offender. It proved to be unjust in preventing the more severely injured victims of

---

66 *R.* v. *Yacoob* (1981) 72 Cr.App.R. 313; [1981] Crim.L.R. 248. The same principle applies to parties to a bigamous marriage: see *R.* v. *Khan, The Times,* June 10, 1986. See also Brownlee, "Compellability and Contempt in Domestic Violence Cases" [1990] J.S.W.L 107.

67 See Police and Criminal Evidence Act 1984, s.80, reversing *Hoskyn* v. *Metropolitan Police Commissioner* [1979] A.C. 474.

68 For details see Parker, *Cohabitees* (3rd. ed., 1991), pp. 92-94.

69 s.35 (as amended).

70 For an example of a compensation order where the accused had had a relationship with the victim, see *R.* v. *Dorton* [1988] Crim. L.R. 254.

71 Run by the Criminal Injuries Compensation Board (The Board), Blythswood House, 200 West Regent Street, Glasgow G2 4SW.

72 ss.108-117, Scheds. 6 and 7: see below, p. 182.

intra-family violence from obtaining compensation and a revised Scheme removed the exclusion but imposed a number of safeguards.

Under the current Scheme[73] if the victim and any person responsible for the injuries which are the subject of the application were living in the same household at the time of the injuries as members of the same family, compensation can be paid only where:

(a) the person responsible has been prosecuted in connection with the offence, except where the Board consider that there are practical, technical or other good reasons why a prosecution has not been brought; and

(b) in the case of violence between adults in the family, the Board are satisfied that the person responsible and the applicant stopped living in the same household before the application was made and seem unlikely to live together again; and

(c) in the case of an application by or on behalf of a minor, the Board are satisfied that it would not be against the minor's interests to make a full or reduced award.

For the purposes of the Scheme, a man and a woman who are not married to each other but are living together as husband and wife are to be treated as members of the same family.

The 1990 Scheme remains subject to limitations and problems of interpretation, most notably in requiring that the person responsible and the victim stopped "living in the same household" before the application was made. The original Scheme prevented the victim from receiving compensation if she and the person responsible were "living together" at the time as members of the same family. In *R. v. Criminal Injuries Compensation Board, ex p. Staten*[74] it was decided that the original phrase should be given its ordinary meaning and not that which it has in matrimonial law, where the test is that which now appears in the revised Scheme. The change of wording should have made it easier to gain compensation, because the fact that two people are living under the same roof does not necessarily mean they are living in the same household, for that requires the sharing of a domestic life.[75] Thus, whereas Mr. and Mrs. Staten were "living together" although they slept apart, had no sexual relationship and she did not cook or clean for him, it is very doubtful that they were "living in the same household".

The Board may withhold or reduce compensation if they consider that the applicant has not taken, without delay, all reasonable steps to inform the police or other appropriate authority; has failed to give reasonable assistance to the Board; or, having regard to the applicant's criminal convictions and unlawful conduct or his character or way of life, it is inappropriate that a full award, or any award, be granted.

---

73 "The 1990 Scheme", applicable to applications received on or after February 1, 1990.
74 [1972] 1 W.L.R. 569.
75 See, *e.g. Hopes* v. *Hopes* [1949] P. 227; *Mouncer* v. *Mouncer* [1972] 1 W.L.R. 321; *Fuller* v. *Fuller* [1973] 1 W.L.R. 730.

The statutory Scheme is similar to the current one, with minor variations of nomenclature rather than principle. Reference to membership of the same family is omitted so that the equivalent provision[76] refers to any criminal injury "sustained by a person not under the age of 18 years who, when he sustains the injury, is living in the same household as the person . . . responsible for causing it . . . ". Hence, the basis of the test continues to be living in the same household. The injury is not a qualifying injury unless the person responsible for causing it has been prosecuted in connection with the injury, or there is *sufficient* reason why he has not been prosecuted. The Board must be satisfied that the victim has ceased to live, and does not intend to live again, in the same household as the person responsible for causing the injury or that circumstances prevent her from doing so. If the victim is a minor who was living in the same household as the person responsible for causing the injury, the Board must consider whether in all the circumstances it is in the interest[77] of the person who sustained the injury to make an award of compensation to the victim and shall not make an award unless they are satisfied that it is in the victim's interest.[78]

Compensation may be refused or reduced unless the claimant satisfies the Board, on a balance of probabilities, that:

(i) she took all reasonable steps within a reasonable time to inform the police or other authority of the circumstances of the injury and has co-operated fully in bringing the offender to justice;

(ii) she has given the Board or such other authority all reasonable assistance with the claim; and

(iii) there is no possibility that the offender will benefit from an award.[79]

So a cohabitee's reluctance to involve the police, believing that they will regard it as only a domestic dispute, may jeopardise her claim.[80] An award may also be reduced or refused because of the victim's conduct in connection with the injury, including conduct after the injury.[81]

Housing

In addition to the remedies discussed so far, if as a result of violence a cohabitee becomes homeless, she may look to the local authority for rehousing or accommodation. In the short term she may turn to a Women's Aid Centre. If she does so, that will not relieve the local

---

76 s.110(5).
77 Rather than not against the interest, so if the balance is even the statutory test is not satisfied.
78 s.112(5).
79 s.112(1).
80 See above, p. 181.
81 s.112(2)(*b*) and (3).

authority of its duty under Part III of the Housing Act 1985.[82] The limited duration of exclusion orders granted under the Domestic Violence and Matrimonial Proceedings Act 1976 is often based on the expectation that the local authority will discharge its obligations under the 1985 Act and the acceptance by the courts that the applicant's claim is essentially a housing matter, rather than one capable of long-term resolution by the grant of an exclusion order.[83] It is important, however, that the courts and local authorities do not abdicate to each other their individual responsibilities towards the applicant.

3. REFORM

The law can, at best, only provide a partial remedy for the victim of family violence and in that it is currently deficient. The law and procedure need rationalisation for, in the words of one commentator, "the hurdles now facing the general practice solicitor are at best a headache, at worst a nightmare."[84] The same can be said also of the hurdles facing his client, particularly if she is not married to the perpetrator. To this end the proposals of the Law Commission in their Report, *Domestic Violence and Occupation of the Family Home*,[85] are to be broadly welcomed, although they do not address all the issues, for example, the criminal law relating to domestic violence[86] and public housing law are excluded. In general the Law Commission propose no departure in principle from the two kinds of remedy, a non-molestation order and a newly-termed occupation order (orders relating to occupation of the home), each with its own criteria and being capable of combination with one another and other remedies. The improved remedies and procedures under the new statutory code would, as currently, coexist with injunctions under the inherent jurisdiction but should, it is anticipated,[87] eliminate the need to rely on the inherent jurisdiction unless there is a particular reason for so doing. The following analysis will concentrate upon those proposals of particular relevance to cohabitation.

Regarding non-molestation orders,[88] all courts[89] should have power to grant an order where it is just and reasonable to do so having regard to all

---

82 See above, p. 65.
83 See *Freeman* v. *Collins* (1983) 4 F.L.R. 649; *Wooton* v. *Wooton* [1984] F.L.R. 871; *Warwick* v. *Warwick* (1982) 12 Fam. Law 60.
84 Robinson, "Domestic Violence: No Ansah" (1979) 129 N.L.J. 896.
85 Law Com. No. 207 (1992), following Working Paper No. 113. See Hayes and Williams, [1992] Fam. Law 497.
86 It is recommended, somewhat controversially, however, that where the police have been involved in an incident of molestation or actual or threatened violence they should have the power to apply for civil remedies on behalf of the victim: see Report, paras. 5.18-5.23. See also Home Office Select Committe Report on Domestic Violence, summarised at [1993] Fam. Law 307.
87 Report, para. 1.6.
88 See Pt. III.
89 Hence cohabitees will be able to use the Magistrates' Court, whose jurisdiction will extend to molestation.

the circumstances including the need to secure the health, safety or well-being of the applicant or a relevant child.[90] Protection, it is recommended, should extend to those who are associated with each other in any of a number of ways (associated persons) which can broadly be classified as an actual or intended domestic connection, for example, marriage or former marriage, parenthood, parental responsibility, or being parties to the same family proceedings. Of particular note is the inclusion, not only of cohabitees, *i.e.* "cohabitants" in the Commission's terminology,[91] but also:

- former cohabitants[92];
- those who live or have lived in the same household,[93] otherwise than merely as employee, tenant or lodger or boarder;
- certain close relatives[94];
- those who have at any time agreed to marry each other (whether or not that agreement has been terminated); and
- those who have or have had a sexual relationship (whether or not including sexual intercourse).[95]

Orders would be capable of being made for any specified period or until further order.

Regarding occupation orders[96] the Commission recommend that the court should have power to make an occupation order with a variety of possible terms, either declaratory[97] or regulatory.[98] Distinctions in the nature of the orders are seen as necessitating different criteria. All courts would have jurisidiction to make occupation orders, but Magistrates' Courts would be required to transfer a case or refuse jurisdiction if it were necessary to decide a dispute as to whether either party has a pre-existing legal, beneficial or statutory right to occupy the home before dealing with the matter. This is linked with the fact that the Commission's proposals differ depending upon whether or not the applicant has a right to occupy by virtue of a legal or beneficial interest or a contractual or statutory

---

90 For meaning of relevant child, see Report, para. 3.27.
91 See above, p. 1, defined as meaning "a man and a woman who, although not married to each other, are living with each other as husband and wife": see Report, para. 3.18 and Draft Family Homes and Domestic Violence Bill, cl.1(*a*).
92 See cl.1(*b*), overcoming the problem in *Pidduck* v. *Molloy* [1992] 2 F.L.R. 202: see above, p. 16. The Commission's terminology will be used in this discussion of their proposals.
93 The phrase "living in the same household" is expected to retain its current meaning in matrimonial proceedings: see above, p. 162.
94 Which includes relationships arising through cohabitation if the relationship would have arisen if the parties were married to each other (see cl. 27), and would extend protection to parties to a family cohabitation: see above, p. 4.
95 Hence including a homosexual relationship: see Report, para. 3.19, whether or not within cohabitation.
96 See Pt. IV.
97 *I.e.* orders which declare, confer or extend occupation rights.
98 *I.e.* other orders, including ouster orders, which just control the exercise of existing rights.

right. The distinction is favoured because an occupation order can severely restrict the enjoyment of property rights and because, in the case of an applicant who has a right to occupy, an occupation order has a purpose beyond short-term protection.[99]

Someone who has such a right (an "entitled applicant") may apply for an occupation order against anyone against whom she could obtain a non-molestation order,[1] provided that the dwelling-house is, was, or was intended to be the joint home of the parties.[2] This is seen as being of considerable practical importance because both types of order are often sought at the same time. An occupation order made between co-owners, whether cohabitants or not, would be capable of being made for any specified period or until further order.[3]

Where the applicant has no existing right to occupy (a "non-entitled" applicant) the Commission defines the qualified applicants far more narrowly and also further distinguishes between the case where the respondent is entitled and where he is not, because in the latter case the court is only adjusting property rights between the parties themselves who may be subject to almost immediate ejection by a third party.[4] Where the respondent is entitled, an application can only be made between cohabitants, former cohabitants and former spouses. Hence there must have been a relationship of marriage or quasi-marriage, so parties to a family cohabitation or homosexual cohabitation are excluded. In the case of cohabitants and former cohabitants, the application must relate to the home in which they lived, are living or both intended to live together as husband and wife.[5] In such cases the court, in deciding whether to exercise its powers to make an order, must have regard, *inter alia*, to:

- the nature of the parties' relationship;
- the duration of the cohabitation;
- whether there are children of both parties or for whom they have, or have had, parental responsibility;
- in the case of former cohabitants, the length of time since the parties ceased cohabitation; and
- the existence of any pending proceedings between the parties for financial provision for the children or relating to the legal or beneficial ownership of the home.[6]

The extension to former cohabitants will fill the current lacuna exemplified by *Ainsbury* v. *Millington*[7] and meet one of the major deficiences

---

99 See Report, para. 4.7.
1 See above, p. 183.
2 See cl.7(1).
3 cl.7(9)(*a*).
4 Report, para 4.10.
5 cl.9(1).
6 cl.9(4).
7 See above, p. 176.

of the current law. Granting an occupation order in favour of a non-entitled applicant would have an effect similar to spouses' automatic rights of occupation under section 1 of the Matrimonial Homes Act 1983, but would be personal rights only and not capable of registration as a charge against the property or be valid against a purchaser.[8] An order in favour of a non-entitled applicant would be limited for up to 6 months initially, with the possibility of renewal for up to 6 months at a time.[9]

Where neither party is entitled to occupy, for example, they are bare licensees or squatters, it is proposed to preserve the effect of the Domestic Violence and Matrimonial Proceedings Act 1976 and extend it to make occupation orders between former spouses and former cohabitants as well as spouses and cohabitants, provided they occupy a dwelling-house which, in the case of cohabitants or former cohabitants, is the home in which they live, or lived, together as husband and wife.[10]

The enforcement provisions would be strengthened so that the court would be required to attach a power of arrest where there has been violence or threatened violence, unless the applicant or any child will be adequately protected without such a power.[11]

Of particular significance in the context of "other issues" in Part VI is the recommendation[12] that the power to transfer tenancies[13] should be extended to cohabitants on the breakdown of cohabitation, whether they are joint tenants or whether one party is sole tenant and the other is non-entitled, if circumstances justify it. The court would have the power to order the transferee to compensate the transferor so as to compensate the tenant for loss of his tenancy, and the proposal would apply between spouses as well as between cohabitants. Cohabitants would not, however, be barred from applying by subsequent marrriage and hence there would be a distinction in that regard between former spouses and former cohabitants as the latter may well be ignorant of their legal position, whereas spouses are more likely to have received legal advice on breakdown of their relationship.

It is also recommended that the summary procedure[14] for determining claims to a beneficial interest should be extended to allow cohabitants to apply for an order within three years of the end of cohabitation.

---

8 Report, paras. 4.18-4.19.
9 cl.9(8).
10 cl.10(1).
11 cl.15.
12 Report, para. 6.6.
13 In Matrimonial Homes Act 1983, s.7: see above, p. 61.
14 In Married Women's Property Act 1882, s.17: see above, p. 13.

CHAPTER 7

MARRIAGE BREAKDOWN AND COHABITATION

Marriage confers upon the spouses mutual rights and duties,[1] the chief of which is a mutual duty to live together or cohabit. The law sees cohabitation and the sharing of lives and a home as the essence of marriage[2] and recognises rights and duties arising from the cohabitation, for example, the mutual right to consortium and the mutual duty to maintain. None of these applies to the unmarried, even though the term cohabitation is frequently used to describe a stable relationship outside marriage. Although the law has ceased to enforce the marital duty to cohabit,[3] it still recognises the matrimonial "wrong" of desertion. A deserted spouse can base a claim on desertion either in divorce proceedings[4] or in proceedings in the Magistrates' Court for maintenance during marriage.[5]

Many couples who cohabit as man and wife do so because they are unable to marry, one or both of them being already married. The cohabitation may be the cause of the marriage breakdown or it may be a symptom of an already broken marriage. Whatever the reason for the cohabitation, its existence is likely to encourage the end of the marriage by divorce.

There is now only one ground for divorce, namely that the marriage has broken down irretrievably.[6] Irretrievable breakdown must be proved by the petitioner showing one of five facts, namely that the respondent has committed adultery and the petitioner finds it intolerable to live with the respondent[7]; the respondent has behaved in such a way that the petitioner cannot reasonably by expected to live with the respondent[8]; desertion[9]; that the parties to the marriage have lived apart for a

---

1 For a comparison of marriage and cohabitation, see above, p. 4.
2 See, *e.g. Thomas* v. *Thomas* [1948] 2 K.B. 294 at 297, *per* Lord Goddard.
3 Since the abolition of the decree of restitution of conjugal rights by the Matrimonial Proceedings and Property Act 1970, s.20.
4 If the respondent has deserted the petitioner for a continuous period of at least two years immediately preceding the presentation of the petition: see Matrimonial Causes Act 1973, s.1(2)(*c*).
5 See Domestic Proceedings and Magistrates' Courts Act 1978, s.1(*d*), which prescribes no time limit.
6 Matrimonial Causes Act 1973, s.1(1).
7 *Ibid.* s.1(2)(*a*).
8 *Ibid.* s.1(2)(*b*).
9 See n. 4 above.

continuous period of at least two years immediately preceding the presentation of the petition and the respondent consents to a decree being granted[10] and that the parties to the marriage have lived apart for a continuous period of at least five years immediately preceding the presentation of the petition.[11] The five years' separation fact was condemned at the time of its introduction as a "Casanova's Charter", the fear being, in particular, that middle-aged wives would be divorced against their wishes and would suffer financial hardship. Those fears were not realised. It is true that in the first year of the provision's operation, it was the basis for one-quarter of the divorce petitions and many cohabitees, particularly elderly couples, who had been living together were able to marry and thereby legitimate their children. The intention of the Law Commission (that the provision would enable couples to regularise by marriage their "stable illicit unions")[12] was thus realised, but only in the short term. Once the initial demand by those who had been unable to marry for some years had been met, however, the use of the provision and the increase in legitimation of children declined. Currently, less than one in ten divorces is granted on this basis. The provision has not proved a "Casanova's Charter" for, of those petitioning, there is an equal number of husbands and wives.

1. COHABITATION BETWEEN SPOUSES

Cohabitation between the spouses can have important consequences in relation to their divorce.[13] If they cohabit after the event which is being relied upon for the divorce, and do so for more than six months, the cohabitation will bar the granting of a decree in a case based on the respondent's adultery,[14] desertion or either of the separation facts[15] and may bar the granting of a decree if the petitioner's case is based on the respondent's behaviour.[16] This is also the case if the parties cohabit for more than six months after the decree nisi but before the decree absolute, because the marriage does not end until the decree absolute. So, for example, if as in *Biggs* v. *Biggs*[17] the parties do so cohabit, the cohabitation operates as a bar to a decree absolute based on adultery. If the decree is based upon the respondent's behaviour then the court has a

---

10 Matrimonial Causes Act 1973, s.1(2)(*d*).
11 *Ibid*. s.1(2)(*e*). For proposals for reform, see Law Com. No. 192, *The Ground for Divorce* (1990).
12 See Law Commission, *Reform of the Grounds of Divorce: The Field of Choice*, Cmnd. 3123 (1966), paras. 33-37 and Deech, "Divorce Law and Empirical Studies" (1990) 106 L.Q.R. 229.
13 For the possible effect of pre-marital cohabitation when the court is assessing financial obligations on divorce, see above, p. 74.
14 Time begins to run after it became known to the petitioner that the respondent had committed adultery: see Matrimonial Causes Act 1973, s.2(1) and (2).
15 Matrimonial Causes Act 1973, s.2(5).
16 *Ibid*. s.2(3).
17 [1977] Fam. 1.

discretion[18] and the issue is whether or not it has been reasonable for the petitioner to cohabit with the respondent after the decree nisi.[19]

During the marriage if either spouse obtains certain Magistrates' Court orders for periodical payments[20] under the Domestic Proceedings and Magistrates' Courts Act 1978 the order is enforceable notwithstanding that the parties are living with each other or resume living with each other, but the order ceases to have effect if they continue or resume living with each other for more than six months after the order.[21]

2. COHABITATION WITH ANOTHER BEFORE DIVORCE

The fact that one spouse is cohabiting with someone else may be used by the other spouse as evidence of adultery in divorce proceedings.[22] Direct evidence is by its nature rarely available and so reliance is usually to be placed on circumstantial evidence which shows both an opportunity and inclination to commit adultery, for example, that the couple concerned are cohabiting.[23]

In addition to providing evidence of adultery, the fact that a spouse is cohabiting may be of importance in relation to any claim for financial provision[24] and property adjustment.[25] The court is under a duty to have regard to all the circumstances of the case,[26] first consideration being given to the welfare, while a minor, of any child of the family[27] when the court is exercising its powers in relation to the parties to a marriage. The

---

18 If the application to make the decree absolute is lodged out of time, see the proviso to Family Proceedings Rules 1991, r. 2.49.
19 See *Court* v. *Court* [1982] Fam. 105; *Savage* v. *Savage* [1982] 3 W.L.R. 418.
20 Made under the Domestic Proceedings and Magistrates' Courts Act 1978, s.2, 6, 11(2) or 19 (other than one made on an application under s.7). Orders in favour of a child of the family are unaffected: see s.25(2).
21 s.25(1). Any order under s.7 and any interim order made on an application for an order under that section ceases to have effect if the parties resume living with each other: see s.25(3).
22 Under the Matrimonial Causes Act 1973, ss.1(2)(*a*) and 17.
23 If that person is named in the petition, he or she must be made a party to the proceedings unless the court otherwise directs: see Matrimonial Causes Act 1973, s.49(1); Family Proceedings Rules 1991, r. 2.7(1) and *Bradley* v. *Bradley* [1986] 1 F.L.R. 128.
24 Whether during the subsistence of the marriage (see the Domestic Proceedings and Magistrates' Courts Act 1978, ss.1-3; Matrimonial Causes Act 1973, s.27 (as substituted)) or on divorce, nullity or judicial separation (see the Matrimonial Causes Act 1973, s.23).
25 On divorce, nullity or judicial separation: see the Matrimonial Causes Act 1973, ss.24 and 24A.
26 Domestic Proceedings and Magistrates' Courts Act 1978, s.3(1) (as substituted) and Matrimonial Causes Act 1973, s.25(1) (as substituted).
27 *I.e.* a child of both parties to a marriage and any other child, not being a child placed with those parties as foster parents by a local authority or voluntary organisation, who has been treated by both of those parties as a child of their family: see Domestic Proceedings and Magistrates' Courts Act 1978, s.88(1) (as substituted); Matrimonial Causes Act 1973, s.52(1) (as substituted). See *R.* v. *R.* [1988] 1 F.L.R. 89.

interests of such children thus take priority over the claims of other dependants, including a cohabitee, and any child who is not a child of the family, such as a child of a cohabitee.

Since the Matrimonial and Family Proceedings Act 1984, the court in divorce and nullity proceedings[28] must consider whether it would be appropriate to exercise its powers in favour of a spouse so that the financial obligations of each party towards the other will be terminated as soon after the grant of the decree as the court considers just and reasonable.[29] Where the court does make a periodical payments order[30] it must consider whether it would be appropriate to require those payments to be for a limited period so as to enable adjustment without undue hardship to the termination of financial dependence.[31] If the court considers that no continuing obligation should be imposed on either party to make periodical payments in favour of the other, for example, in the light of the financial support provided by a new partner, it may dismiss the application with a direction that the applicant shall not make any further application.[32]

These provisions are designed to encourage a "clean break", either immediate or deferred, and may facilitate the development of relationships between a spouse and a new partner, whether by way of remarriage or cohabitation. Such encouragement is, however, limited. Where a marriage has lasted for some years and the wife has sacrificed her financial independence in order to look after the home and the family, the court is unlikely to consider it "just and reasonable" that the husband's financial obligations to his wife should cease. Only in those cases where the wife is capable realistically of being or becoming self-sufficient will a clean break be appropriate, for example, in the case of a short and childless marriage. It must be remembered also that the clean break principle is subject to the court's duty to give first consideration to the welfare of the minor children of the family.

The legislation sets out some of the matters which the court has to consider in deciding whether or not to make an order[33] and, if so, for how much or of what type. The court must consider, *inter alia*,[34] the financial resources, needs, obligations and responsibilities which each of the spouses has or is likely to have in the foreseeable future.[35]

---

28 But not judicial separation, Matrimonial Causes Act 1973, s.27 proceedings, or proceedings in the Magistrates' Court under the Domestic Proceedings and Magistrates' Courts Act 1978.

29 Matrimonial Causes Act 1973, s.25A(1) (as inserted).

30 Secured or unsecured.

31 Matrimonial Causes Act 1973, s.25A(2) (as inserted).

32 *Ibid.* s.25A(3) (as inserted).

33 The same principles apply in both the Magistrates' Court and the higher courts: see *Macey* v. *Macey* (1982) 3 F.L.R. 7.

34 See Domestic Proceedings and Magistrates' Courts Act 1978, s.3(2)-(4) (as substituted); Matrimonial Causes Act 1973, s.25(2)-(4) (as substituted).

35 *Ibid.* ss.3(2)(*a*) and (*b*), 25(2)(*a*) and (*b*).

In so doing, the approach is a practical one since the court "is faced with essentially a financial and not a moral exercise".[36] If the husband is being financially supported by another woman, that fact will be taken into account in assessing the husband's ability to provide for his wife, for his own cost of living will be reduced as, for example, in *Ette* v. *Ette*,[37] where the husband was cohabiting rent-free with another woman in accommodation which she provided.[38] Any maintenance payable by the husband to his wife must come, however, from his resources and not from those of his cohabitee[39] because it is not his cohabitee's responsibility to maintain his wife. The cohabitee's resources may be taken into account to the extent that she is self-supporting and thus relieving the husband of financial responsibilities that he would otherwise have to meet. Her resources are thus relevant indirectly but not directly, in a way analagous to that where a husband remarries, for the second wife's resources and needs are relevant in considering the extent to which she is financially dependent upon the husband or able to contribute to the household sufficient to enable him to use his own resources to support his first wife.[40]

If the husband is cohabiting with another woman and supporting her financially, the consequent drain on his financial resources will also be considered, particularly if the woman has children, whether or not they are the man's children. The extent to which such responsibilities will be taken into account was considered in *Roberts* v. *Roberts*[41] where it was decided that the court should have regard to all the relevant circumstances including obligations which may not be legally enforceable.[42] When considering the order of priority to be accorded to the various obligations, however, it was held that it must rarely be right that a wife's claim to support should be postponed to the claim of a mistress,[43] even though this must be taken into account for whatever weight it is held to bear.

The same principle applies if it is the wife who is cohabiting. If she is being financially supported by a new partner her resources will be that much greater and her financial needs in respect of which she is likely to be claiming against her husband will be that much less. Thus in *Ibbetson* v.

---

36 *Per* Ackner L.J. in *Duxbury* v. *Duxbury* [1987] 1 F.L.R. 7 at 14. See also *Atkinson* v. *Atkinson* [1987] 3 All E.R. 849, below, p. 197 and Johnson, "Arithmetic v. Morality" [1990] Fam. Law. 3.
37 [1964] 1 W.L.R. 1433.
38 See also *Ward* v. *Ward and Greene*, reported on this point only at (1980) 1 F.L.R. 368.
39 *Brown* v. *Brown* (1981) 11 Fam. Law 247; *Macey* v. *Macey* (1982) 3 F.L.R. 7. See also *Re L. (Minors) (Financial Provision)* (1980) 1 F.L.R. 39, below, p. 204; *Walker* v. *Walker* (1982) 4 F.L.R. 44 at 47.
40 *Slater* v. *Slater* (1982) 3 F.L.R. 364.
41 [1970] P. 1.
42 See also *Blower* v. *Blower* [1986] 1 F.L.R. 292 where the same principle was held to apply on a variation application, and *Fisher* v. *Fisher* [1989] 1 F.L.R. 423, below, p. 196, n. 75.
43 See *Tovey* v. *Tovey* (1978) 8 Fam. Law 80.

Ibbetson[44] the court took into account the wife's expectancy of a half share in her cohabitee's house as a financial resource which she was likely to have in the foreseeable future. Conversely, if she is cohabiting with a man of modest resources in comparison to those of her husband, the fact that her cohabitee will benefit from the maintenance which the husband is ordered to pay is irrelevant.[45] Indeed if the cohabitee is dependent upon her this increase in her obligations and responsibilities will result in a drain on her resources.

In exercising their powers the courts are required to have regard to the conduct of each of the parties to the marriage "if that conduct is such that it would in the opinion of the court be inequitable to disregard it".[46] The form of wording was amended by the Matrimonial and Family Proceedings Act 1984[47] in line with the judicial interpretation given to the original wording and hence it is suggested that the case law prior to that Act remains authoritative. The courts will be concerned with conduct only in exceptional cases. The type of conduct envisaged includes, for example, the case where the parties may each not have been blameless but where the imbalance of conduct would make it inequitable to ignore the comparative conduct. The test approved by the Court of Appeal in the post-1984 Act case of *Kyte* v. *Kyte*[48] is whether a right-thinking member of society would say that the conduct was such as to reduce entitlement. In that case, the wife's conduct in assisting her husband's suicide attempts and also in forming a deceitful relationship with another man was held to be such that it would be inequitable to disregard it. It has been referred to also as conduct such that it would be repugnant to a sense of justice for it not to be taken into account.[49] Such an evaluation clearly involves a value judgment precluding any precise formulation of relevant conduct. It is suggested, however, that the fact that a spouse is cohabiting with someone else and committing adultery ought not, in the absence of other conduct, to justify a conclusion that it would be inequitable to disregard such cohabitation.

Each case will depend upon its own circumstances and the particular court's assessment. Thus in *Leadbeater* v. *Leadbeater*[50] it was held not to be inequitable to disregard both spouses' conduct where the husband, having become sexually attracted to a 16-year-old girl-friend of his wife's daughter, introduced her into the matrimonial home and where as a

---

44 [1984] F.L.R. 545. See also *S.* v. *S.* [1987] 2 W.L.R. 282; *Suter* v. *Suter and Jones* [1987] 2 W.L.R. 9, below, p. 193, where the court took into account financial support which the wife should have received from her cohabitee.
45 *Duxbury* v. *Duxbury* [1987] 1 F.L.R. 7.
46 Domestic Proceedings and Magistrates' Courts Act 1978, s.3(2)(*g*) (as substituted) and Matrimonial Causes Act 1973, s.25(2)(*g*) (as substituted).
47 ss.9 and 3 respectively: see also above, p. 74. In *Kyte* v. *Kyte* [1987] 3 All E.R. 1041 the Court of Appeal declined to decide whether the amended wording gave the court a broader discretion.
48 [1987] 3 All E.R. 1041.
49 See, *e.g. Backhouse* v. *Backhouse* [1978] 1 W.L.R. 243; and *cf. Cuzner* v. *Underdown* [1974] 1 W.L.R. 641.
50 [1985] F.L.R. 789.

result the wife, who already had a severe drink problem exacerbated by difficulties with her adopted son, went on holiday and committed adultery with two or three men, whereas in *Suter* v. *Suter*[51] the fact that the wife had invited her lover to cohabit for the foreseeable future in the former matrimonial home, without seeking or receiving any contribution to the expenses of maintaining the home, was regarded as conduct such that it would be inequitable to disregard and the maintenance payable by the husband was reduced to a nominal £1 per year. The decision suggests that financial inequity is the most likely factor to lead the court to take into account a spouse's cohabitation with another. Where it does so, the extent to which the cohabitee should have contributed is relevant as well as his actual contribution. Cohabitation, however, ought rarely to warrant imposing a clean break, the preferred solution being the making of a nominal order in view of the lack of financial security associated with cohabitation compared with marriage.

The result in many cases is that one income will now have to provide for two families, so inevitably there will be a reduction in the parties' standard of living. A husband who leaves his wife and children, for whatever reason, and lives with another woman can expect to have to provide for his first family. This is so, whether or not he plans to remarry. The duty to the first family will limit the income available for the second. A cohabitee, like a second wife, takes her partner subject to the partner's obligations to his first family.

The need for one income to provide for two families may mean that one or both of the spouses has to rely on welfare benefits. As they have ceased to be members of the same household their requirements and resources will no longer be aggregated, but the resources of the second family will be aggregated. The fact that one spouse is receiving benefit does not relieve the other of his obligation to maintain. The courts do not allow a husband to shift his responsibility to maintain his wife onto the State, thus any benefit received will generally be ignored in assessing maintenance. The court, in ordering one spouse to maintain the other, ought not, however, to reduce the payer and his new family below subsistence level[52] and when the case is one in which the parties' means are so modest that an order would result in the husband being left with inadequate funds to meet his financial commitments, the court may have regard to such benefits.[53] The same principles apply whether a man is having to divide his resources between his wife and former wife or

---

51 [1987] 2 W.L.R. 9, discussed by Douglas, (1987) 50 M.L.R. 516. See also *Hepburn* v. *Hepburn* [1989] 1 F.L.R. 373; *Atkinson* v. *Atkinson* [1987] 3 All E.R. 849, below, p. 197 and the pre-1984 Act case of *Ibbetson* v. *Ibbetson* [1984] F.L.R. 545.

52 There is some uncertainty as to what constitutes subsistence level: see *Smethurst* v. *Smethurst* [1978] Fam. 52; *Shallow* v. *Shallow* [1979] Fam. 1; *Tovey* v. *Tovey* (1978) 8 Fam. Law 80; *Allen* v. *Allen* [1986] 2 F.L.R. 265.

53 *Barnes* v. *Barnes* [1972] 1 W.L.R. 1381. In *Ashley* v. *Blackman* [1988] Fam. 85, however, Waite J. held that he could make a clean break order notwithstanding the principle in *Barnes* v. *Barnes*. See also *Peacock* v. *Peacock* [1984] 1 W.L.R. 532.

between his cohabitee and former wife.[54] In *Delaney* v. *Delaney*[55] the husband and his cohabitee bought a house, the outgoings on which left insufficient to support his former wife and children. The Court of Appeal held that a former spouse is entitled to balance future aspirations for a new life against responsibilities to the former family in the light of the realities of the world, including "that there is life after divorce".[56] Having regard to the reasonable financial commitments undertaken by the husband with due regard to the contribution made by his cohabitee, there was insufficient left to maintain the former family properly and the court could take into account that social security benefits were available to the wife and children. Accordingly, implementing the spirit of the clean break, the wife's periodical payments order was discharged and a nominal order made for the children. The Court's preparedness to regard the husband's obligations to the children as having been met by the purchase of a house in which staying access could take place is noticeably out of line with the policy of the Child Support Act 1991, under which the scope for any such clean break order is restricted, particularly if the carer parent is in receipt of income support, family credit or disability working allowance.[57]

In divorce, nullity and judicial separation proceedings[58] the courts have extensive powers to make property adjustment orders irrespective of ownership.[59] The courts place emphasis on the need to provide a home for the parties.[60] If the husband is provided with accommodation by his cohabitee, his wife's need for a home in the former matrimonial home is likely to be seen as being of greater significance than the husband's wish to realise his share in it. The needs of any children are of particular importance.[61] If a husband leaves his wife to cohabit with another woman, he may well find the court transferring the matrimonial home to the wife if she has care of the children. If the husband cohabits in the matrimonial home and the wife leaves, an order may be made transferring the home to her if she has care of the children. The husband's maintenance to his wife may be reduced correspondingly.

If one spouse tries to defeat the claims of the other for financial relief, by disposing or dealing with any property, for example, by transferring it into the name of a cohabitee, the court has power to restrain or set aside dispositions about to be made or already made with the intention of defeating or reducing a claim to financial relief. Any such disposition is reviewable unless it was made for valuable consideration to a person who acted in good faith and without notice of any intention to defeat the

---

54 See, *e.g. Chase* v. *Chase* (1983) 13 Fam. Law 21.
55 [1990] 2 F.L.R. 457, applying *Stockford* v. *Stockford* (1982) 3 F.L.R. 58: see Bryan, [1990] J.C.L. 16.
56 *Per* Ward J. at 461.
57 See above, p. 145.
58 But not domestic proceedings or Matrimonial Causes Act 1973, s.27 proceedings.
59 The court also has jurisdiction to determine the interests of third parties: see *Tebutt* v. *Haynes* [1981] 2 All E.R. 238.
60 *Martin* v. *Martin* [1978] Fam. 12; *Clutton* v. *Clutton* [1991] 1 All E.R. 340.
61 See *Hanlon* v. *Hanlon* [1978] 1 W.L.R. 592.

applicant's claim for financial relief.[62] Where the transferee is a cohabitee, the disposition is likely to come in for particularly close scrutiny by an aggrieved spouse.

Ascertaining resources

If precise details of a cohabitee's resources are not laid before the court, the Family Proceedings Rules 1991[63] provide that the district judge "may at any stage of the proceedings, whether before or during the hearing, order the attendance of any person for the purpose of being examined or cross-examined and order the discovery and production of any document or require further affidavits". The rule raises three separate issues:

(1) attendance at court for examination or cross-examination;
(2) the discovery and production of documents; and
(3) the filing of affidavits.

On (1), it is submitted that notwithstanding contrary judicial dictum[64] in relation to the predecessor of the rule, the power to "order the attendance of any person for the purpose of being examined or cross-examined" does enable the court to order the attendance of a cohabitee as a witness. As such he or she will be a witness of the court, rather than the person who sought the order compelling attendance, and will be available for examination or cross-examination by any party.

On (2), power to order non-parties to produce documents is now conferred by the Rules.[65] However, it does not extend to compelling a person to produce any document at a production appointment which he could not be compelled to produce at the hearing of the ancilliary relief application.[66]

On (3), the reference in the Rules to "further affidavits" is consistent with the continued limiting of the power to the making of orders against parties to the proceedings. A cohabitee is not a party to proceedings for ancillary relief even if named as co-respondent in the main suit and so cannot be ordered to file an affidavit of means.[67] A spouse who is

---

62 See further Matrimonial Causes Act 1973, s.37.
63 See r. 2.62(4).
64 W. v. W., *The Times*, March 21 and 27, 1981 where it was said that a party could seek leave under R.S.C., Ord. 32, r. 7 to issue a *subpoena ad testificandum* or *duces tecum*. See also *H. v. H.* (1981) Fam. Law 209.
65 Family Proceedings Rules 1991, r. 2.62(7): see Mostyn and Moor, "The production appointment" [1991] Fam. Law 506.
66 *Ibid.* r. 2.62(8).
67 *Wynne* v. *Wynne and Jeffers* [1980] 1 W.L.R. 69. See also *Re T.* [1990] 1 F.L.R. 1; *G.* v. *G. (Financial Provision: Discovery)* [1992] Fam. Law 66.

cohabiting, however, may be ordered to file an affidavit disclosing his cohabitee's means in so far as they are known to him.[68]

3. COHABITATION WITH ANOTHER AFTER DIVORCE

The effect of post-divorce cohabitation on an existing maintenance or property order depends upon whether the original order was of a capital or income nature. A maintenance order in the form of a lump sum is a once and for all capital payment[69] and is unaffected by later cohabitation. A periodical payments order, however, is a continuing order and therefore subject to later variation or termination. An ex-spouse who remarries[70] loses the benefit of secured or unsecured periodical payments in her favour[71] except for arrears[72] as financial obligations now fall exclusively within the remarriage. Cohabitation does not have this effect, but a periodical payments order may be for such term as specified,[73] for example, determinable on cohabitation and will be subject to the payer's applying for variation of the order[74] in the light of the recipient's cohabitation. If the court is asked to vary the order it will have regard to all the circumstances, including any change in any of the matters which the court had to consider when making the original order.[75] The court is thus not limited to a change of a financial nature although it is likely to concentrate upon any financial inequity in consequence of the cohabitation, as it would when making an original order. Hence the same general principles apply to post-divorce cohabitation.

In *M.H.* v. *M.H.*[76] it was held that as the fact that the wife was living with another man as husband and wife would have been relevant to an original application, it was therefore relevant to an application to vary. The judge considered that it was not fair, just and reasonable that a divorced woman's financial position should be better if she cohabited with another man in a stable relationship than if she was married to him.

---

68 Failure to file such evidence may result in adverse inferences being drawn (see, *e.g.* *Ette* v. *Ette* [1964] 1 W.L.R. 1433) and reliance being placed upon the parties' life-style as evidence of their resources.

69 If payable by instalments, their size and frequency can be varied but not the capital sum.

70 Including a marriage which is void or voidable: see Matrimonial Causes Act 1973, s.52(3).

71 Orders for children of the family are unaffected.

72 Matrimonial Causes Act 1973, s.28(1) and (2).

73 Matrimonial Causes Act 1973, s.23(1); Domestic Proceedings and Magistrates' Courts Act 1978, s.2(1)(*a*).

74 Under Matrimonial Causes Act 1973, s.31, and see *Wachtel* v. *Wachtel* [1973] Fam. 72; *Atkinson* v. *Atkinson* [1987] 3 All E.R. 849. A similar power is available in the Magistrates' Court: see Domestic Proceedings and Magistrates' Courts Act 1978, s.20.

75 Matrimonial Causes Act 1973, s.31(7) (as substituted): see also *Lewis* v. *Lewis* [1977] 1 W.L.R. 409; *Atkinson* v. *Atkinson* [1987] 3 All E.R. 849. In *Fisher* v. *Fisher* [1989] 1 F.L.R. 423 the Court of Appeal took into account the wife's child by another man after separation from her husband as a factor affecting her earning capacity.

76 (1982) 3 F.L.R. 429.

The wife was in receipt of £3,900 annual periodical payments and a secured provision of £4,800. Taking into consideration the earning capacity of the wife's cohabitee, the periodical payments order was reduced to £500 per annum. One difference in cases where an ex-spouse cohabits rather than remarries is that the cohabitee, unlike a spouse, is under no duty to maintain a partner. For this reason it seems correct that the judge did not reduce the order to a nominal one as would have been appropriate, as the law then stood,[77] if he had sought to put her in the position she would have been in had she remarried rather than cohabited. Thus in *Atkinson* v. *Atkinson*[78] the Court of Appeal did not accept that settled cohabitation by an ex-wife should be equated to marriage. The court will look at the overall circumstances of the cohabitation, particularly the financial consequences, which may be such that it would be inappropriate for maintenance to continue, but it was held that in general there is no statutory requirement that the court should give decisive weight to the fact of cohabitation. If the court were to do so it would impose an unjustified fetter on the freedom of the ex-wife to lead her own life as she chooses.

Where it is inappropriate for maintenance to continue, it is submitted that, as a general principle, the appropriate order is a nominal one so as to reflect the lack of financial security arising from cohabitation, whilst acknowledging that cohabitation is an important change of circumstances. It has been acknowledged also that "it is not the job of a court to put pressure on parties to regularise their irregular unions".[79] A deliberate decision to remain unmarried solely to keep the benefit of periodical payments, however, may be conduct which it is inequitable to disregard.[80]

Just as the recipient's cohabitation will be relevant to an application to vary as well as to an application for an original order, so too if the payer cohabits. Either ex-spouse can apply for a variation in the light of the cohabitation, depending upon whether the cohabitation has increased the payer's obligations or resources.

If an ex-spouse cohabits after divorce but before applying for maintenance, the cohabitation will not bar an application, but will be taken into account when deciding what order, if any, to make. The court may well decide to make a nominal order.[81] An ex-spouse who remarries before applying for maintenance, whether in the form of periodical payments or lump sum, is barred from making an application.[82] An ex-spouse who

---

77 There being no power to dismiss the wife's right to claim periodical payments without her consent: see now Matrimonial Causes Act 1973, s.25A(3).
78 [1987] 3 All E.R. 849.
79 *Per* Butler-Sloss L.J. in *Hepburn* v. *Hepburn* [1989] 1 F.L.R. 373 at 378: see Mears, "The Clean Break v. The Courts: The Illogical Backstop" [1989] Fam. Law 398. See also *Stead* v. *Stead* [1968] 1 All E.R. 989.
80 *Atkinson* v. *Atkinson* [1987] 3 All E.R. 849, and see above, p. 192.
81 See, *e.g. W.* v. *W.* [1976] Fam. 107.
82 Matrimonial Causes Act 1973, s.28(3).

contemplates remarriage is best advised, therefore, to seek a lump sum order which is unaffected by remarriage and must apply before remarrying, but not necessarily before cohabiting. Any cohabitation, however, will not be ignored. If an ex-spouse plans to remarry, the effect of remarriage on his financial position will be considered,[83] but if there are no remarriage plans the courts will not assess the parties' remarriage prospects[84] when determining maintenance and property adjustment.

A property adjustment order in favour of an ex-spouse is unaffected by cohabitation or remarriage. It is a once and for all order and as such cannot be varied or terminated. A property order is thus akin to a lump sum maintenance order, both being of a capital rather than income nature, and an ex-spouse in whose favour such an order is made is in a better position, in the event of remarriage or cohabitation, than an ex-spouse with a periodical payments order. It remains important, however, to apply[85] for the order before remarrying, for no application is possible after remarriage.[86] Cohabitation does not bar an application but will be considered.

It is important to note, however, that "it is becoming a more frequent practice for orders under sections 23 and 24 [of the Matrimonial Causes Act 1973] to include provision for extinction or review upon cohabitation with someone else whether those orders relate to property provisions or to purely money payments"[87] thus narrowing the distinction between the effect of remarriage and cohabitation. In *Harvey* v. *Harvey*[88] the Court of Appeal made an order transferring the matrimonial home into the joint names of the wife and the husband on trust for sale in shares of two-thirds to the wife and one-third to the husband and providing that the sale be postponed *inter alia* until the wife became "dependent on another man". The Court took the view that if the wife cohabited with another man in the premises he ought to take over the responsibility of providing accommodation for her. This view, however, disregards both the absence of any legal duty upon him to do so and the possibility that he may not in any event be able to do so. The effects of such an order could be very serious[89] not only upon the wife but also any children who would stand to lose the security of their home.[90]

---

83 *H.* v. *H.* [1975] Fam. 9; *Smith* v. *Smith* [1975] 2 All E.R. 19; *Tinsdale* v. *Tinsdale* (1983) 4 F.L.R. 641. Where there is a failure to disclose plans to remarry or cohabit, see below, p. 200.

84 *Duxbury* v. *Duxbury* [1987] 1 F.L.R. 7.

85 An application already made can be pursued: see *Jackson* v. *Jackson* [1973] Fam. 99.

86 Matrimonial Causes Act 1973, s.28(3).

87 *Per* Wood J. in *M.H.* v. *M.H.* (1982) 3 F.L.R. 429 at 437.

88 [1982] 2 W.L.R. 283. See also *Tinsdale* v. *Tinsdale* (1983) 4 F.L.R. 641.

89 See Hayes and Battersby, "Property Adjustment Order or Disorder in the Former Matrimonial Home?" [1985] Fam. Law 213 at 215.

90 In which event the issue arises of whether there is property available for occupation by the wife and cohabitee within the meaning of the Housing Act 1985, s.75: see *R.* v. *Wimborne District Council, ex p. Curtis* [1986] 1 F.L.R. 486 and above, p. 70.

The courts' response to such cohabitation clauses has been mixed. In *Hembrow* v. *Hembrow*[91] the sale was postponed until the wife's remarriage or death but the Court of Appeal declined to impose a condition covering cohabitation. It was felt that to do so would incite supervision and inquiry agents. In *Eagle* v. *Eagle*[92] the Court of Appeal lifted a restriction that a sale should take place if the wife cohabited in the former matrimonial home for more than 28 days in any six months. In *Grimshaw* v. *Grimshaw*[93] Ormrod L.J. was "not enthusiastic" that cohabitation of the wife with another man as husband and wife would entitle the husband to enforce a charge in his favour[94] on the matrimonial home but as it was cohabitation for six months "that should be all right". More enthusiasm was displayed in *Chadwick* v. *Chadwick*[95] when the Court of Appeal upheld the postponement of sale without the wife's consent unless she remarried, cohabited or died.[96] It was considered necessary in order to do justice to the husband to impose some real inconvenience on the wife to select, as her future partner, a man who was able to provide her with suitable alternative accommodation. If she chose a partner who could not provide such accommodation, that was to be regarded as a grave misfortune which she would have brought upon herself. This misfortune is of course especially grave if she cohabits rather than remarries, as a cohabitee is under no duty to provide accommodation. The Court of Appeal expected the wife to choose a partner upon whom she could depend financially. The preferable approach, it is submitted, is that in *Atkinson* v. *Atkinson*,[97] where the Court of Appeal refused to impose such an unjustified fetter on the freedom of the ex-wife.

The diversity of approach relates not only to the desirability of a cohabitation clause but also, if one is inserted, the circumstances giving rise to its operation. In *Chadwick* v. *Chadwick*[98] the mere commencement of cohabitation would precipitate a sale, whereas in *Grimshaw* v. *Grimshaw* the cohabitation had to have lasted for six months. The problem in either case is the determination of cohabitation. At least the approach in *Grimshaw* requires some degree of permanence and stability in the relationship so that there is no question of a casual relationship satisfying the requirement. The test adopted in *Harvey* v. *Harvey* was not

---

91 Reported on this point in *The Times*, October 28, 1981. See also *Holtom* v. *Holtom* (1981) 11 Fam. Law 249 (an undertaking given by a wife not to cohabit with another man at the matrimonial home held to be bad and ought not to have been accepted).
92 Referred to briefly in *The Times*, February 2, 1983; (1983) 13 Fam. Law 101.
93 (1983) 11 Fam. Law 75.
94 See also *Carter* v. *Carter* [1980] 1 W.L.R. 390 and Hayes and Battersby, "Property Adjustment Orders and the Matrimonial Home" [1981] Conv. 404 at 414.
95 [1985] F.L.R. 606.
96 Often referred to as a *Martin* order: see *per* Lloyd L.J. in *Clutton* v. *Clutton* [1991] 1 All E.R. 340 at 342, following *Martin* v. *Martin* [1978] Fam. 12, although the order in that case was that the home be settled on trust for the wife during her life, or until remarriage or such earlier date as she should cease to live there.
97 Above, p. 197.
98 See also *Lewis* v. *Lewis* (1982) 132 N.L.J. 589; (1982) 79 L.S. Gaz. 953.

cohabitation but dependence on another man. The tests are distinguishable in that a wife may be cohabiting with another man without being dependent upon him and may be dependent upon him without cohabiting with him. The former is a matter more of status, *i.e.* the unmarried housewife, whereas the latter connotes more the mistress. Whilst dependence has the attraction that if the cohabitee is unwilling or unable to maintain or provide accommodation the clause does not come into effect, it is likely to be no easier to determine than cohabitation.

As the court already has the power to vary periodical payments taking into account all the circumstances, there seems an advantage in dealing with subsequent cohabitation by variation proceedings.[99] A property adjustment order is not capable of variation[1] but a similar result may be achieved by either creating a trust for sale coupled with a clause providing for the sale to be postponed until remarriage or until further order,[2] or by a clause conferring on the husband liberty to apply for a sale if the wife should remarry or cohabit.[3] The court would then have power to review the case in the light of all the interests and circumstances at the time of the proposed sale. This would enable proper consideration to be given to the interests of any children for whom it might be necessary to secure a home. Notwithstanding the uncertainty of such a clause it has the attraction that the court retains the necessary discretion.

In line with the principle of encouraging private ordering of financial matters on marital breakdown, the legislation[4] provides that on an application for a consent order the court may make an order in terms agreed on the basis of prescribed information supplied with the application. This information includes, *inter alia*, whether either party has remarried or has any present intention to marry or cohabit with another person.[5] If a party fails to make full and frank disclosure of material information[6] the other party may apply for the order to be set aside. The circumstances must be such, however, that had the facts been known, a substantially different order would have been made by the court. Thus in *Cook* v. *Cook*[7] shortly after the making of a consent order the husband discovered the information supplied by his wife as to her intentions regarding cohabitation was inaccurate and he sought a rehearing. The Court of Appeal found, however, that there had not been a complete change of circumstances but rather a development of a close relationship of which the husband was aware. Although the non-disclosure constituted a change of circumstances, it would have made no substantial

---

99 See Wright, "Remarriage and Cohabitation" (1983) 13 Fam. Law 262 at 264.
1 See, *e.g. Norman* v. *Norman* [1983] 1 W.L.R. 295.
2 See, *e.g. Lewis* v. *Lewis* (1982) 132 N.L.J. 589; (1982) 79 L.S. Gaz. 953.
3 See Hayes and Battersby, "Property Adjustment Order and Disorder in the Former Matrimonial Home?" [1985] Fam. Law 213 at 216; *Thompson* v. *Thompson* [1986] Fam. 38.
4 Matrimonial Causes Act 1973, s.33A.
5 Family Proceedings Rules 1991, r. 2.61, replacing Matrimonial Causes Rules 1977, r. 76A. See also *Registrar's Direction* [1976] 1 F.L.R. 337.
6 See *Livesey* v. *Jenkins* [1985] A.C. 424.
7 [1988] 1 F.L.R. 521.

difference to the order. Similarly, if an application to appeal out of time is made because of a change of circumstances since the order was made, for example, cohabitation, the change must be such as to invalidate the basis, or fundamental assumption, on which the order was made so that the appeal would be likely to succeed. The change should have occurred within a relatively short time of the order and the application for leave made reasonably promptly.[8]

4. CHILDREN

Upbringing

The issue of bringing up children and the relevance of cohabitation by a parent with a non-parent may arise during marriage as part of a matrimonial dispute, in which case the upbringing of children of the family[9] will be decided by a Magistrates' Family Proceedings Court.[10] A child's upbringing may arise as an independent issue, in which case application can be made for an order under the Children Act 1989, s. 8.[11] If there are divorce, nullity or judicial separation proceedings the court must consider whether, in the light of the arrangements which have been, or are proposed to be, made for the upbringing of any child of the family, it should exercise any of its powers under the Children Act 1989.[12] Whatever the context in which a child's upbringing is in issue, the Children Act 1989 prescribes the court's powers and the principles applicable to their exercise. The court's powers are in terms of practicalities, in particular residence and contact,[13] and the guiding principle remains the paramountcy of the child's welfare.[14] If either spouse is cohabiting, the cohabitation will be a factor to be taken into account as part of that principle, but the conduct of the parties to the marriage is relevant only in so far as it relates to the child's welfare. The courts are no longer concerned with doing justice between the parties, so adultery by one is relevant only in so far as it is likely to have an effect on the children. The same principle applies if one of the parties is cohabiting.[15] If a parent cohabits in a homosexual relationship that factor will be a relevant, but not a decisive, consideration in relation to the welfare of the children. The significance attached by the courts to such relationships

8 See *Barder* v. *Barder* [1988] A.C. 20; *Chaudhuri* v. *Chaudhuri* [1992] 2 F.L.R. 73.
9 See above, p. 189, n. 27.
10 Exercising its powers under the Domestic Proceedings and Magistrates' Courts Act 1978 and the Children Act 1989.
11 See above, p. 120.
12 Matrimonial Causes Act 1973, s.41(1) (as substituted). Only exceptionally may the court withhold the granting of a decree.
13 See above, pp. 123 and 127.
14 See above, p. 125.
15 See, *e.g.* the pre-Children Act 1989 cases *Re K.* [1977] Fam. 179; *S. (B.D.)* v. *S. (D.J.)* [1977] Fam. 109.

appears to be lessening. In *S*. v. *S*.[16] the wife left her husband, who continued to care for their two children aged seven and five, and went to live in a lesbian relationship with a married woman. The Court of Appeal rejected the wife's claim for care of the children because of the social embarrassment and hurt which could be caused to them if their mother's lesbian relationship became known in the locality and the children were living with her. In *C*. v. *C*.[17] the Court of Appeal held that a mother's lesbian relationship does not disqualify her from having care of her child but is an important factor to be put into the balance when determining what is in the child's best interests. The trial judge in excluding the lesbian relationship as a factor was found to have been plainly wrong and the case was remitted for rehearing where the mother was granted care and control.[18] At the rehearing, the court considered the issue of parental sexual orientation to be just one factor to be taken into account and found that the child needed the mother's support in meeting the effect on the child of being teased by her peers. Moreover, empirical research indicates that a mother's sexual orientation does not appear to influence the child's well-being[19] as was judicially acknowledged in *B*. v. *B*.[20] where a caring and loving lesbian mother with a good understanding of the children's psychological needs was granted care and control.

Not only is the nature of the cohabitation a relevant factor, the court will also investigate the stability of the cohabitation[21] and whether or not there is any possibility of the parents being reconciled. Consideration will be given to the suitability of the cohabitee as a parent substitute,[22] the permanence of the relationship between the parent and the cohabitee[23] and the likelihood of their eventual marriage. In view of the importance which the court is likely to attach to the suitability of a cohabitee as a parent substitute, the cohabitee will usually be required to attend the hearing[24] in order that the court can properly determine whether or not the cohabitee is a fit and proper person to look after the child.[25]

If a spouse with the care of a child cohabits after the making of an order relating to the child's upbringing, the fact of cohabitation will be relevant

---

16 (1980) 1 F.L.R. 143. See also *G*. v. *G* (1981) 11 Fam. Law 148; *Re P*. (1983) 4 F.L.R. 401; Bradley, "Homosexuality and Child Custody in English Law" (1987) 1 I.J.L.F. 155.

17 [1991] 1 F.L.R. 223: see Fox, [1991] J.S.W.F.L. 155; Boyd, [1992] 55 M.L.R. 269; Catley, [1992] J.S.W.F.L. 249.

18 *C*. v. *C*. *(No. 2)* [1992] F.C.R. 206.

19 See Tasker and Golombok, "Children Raised by Lesbian Mothers" [1991] Fam. Law 184

20 [1991] 1 F.L.R. 402; Standley, "Children and Lesbian Mothers" (1991) 4 J.C.L. 134.

21 *Dickinson* v. *Dickinson* (1983) 13 Fam. Law 174; *Stephenson* v. *Stephenson* [1985] F.L.R. 1140; *T*. v. *T*. *(Minors: Custody Appeal)* [1987] 1 F.L.R. 374.

22 *Re F*. [1969] 2 Ch. 239; *Hutchinson* v. *Hutchinson* (1978) 8 Fam. Law 140; *S*. v. *S*. [1986] 1 F.L.R. 492 and see Hodson, "The New Partner After Divorce: Part II Children and Step-Parents" [1990] Fam. Law 68.

23 *May* v. *May* [1986] 1 F.L.R. 325; *Re R*. [1986] 1 F.L.R. 6.

24 *S*. v. *S*. (1972) 117 S.J. 34.

25 See, *e.g. Scott* v. *Scott* [1986] 2 F.L.R. 320; *Butler* v. *Butler* (unreported, December 11, 1987, C.A.).

to an application to vary an order in the same way as it would be to the making of an original order. If the cohabitation takes place within a short time after making the original order such that the basis upon which the court reached its decision, although not plainly wrong on the evidence before it, was ill-founded, then the case should be remitted for reconsideration in light of the fresh evidence.[26]

The court's powers include making orders regarding contact.[27] The child's interests are frequently best served by an order for contact in favour of the non-residential parent.[27a] Such contact will be refused, however, if it is likely to be harmful to the child. The behaviour of the non-residential parent may result in the refusal of contact and if the residential parent is cohabiting in a stable relationship,[28] then a relevant factor will be the impact, upon that parent and the cohabitee, of the non-residential parent's behaviour when exercising contact.

Discussion so far has proceeded on the basis that a child's upbringing is in issue between spouses both of whom are the child's parents, because parental responsibility normally rests with the parents.[29] If the child's parents are not married to each other but either of them is married to a third party, it is possible for the child to be a child of the family[30] for the purposes of matrimonial law and for the third party (*i.e.* the step-parent) to be able to seek an order relating to the child's upbringing[31] or, more usually, be liable to maintain the child. For example, a wife has a child by another man, she and her husband treat the child as a child of their family, the marriage breaks down and the mother cohabits with the child's father. In any matrimonial proceedings between the husband and wife the child is a child of the husband's family. The fact that the husband was ignorant of the child's paternity will not prevent the child being a child of his family.[32] So far as the responsibility to maintain is concerned, however, the court must consider, *inter alia*, whether he assumed any responsibility for the child's maintenance and, if so, to what extent and for how long, whether he did so knowing the child was not his own and the liability of anyone else, for example, the father, to maintain the child.[33]

A different situation arises if a divorced or separated spouse, who has children of the marriage living with him or her, cohabits with a third party. The non-parent cohabitee is under no corresponding duty to

---

26 *A. v. A. (Custody Appeal: Role of Appellate Court)* [1988] 1 F.L.R. 193.
27 See above, p. 127.
27a Even if the child believes that the residential parent's cohabitee is his or her parent: see *Re R.(A Minor)(Contact)* [1993] 1 F.C.R. 954.
28 See, *e.g. Re C. (Minors) (Access)* [1985] F.L.R. 804.
29 See above, p. 116.
30 See above, p. 189, n. 27.
31 For an unsuccessful application by a step-father for access, see *Re C.(A Minor)(Access)* [1992] 1 F.L.R. 309.
32 *W.(R.J.) v. W.(S.J.)* [1972] Fam. 152.
33 Matrimonial Causes Act 1973, s.25(4); Domestic Proceedings and Magistrates' Courts Act 1978, s.3(4). There is a similar provision in proceedings under the Children Act 1989: see Sched. 1, para. 4(2).

maintain the children of his or her partner's marriage, because there must be a marriage between the parties before the child can be a child of the family. The parent cohabitee and the parent's spouse or ex-spouse are alone under a liability to maintain their child. In *Re L. (Minors) (Financial Provision)*[34] the parents of three children separated and the mother went to live with another man. The father was granted custody of the children and sought maintenance for them from the mother. She had no income and her cohabitee, who was working, refused to disclose his means. The magistrates felt entitled to take his earnings into account and made an order against the mother. The mother's appeal was allowed because the effect of the order was to require her cohabitee to pay the maintenance. An order ought not to be made against a parent or a spouse unless the court is satisfied that the person against whom the order is made has the means to pay it. In those cases where, however, a cohabitee's support of a partner relieves the partner of self-support, that fact should, it is submitted, be relevant when assessing the ability of the partner to maintain his or her children, just as it is in relation to a cohabitee's financial support for a married partner when assessing financial provision for that partner by his or her spouse or ex-spouse.[35]

Surname

One problem of particular significance on divorce is that which occurs when the wife has the children living with her and forms a relationship with another man and she wishes to change her children's surname to that of her new partner. The problem usually arises on remarriage but also occurs if the wife cohabits. Although a wife on remarriage or cohabitation is free to change her surname to that of her new partner, she does not have the same freedom with regard to the children. If there is a residence order or care order in force with respect to the child, the mother is not entitled to change her children's surname except with the written consent of every person with parental responsibility for the child or with the leave of the court.[36]

Case law has reflected a difference of emphasis. On one view a change is an important matter and the courts rarely gave leave for a change except where it was felt that a complete severance from the father was desirable.[37] There followed a line of cases,[38] however, which suggested a greater preparedness to permit a unilateral change of name, on the basis that too much attention had been paid to the question of names at the

---

34 (1980) 1 F.L.R. 39.
35 See above, p. 191.
36 Children Act 1989, ss.13(1)(*a*) and 33(7)(*a*). In the absence of such an order a parent wishing to prevent such a change would have to seek a prohibited steps order: see above, p. 131.
37 See, *e.g. Re T.* [1963] Ch. 238; *Y.* v. *Y.* [1973] Fam. 147; *Re W.G.* (1976) 6 Fam. Law 210.
38 *Crick* v. *Crick* (1977) 7 Fam. Law 239; *R.* v. *R.* [1977] 1 W.L.R. 1256; *D.* v. *B.* [1979] Fam. 38.

expense of what was best for the child, for example, the effect of being known by a different surname from brothers and sisters and the embarrassment this can cause at school. Subsequently the earlier approach was revived and the issue has been seen as one of great substance and not to be regarded as a minor matter.[39]

Ultimately it is a question of balancing the need to preserve the child's links with his natural father against the desire to facilitate the child's integration within the new family. In so far as there is an answer it lies in the principle of the paramountcy of the child's welfare. In accordance with that principle any preference in favour of one parent over the other and over the child's interests is inappropriate. The problem remains, however, of determining what is in the child's best interests in the particular circumstances. There has been a tendency for the courts to presume that it is in the child's best interests that his surname should not be changed, and the courts are likely to be particularly reluctant to sanction a change if the mother and her new partner are not married. Much will depend upon the stability of the cohabitation, as for example, in *R. v. R.*,[40] where the court found a strong relationship between the mother and her cohabitee. The mother had been granted custody of the three eldest children on divorce and they were known by her cohabitee's surname. She later applied for custody of the youngest child who had been living with his father since the divorce. The Court of Appeal held that in deciding the custody of the child, the fact that the three eldest children had taken the cohabitee's surname was not of significance, it was merely more convenient that they should be known by that name. The observations in that case were subsequently seen, however, as being confined to their context and not establishing a general proposition. In *W. v. A.*,[41] the Court of Appeal stressed that the matter is one of discretion for the judge. The child's welfare is the paramount consideration. A change of name is an important matter so far as the child's welfare is concerned and a change will not be sanctioned lightly. The law remains in a state of uncertainty and the unsuitability of the judicial process as a means of resolving such issues has been recognised.[42] The case law must also be viewed in the light of the *Gillick*[43] principle and the need for the court to pay regard to the child's wishes.

---

39 *L. v. F., The Times*, August 1, 1978; *W. v. A.* [1981] Fam. 14.
40 [1977] 1 W.L.R. 1256.
41 [1981] Fam. 14.
42 See, *e.g. R. v. R.* (1982) 3 F.L.R. 345.
43 See above, p. 9.

CHAPTER 8

DEATH

The informal nature of cohabitation means the parties may not have addressed their legal relationship or that of the survivor in the event of death. Issues which may need to be addressed, and which are considered in other Chapters, include inheritance tax,[1] parental responsibility for, and inheritance rights of, children[2] and rights arising under contract.[3] This Chapter focuses upon entitlement to a deceased cohabitee's estate; a surviving cohabitee's rights in the family home; pension rights; widow's benefits and compensation for death.

1. THE DECEASED'S ESTATE

If a cohabitee is to succeed to a deceased partner's estate, it is essential that the deceased made a valid will, because the rules of intestate succession do not confer any entitlement upon cohabitees. The only way, other than under the rules of testate succession, in which a cohabitee could seek to benefit would be by application to the court for financial provision from the deceased's estate. The cost and uncertainty associated with any such application is in marked contrast to the simplicity and certainty of inheritance under a will, where it is not necessary either to apply or prove a case.

Inheritance and succession

In line with the general principle of freedom of testation if the deceased dies testate the property forming his estate will be disposed of in accordance with the terms of the will.

Will

A testator who wishes to leave property to a specific person should identify that person by name, rather than by status. A gift in a will to "my wife" or "my husband" will, in the absence of contrary evidence, be taken to mean the person to whom the deceased was married at the date

---

1 See above, p. 101.
2 See above, pp. 133 and 156.
3 See below, p. 239.

of the will.[4] Cases have occurred where such a gift has been intended not for a spouse but for a cohabitee. It is possible for the prima facie meaning to be over-ridden in the context of the particular gift, even to the extent that a person who was not married to the deceased has been held entitled to benefit. It is essential, however, that the testator has made it clear that he is describing that particular person. So, in *Re Brown*[5] the testator, a widower, left a legacy to "my wife" and the court decided that the woman with whom the testator lived, but to whom he was not married, was entitled to the legacy. It is not essential, therefore, for the testator to have named the person, but his intention will be that much clearer if he has done so. Each case will depend upon the construction of the particular will in the light of the particular circumstances, including extrinsic evidence. In *Re Smalley*[6] a testator by his will left all his property to "my wife E.A.S.". At his death he was survived by a wife M.A.S. and by a woman E.A.M. with whom he had contracted a later, bigamous marriage and who lived with him as his wife. E.A.M. was known as E.A.S. and believed she was his wife. The Court of Appeal held that the testator intended to benefit E.A.M. and she was entitled to his property. Similarly in *Re Lynch*[7] the testator, a widower, appointed "my wife Annie Ethel Lynch" one of his executors and left part of his estate "to my wife during her widowhood". The parties were not married and could not marry because they were within the prohibited degrees of relationship. They had cohabited as man and wife for five years and represented themselves as man and wife. The court decided that on the construction of the will the testator had provided his own dictionary and when he referred to "my wife" he intended Annie Ethel Lynch, so she was entitled to benefit. In view of the increase in the incidence of cohabitation, the chance of cases of the kind just discussed arising must also increase. Hence the need for the testator to identify clearly the beneficiary.

If cohabitees marry, the marriage will revoke any existing will of either party unless the will was made in contemplation of the particular marriage.[8] A will is not revoked either by divorce[9] or by cohabitation. A witness who attests a will is disqualified from benefiting under the will, as is the spouse of any such witness.[10] The rule does not apply to the cohabitee of a witness. The provision [11] whereby a bequest to a spouse with a gift over to the testator's issue gives an absolute interest to the

---

4 *Re Coley; Hollinshead* v. *Coley* [1903] 2 Ch. 103.
5 (1910) 26 T.L.R. 257.
6 [1929] 2 Ch. 112.
7 [1943] 1 All E.R. 168.
8 Wills Act 1837, s.18 (as substituted). For full details of the exceptions, see s.18(2)-(4) (as substituted).
9 But where a decree of divorce or nullity is granted after the will is made any devise or bequest to a former spouse lapses and any appointment of the former spouse as an executor or trustee of the will is ineffective, except in so far as a contrary intention appears in the will: Wills Act 1837, s.18A (as inserted).
10 Wills Act 1837, s.15.
11 See further Administration of Justice Act 1982, s.22.

spouse unless a contrary intention is shown does not apply to such a bequest to a cohabitee.

When making a will consideration should be given to the exercise of parental responsibility in the event of death and the appointment of testamentary guardians for any minor children of the relationship.[12] Provision can also be made for funeral arrangements thereby avoiding the dispute which arose in one case[13] where the deceased's wife wanted him cremated and the woman with whom he had been living wanted a burial. The hospital refused to release the body until the High Court gave a ruling which it did in favour of the widow.

Intestacy

The importance of making a will in order to benefit a cohabitee is illustrated by the rules of intestate succession,[14] whereas on the death of a spouse intestate the surviving spouse has rights of inheritance from the deceased's estate; not so a surviving cohabitee on the death of a partner.

A surviving spouse has a right on intestacy to the deceased's personal chattels[15] and to a statutory legacy, the amount of which depends upon the existence of other relatives of the deceased. If there are no children (marital or non-marital), no parents, brothers, sisters, or children of any brothers or sisters, the surviving spouse receives the whole estate. If there are children, the spouse's statutory legacy is the first £75,000 and a life interest in half the rest of the estate, the other half going to the children, who also get the half share of the surviving spouse on his or her death. If there are no children, but a parent, brother or sister or nieces and nephews, the surviving spouse's legacy is increased to £125,000 and an absolute interest in half the rest; the other half goes to the parent or equally to the parents if more than one, and if both are dead then equally between the brothers and sisters. The result of these complex rules is that in most cases the surviving spouse inherits the whole estate.

If the deceased's estate includes a house in which the surviving spouse was living at the date of the deceased's death, the surviving spouse may require the house to be transferred to him, or her, in, or towards, satisfaction of his or her entitlement to the deceased's estate.[16]

On the intestate death of a cohabitee, the surviving cohabitee inherits nothing. However, the Law Commission has reviewed this rule and does not favour the inclusion of cohabitees within the intestacy rules because of the loss of simplicity and clarity. Such a change is seen as likely to increase the costs of, and cause delays in, the administration of estates because of disputes as to whether a given individual was a cohabitee. The

---

12 See above, p. 133.
13 Referred to in *The Times*, December 18, 1986.
14 See the Administration of Estates Act 1925, s.46 (as amended), dealing with total and partial intestacy; on the latter, see s.49. For recommendations for reform, see Law Commission Report Law Com. No. 187, *Family Law; Distribution On Intestacy* (1989).
15 *Ibid*. s.55(x).
16 Intestates' Estates Act 1952, s.5 and Sched. 2.

Commission favours instead allowing certain cohabitees to apply for discretionary provision under the Inheritance (Provision for Family and Dependants) Act 1975, without the need to show dependency.[17] The deceased's estate, in the absence of a surviving spouse, will be held on trust for the deceased's children.[18] In the absence of children the estate will pass to the parents (in equal shares if both survive) and, in the absence of children and parents, to the following relatives in order: brothers and sisters, grandparents, uncles and aunts.

The only circumstances in which a surviving cohabitee could benefit is if there is no one in the family to inherit, in which case the estate passes to the Crown and the Crown has a discretion to make payments for dependants and "other persons for whom the intestate might reasonably have been expected to make provision".[19] This could include a cohabitee, although a claim is more likely under the Inheritance (Provision for Family and Dependants) Act 1975, for any property which passes to the Crown is subject to claims under that Act.[20] So far as intestate succession is concerned, it is therefore to a cohabitee's benefit to marry a partner.

A cohabitee is not entitled to apply for letters of administration for the order of priority is in terms of a relationship by either marriage or by blood.[21] If there is no member of the deceased's family available or willing to take a grant of letters of administration the Official Solicitor may be willing to take out a grant should the cohabitee wish to make a claim against the deceased's estate.

Claim for financial provision

A claim against the deceased's estate, including a claim by a cohabitee, may be possible under the Inheritance (Provision for Family and Dependants) Act 1975 (the 1975 Act), notwithstanding the rules of testate and intestate succession.

A cohabitee can claim under the 1975 Act on the death of a partner on the ground that the deceased's will and/or the law of intestacy do not "make reasonable financial provision for the applicant".[22] The Act[23] applies only if the deceased died domiciled in England and Wales. The place of death is irrelevant.

Claims under earlier legislation[24] were limited to members of the deceased's family. Qualified applicants now include "any person . . .

---

17 See Law Com. No. 187, para. 58 and below, p. 212.
18 For the inheritance rights of children on intestacy, see further above, p. 157.
19 Administration of Estates Act 1925, s.46(1)(vi). See further Chatterton, "In Bona Vacantia: Ex Gratia Payments" (1987) 84 L.S. Gaz. 3315.
20 s.24.
21 See the Non-Contentious Probate Rules 1987 (S.I. 1987 No. 2024), r. 22.
22 s.1(1).
23 Implementing the recommendations of the Law Commission: see Second Report on Family Property, *Family Provision on Death* (Law Com. No. 61).
24 Inheritance (Family Provision) Act 1938 (as amended); Matrimonial Causes Act 1965, ss.26-28.

who immediately before the death of the deceased was being maintained, either wholly or partly, by the deceased".[25] Other qualified applicants (*i.e.* a spouse, a former spouse who has not remarried, a child,[26] or anyone who, in the case of any marriage to which the deceased was at any time a party, was treated by the deceased as a child of the family in relation to that marriage[27]) are defined by reference to a family relationship. The extension to a relationship defined in terms of dependency was designed to include cases where failure to provide was accidental or unintentional: "In these cases an order for family provision would be doing for the deceased what he might reasonably be assumed to have wished to do himself. This argument carries particular weight when the 'dependant' is a person with whom the deceased has been cohabiting."[28]

The matters upon which the applicant will need to satisfy the court[29] can be formulated in a series of inter-related questions[30]:

- Does the applicant cohabitee qualify as a person who immediately before the deceased's death was being maintained either wholly or partly by the deceased?
- If so, did the deceased's will and/or the law of intestacy make reasonable financial provision for the applicant?
- If not, should the court in its discretion exercise its power to order some financial provision to be made?
- If so, in what manner should the provision be ordered?

Cohabitees as qualified applicants

Currently a cohabitee may qualify to apply by virtue of dependency but not status.[31] An applicant under section 1(1)(*e*) is to be treated as being maintained either wholly or partly by the deceased "if the deceased, otherwise than for full valuable consideration, was making a

---

25 s.1(1)(*e*): see below.
26 Including a child whose parents are not married to each other. Children are to be treated on the same basis regardless of their parents' marital status: see *C.A.* v. *C.C.*, *The Times*, November 17, 1978, *sub nom. In the estate of McC.* (1979) 9 Fam. Law 26. Whilst claims are not limited to minor children, the courts are less sympathetic to the claim of an adult child who is under no disability: see *Re Coventry, dec'd* [1989] Ch. 461.
27 Treatment as a child of the family can include events which preceded or followed the marriage, provided the treatment can be said to be in relation to that marriage: see *Re Leach, dec'd; Leach* v. *Linderman* [1986] Ch. 226.
28 Law Com. No. 61, para. 90.
29 The burden of proof is on the applicant, whose position can be contrasted with that of a beneficiary under a will or intestacy who is entitled by operation of law without the need to make a claim and prove a case: see, *e.g. Williams* v. *Roberts* [1986] 1 F.L.R. 349.
30 See *Re Coventry, dec'd* [1980] Ch. 461; *Kourkgy* v. *Lusher* (1983) 4 F.L.R. 65 at 72. It has been cogently argued that the first question is whether or not the deceased's net estate justifies a claim: see Parker, *Cohabitees* (3rd. ed.), p.176 and below, p. 218.
31 For proposals for reform, see below, n. 36.

substantial contribution in money or money's worth towards the reasonable needs of that person".[32] In short, the applicant must have been largely financially dependent upon the deceased.[33] It is not sufficient if the parties merely shared their lives and equally contributed to the maintenance of each other. So in *Re Beaumont*[34] the applicant and the deceased, Mrs. Beaumont, lived together as husband and wife in Mrs. Beaumont's bungalow for 26 years up to her death. He paid for his accommodation and contributed to the shopping bill. Mrs. Beaumont paid the outgoings on the home. She did the cooking and housework and the applicant did various household and gardening jobs. He bought a car for their use and paid its running costs whilst the deceased paid the insurance. She left her estate of £17,000 to her three sisters. The applicant who received nothing other than £550 worth of previously nominated savings certificates claimed under subsection 1(1)(*e*) of the 1975 Act. The executors successfully sought to have the action struck out on the ground that the applicant did not qualify within that subsection. Megarry V.-C. held that section 1(3) qualifies section 1(1)(*e*) and is not an alternative to it. Thus an applicant qualifies only if the deceased, otherwise than for full valuable consideration, was making a substantial contribution in money or money's worth towards the applicant's reasonable needs.[35] These difficult issues of interpretation will be overcome in cases of long-term cohabitations if the Law Commisson's recommendation that cohabitees should be qualified to apply without having to show dependence is enacted.[36] The recommendation defines cohabitation in the same way as the Fatal Accidents Act 1976[37] and hence will not apply to all cohabitations,[38] and excluded applicants will still need to rely upon section 1(1)(*e*) of the 1975 Act.

With regard to what constitutes a substantial contribution towards the applicant's needs otherwise than for full valuable consideration, it was said in *Bishop* v. *Plumley*[39] that there are two issues:

(i) was the deceased making a substantial contribution in money or money's worth towards the applicant's reasonable needs and,

(ii) if so, was the contribution made for full valuable consideration by the applicant?

If the answer to (i) is yes and to (ii) is no, the applicant qualifies as being maintained either wholly or in part. Earlier cases seem to have combined

---

32 s.1(3).
33 See, *e.g. Re Wilkinson, dec'd* [1978] Fam. 22.
34 [1980] Ch. 444. See Naresh, "Dependants' Applications Under The Inheritance (Provision for Family and Dependants) Act 1975" (1980) 46 L.Q.R. 534.
35 See also *Jelley* v. *Iliffe* [1981] Fam. 128 and compare *Bishop* v. *Plumley* [1991] 1 All E.R. 236, below, p. 213.
36 See Law. Com. No. 187, para. 59.
37 s.1(3)(*b*).
38 See below, p. 230.
39 [1991] 1 All E.R. 236 at 241, *per* Butler-Sloss L.J.

the two issues. Thus the exclusion of claims was held in *Re Beaumont* not to be restricted to contributions supplied under a contract but extends to any contribution provided for full valuable consideration,[40] and so if a couple living together make equal contributions towards each other's maintenance then although both will be making a substantial contribution in money or money's worth towards the reasonable needs of the other they will be doing so for full valuable consideration and the applicant will not qualify.[41] The desirability of the court having to undertake a commercial evaluation of the reciprocal benefits in a personal relationship, including benefits of a non-monetary nature if constituting money's worth, such as domestic services, support and even companionship,[42] rather than an evaluation of whether the relationship was such that in broad terms the applicant was dependent on the deceased, is, it is suggested, questionable.

The better approach is to give the legislation a purposive interpretation as applied by the Court of Appeal in *Bishop* v. *Plumley*[43] where the comparison of the benefits which had flowed between a couple living together as husband and wife was made in a commonsense way without fine balancing computations involving the normal exchanges of domestic care and support within such a relationship.

> "If a man or a woman living as man and wife with a partner gives the other extra devoted care and attention, particularly when the partner is in poor health, is he or she to be in a less advantageous position on an application under the Act than one who may be less loving and give less attention to the partner? I do not accept that this could have been the intention of Parliament in passing this legislation." [44]

Since the deceased had provided the applicant with a secure rent-free home, he had made a substantial contribution to her needs and her care of, and attention to, him considered in the context of their relationship, and not in isolation, did not constitute full valuable consideration but was part of the mutuality of that relationship.

If the surviving cohabitee maintained the deceased, the survivor has no claim against the deceased's estate however meritorious such a claim might be. The fundamental issue is the extent of the applicant's financial dependency on the deceased.[45] If the balance of their respective contributions comes down clearly in favour of the applicant's being the greater, or if the contributions are clearly equal, the application should be struck

---

40 See also *Jelley* v. *Iliffe* [1981] Fam. 128.
41 See also *H.* v. *G. and D.*, noted briefly at (1980) 10 Fam. Law 98.
42 See, *e.g. Re Wilkinson, dec'd* [1978] Fam. 22.
43 [1991] 1 All E.R. 236; Bridge, [1991] C.L.J. 42.
44 *Per* Butler-Sloss L.J. at 242.
45 See *Williams* v. *Roberts* [1986] 1 F.L.R. 349. For an example of overwhelming evidence to support a finding that the cohabitee applicant had been wholly maintained by the deceased, see *Harrington* v. *Gill* (1983) 4 F.L.R. 265.

out.[46] To do so, however, is a Draconian step[47] to be taken only where it is clear that the claim will not succeed. Otherwise the applicant's claim should be heard on its merits.[48]

The legislation requires that the applicant was largely financially dependent upon the deceased "immediately before the death."[49] This was interpreted in *Re Beaumont* and *Jelley* v. *Iliffe*[50] as requiring a settled basis or arrangement between the parties whereby the deceased was substantially maintaining the applicant at that time, rather than that the deceased was actually providing maintenance for the applicant at the time of death. Should the settled arrangement have ceased prior to the deceased's death the applicant will not qualify.[51] There is no need, however, to establish that the deceased intended that he should maintain the applicant after his death. Similarly the fact that there has been mutuality of dependence at some earlier time does not preclude a finding of dependency on the deceased immediately before his death, if such dependency has arisen prior to the death.[52]

It has been suggested that section 1(1)(e) is qualified also by section 3(4) so that it is not sufficient that the deceased was maintaining the applicant at the date of death unless the deceased had assumed responsibility for the maintenance of the applicant and was maintaining him under that assumption. The Court of Appeal in *Jelley* v. *Iliffe* adopted a less restrictive approach on this point than that adopted in *Re Beaumont* and held that the fact that the applicant was being maintained by the deceased under an arrangement subsisting at the deceased's death generally did raise a presumption that the deceased had assumed responsibility for the applicant's maintenance. Mr. Jelley, the applicant, a widower, went to live with Mrs. Iliffe, the widow of his brother-in-law, in her house. They shared the accommodation and pooled their incomes. The applicant provided some furniture for the house, looked after the garden and did household jobs. He provided her with companionship, although the evidence was equivocal as to whether or not they were living as husband and wife. She provided him with rent-free accommodation, cooked and washed for him. Their relationship continued for eight years until Mrs. Iliffe's death. All her property passed under her will to her children and Mr. Jelley applied under section 1(1)(e). The Court of

---

46 *Jelley* v. *Iliffe* [1981] Fam. 128. It has been argued that this interpretation yields results quite inconsistent with the purposes of the Act: see Dewar, "Cohabitees: Contributions and Consideration" (1982) 12 Fam. Law 158.

47 *Re Kirby, dec'd; Hirons* v. *Rolfe* (1982) 3 F.L.R. 249 (deceased contributed 50 per cent. more than cohabitee applicant).

48 Which should not of itself, however, be taken as endorsing the applicant's chances of eventual success. See *per* Stephenson L.J. in *Jelley* v. *Iliffe* [1981] Fam. 128 at 140.

49 s.1(1)(e).

50 [1981] Fam. 128: see Coldham, (1982) 45 M.L.R. 100; Pople, [1981] J.S.W.L. 364.

51 See, *e.g. Kourkgy* v. *Lusher* (1983) 4 F.L.R. 65 (deceased left the applicant after a number of years' intermittent cohabitation returning to live with his wife a mere nine days before dying of a heart attack); *Layton* v. *Martin* [1986] 2 F.L.R. 227 (applicant's relationship with the deceased ended two years before his death).

52 *Bishop* v. *Plumley* [1991] 1 All E.R. 236.

Appeal, allowing the applicant's appeal against the striking out of his application, held that the deceased's provision of rent-free accommodation did, in all the circumstances, amount to an assumption of responsibility for the applicant's maintenance. As it was not clear whether his contributions had equalled or outweighed that benefit, his application ought not to have been struck out and was sent back for decision on its merits.

As section 1(1)(e) is concerned with dependency, claims are not limited to those whose relationship is that of *de facto* spouse and may be made by anyone who comes within the terms of the section, including a mistress, lover or homosexual partner. The subsection essentially caters for parties to a stable relationship where a moral duty is owed to the survivor of that relationship. The Act is hardly thereby becoming a "mistresses' charter."[53] If the relationship between the applicant and the deceased is one of housekeeper and employer, dependency will be very difficult for the applicant to prove, whereas there will be a stronger claim in the case of a stable cohabitation where the parties have lived together as man and wife,[54] rather than as employer and employee.

A claim under the 1975 Act is a personal one, so if a surviving cohabitee applicant dies before the application is decided, it cannot be continued by the applicant's personal representatives.[55]

Reasonable financial provision

Once a person has shown that he or more usually she (it will be assumed that the woman is the applicant) is qualified to apply, she must then show that the deceased's estate has failed to make reasonable financial provision for her and that the court should order some financial provision to be made. There is here an important distinction. If the applicant is a spouse, reasonable financial provision means such as it would be reasonable in all the circumstances to receive, whether or not for the applicant's maintenance. In the case of any other applicant, including a cohabitee, reasonable financial provision is limited to maintenance.[56] A spouse is treated as though the marriage had ended in divorce[57] and therefore entitled to be considered for a share of the deceased's capital, but a cohabitee can look only for maintenance.[58]

---

53 H.C. Deb. Vol. 898, col. 172. For an early discussion of the issue, see Cadwallader, "A Mistresses' Charter?" [1980] Conv. 46.
54 As for example in *C.A.* v. *C.C.*, *The Times*, November 17, 1978, *sub nom. In the estate of McC.* (1979) 9 Fam. Law 26.
55 See *Re R., R.* v. *O.* [1986] Fam. Law 58; *Whytte* v. *Ticehurst* [1986] Fam. 64; *Re Bramwell, dec'd; Campbell* v. *Tobin* [1988] 2 F.L.R. 263.
56 1975 Act, s.1(2).
57 *Ibid.* s.3(2), and see *Moody* v. *Stevenson* [1992] 2 All E.R. 524.
58 The Law Commission has recommended that this distinction should continue, as the claim which a cohabitee should have is to some recognition for the deceased's contribution to the common household rather than for the, perhaps greater, share in the deceased's accumulated assets which a spouse may reasonably expect when the marriage ends by death or divorce: see Law. Com. No. 187, para. 60.

If a deceased cohabitee has adequately provided for his partner in his will, but has not adequately provided for his spouse, then the surviving spouse can seek an order that some part of the estate be given for her benefit. The outcome of any claim by a surviving spouse will depend upon the reasonableness of the deceased's failure to provide for his marriage partner.[59] It may be, for example, that the estate is too small to provide adequately for both his spouse and his cohabitee and so a choice has to be made between the moral obligation to the cohabitee and the legal obligation to the spouse. Thus, if the spouse has adequate means whereas the cohabitee is destitute, it will be reasonable for there to be no provision for the surviving spouse. Even before the 1975 Act the courts recognised that in such circumstances the deceased's moral obligation to a cohabitee may defeat a widow's application.[60] It may be, however, that in many cases the deceased also had a moral obligation to the spouse if they had lived together for a lengthy period before the deceased's cohabitation with someone else began. Moreover the Act provides for a higher standard of financial provision for spouses than for cohabitees. So if a cohabitee is self-supporting, her claim is weakened against that of a surviving spouse.

An application can be made by a former spouse of the deceased provided that the applicant has not remarried.[61] There will be few cases, however, where a former spouse will be able to satisfy the requirement that the deceased's estate did *not* make reasonable financial provision for the applicant[62] in view of the court's powers on divorce to make capital adjustments between spouses.[63] Any claim by a former spouse is limited to maintenance. On granting a decree of divorce, nullity or judicial separation or at any time thereafter, the court may on the application of either spouse order that the other spouse shall not, on the death of the applicant, be entitled to apply for an order.[64] A cohabitee who has an ex-spouse in respect of whom such an order is in force will be able to leave his property free from any claim under the 1975 Act by the former spouse.

The principles to be applied in deciding whether or not reasonable financial provision has been made for the applicant were considered in *Re Coventry*.[65] The Court of Appeal emphasised that each case depends upon its own facts, but that it is not sufficient that the applicant is in financial need, for that fact alone will not necessarily make it unreasonable that no financial provision has been made for the applicant. The

---

59 On provision for surviving spouse generally, see Miller, (1986) 102 L.Q.R. 465.
60 *Re Joslin* [1941] Ch. 200. In *Moody* v. *Stevenson* [1992] 2 All E.R. 524 the Court of Appeal indicated that the pre-1975 Act case law should be approached with caution, particularly where a surviving spouse is involved.
61 The 1975 Act, s.1(1)(*b*). Remarriage includes a reference to a marriage which is void or voidable: see s.25(5). A former cohabitee cannot apply: see above, p. 214.
62 For an example of such a case, see *Re Crawford, dec'd* (1983) 4 F.L.R. 273.
63 *Re Fullard, dec'd* [1981] 3 W.L.R. 743. See Shindler, [1982] Conv. 75. *Cf. Re Farrow, dec'd* [1987] 1 F.L.R. 205.
64 1975 Act, s.15 (as substituted).
65 [1980] Ch. 461.

court, in deciding whether or not reasonable financial provision has been made, has to make a value judgment. It is not a question of the court deciding how the deceased's assets should be fairly divided, nor is it a question of whether it might have been reasonable for the deceased to have provided for the applicant, but whether in all the circumstances, looked at objectively, it is unreasonable that the deceased's estate does not so provide.

It is only when the applicant has shown that the deceased's estate has failed to make reasonable financial provision that the court can proceed to decide the next issue of how, if at all, to exercise its discretionary powers under the 1975 Act.

Considerations when deciding a claim

Section 3 sets out the matters which the court must consider in deciding, first, whether or not reasonable financial provision has been made for the applicant's maintenance and, secondly, if such provision has not been made, what order, if any, the court in the exercise of its discretion should make. These matters, which are the same for both considerations, are:

- the financial resources and financial needs which the applicant, any other applicant, or any beneficiary of the deceased's estate, has or is likely to have in the foreseeable future;
- any obligations and responsibilities which the deceased had towards any applicant or beneficiary;
- the size and nature of the net estate;
- any physical or mental disability of any applicant or beneficiary; and
- any other matter, including the conduct of the applicant or anyone else, which the court may consider relevant.

Reference has already been made to the additional consideration applicable in the case of an application under section 1(1)(e) that the court must have regard to the extent to which, and the basis upon which, the deceased assumed responsibility for the applicant's maintenance and to the length of time for which the deceased discharged that responsibility.[66] In *Harrington* v. *Gill*[67] the task facing the court was put in the form of the question: "What testamentary provision would a reasonable man in the position of this deceased have made for the plaintiff in all the circumstances, including the matters set out in section 3?" In considering the matters to which the court is required to have regard, it is the facts as known at the date of the hearing which are material.[68] So the court can take into account any change of circumstances after the deceased's

---

66 1975 Act, s.3(4): see above, p. 214.
67 (1983) 4 F.L.R. 265 at 271.
68 *Ibid*. s.3(5). The court is not entitled to take account of legally unenforceable assurances given by other beneficiaries: see *Rajabally* v. *Rajabally* [1987] 2 F.L.R. 390.

death, for example, the fact that the applicant is being maintained by someone else. When the court is deciding whether or not the deceased's estate makes reasonable financial provision for the applicant, the test is an objective one, *i.e.* in the light of the circumstances as viewed by the court at the date of the hearing and not as viewed by the deceased at the time of his death. The court may, however, take into account any wish of the deceased expressed before his death, including, if and so far as is relevant, any unexecuted will of the deceased.[69]

Section 3 of the 1975 Act makes it clear that the issues of whether or not there has been reasonable financial provision from the deceased's estate for the applicant, and, if not, whether and how the court should exercise its discretion, are inter-related. It will be unusual if the court finds that there has been a failure to make reasonable financial provision for it not to order some financial provision for the applicant. The size of the deceased's estate is clearly an important factor and in the case of small estates the cost of litigation may well make a claim unprofitable.[70] The court must take into account the alternative sources of income which are available to any applicant, for example, welfare benefits. Likewise the income of any beneficiaries of the estate must be considered, for the amount the beneficiaries will receive may be reduced by any order under the Act. The issue of failure to provide reasonable maintenance for the applicant must be considered in relation to the deceased's net estate and the legitimate claims of the beneficiaries to that estate.[71]

Competing claims are particularly likely where, for example, a husband and wife separate, the husband cohabits with another woman and then dies without making provision for his cohabitee. If she applies under the Act the court, in balancing the competing claims, will consider, *inter alia*, the income, capital and earning capacity of the applicant and the wife as well as any other beneficiary, together with their financial obligations and responsibilities.[72] The length of the cohabitation and of the marriage, the age of the parties and their contributions to the welfare of the families are not specifically referred to, as they are on an application by a spouse or former spouse,[73] but are likely to be relevant as "any other matter".[74] The deceased's reasons for his dispositions can also be considered as "any other matter".[75] Competing claims may arise also between a *de facto* spouse and a mistress.[76]

---

69 *Re Collins, dec'd* [1990] Fam. 56.
70 See, *e.g. Re Coventry* [1980] Ch. 461.
71 See, *e.g. Williams* v. *Roberts* [1986] 1 F.L.R. 349; *Clark* v. *Jones* (unreported, December 2, 1985, C.A.).
72 1975 Act, s.3(6).
73 *Ibid.* s.3(2). The Law Commission has recommended that the relevant factors should be the same for cohabitees as for spouses: see Law. Com. No. 187, para. 60.
74 *Ibid.* s.3(1)(g).
75 See also *ibid.* s. 21.
76 See, *e.g. Malone* v. *Harrison* [1979] 1 W.L.R. 1353 where Hollings J. accepted that the order in favour of the mistress should not be at the expense of the *de facto* wife and was ordered to be taken from the legacy to the deceased's brother.

Specific statutory reference is made to the conduct of the applicant or any other person. In so far as section 3 of the 1975 Act is modelled on section 25 of the Matrimonial Causes Act 1973 it is to be expected that conduct is to be given the same meaning in both sections. The matrimonial causes legislation (but not the inheritance legislation) has, however, been amended[77] to make it clear that it is only conduct such that it would, in the opinion of the court, be inequitable to disregard that is relevant. That amendment seems merely to codify the judicial approach to the issue of conduct.[78] In line with the Law Commission's suggestion, it will remain consistent for the court to limit conduct to that which it would be inequitable to disregard, at least on the application of a surviving spouse.[79] It is submitted that the test to be applied on the application of a surviving cohabitee should be the same,[80] at least in so far as concerns allegations of blameworthy conduct.

Orders

Having considered the matters set out in section 3, the court may, if it is satisfied that the disposition of the deceased's estate is not such as to make reasonable financial provision for the applicant, make one or more of the orders in section 2. An order in favour of a cohabitee can only be for her maintenance[81] but can take the form of periodical payments, a lump sum[82] (in one or more instalments),[83] transfer or settlement of property,[84] or acquisition and transfer or settlement of property.[85]

Where the deceased was, immediately before his death, beneficially entitled to a joint tenancy of any property, then, if before the end of the period of six months from the date on which representation to his estate was first taken out, an application is made for an order under section 2, the court, "for the purpose of facilitating the making of financial provision for the applicant", has a discretion to order that the deceased's

---

77 By the Matrimonial and Family Proceedings Act 1984, s.3.
78 See above, p. 192.
79 Law Com. No. 61, paras. 35 and 36: see, *e.g. Re Snoek, dec'd* (1983) 13 Fam. Law 18.
80 For a case concerning cohabitees where conduct was considered, but without any discussion of the concept, see *Williams* v. *Roberts* [1986] 1 F.L.R. 349.
81 See above, p. 215.
82 See, *e.g. C.A.* v. *C.C.*, *The Times*, November 17, 1978, *sub nom. In the estate of McC.* (1979) 9 Fam. Law 26 (from a net estate of some £20,000-£35,000 a figure of £5,000 was "plucked out of the air"); *Malone* v. *Harrison* [1979] 1 W.L.R. 1353 (from a net estate of £480,000 a figure of £19,000 was carefully calculated using the method of the multiplier: see Bryan, "The Mistress and The Multiplier" (1980) 96 L.Q.R. 165); *Williams* v. *Roberts* [1986] 1 F.L.R. 349 (£20,000 from a net estate of between £110,000-£120,000).
83 See further 1975 Act, s.7.
84 See, *e.g. Harrington* v. *Gill* (1983) 4 F.L.R. 265 (a settlement on the applicant cohabitee for life of the house in which she and the deceased had been living and the transfer of the contents absolutely in addition to a lump sum of £5,000 and a further £5,000 to be used to provide income from a net estate of £65,000).
85 See, *e.g. Re Haig* (1979) 129 N.L.J. 420.

severable share of that property shall be treated as part of the net estate,[86] rather than passing to the surviving joint tenant. So, for example, a surviving spouse's right of survivorship in the home could be subject to a claim by a cohabitee and vice versa. In *Kourkgy* v. *Lusher*[87] it was held that this discretion should not be deferred until the court was deciding what order should be made but should be exercised when the court is deciding the preliminary issue as to whether reasonable financial provision has been made for the applicant. This approach was followed in *Jessop* v. *Jessop*[88] where the deceased, a petty officer, maintained and kept contact with two families. His wife and three children in Cleveland knew nothing of his long-standing cohabitee and their daughter in Portsmouth. The cohabitee knew of the wife's existence but not of the three children and had been misled into thinking the marriage was a legal shell. The deceased's beneficial half interest in the home he shared with his cohabitee passed to her by survivorship. On the wife's claim under the 1975 Act the Court of Appeal held that there was jurisdiction under section 9 to treat the deceased's severable half share in the home as part of his estate and could do so when considering whether there was a failure to make reasonable financial provision.

The deceased's estate may also include property disposed of during his lifetime with the intention of defeating an application for financial provision. If certain conditions are satisfied the donee may be ordered to provide money or property up to the value he received, for the purpose of providing financial provision, irrespective of whether or not the donee still has any of the property given to him. The court also has power to review contracts made with the intent of defeating an application for financial provision.[89] An order for financial provision operates retrospectively from the date of the deceased's death.[90] A periodical payments order in favour of a former spouse of the deceased, or a spouse where the marriage was the subject of a decree of judicial separation, ceases on remarriage[91] but not on cohabitation. An order in favour of a surviving spouse is not so affected by remarriage.

An order can only be made out of the deceased's net estate as defined in the Act.[92] Where the deceased has, in accordance with any statute, nominated someone to receive money or property on his death it is to be treated as part of the net estate.[93] In *Re Cairnes, dec'd,*[94] the deceased

---

86 1975 Act, s.9 and see *Powell* v. *Osbourne* [1993] 1 F.C.R. 797.
87 (1983) 4 F.L.R. 65: see also *Re Crawford, dec'd* (1983) 4 F.L.R. 273.
88 [1992] 1 F.L.R. 591.
89 1975 Act, ss.10 and 11, respectively. The ambit of these sections is outside the scope of this work.
90 *Ibid.* s.19(1).
91 *Ibid.* s.19(2).
92 *Ibid.* s.25, and see *Re Dr. Kozdrach, dec'd* [1981] Conv. 224.
93 *Ibid.* s.8(1).
94 (1983) 4 F.L.R. 225.

had nominated his wife as beneficiary under his employers' pension scheme. On their divorce the deceased lived for varying periods with both his former wife and another woman, Mrs. Howard. On his death Mrs. Howard applied under the 1975 Act and claimed that the death benefit formed part of the estate. The estate was otherwise exceedingly small. Her claim failed because the deceased's power to dispose of the death benefit was strictly circumscribed and also because the nomination was under a pension scheme and not "in accordance with the provisions of any enactment".

If the court considers that the applicant is in immediate financial need, but it is not yet possible to determine what order, if any, should be made under section 2 and that property forming part of the net estate is or can be made available, the court has power to make an interim order.[95]

Procedure

The County Court and the High Court have jurisdiction to hear an application for financial provision under the 1975 Act and the County Court's jurisdiction is unlimited.[96] In the High Court, proceedings may be issued in either the Chancery Division or the Family Division. As the matter is of a family nature it is to be regretted that the Law Commission's recommendation that the High Court jurisdiction should be assigned exclusively to the Family Division[97] has yet to be implemented. Application in the County Court must be by originating application[98] and in the High Court by originating summons supported by affidavit.[99]

A grant of probate or letters of administration must have been obtained before an application can be made.[1] Application must be made within six months from the date on which representation[2] to the deceased's estate was first taken out,[3] unless the court gives permission for a later application.[4] If it is wished to apply after the six-month period the court's leave must be requested in the application stating the grounds for the request.[5] An order under section 9 in relation to property of

---

95 *Ibid.* s.5, and see *Re Ralphs* [1968] 1 W.L.R. 1522.
96 County Courts Act 1984, s.25 (as amended).
97 Law Com. No. 61, rec. 63.
98 The procedure to be followed is prescribed by C.C.R. 1981, Ord. 48 and see below, p. 259.
99 The relevant procedure is to be found in R.S.C., Ord. 99. See also *Practice Direction* [1976] 1 W.L.R. 418.
1 See *Re McBroom, dec'd* [1992] 2 F.L.R. 49.
2 *I.e.* effective representation: see *Re Freeman, dec'd* [1985] F.L.R. 543.
3 The personal representatives are not liable for having distributed the estate after the six-month period but property may be recovered from the beneficiaries to whom it has been distributed: see s.20(1).
4 1975 Act, s.4 and see *Re Ruttie* [1970] 1 W.L.R. 89; *Re Salmon, dec'd; Coard v. National Westminster Bank Ltd.* [1981] Ch. 167.
5 C.C.R. 1981, Ord. 48, r. 2(1)(*h*); *Practice Direction* [1976] 1 W.L.R. 418, and see below, p. 259.

which the deceased was joint tenant can only be made if the application was made within the six-month period.

2. THE HOME

A main concern of a surviving cohabitee will be his or her[6] rights in the family home. Their nature and scope will depend upon the type of occupation, in particular whether the home was owned or rented by one or both of the parties.

Owned

If the home was owned solely by the deceased cohabitee, then it will be disposed of according to the deceased's will or, if there is no valid will, according to the law of intestacy. The surviving cohabitee will succeed to the home only if it is left to her in the will, for a cohabitee has no rights of succession on a partner's intestacy.[7] If the survivor can establish a beneficial interest in the property,[8] however, this can be enforced against the deceased's personal representatives. The survivor should seek the appointment[9] of an additional trustee to protect her interest. In the event of disagreement as to the disposition of the property, application will have to be made under the Law of Property Act 1925, s.30.[10] In the absence of any beneficial interest the survivor will need to consider whether there is any proprietary estoppel[11] or rights arising under a licence[12] in her favour.

A gift of land by delivery of title deeds[13] may be valid as a *donatio mortis causa* notwithstanding the absence of writing if three conditions are satisfied:

(1) the gift is in contemplation, although not necessarily expectation of impending death;
(2) the gift was made upon the condition that it was to be absolute and perfected only on the testator's death, being revocable until death occurred and ineffective if it did not; and
(3) there must be delivery of the subject-matter of the gift or the essential indicia of title thereto, which amounts to a parting with

---

6 Examples will have the woman as survivor.
7 See above, p. 209.
8 See above, p. 19.
9 Under the Trustee Act 1925, s.41. On other methods of protecting rights arising from a beneficial interest, see above, p. 31.
10 See *Stott* v. *Ratcliffe* (1981) 126 S.J. 310; (1983) 133 N.L.J. 303, and above, p. 45.
11 See above, p. 37 and Davey, "Testamentary promises" (1988) 8 L.S. 92.
12 See above, p. 52.
13 *Quaere* the position if it is registered land.

domain, and not mere physical possession, over the subject-matter of the gift.

In *Sen* v. *Headley*[14] the deceased, while very ill, told the plaintiff, his former cohabitee, that his house was hers, that the deeds were in a steel box and that she had the keys in her bag. He died three days later. The plaintiff found the box in the house and using a key which she thought the deceased had slipped into her handbag she opened it and took possession of the deeds. The Court of Appeal held that the doctrine of *donatio mortis causa* applied to a gift of land and on the facts the three conditions were satisfied.

If the property is left to the surviving cohabitee it might still be subject to a claim by a spouse or former spouse of the deceased, particularly if the property is the former matrimonial home, either on the ground that the surviving spouse has a beneficial interest in the property or under the Inheritance (Provision for Family and Dependants) Act 1975.[15]

If the home was owned solely by the surviving cohabitee, ownership will remain unchanged, unless it can be shown that the deceased had a beneficial interest in the property, or unless the property had formerly belonged to the deceased and had been conveyed to the surviving cohabitee as a means of defeating a claim by a third party, for example, a member of the deceased's family under the Inheritance (Provision for Family and Dependants) Act 1975,[16] or creditors under the Insolvency Act 1986.

If the home was jointly owned by the deceased and the surviving cohabitee, the succession rights depend upon the nature of the beneficial ownership.[17] If the property was beneficially owned by the parties as joint tenants the right of survivorship between joint tenants operates and on the death of one the survivor automatically inherits the other's share. This *jus accrescendi* is subject to claims against the deceased's share under the Inheritance (Provision for Family and Dependants) Act 1975.[18] The right of survivorship does not operate if either of the parties severed the joint tenancy during their lifetime,[19] in which case the parties then become beneficial tenants in common. If the property was beneficially owned by the parties as tenants in common each is regarded as owning a separate share, so on the death of one of the parties his share forms part of his estate and does not pass automatically to the survivor. Hence the importance of clearly identifying the nature of the shared beneficial ownership at the time of purchase.[20]

---

14 [1991] 2 All E.R. 636; Thornley, [1991] C.L.J. 404; Halliwell, [1991] Conv. 307; Baker, (1993) 109 L.Q.R. 19.
15 See above, p. 210.
16 s.10: see above, p. 220.
17 See above, p. 14 and Roberts, "Will Drafting and Property Ownership: Bearing in mind Cohabitees and Lesbian and Gay Couples" [1992] Fam. Law. 77.
18 s.9: see above, p. 220.
19 See above, p. 17.
20 See above, p. 14.

Rented

If the tenancy was in the surviving cohabitee's name, his or her rights are unaffected. If the tenancy was a joint one, with the surviving cohabitee, the tenancy will continue in favour of the survivor.

If the home was rented by the deceased cohabitee alone then, in contrast to the precarious position of a cohabitee who is deserted by, or required to leave by, a sole tenant partner,[21] the surviving cohabitee may be able to continue in occupation and become a statutory tenant by succession. There are different provisions applicable to private sector and public sector tenancies.

Private sector tenancies
Rent Act 1977 tenancies Statutory succession to protected or statutory tenancies[22] was amended significantly by the Housing Act 1988 where the tenant died after January 15, 1989, and usually allows a tenancy to pass by succession only once. Where the death was on or before that date, the applicable law was not amended[23] and permitted up to two successions.

Where an original protected or statutory tenant dies after January 15, 1989, a spouse residing in the dwelling-house immediately before the tenant's death becomes the statuory tenant so long as she continues to occupy it as her residence.[24] Moreover "a person who was living with the original tenant as his or her wife or husband shall be treated as the spouse of the original tenant".[25] The issue under the amended law is whether or not the claimant cohabitee's relationship with the deceased tenant was of sufficient stability and permanence to constitute living as husband and wife and not, as previously, whether or not she was a member of the tenant's family residing with him at the time of death and for the six months up to the death. The case law on the original wording[26] is relevant only in so far as the courts concentrated upon relationships akin to marriage when seeking to ascertain membership of a family. The current test of living together as husband and wife is the more usual one applicable to the evaluation of cohabitation.[27] A similar, but not identical, wording is used in relation to public sector tenancies, where it has been held, for example, that a homosexual cohabitation cannot constitute living as husband and wife.[28] The similarity of wording would no

---

21 See above, p. 59.
22 For meaning, see above, p. 58.
23 See Rent Act 1977, Sched., Pt. I, discussed in the second edition of this book, paras. 8-27 to 8-30.
24 *Ibid*. Sched. 1, para. 2 (as amended).
25 Housing Act 1988, Sched. 4, para. 2(2), amending Rent Act 1977, Sched. 1.
26 See the second edition of this book, paras. 8-27 to 8-29.
27 See, for example, in the context of protection from domestic violence, above, p. 161 and the cohabitation rule in social security law, above, p. 81.
28 See below, p. 228.

doubt lead to the same interpretation of the amended Rent Act 1977 provision.[29]

In one respect a surviving spouse is more favourably treated than a surviving cohabitee. Either claimant must have been residing in the dwelling-house immediately before the tenant's death, but a cohabitee must also have been so living with the tenant whereas a spouse need not. If the tenant's cohabitation has been of a pluralistic nature so that more than one partner qualifies, whether as spouse and cohabitee or both as cohabitee, there is no provision for joint succession and they are required to agree amongst themselves who will be the successor. If they cannot agree the County Court has the power to decide.[30]

In the absence of either a surviving spouse or surviving cohabitee, there can be a succession by any member of the tenant's family who was residing with him in the dwelling-house at the time of the tenant's death, and for the two years immediately before his death.[31] The House of Lords considered the meaning of the term "family" in *Carega Properties* v. *Sharratt*[32] in relation to a cohabitation of a platonic nature between a man and a childless widow, 50 years his senior. It was decided that two adults who lived together in a platonic relationship could not, in the absence of any other relationship, be a family for the purpose of the Rent Act. The following have constituted a family for the purpose of the Rent Act:

- brother and sister[33];
- parent and child, (including a child of unmarried parents, a step-child and adopted child)[34];
- a grandchild,[35] nephews and nieces[36] and in-laws living together.[37]

Protection does not extend to a *de facto* adoption of an adult, for being treated as a member of the family does not constitute being a member of the family.[38] There is no authority under the Rent Act as to whether or not a homosexual cohabitation can constitute a family. It has been held that it cannot in relation to a public sector tenancy,[39] but in that context the issue is slightly different for that legislation requires that "they live together as husband and wife". The courts have, however, tended to regard the issues as the same and it seems likely that a homosexual

---

29 See also below in the context of member of the tenant's family.
30 Housing Act 1988, Sched. 4, para. 2(3), amending Rent Act 1977, Sched. 1, para. 3.
31 Succession is to a periodic assured tenancy and not a statutory tenancy: Housing Act 1988, s.39(5).
32 [1979] 1 W.L.R. 928. See also *Ross* v. *Collins* [1964] 1 W.L.R. 425.
33 *Price* v. *Gould* (1930) 143 L.T. 333.
34 Whether or not there has been a legal adoption (see *Brock* v. *Wollams* [1949] 2 K.B. 388) so presumably also foster children.
35 *Collier* v. *Stoneman* [1957] 1 W.L.R. 1108.
36 *Jones* v. *Whitehill* [1950] 2 K.B. 204.
37 *Standingford* v. *Probert* [1950] 1 K.B. 377.
38 See *Sefton Holdings Ltd.* v. *Cairns* [1988] 2 F.L.R. 109.
39 See below, p. 228.

cohabitation would not be regarded as constituting a family for this purpose.

Housing Act 1988 assured tenancies[40] Statutory succession to an assured periodic tenancy[41] is possible only in favour of a sole tenant's "spouse". Where immediately before the sole tenant's death the tenant's "spouse" was occupying the dwelling-house as her only or principal home and the tenant was not himself a successor, then the tenancy vests in the spouse and does not devolve under the tenant's will or intestacy.[42] In line with the amended Rent Act 1977 provision, and in contrast to succession to a public sector tenancy,[43] "a person who was living with the tenant as his or her wife or husband shall be treated as the tenant's spouse".[44] A married spouse is not required to have been living with the tenant but if the claimant was not married to the deceased she must show, in addition to the fact that she was occupying the house as her only or principal home immediately before the tenant's death, that she was living with the tenant as his spouse. The Act does not indicate whether or not the living with the tenant as spouse and the occupation of the home (which must immediately precede the tenant's death) need coincide. Indeed section 17(4) does not stipulate a time requirement for the cohabitation, although when read together with section 17(1)(*b*) the implication is that the living with the deceased as spouse must immediately precede the tenant's death. It is submitted that this should be interpreted in a similar way to the "immediately before the death" in the Inheritance (Provision for Family and Dependants) Act 1975,[45] so as to require a settled basis or arrangement between the parties, so that, for example, disruption by hospitalisation would not defeat that basis or arrangement.

If more than one person qualifies as a "spouse" who was occupying the premises as his or her only or principal home, for example, if there was a *ménage à trois*, they may agree between themselves who is to be treated as the tenant's spouse and in default of agreement the County Court may decide.[46] Unlike the Rent Act 1977 succession provisions, there is no possibility of a member of the tenant's family other than a "spouse" being entitled to succeed.

There can be no succession if the deceased tenant was a successor, which will have been the case if the tenancy was vested in him by succession under the Act, under the Rent Act 1977, under the Rent (Agriculture) Act 1976, under the will or intestacy of a previous tenant,

---

40 Including assured agricultural occupancies: see s.24(3).
41 Not a fixed-term tenancy, which devolves by will or intestacy and the recipient will be a successor, so as to preclude any further succession: see below. For meaning of periodic tenancy, see above, p. 60.
42 Housing Act 1988, s.17(1).
43 Where a cohabitee must come within the category of a member of the deceased's family, in order to qualify: see below, p. 227.
44 *Ibid.* s.17(4) and see above, p. 224.
45 s.1(1)(*e*): see above, p. 214.
46 Housing Act 1988, s.17(5).

or by survivorship.[47] Thus where one of a married couple dies and the other succeeds to the tenancy, there can be no succession in favour of any new partner of the survivor.

Public sector tenancies

A person is qualified to succeed to a local authority or housing association secure tenancy[48] if he occupied the property as his only or principal home at the date of the tenant's death *and* he is either (a) the tenant's spouse or (b) another member of the tenant's family who has resided with the tenant throughout the period of 12 months ending with the tenant's death.[49] In contrast to private sector tenancies a spouse is limited to the tenant's partner by marriage and has no extended meaning, so for a cohabitee to qualify it must be as a member of the tenant's family. Moreover, a spouse does not have to have been residing with the deceased tenant whereas any other member of his family has to have done so for at least a year up to the date of death, unlike the private sector where there is no minimum residence period. The Housing Act 1985 does not state where the parties must have lived throughout the period, but it was held by the House of Lords in *Waltham Forest London Borough Council* v. *Thomas*[50] that the requirement of 12 months' residence with the tenant does not require residence at a particular house or even in a house which was subject to a secure tenancy but simply that the successor occupied the council house as his home at the death of the tenant and made his home for 12 months as a member of the tenant's family. It does not matter where the successor and the tenant lived together for that period.

A person is defined as a member of another's family[51] if:

(a) he is the spouse of that person, or he and that person live together as husband and wife; or
(b) he is that person's parent, grandparent, child, grandchild, brother, sister, uncle, aunt, nephew or niece.[52]

For a cohabitee to qualify the parties must have lived together as husband and wife, so the test of cohabitation is analagous to that

---

47 *Ibid.* s.17(2). Under s.17(3) a person is a successor even if granted a new tenancy of the same house following an earlier tenacy to which he succeeded.
48 For meaning, see Housing Act 1985, ss.79-81; s.89 provides for succession to a periodic tenancy. Section 90 provides for the devolution of a certain term tenancy in accordance with the deceased's will or the law of intestacy.
49 Housing Act 1985, s.87.
50 [1992] 3 All E.R. 244, overruling *South Northamptonshire District Council* v. *Power* [1987] 3 All E.R. 831.
51 Housing Act 1985, s.113. The Housing Associations Act 1985 uses the same definition for the purposes of s.13 of that Act.
52 Including for the purposes of (b) relationships by marriage, relationships of the half blood, step-children and children whose parents have not married (*Ibid.* s.113(2)). Adopted children will be included by virtue of the Adoption Act 1976, ss.12 and 39. No provision is made to include the foster child.

applicable to private sector tenancies. Although the Housing Act 1985 does not state that the parties must not be of the same sex, the Court of Appeal in *Harrogate Borough Council* v. *Simpson*[53] held that two women who lived together in a committed homosexual relationship could not in law be described as living together as husband and wife so as to entitle the survivor to succeed to the secure council tenancy on the tenant's death. In the words of Watkins L.J.[54]:

> " . . . it would be surprising in the extreme to learn that public opinion is such today that it would recognise a homosexual union as being akin to a state of living as husband and wife. The ordinary man and woman . . . would in my opinion not think even remotely of there being a true resemblance between these two very different states of affairs."

Where more than one person qualifies to succeed, preference is given to the tenant's spouse over another member of the tenant's family, including a cohabitee. If there is more than one other member of the tenant's family they must agree between them and in the absence of such agreement the landlord, rather than the County Court, may select.[55] So if there were children of the deceased tenant living in the premises as their only or main home as well as a cohabitee, they would rank equally. If they could not agree, the landlord could ultimately decide.

There can be only one succession and not two as under the Rent Act.[56] There cannot be a succession where the tenant himself is a successor which includes, *inter alia*, a surviving joint tenant.[57]

3. Pensions and State Benefits

Pension funds[58]

Many pension funds provide for payment to the deceased's widow (and sometimes widower) but not to a surviving cohabitee. In all cases it is necessary to look at the provisions of the scheme concerned. So, for

---

53 [1986] 2 F.L.R. 91. See McLeod, "Gays and Succession to Council House Tenancies" (1985) 82 L.S. Gaz. 3517. For rejection of a complaint to the European Commission on Human Rights, see *Application No. 11716/85* v. *U.K.*
54 [1986] 2 F.L.R. 91 at 95.
55 Housing Act 1985, s.89.
56 Housing Act 1985, s.87.
57 See *ibid.* s.88 for that and other definitions of successor. If a joint tenancy is determined and the landlord grants a sole tenancy to one of the joint tenants, the latter is not a successor: see *Bassetlaw District Council* v. *Renshaw* [1992] 1 All E.R. 925.
58 See Rosettenstein, "Cohabitation and English Public Sector Occupational Pension Schemes: Problems and Policy in Pursuit of the New Property" in Eekelaar and Katz (eds.), *Marriage and Cohabitation in Contemporary Societies* (1980), Chap. 32.

example, some provide payment to the person nominated[59] by the deceased, which could include a cohabitee. Others make provision for payment to a "dependent relative" in the absence of a surviving spouse, but such payments are often at the discretion of the pension fund. Moreover, a cohabitee (other than in a family cohabitation) will be unlikely to come within the scheme's definition of a relative. If the scheme provides for payments to a "dependant", it will depend upon the scheme's definition as to whether or not a cohabitee is included; for example, a definition that "dependants means persons who in the opinion of the trustees shall have been wholly or partly maintained or financially assisted by the member" may well include a cohabitee, whereas a definition based on a relationship by blood or by marriage would not.

A surviving spouse in receipt of a pension should note that some schemes provide for the pension to be payable until death, marriage, or living with another as man and wife. So, not only may a surviving cohabitee receive no pension, but also a surviving spouse who becomes a cohabitee may lose one.

Widow's benefits

It has been seen[60] that cohabitees acquire no national insurance pension rights as a result of their partner's contributions. So a surviving cohabitee is not entitled to a widow's payment, a widowed mother's allowance or a widow's pension, for "widow" is limited to a woman who has lost a husband by death. The social security legislation makes no provision for the extension of the term to include those who were living together as husband and wife at the time of the man's death. It is ironic, therefore, that the lump sum widow's payment is not payable to a widow if she and a man to whom she is not married are living together as husband and wife at the time of her husband's death.[61] Similarly a widowed mother's allowance and a widow's pension are suspended for any period during which she is so living.[62] So once again, in the context of State benefits, cohabitation is recognised only so as to deny benefit. Cohabitation has the advantage over remarriage, however, in that the former suspends these benefits whereas the latter terminates them.

---

59 A pension scheme is not an enactment for the purposes of s.8 of the Inheritance (Provision for Family and Dependants) Act 1975: see *Re Cairnes, dec'd* (1983) 4 F.L.R. 225 and above, p. 220. The nomination of a beneficiary to receive a non-assignable "death in employment" benefit subject to the prior approval of the trustees or management committee of the scheme is not a testamentary disposition and does not have to be executed as if it is a will: see *Baird* v. *Baird* [1990] 2 All E.R. 300.

60 See above, p. 93.

61 Social Security Contributions and Benefits Act 1992, s.36(2). Interpretation is the same as for income-related benefits: see *R(SB) 17/81* and *R(G) 3/81*, above, p. 82.

62 Social Security Contributions and Benefits Act 1992, ss.37(4)(*b*) and 38(3)(*c*). See Bonner *et al*, *Non-Means Tested Benefits: The Legislation* (1993) for further discussion. See also *R(G) 3/81*; *R(S) 4/85*.

Differential treatment in favour of cohabitation applies also under the Naval, Military and Air Forces etc. (Disablement and Death) Services Pensions Order 1983.[63] Any pension to or allowance in respect of a female person, other than a parent, ceases if that person remarries[64] or lives with a man as his wife.[65] If the cohabitation ceases there is a discretionary provision for the pension or allowance to be restored forthwith either wholly or in part[66] whereas in the case of remarriage, the discretion only arises after the death of the second husband.[67]

4. COMPENSATION FOR DEATH

The Fatal Accidents Act 1976 provides that if a person's death is caused by the wrongful act, neglect or default of another such as would (if death had not ensued) have entitled the injured person to bring an action and recover damages, then the person who would have been liable if death had not ensued is liable to an action in damages.[68] Such action is for the benefit of the deceased's dependants, a class of persons which as originally defined excluded a cohabitee, but which has since been extended to include any person who was living with the deceased in the same household as husband and wife immediately before the date of death and had been so living for at least two years before that date.[69] This extended category is thus defined in terms of status as well as dependency.[70] The concepts of living in the same household and living as husband and wife are comparable with those in other contexts,[71] and the latter excludes parties to a homosexual cohabitation. Additionally and unusually there is a temporal requirement, the length of which is likely to exclude some stable relationships.[72]

A claim under this Act is for "the injury resulting from the death to the dependants respectively"[73], *i.e.* "in reference to a reasonable expectation

---

63 S.I. 1983 No. 883.
64 Including a voidable marriage: see *Ward* v. *Secretary of State for Social Services* [1990] 1 F.L.R. 119.
65 S.I. 1983 No. 883., art. 42(1).
66 *Ibid.* art. 42(7).
67 *Ibid.* art. 42(3).
68 Fatal Accidents Act 1976, s.1(1) (as substituted by the Administration of Justice Act 1982, s.3(1)).
69 See Fatal Accidents Act 1976, s.1(3)(*b*) (as substituted). A dependant is otherwise defined as the spouse or former spouse of the deceased; any parent or other ascendant of the deceased; any person treated by the deceased as his parent; any child or other descendant of the deceased; any person who was treated by the deceased as a child of the family in relation to a marriage of the deceased; and any person who is, or is the issue of, a brother, sister, uncle or aunt of the deceased.
70 *Cf.* Inheritance (Provision for Family and Dependants) Act 1975, s.1(1)(*e*), above, p. 211.
71 In particular domestic violence (see above, p. 161), social security (see above, p. 81) and succession to tenancies (see above, p. 224).
72 See below, p. 244.
73 s.3(1) (as substituted).

of pecuniary benefit as of right or otherwise, from the continuance of the life".[74] It will be taken into account that a dependent cohabitee had no enforceable right to financial support by the deceased as a result of their living together.[75] Any children of the relationship can bring an action and may also be able to recover for loss of payment by the deceased to the surviving parent which was for their benefit, in so far as that parent is denied a claim.[76] Claims in respect of the death of a minor child are limited to damages for bereavement,[77] which in the case of the child of unmarried parents are payable only for the child's mother. A spouse, but not a cohabitee, can claim bereavement damages on the death of a partner.

An action under the 1976 Act is brought by dependants to compensate them for their loss of financial support by the deceased. In addition there is the possibility of an independent action against the negligent party by the deceased's estate under the Law Reform (Miscellaneous Provisions) Act 1934 for damages for the deceased's losses up to the time of death. Any damages so recovered, which may not be large, would go to the deceased's estate and could benefit a cohabitee or child who stands to inherit from, or has a claim against, the deceased's estate.

If the deceased has died as a result of criminal injuries coming within the Criminal Injuries Compensation Scheme, a dependant of the victim within the meaning of section 1(3) of the Fatal Accidents Act 1976 may seek compensation under the Scheme.[78] Dependent children of the deceased can also apply.

If the deceased's death was a result of pneumoconiosis or a related disease and the conditions of the Pnuemoconiosis etc. (Workers' Compensation) Act 1979 are satisfied, certain "dependants"[79] are entitled to claim a lump sum payment. In the absence of a qualified spouse or child, a dependant means "a reputed spouse", who was residing with the deceased. The Act does not define "a reputed spouse", thereby adding to the uncertainty in the law relating to cohabitation.

---

74 *Franklin* v. *S.E. Rly.* (1858) 3 H. and N. 211 at 213-214.
75 *Ibid.* s.3(4).
76 *K.* v. *J.M.P. Co. Ltd.* [1976] Q.B. 85.
77 Fixed at £7,500: see Fatal Accidents Act 1976, s.1(3) (as amended by S.I. 1990 No. 2575).
78 See Criminal Justice Act 1988, s.111(1). The statutory provisions are not yet in force; (see above, p. 180), but this revision has been incorporated within the current guidelines.
79 See s.3.

CHAPTER 9

CONTRACTS

A cohabitee can enter into a contract with his or her partner, or with a third party, but it is necessary to consider the extent to which any particular legal consequences follow as a result of the cohabitation.

I. CONTRACTS BETWEEN COHABITEES

Cohabitees are free to enter into contracts with each other in accordance with the ordinary principles of contract law. Hence there must have been an intention to create a legal relationship, an offer and acceptance, clear terms of agreement, consideration, and the agreement must not be illegal or contrary to public policy.

As with contracts between spouses, any such contract may be regarded as an agreement which was not intended to create a legal relationship and is therefore unenforceable.[1] This is particularly so if a cohabitee seeks to rely on an implied contract based on vague assurances. For example, in *Layton v. Martin*[2] the plaintiff had been the mistress of a married man over a number of years. He wrote in 1975 asking her to be his wife in everything but name and offered "financial security during my life, and financial security on my death". Thereafter they cohabited as husband and wife and he paid her a salary plus housekeeping. After his wife's death their unmarried relationship continued for a further three years until it broke down, whereupon he gave the plaintiff written notice of dismissal and, unknown to her, cut her out of his will. They parted without rancour with the plaintiff making no claim against him until his death some two years later. She then claimed, *inter alia*, that the deceased's representation in his letter in 1975 constituted an offer which she, by her subsequent conduct, had accepted and that she was entitled to enforce the contract against his estate. Scott J. held that the evidence did not justify a conclusion that she thought that by going to live with the deceased she was accepting an offer of financial provision, nor that she was induced by his promise to pursue a course of conduct that she would

---

1 See Treitel, *The Law of Contract* (8th ed., 1991), pp. 151-153. An agreement in the case of a family cohabitation, for example, between a brother and a sister, is likely to be unenforceable on this basis, unless there is clear evidence to the contrary.
2 [1986] 2 F.L.R. 227.

not otherwise have embarked upon. Even if she had gone to live with him in reliance on his representation that he would make financial provision for her, the offer was no more than a statement of intention in general terms, not capable of being turned by acceptance into a binding contract. Moreover:

> "in family or quasi-family situations there is always the question whether the parties intended to create a legally binding contract between them. The more general and less precise the language of the so-called contract, the more difficult it will be to infer that intention."[3]

As the deceased was a businessman accustomed to contractual negotiations the judge did not accept that in offering "financial security" he was making an offer which could lead to contractual enforceability.

Parties to a relationship outside marriage who wish to create a legally enforceable agreement should therefore make their intention clear, for example, by entering into a formal written contract to that effect. This should rebut any presumption that the agreement is of a domestic or family nature and the parties did not intend to be bound thereby. The family arrangement cases have for the most part concerned spouses as, for example, in *Balfour* v. *Balfour*[4] where a husband's promise to pay his wife £30 a month maintenance whilst he worked abroad was held to be unenforceable, *inter alia*, on the ground that the parties did not intend the arrangement to be legally binding. This is not to say that every agreement between spouses is not binding. An agreement will be enforceable if, for example, it is clearly a business agreement, or if the parties have separated or are about to separate at the time the arrangements were made.[5]

The fact that cohabitees are not married to each other may strengthen the case that any agreement is not of a purely domestic nature of the type which spouses may be presumed to make. So too the point has been made[6] that contracts entered into by a couple who later marry may be discharged on marriage by a tacit agreement, because the parties do not intend that thereafter their obligations should be legally enforceable.

The obligations of spouses may be seen as being a public matter regulated primarily by the contract of marriage and the remedies available under matrimonial law.[7] As the obligations of parties to a relationship outside marriage are not so regulated, they ought therefore to be free to make private arrangements for the ordering of their relationship,

---

3 *Ibid.* at 239.
4 [1919] 2 K.B. 571.
5 See, *e.g. Merrit* v. *Merrit* [1970] 1 W.L.R. 1211. For a case of an inferred contract where the separating parties were unmarried, see *Tanner* v. *Tanner* [1975] 1 W.L.R. 1346, above, p. 53.
6 Bromley and Lowe, *Bromley's Family Law* (8th ed. 1992), p. 129.
7 See above, p. 187.

thereby clarifying their mutual obligations and expectations, and conferring powers and responsibilities which the law otherwise denies them.[8] Such an agreement could reduce recourse to litigation in the event of breakdown of cohabitation, for even if the agreement is not legally binding, it may serve as a basis for settlement.

Cohabitation contracts

One type of contract between cohabitees is becoming increasingly common, namely a "cohabitation contract", *i.e.* an agreement to cohabit and to provide for the parties' rights on breakdown of cohabitation. In this respect cohabitees are in a different position from spouses. Marriage is certain; the spouses have contracted a marriage evidenced by a marriage ceremony. Cohabitation is uncertain and is not self-evident. To some cohabitees the lack of ties and commitments is the advantage of cohabitation, whereas others may wish to regularise their relationship. Should they be able to enter into an agreement to that effect? As with any contract between cohabitees, it might be argued that the agreement was not intended to be legally binding,[9] but this argument is without force if the parties have clearly expressed their intention to be bound legally.

If it is accepted that a cohabitation contract was intended to create a legal relationship, the courts may still refuse to enforce it on the basis that it is an immoral contract[10] and thus illegal. Such contracts are not new. In 1764 in *Walker* v. *Perkins*[11] a man and a woman contracted to live together and agreed that he should provide her with board, lodging, clothes and a servant and if he predeceased her or refused to live with her he should pay her an annuity of £60 per annum. If she left him or kept company with another man he should not be obliged to pay the annuity or to provide her board. The court drew a distinction between a contract of the type under consideration, entered into with a view to procure or continue a relationship, which was illegal and one entered into after cohabitation, which was legal as it did not promote immorality.[12] The latter would nevertheless fail because the consideration was past[13] unless the contract was made by deed[14] for, as with any contract, a cohabitation contract must be more than a gratuitous promise and it is doubtful whether cohabitation *per se* is sufficient consideration.

---

8 Such freedom is consistent with the encouragement given to spouses to regulate their obligations by consent orders and separation agreements (see, *e.g.* Matrimonial Causes Act 1973, ss. 33A, 34, and 35) but not currently marriage contracts: see below, p. 240.
9 See above, p. 233.
10 See *Diwell* v. *Farnes* [1959] 1 W.L.R. 624 at 631, *per* Ormrod L.J.; Dwyer, "Immoral Contracts" (1977) 93 LQ.R. 386; Treitel, *op. cit.*, pp. 390-392.
11 (1764) 1 Wm. Bl. 517.
12 See, *e.g. The Lady Cox's case* (1734) 3 P. Wms. 339.
13 See, *e.g. Binnington* v. *Wallis* (1821) 4 B. and Ald. 650.
14 For the meaning of which see Law of Property (Miscellaneous Provisions) Act 1989, s.1.

The case law cited in argument against the recognition of cohabitation contracts on grounds of immorality[15] is of such vintage as to cast serious doubt on its current applicability. This is particularly so in view of the increasing acceptability of the private ordering of family matters. Recognition has been given to agreements between cohabitees over rights to property.[16] Although this recognition does not directly support the validity of cohabitation contracts it does strengthen the argument in favour of their acceptance. In *Layton* v. *Martin*[17] the vague nature of the arrangement was such as to preclude a finding that there was any intention to create a legal relationship but there was no suggestion that, had there been such an intention, any contract so created would have been struck down on grounds of immorality. Indeed in the words of the judge[18]: "An agreement by one party to pay to the other, say £5,000 a year, or a lump sum of £15,000, is enforceable, if it complies with the requirements of contracts, as a contract." Provided that the agreement is not one merely for the provision of a sexual relationship, the court will be better able to find the requisite consideration as it has done, for example, in the context of the contractual licence.[19] For the avoidance of doubt, however, the contract shoud be executed by deed.

It is suggested that a distinction must be drawn between a contract, the purpose of which is to provide for a sexual relationship, and a contract to regulate a stable cohabitation outside marriage. Whilst the former may be viewed as contrary to public policy[20] the same need not be said of the latter. If the agreement is a genuine attempt by the parties to regulate their obligations towards each other and their children, for example, by way of maintenance or the provision of a home, rather than the provision for payment for a sexual relationship, the courts should have regard to the agreement. In so doing, they should have a discretion whether or not to give effect to the agreement, so that it would not be enforced if to do so would not be in the interests of justice, for example, if the agreement were not in the children's interests.

The freedom to contract in respect of matters affecting the children's interests is limited also by the Children Act 1989. A person who has parental responsibility for a child,[21] for example, an unmarried mother, may not as a general principle surrender or transfer any part of that responsibility to another person, although she may delegate some or all of it to others.[22] The unmarried mother and father may enter into "a parental responsibility agreement", provided it is in the prescribed form

---

15 See further Barton, *Cohabitation Contracts* (1985), pp. 38 *et seq.*
16 See above, p. 20.
17 [1986] 2 F.L.R. 227: see above, p. 233.
18 *Ibid.* at 238.
19 See *Tanner* v. *Tanner* [1975] 1 W.L.R. 1346, and above, p. 53.
20 See *Upfill* v. *Wright* [1911] 1 K.B. 506: *Fender* v. *St. John Mildmay* [1938] A.C. 1 at 42, *per* Lord Wright. For a detailed analysis, see Poulter, "Cohabitation Contracts and Public Policy" (1974) 124 N.L.J. 999 at 1034.
21 See above, p. 116.
22 Children Act 1989, s. 2(9), above, p. 117.

and duly recorded.[23] Any provision purporting to deal with the future upbringing of children would be subject to the court's duty, when determining any question with respect to a child's upbringing, to give his welfare paramount consideration.[24] Any agreement relating to child maintenance is subject to the Child Support Act 1991[25] and is also open to review by the courts. It ought to be open to the courts similarly to review any aspect of a cohabitation agreement, for example, in relation to future entitlement to the family home, to see whether or not it accords with the children's welfare; just as the welfare of the minor children of the family must be given first consideration when the court is exercising its adjustive powers in relation to financial relief on divorce.[26]

One danger associated with cohabitation contracts is the potential for exploitation of a weaker partner where there is an absence of equality of bargaining power, for only if there is evidence of undue influence may the contract be set aside. Whilst there is no such presumption in contracts between husband and wife[27] it has been held to operate in certain transactions between parties who are engaged to be married, where the transaction appears much more favourable to one party than to the other. In such circumstances the court may find a fiduciary relationship so as to shift the burden on to the party benefiting to prove that the transaction was completed by the other party with "full, free and informed thought"[28] which usually requires that the other party received genuinely independent advice. In the absence of an engagement the courts would probably not apply a presumption of undue influence to a cohabitation contract[29] but it must remain open to either party to adduce evidence that his or her will has been overborne by the other such that the contract should be set aside.

The refusal to recognise cohabitation contracts as being detrimental to marriage is inconsistent with the change in social and legal attitudes to unmarried partnerships.[30] Where neither party is already married there can be no threat to an existing marriage but only to a possible future marriage, for example, between the parties or between one of them and someone else or between two others who may be encouraged to cohabit by the recognition of cohabitation contracts. Where either party is

---

23 *Ibid.* s.4: see above, p. 117.
24 *Ibid.* s. 1(1): see above, p. 125.
25 See above, p. 150.
26 See above, p. 189.
27 *Howes* v. *Bishop* [1909] 2 K.B. 390: the burden of proving undue influence thus lies on the spouse alleging it. A presumption of undue influence between spouses may arise from special circumstances of dependency: see *Simpson* v. *Simpson* [1992] 1 F.L.R. 601. On undue influence generally, see *National Westminster Bank* v. *Morgan* [1985] A.C. 686; *Barclays Bank plc* v. *O'Brien* [1993] 1 F.L.R. 124.
28 See *Zamet* v. *Hyman* [1961] 1 W.L.R. 1442 at 1446.
29 Barton, *op. cit.*, p. 46.
30 It has been suggested that where a cohabitation contract is between homosexual partners, neither party would wish to marry a person of the opposite sex and therefore the contract of itself is not prejudicial to the state of marriage: see Barlow, *Living Together: A Guide to the Law* (1992), p. 19.

already married then the doctrine is of more relevance.[31] It is doubted, however, whether the outlawing of cohabitation contracts would have any effect on either the incidence of marriage breakdown or the incidence of cohabitation. In view of the frequency of relationships outside marriage[32] it seems desirable that (at least unmarried) parties should be able to regulate their mutual responsibilities if they so wish. It has been "confidently suggested that the modern cohabitation contract is not threatened by this doctrine".[33]

It is not suggested that an agreement to live together could be enforced but that an agreement which provides for the parties' obligations in the event of breakdown of the cohabitation could be enforced. The present law may "deter couples who do not wish to be subject to the rights and duties attached by law to the status of marriage from making proper arrangements to govern the financial and other consequences of their relationship". In so saying, the Law Commission expressed the initial view:

> "that it might be appropriate at some stage to examine, with a view to reform, the rules now governing contracts between couples who live together outside marriage, since it is perhaps in that area that the law is most uncertain and outdated."[34]

A first unsuccessful attempt to reform the law was the Cohabitation (Contract Enforcement) Bill 1991, a Private Member's Bill which sought to provide for the enforcement of cohabitation contracts to regulate financial arrangements and define the parties' respective rights in and ownership of property.[35] The Scottish Law Commission has recommended statutory provision that a contract relating to property or financial matters should not be void or unenforceable solely because it is concluded between parties who are, or are about to, cohabit.[36]

One difficulty with cohabitation contracts is that where the relationship lasts for a considerable time the parties are unlikely to have contracted in the light of changing circumstances. Such a problem is not insurmountable. First, the agreement should be subject to periodic review by the parties and their professional advisors as circumstances change. Secondly, the courts constantly deal with variation of maintenance orders and agreements between spouses in the light of changed

---

31 Barton suggests that a cohabitation contract should be void if either of the parties is married at its inception: see p. 92.
32 See above, p. 6.
33 Barton, *op. cit.*, p. 44.
34 Law Com. No. 97, para. 32. For a subsequent study on behalf of the Law Commission, see Barton, *op. cit.*, which provides a comprehensive critical analysis of the current law together with proposals for reform. See also below, p. 246.
35 See Jackson, [1991] Fam. Law 294.
36 Scot. Law Com. No. 135, para. 16.46.

circumstances. It is unnecessary and impractical for the parties to have to contract in detailed terms at the outset to cover every eventuality. In those cases where circumstances change to such an extent as to render the original agreement unjust, it would be possible to confer upon the courts power to vary or override the agreement.

Until such time as cohabitation contracts are accepted by the courts it is advisable for such agreements to be drafted with caution. It seems preferable to concentrate upon ownership of property,[37] both previously acquired and acquired during the subsistence of the relationship. In the absence of a deed, a contract for the disposition of land or any interest in land must generally be made in writing, signed by each party and incorporating all the express terms.[38] An implied contract in respect of land would have to be based upon the creation of resulting, implied or constructive trusts[39] or alternatively estoppel.[40]

Provision could be made also with regard to savings[41] and financial obligations as between the parties and towards any children,[42] both during the subsistence of the relationship and in the event of its termination.[43] Reference to minute details of a more intimate personal nature, for example, living arrangements, sexual, personal and social relationships, should be avoided because such matters, although evidencing the parties' expectations, are unlikely to have any legal effect. In disregarding them a court may be inclined to hold the entire agreement to be unenforceable rather than to apply the doctrine of severance and strike out the offending clauses on the basis that part of the consideration is illegal.[44]

Barton argues[45] that provided the parties take care to show an intention to create legal relations, avoid the appearance of undue influence, eschew references to sexual matters and attempts to tamper with existing rights and duties over children[46] and ensure some reciprocity then agreements between (at least) heterosexual couples are binding. This sound advice should form the basis of any written contract

---

37 See above, Chap. 2.
38 See the Law of Property (Miscellaneous Provisions) Act 1989, s.2, superseding the Law of Property Act 1925, s.40. For the requirements relating to a declaration of trust, see above, p. 19.
39 See above, p. 20.
40 See above, p. 37.
41 See above, p. 77.
42 See above, pp. 76 and 150.
43 Such would be in line with Recommendation R(88)3 of the E.C. Council of Ministers that Member States should not preclude cohabitation contracts dealing with property and money on the ground that the parties are not married to each other. That type of approach has been adopted by the Scottish Law Commission: see Scot. Law. Com. No. 135, para. 16.46.
44 See *Bennett* v. *Bennett* [1952] 1 K.B. 249 at 254, *per* Somervell L.J.
45 *Op. cit.*, p. 49.
46 But see above, p. 236.

drawn up between cohabitees, the form of which has been suggested[47] but the validity of which is as yet untested.

Any agreement should, it is suggested, merely recite that the parties have agreed to live together rather than make cohabitation part of the agreement as that is not a matter which could be enforced and could possibly taint the whole contract with immorality. This would enable the agreement to concentrate upon the financial aspects of the relationship in respect of which the parties express their intention to be bound legally. It seems unnecessary to describe the parties in terms of status, that matter not being of relevance to the parties' contractual obligations. It seems preferable to avoid calling the parties, for example, the husband and the wife. This would enable such a contract to be adapted for use by a homosexual cohabiting couple should the courts be prepared so to extend the operation of a cohabitation contract, rather than (more likely) strike it down on grounds of immorality.

A cohabitation contract is an agreement entered into either at the inception of or during the subsistence of cohabitation. It may be possible as an alternative for the parties to contract on breakdown of cohabitation in a similar manner to spouses who enter into a separation agreement. A separation agreement between spouses is valid if it provides for immediate separation or if separation has already occurred, but such an agreement between cohabiting spouses making arrangements in case of future separation is void as being prejudicial to the institution of marriage and contrary to public policy.[48] Hence spouses are currently precluded from entering into a marriage contract of a type equivalent to a cohabitation contract but any such marriage contract may be relevant, however, as part of all the circumstances of the case and the court may take note of the parties' intention in the exercise of its discretionary powers.

In this context it is interesting to note that in response to the growing demand for facilities for out-of-court conciliation and mediation in disputes relating to property and maintenance which can arise on the breakdown of marriage and relating to claims under the Inheritance (Provision for Family and Dependants) Act 1975,[49] the Family Law Bar Association has set up a Conciliation Board to provide and administer a conciliation procedure.[50] This procedure is not limited to spouses and former spouses but applies also to formerly engaged couples and persons

---

47 See Gray, "A New Lease of Life" (1973) 123 N.L.J. 596 and the precedent at 591. See also correspondence at 705 and analysis by Poulter, "Cohabitation Contracts and Public Policy" (1974) 124 N.L.J. 999 at 1034. For a more comprehensive example, see Bottomley et al., *The Cohabitation Handbook* (2nd ed., 1984), pp. 191-192. See also Hoggett and Pearl, *The Family, Law and Society* (3rd ed., 1991), pp. 344-345 and Weitzman, *The Marriage Contract* (1981) for an American perspective.

48 See *Wilson* v. *Wilson* (1848) 1 H.L. Cas. 538.

49 See above, p. 210.

50 The procedure is in effect a type of arbitration. Details and application forms are available from the Secretary to the F.L.B.A. Conciliation Board, 4 Paper Buildings, Temple, London EC4Y 7EX. See also "The Family Law Bar Association Conciliation Board" [1992] Fam. Law 573.

who have lived together.[51] The Board makes a recommendation based on the likely result if the case had gone to court. The parties can agree either before or after the recommendation whether it is to be regarded as binding upon them.

Quasi-contract

It may be possible to extend the recognition already given to implied agreements with regard to ownership of the home,[52] so that a cohabitee who cohabits to his detriment on the understanding that he would be supported has a "quasi-contractual" claim, *i.e.* a claim for recompense for services rendered, liability for which is imposed by law rather than arising under contract. Such an extension of the restitutional remedy of *quantum meruit* is currently without authority but there is some support for the emergence of a principle of restitution if the plaintiff's services have been freely accepted by the defendant.[53] The principle could be argued as applicable between cohabitees where the claimant's resources have operated to the benefit of the defendant. In *Windeler* v. *Whitehall*[54] Miss Windeler's entitlement to a *quantum meruit* claim was rejected because what she did "was not work for which Mr. Whitehall would have paid anyone to do in any circumstances whatever".[55] The suggestion is that, had it been, her claim might have succeeded.

2. CONTRACTS WITH OTHERS

A wife who is cohabiting with her husband is presumed to have his authority to pledge his credit for necessary goods and services,[56] for example, food, clothing and household goods. This presumption of agency from cohabitation[57] arises out of the cohabitation and can therefore be said to apply to an unmarried couple who are cohabiting as husband and wife.[58] As the woman is regarded as her partner's agent, he is liable to the supplier.

---

51 It is also available to adult parties involved in and application under the Inheritance (Provision for Family and Dependants) Act 1975.
52 See above, p. 20.
53 See Jones, "Restitutionary Claims for Services Rendered" (1977) 93 L.Q.R. 273; Gardner, "Rethinking Family Property" (1993) 109 L.Q.R. 263.
54 [1990] 2 F.L.R. 505: see above, p. 40.
55 *Ibid.* at 516.
56 *Phillipson* v. *Hayter* (1870) L.R. 6 C.P. 38. See Bromley and Lowe, *op. cit.,* pp. 130-133.
57 To be distinguished from the wife's agency of necessity abolished by the Matrimonial Proceedings and Property Act 1970, s.41(1).
58 *Blades* v. *Free* (1829) 9 B.&C. 167.

If a man leads a supplier to believe that his cohabitee is acting as his agent, for example, by paying for goods which she has ordered, he will be regarded as holding her out as his agent. If she orders further goods from that supplier, her partner will be liable to the supplier for the price.[59]

---

59 *Ryan* v. *Sams* (1848) 12 Q.B.D. 460.

CHAPTER 10

CONCLUSION

Those who live together outside marriage have not, as yet, achieved the same extent of legal recognition as those who live together within it. Nevertheless, some judicial and statutory recognition is being given to cohabitation, although its extent is uncertain and inconsistent. The law recognises, for example, contributions towards the acquisition of the home and its contents, and the right of a cohabitee to live in the home free from violence. A cohabitee, unlike a spouse, however, has no right as such to maintenance and no right to a home by virtue of the relationship alone. Yet, for income support purposes, a couple living together as husband and wife are treated in the same way as spouses.

The uncertainty and inconsistency of recognition is due to its having been secured on an ad hoc basis, with a view to achieving justice in the particular context and with little thought for public policy and the social implications. The tendency has been to treat cohabitees as spouses, not, it seems, because of a desire to equate marriage and cohabitation, but to avoid the necessity for considering what policy should apply to the law relating to cohabitation. Recognition, in so far as it is given, is given in part on the basis of living together as husband and wife (for example, entitlement to income support and protection from violence), in part on the basis of the parties' agreed intention (rights in the home) and in part on the basis of dependency (rights on death). If recognition is to be given to cohabitation,[1] should the law continue to develop on an ad hoc basis, or should the legal test be one of status, contract, dependence or perhaps a combination thereof?

It is not within the scope of this book to undertake a detailed consideration of issues of social policy[2] but only to review briefly some of the many and varied arguments[3] which have been presented for, and are likely to be influential upon, the future development of the law relating to cohabitation.

One major problem with the status approach to cohabitation lies in identifying the types of cohabitation to which recognition is to be given.

---

1 For an analysis of the arguments for and against further intervention, see Barton, *Cohabitation Contracts* (1985), Chap. 8.
2 On which see O'Donovan, *Family Law Matters* (1993).
3 For a valuable international and interdisciplinary study extending to some 43 Chapters, see Eekelaar and Katz (eds.), *Marriage and Cohabitation in Contemporary Societies - Areas of Legal, Social and Ethical Change* (1980).

The tendency has been to recognise relationships in which the parties have performed the roles of husband and wife. To define cohabitation in terms of living together as husband and wife would necessitate a close investigation of each relationship to ascertain whether or not the relationship has the necessary personal qualities. This would produce all the difficulties associated with the operation of a cohabitation rule[4] and the danger of encouraging litigation in order to ascertain the types of relationship encompassed by the definition. A definition in terms of marriage would exclude family cohabitations and, presumably, homosexual cohabitations,[5] notwithstanding that the parties to such a relationship are just as likely to have inter-personal legal problems as those who cohabit as husband and wife. If the resolution of the problems of the former cannot be assimilated within the resolution of those of the latter, separate means will have to be found either within the existing ad hoc model or on some other basis. The Scottish Law Commission consider, on pragmatic grounds, that it is likely to be more productive to concentrate on relationships of a man and a woman who are not legally married but are living together as husband and wife, as it this type of cohabitation which is statistically more important.[6] The European Court of Human Rights has held that a homosexual couple cannot be equated to a man and a woman living together.[7] By contrast in 1989 Denmark introduced a special legal régime closely modelled on marriage, the "registered partnership", which can be entered into only by couples of the same sex, whether or not they are cohabiting.[8]

It has been suggested that cohabitation for a specified minimum period justifies equating the relationship with marriage. This occurs already in certain contexts, for example, the Mental Health Act 1983 definition of nearest relative[9] identifies the first qualifying relative as the patient's husband or wife. This includes:

> "a person who is living with the patient as the patient's husband or wife, as the case may be (or, if the patient is for the time being an in-patient in a hospital, was so living until the patient was admitted), and has been or had been so living for a period of not less than six months . . . [10]

Time limits by their nature are arbitrary. If a relationship has the qualities of marriage, what does the fact that the relationship has

---

4 See above, p. 82. Such a definition is used in the Matrimonial Homes (Family Protection) (Scotland) Act 1981, s.18.

5 See above, p. 4.

6 See Scot. Law Com. No. 135, para. 16.3.

7 See *Kerkhoven* v. *Netherlands* (1993) L.A.G. 17.

8 See further Nielsen, "Family Rights and the 'Registered Partnership' in Denmark" (1990) 4 I.J.L.F. 297.

9 s.26(1) and (3); see Jones, *Mental Health Act Manual* (1991).

10 s.26(6). A person is excluded if the patient is married unless the patient's husband or wife is permanently separated from the patient either by agreement or court order, or has deserted or has been deserted by the patient and the desertion is continuing: see s.26(5)(*b*).

endured for six months, a year, two years or however long give to it which it did not already have? The Fatal Accidents Act 1976 has been extended to include as a dependant any person who was living with the deceased in the same household as husband and wife immediately before the date of death and had been so living for at least two years before that date.[11] It seems unjust to exclude a claimant who, although cohabiting with the deceased in such a relationship, had done so for only one year and 11 months prior to the deceased's death. It seems preferable to avoid arbitrary time limits.[12]

Cohabitation for a specified period has served to give rise to support obligations in other jurisdictions. Since 1837, Tasmania has had a provision[13] enabling a woman who has had a man living with her for at least one year to apply, in certain circumstances, for maintenance. The British Columbia Family Relations Act 1979 provides for maintenance and support obligations between a man and a woman not married to each other, who lived together as husband and wife for a period of not less than two years.[14] Such a policy is one of partial equivalence to marriage. It may be argued that cohabitees should be entitled to the same legal recognition as spouses[15] so that, for example, the power of the matrimonial courts to adjust the balance between the parties should be exercisable whenever parties to a relationship have been fulfilling roles equivalent to the marital roles.[16] In New South Wales the De Facto Relationships Act 1984 confers property rights on unmarried partners comparable with those applicable between divorced spouses.[17] In England and Wales the courts' wide and complex discretionary powers, exercisable on breakdown of marriage, are not available on breakdown of cohabitation. It may be asked, however, whether it is right that those who choose not to enter into matrimony should be entitled to the protection of matrimonial law: it is submitted not. The parties may have chosen to cohabit in order to be free of the complex provisions of matrimonial law and the law ought not to undermine that freedom. Moreover, to equate the treatment of those who do not marry to the treatment of those who do is to undermine marriage. Recognition may be given without, however, equating cohabitation and marriage.

The encouragement of marriage has resulted in resistance to any formulation of a basis of recognition for cohabitation, yet there is no

---

11 See above, p. 230.
12 The Scottish Law Commission recommend either self-limiting rules or rules which would confer sufficient judicial discretion to take account of all the relevant circumstances: see Scot. Law Com. No. 135, para. 16.4.
13 See now Maintenance Act 1967, s.16.
14 For a review of the Canadian legislation, see the Institute of Law Research and Reform, Alberta, *Towards Reform of the Law Relating to Cohabitation Outside Marriage* (Issues Paper No. 2, 1987), pp. 59-62.
15 For the justifications advanced in England and other jurisdictions, see Freeman and Lyon, *Cohabitation Without Marriage* (1983), Chap. 6.
16 Eekelaar, "The Place of Divorce in Family Law's New Role" (1975) 38 M.L.R. 241 at 246.
17 See below, p. 250.

need to assimilate the rights of spouses and the rights of cohabitees.[18] The tendency to do so has meant that cohabitation has been seen as a challenge to marriage and therefore undesirable. Cohabitation is not becoming a replacement for marriage; once it is seen as an alternative to marriage, and one which does not constitute a threat to marriage, the basis for recognition could be developed accordingly.

That development need not be subject to the restraints of the status approach where recognition means the granting of rights solely on the strength of cohabitation. Such an approach has been criticised because it can produce unjust results, for example, where one cohabitee, whether the woman or the man, makes no financial or physical contribution to the home acquired by the other, chooses freely a homebound role rather than work and lives in comfort through the other's support with no agreement on the creation of mutual rights and obligations.[19]

The acceptance of cohabitation as giving rise to a status may be contrary to the expectations of those who cohabit.[20] People marry in the knowledge and expectation of the rights and obligations imposed by marriage. Is it right that those who cohabit in order to be free of marital rights and obligations should have rights and obligations thrust upon them? It can be argued that any further extension of legal recognition is unnecessary and undesirable.

An alternative would be to regard the rights of cohabitees as essentially a private matter of contract[21] rather than a public matter of status so that the law should only confer rights and obligations if such was the parties' agreed intention. The law's reluctance to recognise any such agreement was discussed in Chapter 9 and it was there suggested that a distinction should be drawn between an agreement for a sexual purpose and an agreement to regulate a stable cohabitation outside marriage. If the agreement is a genuine attempt to regulate the parties' obligations, the courts should be prepared to give effect to it unless to do so would not be in the interests of justice, for example, if the parties were of unequal bargaining power. Any such danger could be met, if necessary, by requiring the parties to receive independent legal advice before entering the agreement, as a prerequisite to its having legal effect. Indeed, if the principle of accepting cohabitation contracts as valid is adopted, detailed consideration would need to be given to the form and scope of such contracts[22] and whether, for example, that acceptance would apply also between parties to other domestic relationships outside marriage, in particular family cohabitations and homosexual cohabitations.

---

18 For the justifications advanced in England and other jurisdictions for differential treatment, see Freeman and Lyon, *op. cit.*, Chap. 7.

19 See Zuckerman, "Formality and the Family - Reform and Status Quo" (1980) 96 L.Q.R. 268 at 276.

20 See Deech, "The Case Against Legal Recognition of Cohabitation" in Eekelaar and Katz, *op. cit.*, Chap. 30 and also at (1980) 29 I.C.L.Q. 480.

21 For the arguments for and against legal recognition and use of cohabitation contracts, see in particular Barton, *op. cit.*, Chap. 9. See also Blake, "To Marry Or Not To Marry?" (1980) 10 Fam. Law 29.

22 See above, Chap. 9, and Barton, *op. cit.*, Chaps. 5, 6 and 10.

There is a strong case for a review of the rules applicable to contracts between couples who live together outside marriage. As the law already indirectly recognises such contracts as a means of conferring support rights and property rights, as, for example, with the contractual licence,[23] consideration needs to be given also to the recognition of implied agreements[24] where one party has cohabited with another to his or her detriment on the common understanding that the contributor should receive some recognition for the contribution made, whether that contribution was in cash or kind.

To link recognition of cohabitation exclusively with the existence of a contract would not cater for those relationships where the parties have no agreement either express or implied, yet the relationship is just as worthy of recognition. The Scottish Law Commission is right to "doubt whether it is realistic to expect all cohabiting couples to make adequate private legal arrangements".[25] The acceptance of cohabitation contracts need not operate, however, to the exclusion of a wider basis of recognition, independent of any agreement. The parties could be free to opt out of such recognition if they so wish, save in so far as the recognition should be imposed on policy grounds, for example, protection from violence.[26] The point has been well made that cohabitation contracts are a small part of a big problem[27] and would not necessarily constitute a complete legal solution. It would be necessary also to distinguish between matters of public rather than private regulation over which the parties have no control, such as entitlement to welfare benefits.

If parties to a relationship outside marriage are to be allowed to regulate their mutual rights and obligations by agreement, it can be argued that spouses too should be allowed to choose the terms of their marriage contract and define the terms of their relationship[28]; in effect, that the cohabitation contract would replace the marriage contract.[29] Such a fundamental change in our social policy, it is submitted, would seem neither realistic nor desirable. "In short, there should be a mix of public and private law in each relationship but with a prevalence of the former in marriage and of the latter in cohabitation."[30]

One suggestion has been to base rights on "mutual interdependence" in a stable relationship.[31] A similar argument advocates the extension of

---

23 See above, p. 53.
24 See Freeman and Lyon, *op. cit.*, pp. 209 *et seq.*
25 Scot. Law Com. No. 135, para. 16.1.
26 *Ibid.* para. 16.47.
27 Barton, *op. cit.* Chap. 10.
28 See Weitzman, *The Marriage Contract* (1981); Wright, "Marriage from status to contract?" (1984) 13 Anglo-Am. 17.
29 For a consideration of whether the law might ignore marriage altogether, see Clive, "Marriage: An Unnecessary Legal Concept?" in Eekelaar and Katz, *op. cit.*, Chap. 8; Dewar "Is marriage redundant?" (1992) Stud. L.R. 46.
30 Barton, *op. cit.*, p. 88.
31 See Pearl, "The Legal Implications of a Relationship Outside Marriage" (1978) C.L.J. 252.

rights and obligations where a relationship has reduced one party, usually, but not necessarily, the woman, to a position of dependency, normally because of responsibilities for children.[32] Such recognition, it is submitted, should be coupled with, rather than operate as an alternative to, the regulation of rights based on agreement.

A test based on dependency differs from a test based on mutual interdependence in that the latter encompasses relationships where the parties share their lives and equally contribute to the maintenance of each other, whereas the former does not.[33] Such a limitation seems to give inadequate recognition to the essential characteristics of a stable relationship outside marriage, namely the sharing of family life. Mutual contribution towards that life and the support of each other would seem just as worthy of recognition as where one party has been the supporter and the other the supported. Such recognition would enable cohabitation based on dependency to be determined as a two-sided and not just one-sided relationship, thereby avoiding the notion that cohabitation is necessarily a relationship of (female) dependence and (male) dominance. Where there is such dependence, consideration could be given to the provision of compensation by way of rehabilitative financial support. Such compensation could extend to cases of dependency whether or not the parties live together as husband and wife and, like the Inheritance (Provision for Family and Dependants) Act 1975, apply to other domestic relationships.

A problem common to any test of recognition of cohabitation is the significance, if any, to be attached to the marital status of either party to the cohabitation. By giving recognition to a married person's extra-marital relationship, is not the law moving away from accepting marriage as being a monogamous union and accepting instead a form of polygamy? The frequency of marital breakdown and the high incidence of remarriage has virtually destroyed the notion that marriage is a union for life, but the law relating to marriage and divorce does ensure that legally recognised relationships run in series and not in parallel. To recognise a relationship outside marriage between two people, one of whom is already lawfully married, is to recognise a secondary spouse (or concubine) and to give rise to issues of priority of rights and obligations. This is part of a wider issue in that, however apparent the increase in cohabitation appears to be,[34] the same cannot be said of the parties' reasons for cohabiting.[35] Whilst for some it is a preliminary to marriage, for others it is a substitute. Some couples cohabit because they are unable to marry but desire a permanent relationship, whilst others have no intention of forming permanent ties. The equivocal nature of the legal response to

---

32 Oliver, "The Mistress in Law" (1978) 31 *Current Legal Problems* 81.
33 See *Re Beaumont* [1980] Ch. 444, above, p. 212.
34 See above, p. 6.
35 See Freeman and Lyon, *op. cit.*, p. 51.

cohabitation is hardly surprising in view of the varied nature of cohabitation and of the varied expectations of those who cohabit.

The development of the law relating to unmarried couples in other countries, particularly common law countries, is worthy of note.[36] When considering other countries' approach to cohabitation, consideration must be given to the extent to which the approach is based on cultural policies and philosophies which are different from our own. Hence attention will be focused on American, Commonwealth and European jurisdictions. In the United States, some State courts have been prepared to enforce agreements between cohabitees unless the agreement is based on unlawful consideration, following the decision in the celebrated case of *Marvin* v. *Marvin*[37] where the California Supreme Court held that:

> "The fact that a man and a woman live together without marriage, and engage in sexual relationship, does not in itself invalidate agreements between them related to their earnings, property or expenses. Neither is such an agreement invalid merely because the parties may have contemplated the creation or continuation of a non-marital relationship when they entered into it. Agreements between non-marital partners fail only to the extent that they rest upon a consideration of meretricious sexual services."

The court also said that a claim could be upheld on the basis of an implied contract, partnership or equitable remedies.

Certain American courts accept that couples living together outside marriage do have rights arising from their relationship,[38] albeit that the compensation awarded in respect of these rights may be less than would have been awarded had they been married. There is recognition of cohabitation without equating it with marriage. Other jurisdictions have gone further and made specific legislative provision.[39]

The development of the legal response and the policy which the law should adopt, whether, for example, by being neutral and pragmatic (as in Poland[40]), by imposing marriage-like obligations (as in France[41] and to

---

36 See especially Eekelaar and Katz, *op. cit.*; Freeman and Lyon, *op. cit.*, Chap. 5; Muller-Freienfels, "Cohabitation and Marriage Law - A Comparative Study" (1987) 1 I.J.L.F. 259; Scottish Law Commission Discussion Paper No. 86, *The Effects of Cohabitation in Private Law*, paras. 5.2-5.4.

37 18 Cal. (3d) 660 (1976). Ultimately the claimant received nothing: see *Marvin* v. *Marvin 111* 122 Cal.App. (3d) 871 (1981); 176 Cal.Rpt. 555 (1981) where the trial court's award of $104,000 for rehabilitation purposes was reversed.

38 See further Bala, "Family Law in Canada and the United States: Different Visions of Similar Realities" (1987) 1 I.J.L.F. 1 at 24-28; Freed and Walker, "Family Law in the Fifty States: An Overview" [1987] F.L.Q. 439 at 457 and 569.

39 See, *e.g.* in Ontario the Family Law Act 1986, s.29; the New Brunswick Family Services Act 1980, s.112.

40 See Szlezak, "Cohabitation without Marriage in Poland" (1991) 5 I.J.L.F. 1.

41 See Freeman and Lyon, *op. cit.*, pp. 123 *et seq.*

some extent in Scandinavia[42] and particularly in South America[43]), by treating the parties as autonomous,[44] or by distinguishing between those couples who have children and those who do not[45] (as, for example, in Newfoundland where a support obligation arises after one year's cohabitation provided it is accompanied by parenthood[46]) ought, it would seem, to proceed in the light of evidence as to why couples live together.[47] The New South Wales Law Reform Commission, for example, engaged widely in a programme of community consultation in the course of the preparation of its Report on De Facto Relationships.[48]

Consideration must be given also to the nature of the issues which arise during any relationship. As the preceding Chapters have shown, the variety of issues is such as to refute a uniform response. Whilst, for example, a cohabitee's entitlement to a life free from domestic violence seems no more than the recognition of a basic right, the same cannot be said of entitlement to financial support. One option is thus to examine each area of law where injustices or anomalies arise so as to provide the appropriate remedy for each issue. This approach, which has much to commend it, is favoured by the Scottish Law Comission[49] as it was earlier by the New South Wales Law Reform Commission and enacted in the De Facto Relationships Act 1984. That Act seeks to avoid equating marriage and cohabitation whilst providing for the rights of cohabitees in a single legislative code[50] which could operate alongside, and be generally excluded by, private contract.

It has also been argued that the current practice of judicial discretion is preferable to a legislative code of rights for cohabitees as it allows the courts to give effect to rights and obligations created by the parties themselves through agreement and other relevant conduct in accordance with recognised legal principles, thereby minimising uncertainty.[51] Such an approach avoids the difficulties of definition associated with the status approach, which can in addition be seen as undesirable because it treats those who have chosen not to marry as if they had married.

---

42 See Agell, "Cohabitation Without Marriage in Swedish Law" in Eekelaar and Katz, *op. cit.*, Chap. 25; Danielson, "Unmarried Partners: Scandinavian Law in the Making" (1983) 3 O.J.L.S. 159; Lund-Andersen, "Moving Towards an Individual Principle in Danish Law" (1990) 4 I.L.J.F. 328.

43 See Muller-Freienfels, "Cohabitation and Marriage Law - A Comparative Study" (1987) 1 I.J.L.F. 259 at 262.

44 See Deech in Eekelaar and Katz, *op. cit.*, Chap. 30.

45 See Eekelaar, *Family Law and Social Policy* (2nd ed.), Chap. 8.

46 For details of this and other examples, see Deech, *op. cit.*, p. 301. For a consideration of Canadian law generally, see Holland, *Unmarried Couples: Legal Aspects of Cohabitation* (1982).

47 See Oliver, "Why Do People Live Together?" [1982] J.S.W.L. 209.

48 See Astor and Nothdurft, (1985) 48 M.L.R. 61.

49 Scot. Law Com. No. 135, para. 16.1.

50 See Hoggett and Pearl, *The Family, Law and Society* (3rd ed., 1991), pp. 351-353. See also Johnson, "Cohabitation Without Formal Marriage in England and Wales" [1986] Fam. Law 47.

51 See Zuckerman, *op. cit.*

Whilst there is a need for the development of clear principles upon which to base the legal recognition of cohabitation so that those who cohabit can be advised with certainty, first, whether or not their relationship is one of cohabitation and, secondly, if it is, the legal rights and obligations arising from that relationship, the formulation of such principles is a daunting task. The Scottish Law Commission faced up to the task in 1990 with a discussion paper[52] the response to which confirmed their view that there is a stong case for some limited reform of Scottish private law.[53] The English Law Commission has to date been more cautious.[54] Reform and rationalisation of the law is seen as involving enormous problems, not least because of the social and financial implications. The Commission have considered an internal study paper which summarises the English law and reforms in other countries. Their initial view is that a review of the rules governing contracts between couples who live together outside marrriage might be appropriate[55] but they decline to say when, if at all, this could be done, and whether or not it should be seen as a preliminary to a more general review. A preliminary survey on the enforceability of agreements between cohabiting parties has been undertaken on behalf of the Commission[56] which has expressed an intention to give further thought to the issue.[57]

Meanwhile it seems likely that English law will continue to develop as before and concentrate on achieving justice in the particular context as and when it arises, notwithstanding the inconsistencies and uncertainties of such an approach and the failure to give overall consideration to the policies and principles applicable to the law relating to cohabitation.

---

52 No. 86, *The Effects of Cohabitation in Private Law*.
53 See Scot. Law Com. No. 135, Pt. XVI.
54 As part of their duty to keep the law under review, they have given consideration to the legal position of unmarried couples who live together as husband and wife (see Law Com. No. 97, para. 2.32) and noted the inconsistent approach in the different statutory provisions and the risk that difficulties of interpretation will occur.
55 See above, p. 238.
56 See Barton, *op. cit.*
57 Law Com. No. 131, *18th Annual Report 1982-1983*.

PRECEDENTS

Contents

NOTE
    Reference should also be made to the following Children Act 1989 Forms:

Statutory Declaration for Change of Surname

I [name] of [address] do solemnly and sincerely declare as follows:

1. I absolutely relinquish and abandon the use of my said former surname of [former surname] and in substitution therefor I have adopted and hereby formally assume as from the date hereof the surname of [new surname].

2. I shall at all times hereafter in all records, deeds, documents and other writings and in all actions and proceedings as well as in all dealings and transactions and on all occasions whatsoever use and sign the said surname of [new surname] as my surname in substitution for my former surname of [former surname].

3. I hereby authorise and require all persons at all times to designate describe and address me by the adopted surname of [new surname].

IN WITNESS whereof I have hereto signed my forename/s of and my adopted surname of [new surname] and my former surname of [former surname] this day of   19

(Signed) . . . .
formerly known as. . . . .

AND I make this solemn Declaration conscientiously believing the same to be true and by virtue of the provisions of the Statutory Declarations Act 1835.

DECLARED by the above named   )
at   )   [Signature of declarant]
this   day of 19   )
Before me   )
A Solicitor of the Supreme Court
empowered to administer oaths

Originating Application in the County Court under section 30 of the Law of Property Act 1925

In the   **County Court**

No. of Matter

In the matter of section 30 of the Law of Property Act 1925
And in the matter of the trusts of the property [*address*]

Between   Applicant
and   Respondent

[*Name of Applicant*] of [*address and occupation*] hereby applies to the court for an order in the following terms:

1. That the Applicant and the Respondent hold the property [*address*] as [*set out the manner in which it is claimed that the Applicant and Respondent hold the legal and beneficial ownership of the property, for example, as joint tenants in trust for themselves in equal shares or in such other shares as the court shall determine: see above, p.13*].

2. That the said trusts be executed and the said property sold forthwith.

3. Such further and other relief as may be necessary.

4. That the costs of the Applicant be paid by the Respondent.

The grounds upon which the Applicant claims to be entitled to such order are:
[*set out in numbered paragraphs the evidence relied upon*].

The name and address of the person on whom this application is intended to be served is [*name and address of Respondent*].

The Applicant's address for service is

Dated this   day of   19

[*Signature*]
[*Solicitor for the*] Applicant

NOTE
    In the High Court, application is by way of originating summons: see above, p.50, adapting Form No. 8 in R.S.C., Appendix A, setting out the terms of the order sought and with affidavit in support setting out the evidence upon which the applicant relies.

Appointment of Testamentary Guardian/s

I [*name of mother or father*] of [*address*] in accordance with section 5 of the Children Act 1989 appoint [*name/s and address/es of guardian/s*] to be the guardian/s of my child [*name of child*] (and all my children born hereafter) during his/her/their minority.

If (both of) the said [*name/s of guardian/s*] shall refuse or for any reason whatsoever cease to act as such guardian/s then I appoint [*name and address of alternative guardian*] to be such guardian in his/her/their place.

Dated this   day of   19

[*Signature*]

NOTE

The unmarried father has no power to appoint a testamentary guardian unless he has parental responsibility for the child immediately before his death: see above, p.135.

General Form of Application for Injunction

In the		
		County Court
Case Number	*Always quote this*	
Plaintiff's Ref		
Defendant's Ref		

Between . . . . **Plaintiff**
Applicant
Petitioner

and . . . . **Defendant**
Respondent

 Seal

Notes on completion
Tick whichever box applies

☐ By application in pending proceedings
☐ In the matter of the Domestic Violence and Matrimonial Proceedings Act 1976

[1] Enter the full name of the person making the application

The Plaintiff (Applicant/Petitioner)[1] applies to the court for an injunction order in the following terms:

[2] Enter the full name of the person the injunction is to be directed to

That the Defendant (Respondent)[2] be forbidden (whether by himself or by instructing or encouraging any other person)[3]

[3] Set out here the proposed restraining orders (If the defendant is a limited company delete the wording in brackets and insert "Whether by its servants, agents, officers or otherwise")

[4] Set out here any proposed mandatory orders requiring acts to be done

And that the Defendant (Respondent)[4]

[5] Set out here any further terms asked for including provisions for costs

And that[5]

[6] Enter the names of all persons who have sworn affidavits in support of this application

The grounds of this application are set out as in the sworn statement(s) of[6]

This (these) sworn statement(s) is (are) served with this application

<table>
<tr><td>

7 Enter the names and addresses of all persons upon whom it is intended to serve this application

8 Enter the full name and address for service and delete as required

</td><td>

This application is to be served upon[7]

This application is filed by[8]
(the Solicitors for) the Plaintiff (Applicant/Petitioner) whose address for service is

Signed   **Dated**

</td></tr>
<tr><td>

* Name and address of the person application is directed to

</td><td>

This section to be completed by the court

To*
of

**This application will be heard by the (District) Judge
at
on   the   day   of   19   at   o'clock**

If you do not attend at the time shown the court may make an injunction order in your absence

If you do not fully understand this application you should go to a Solicitor, Legal Advice Centre or a Citizens' Advice Bureau

</td></tr>
<tr><td></td><td>

The Court Office at
is open from 10am to 4pm. When corresponding with the court, address all forms and letters to the Chief Clerk and quote the case number.

</td></tr>
</table>

NOTE

This precedent is based upon County Court Form N16A which must be used for all applications for an injunction whether it is sought under the Domestic Violence and Matrimonial Proceedings Act 1976 or ancillary to other proceedings.

Originating Application in the County Court under section 1 of the Inheritance (Provision for Family and Dependants) Act 1975

In the   County Court

No. of Matter

In the matter of an application under section 1 of the Inheritance (Provision for Family and Dependants) Act 1975

Between   Applicant
and   1st Respondent
and   2nd Respondent

1. I, of [address], apply to the court for an order under section 1 of the Inheritance (Provision for Family and Dependants) Act 1975 for reasonable financial provision to be made for me out of the estate of (hereafter called the deceased) who died on the day of   19   being domiciled in England and Wales at that date and resident at [address].

2. I am a person who immediately before the death of the deceased was being maintained, either wholly or partly, by the deceased.

3. A grant of probate [or letters of administration] in regard to the estate of the deceased was first taken out on the   day of   19   and the personal representative/s is/are of [address] and   of [address].

4. The disposition of the deceased's estate affected by his/her will [or the law relating to intestacy, or the combination of his/her will and the law relating to intestacy] was such as to make no provision for me [or to make the following provision for me, namely   ].

5. To the best of my knowledge and belief the persons or classes of persons interested in the deceased's estate and the nature of their interests are as follows: [details].

6. The following are particulars of my present and foreseeable financial resources and financial needs [details together with any other information which the applicant desires to place before the court on the matters to which the court is required to have regard under section 3 of the Act: see above, p.217].

7. [I request the court's permission to make this application notwithstanding that the period of six months has expired from the date on which representation in regard to the deceased's estate was first taken out and the grounds of my request are as follows: see above, p.221.]

8. I ask for reasonable financial provision to be made for me out of the deceased's estate by way of an order for [*give details of order applied for: see above, p.219.*]

9. The names and addresses of the respondents on whom this application is intended to be served are:

10. My address for service is:

Dated this   day of   19

[*Signature*]
Applicant

To The Respondent

Within 21 days after service of this application on you, inclusive of the day of service, you must file in the court office an answer, together with a copy for every other party to the proceedings, containing a statement of your case, and if you are a personal representative of the deceased:

  (a) full particulars of the deceased's net estate;
  (b) the persons or classes of persons beneficially interested in the estate, (including the names and addresses of all living beneficiaries, and whether any of them is a minor or a mental patient); and
  (c) any facts known to you which might affect the exercise of the court's powers under Act.

Note
   This precedent is based upon C.C.R. 1981, Ord 48, r. 2 and County Court Practice Form N.423. Application to the High Court is by way of originating summons in Form No. 10 in R.S.C., Appendix A, with affidavit in support: see R.S.C., Ord. 99, r. 3.

INDEX